AN INSIGHT INTO YOGA

SWAMI SHIVAPREMANANDA

Published by

THE DIVINE LIFE SOCIETY

P.O. SHIVANANDANAGAR—249 192

Distt. Tehri-Garhwal, Uttaranchal, Himalayas, India

Price] **2005** **[150/-**

First Edition: 2005
[1,000 Copies]

ISBN 81-7052-179-3
EO 63

Published by Swami Vimalananda for
The Divine Life Society, Shivanandanagar, and printed by him
at the Yoga-Vedanta Forest Academy Press,
P.O. Shivanandanagar, Distt. Tehri-Garhwal, Uttaranchal,
Himalayas, India

FOREWORD

The book *An Insight into Yoga* is authored by H.H. Revered Sri Swami Shivapremanandaji who has his field of activity in Yoga (theory as well as practical classes) and philosophical lecturing in three South American capital cities, namely, Buenos Aires in Argentina, and Montevideo in Uruguay, both on the South American east coast, and the third in Santiago de Chile, the capital city of the country, on the west coast. He has been doing this Yoga-Vedanta work for over the past 43 years since the year 1962. His work has immensely benefited thousands of earnest seekers who are eager to acquire the knowledge of the science of Yoga as well as its philosophy, both theory and practice. Yoga and Vedanta are highly venerated, since they are regarded as a priceless and precious spiritual gift given to the modern world by ancient India's great Yoga adepts and philosophers of a long bygone and hoary era.

The contents of the book cover a wide-range of the area of knowledge, dealing with more than 115 topics. In its encyclopaedic all-comprehensiveness the book is a mini-library in itself.

I wish this work the widest possible circulation so that it brings immense benefit to the reading public.

May the Divine Grace of God and the sacred benedictions of Holy Master, the late H.H. Sri Swami Sivanandaji Maharaj be upon this book in their abundance! My fullest blessings are upon this book as well as its readers.

Swami Chidananda
ॐ

Rama Navami
17th April, 2005

President
THE DIVINE LIFE SOCIETY

PREFACE

An Insight into Yoga is a collection of interrelated articles which formed the basis of my courses on the various aspects of yoga and other related philosophical and psychological subjects. They were given at seminars held in Britain and Ireland, and New York, Antwerp, Buenos Aires, Montevideo and Santiago de Chile, from 1962 to 2004.

Chapter I deals with philosophical enquiries as to the search for truth, the spirit of yoga without being in conflict with religion, and the definition of a yogi and a guru. Chapter II speaks on the philosophy and practice of Gyana Yoga or Vedanta, in the light of the teachings of the Upanishads. Chapter III covers the first steps in Raja Yoga, such as the ethical values of *yama* and *niyama*. Chapter IV extensively treats of the theory and practice of meditation. Chapter V discusses the nature of the mind and its control through self-education, and various criteria for inner balance. Chapter VI gives some thoughts to ponder, and Chapter VII some resolves to make. Chapter VIII speaks on chants. Chapter IX deals on knowledge through enquiry and Chapter X covers the subject of criterion and inner balance. Chapter XI gives some guiding values of peace and liberty. Chapter XII is on the meaning of culture. Chapter XIII is on the problems of human nature. Chapter XIV is on the Buddha's teachings. Chapter XV deals on Yoga and Christianity. Chapter XVI is on yoga, God and religion. Chapter XVII is on the three *gunas* or qualities of nature. Chapter XVIII ruminates on many themes in two parts. Chapter XIX is on the six systems of Indian philosophy. Chapter XX presents some thoughts for the month. Chapter XXI relates some anecdotes in two parts.

The Appendix is divided into several parts: the first on the detailed explanation of the Gayatri mantra, the second on two

THE AUTHOR

SWAMI SHIVAPREMANANDA

interviews with me by Jane Sill, the present editor of the *Yoga and Health* monthly magazine, published in the United Kingdom, and the second being by her predecessor, the late Ronald Hutchinson, when it was called *Yoga Today.* I consider both of them personal friends sharing similar ideals. There is a transcription of a tape on meditation conducted by me at a seminar in England, and of a lecture on stress management given in London. Following these, there is an article on Yoga in Argentina by Ana Hosmann de Sarasin and by three other authors. The article on How I Came to Yoga by Renate Rikke Gradenwitz speaks on the same subject. Yoga in Uruguay is described by Mario Caffera, Humberto Cairoli, Sofia Aguiar and Olga Gutierrez. The main article on Yoga in Chile is written by the late Anita Palma, which is followed by those of Hector Calderon and Lucila Broughton. An encyclical of Pope John-Paul II, under the title *Know Thyself,* makes a beautiful presentation of the spirit of Christianity and religion as such, and respect for other cultural traditions.

The concluding part of the Appendix describes the formation of the Sivananda Yoga-Vedanta Centres in Buenos Aires, Montevideo and Santiago de Chile by different authors, some of them being quite nostalgic, and two of them having passed away, Ulrich Hartschuh and Anita Palma.

The reiteration of some of the themes could not be avoided, as they were needed under different contexts.

I wish to express my gratitude to H.H. Revered Sri Swami Chidanandaji Maharaj for writing a Foreword to this book. His blessings are always very precious to me as the seniormost living Gurubhai and as I have known him to be the closest disciple of Gurudev H.H. Sri Swami Sivanandaji Maharaj.

I also wish to give my grateful thanks to Sri Kaviraj Nayak for his editorial and proof-reading assistance, and to Sri Swami Narasimhuluji for the final revision of the book.

Buddha Purnima
23rd May, 2005
Rishikesh, Uttaranchal **Swami Shivapremananda**

CONTENTS

APPENDIX:

AN INSIGHT INTO YOGA

Chapter One

WHAT IS YOGA

SEARCH FOR TRUTH

In Latin truth is *veritas*, or that which is determined by verification. The purpose of verification is to be sure about something, a primary human need for security. In Sanskrit truth is *satya.* Its root *sat* means existence, that of an unchanging reality behind changing forms of expression. The purpose of *sat* is also to give security by its principle of constancy and, in addition, to motivate the search for a series of inner truths, such as the existence of the physical body being possible not merely by sustenance through food, a reality in itself, but by the possibility of assimilation through the biochemical aspect of the *prana*, the vital principle, which itself is sustained by a spiritual presence, the *atma*, giving life to the body.

To say that the body or the material world is unreal is to indulge in hypocrisy. The truth is that the grosser reality of the body is dependent on the subtler reality of the *atma*, and a parallel truth is also that the subtler reality of the *atma* needs the grosser reality of the body to express itself, not for its existence, but to say that the *atma* is a greater reality.

Here arises the question of truth as *veritas*. A scientific verification of an energy form as the basis of an element is possible. Nothing can exist without energy, the cosmic *shakti*. Behind this macrocosmic force, the *Purusha*, the cosmic spirit, gives expression to life by its presence, for example, in a microcosmic form such as the body as its *atma* or soul, and once this subtle entity passes out of it, no measurable form of energy can revive it. Thus, the temporary existence of a subtle spiritual presence within a living body is self-evident. The Buddhists do not recognise the soul but in effect, disregarding the semantic interpretation, do so by presupposing a deathless, subtle entity which survives the death of the body and reincarnates again.

That which is derived from an underlying spiritual reality, *sat*, giving a conceptual form to a fact, as apart from an illusion which gives a distorted meaning to a fact, is called *satya*. The much-misunderstood theory of *maya* is not meant to deny the empirical reality of the life around but helps to differentiate the relevance of reality and illusion as per our attitude towards it. A subtle reality is hidden behind a series of illusions created by our infatuation and expectation, pride and prejudice, fear and insecurity. The purpose of truth is to remove these layers of illusion by a discerning search for reality.

The most ugly thing about truth to avoid is the scripture-thumping, dogmatic passion for truth.

NATURE OF TRUTH

There are two levels of reality, the empirical and what does an empirical fact signify, both being deeply interrelated. For example: the inner security of a home, in a loving relationship, within the outer security of the possession of a house, is the true purpose of a household. The fact of a title to a property is an empirical reality, its inner truth being the spiritual satisfaction the owner experiences.

If the spirit behind the letter of a law, or the intention behind assessing and expressing a fact is not in consonance, there is distortion of truth.

It is easy to know an empirical truth, and its purpose is always to serve a common need, such as the denominating factor of temperature measured by a thermometer. However, the experience of an empirical truth is plastic, someone feeling warmer or colder than someone else. In the case of a subtler experience, such as a good or a bad action, the determining factors being the good through benefit and the bad by harm, there are many shades as to what it means individually and collectively.

It is because an empirically verifiable truth does not give us a deeper satisfaction, we seek higher levels of truth. Through a series of dreams we seek a subtler truth, not to escape a hard reality, but to expand its meaning, its relevance, in the fathomless depth of our conscience, although interacting in a dimensional world.

The Spanish philosopher George Santayana said, "Truth is a dream, if my dream is true." It means that, apart from the verification of a fact, a spiritual search for the meaning of life, of the universe around and our relevance to it, an infinite process in itself, is the higher purpose of truth.

We are confronted with two basic facts: our human nature with which we are dissatisfied and our inner longing to be happier, which is possible only by lessening the degree of our imperfection. Behind the public truth of a person known by what he does, the promises he keeps, there is a private truth in the state of his mind, in which he lives most of the time and which is known only to himself. Behind this private truth, there is another hidden layer of a deeper truth, unknown even to himself and which he can only know by a lot of soul-searching.

The public truth is that which is expressed or verifiable by others, the private truth is that which is experienced or verifiable by oneself, and the unknown, inner truth is *sat* or that which is longed for spiritually. *Sat* is a series of dreams meant to be realised, not just to nurse in our fantasy, but to deepen and widen the dimension of the known, of our life, in the process of the search for the unknown.

RELATIVITY OF TRUTH

The saying of Andre Malreaux, the French writer, "the truth of a person is in the first place what he hides" indicates that one is ashamed of an unpleasant truth due to a regard for a wholesome truth, as to what one should be. It shows the relationship between a private truth and *sat*, or the imperfect state of the I and its dormant spiritual longing.

The German philosopher Gotthold Lessing said that if God had 'truth' in one hand and the 'search for truth' in the other, he would ask for the gift for the 'search for truth' because it gives "an infinite possibility for hypotheses." The search for truth opens up the spiritual fountain of life, its meaning, its values, for a mind without curiosity is like a dead wood, a life without purpose is like a dried-up fountain.

The yogic saying "Truth is self-evident; it does not need mystification" is very true. We hide our ignorance behind mystery, our vanity behind transcendentalism. The Western saying that "politics is an art of the possible and philosophy an art of the impossible" is rather silly, because why should one try for something after pre-empting the possibility of its realisation? The saying that "truth is only relative" is also not quite true, because truth in order to give individual security must have a permanent consistency and an unchangeable constancy, and in order to give collective security must have a universal character.

It is the perception of truth by individuals under different circumstances that is relative, due to the difference in the manner and experience of cognition. For example: We arrive at a common agreement as to the measurement of one metre. Multiplying it by one thousand makes the distance of one kilometre. There cannot be two truths about it because its determination is universal, but there can be several opinions formed by individual experience of the distance, such as for a healthy young man it is not a long walk but for a sickly old man it is a long way to go. The difference does not alter the truth of the distance, and what is relative is the experience of it.

Truth is neither hard, nor soft. It feels hard and hurts because our ego does not permit us to recognise and accept an unpleasant reality, or the malicious way we are hit with it by those who use truth as a weapon to hurt us. Like God truth is impartial. Like a mirror truth hides nothing but reflects as things are, beautiful or ugly, good or bad. Like a mirror truth does not judge and is synonymous with honesty. Like God truth embraces all, the virtuous and the sinner, and like rain it washes all, the virtuous of the pride of his virtue and the sinner the impurity of his error. Truth is the light that is hidden by the dark shades of vanity and selfishness in our heart.

CRITERIA OF TRUTH

Unity is the spirit of truth and division of untruth. Promoting individual and collective welfare is the purpose of truth, whereas that which conduces to unhappiness and harm is untruth. Harmony and peace are the two basic ideals of truth, and that is why truth is called beauty because beauty means harmony, and harmony is that which gives peace. When a bad deed of a person is called an ugly truth, it means that it ought not to be so, although it is so.

Truth and beauty are interrelated, because beauty is a balance of lines and contours blending into each other and uniting into a whole. The Italian writer, Umberto Eco, said that "the wholeness or integrity of a form (or a work) is called perfection." Ugliness is that which is unfinished or imperfect. Perfection is the first principle of beauty, either of a concept or a form, a poem or a painting, a sculpture or an architecture, of a work well done. The *Bhagavad Gita* says *yogah karmasu kausalam,* yoga is efficiency in action. The second principle is the balance of proportion or consonance, such as a room is said to be well constructed when one, sitting inside, is not aware of its walls. The third is clarity or light refracting into colours and shades, giving depth and dimension to what is created.

Depth and peace are synonymous, just as superficiality and lack of peace. Life is beautiful if there is depth of insight, together with harmony, in its relatedness. Beauty is harmonious because its expressiveness unites the beholder with the beholden. Ugliness freezes out the beholder, denying the togetherness, the plasticity of one's spirit.

The Vedic saying "Truth is one, spoken of variously" means that truth is universal and that many truths are united by the universality of their pertinence. When it is said that truth is one, it is hard to disregard how much blood has been shed in the name of one God, with scripturally-mandated disapproval of polytheism and idolatry. The relevancy of any singular entity is, indeed, tied down to doctrinal conformity requiring one's subjugation to it.

To say that all religions started well and their followers spoiled them later is to go against the evidence of the built-in imperfection of man in his search for security and identity, as he revealed himself in the pages of his scriptures, in the different stages of his evolution.

"Truth is one; paths are many" is a noble saying, evoking tolerance and upholding the autonomy of the human spirit, but there is no guarantee that all paths supposedly leading to truth will lead to it. The freedom to search for oneself, like a bee drawing honey from many flowers, while maintaining the integrity of one's search, is the universal spirit of truth.

The Vedic saying "Truth alone is victorious, not untruth," adopted as a worthy motto in the national emblem of India, is an inspiring and encouraging ideal, but not necessarily true. Sometimes truth is victorious and sometimes not when untruth rules roughshod. If striving for the unity of India, as Mahatma Gandhi did, is an ideal truth to strive for, which truly it was and still is, he did not succeed. Religious animosity prevailed, over a million died and untruth won. One day the truth of religious unity may make division on the basis of religion irrelevant, but meanwhile who can deny the immense suffering visited upon the people and the hollowness of the claim that truth *alone* is victorious? Any ideal needs constant striving and nursing, vigilance and protection. By itself truth does not grace the human nature.

GUIDING PRINCIPLES

We may use five guiding principles in our understanding of truth:

1. That which can be verified under different circumstances without losing its basic permanent character, in order to have security.

2. An effort to widen and deepen our experience of such values that can make life happier and more meaningful.

3. That which represents freedom of conscience, freedom from any theocratic or ideological servitude or any kind of dogmatism, and from ignorance, fear and passion.

4. To promote collective welfare by the mutual identity of our good, fairness and justice, by knowledge not mystery, by constructive co-operation not confrontation of selfish interests.

5. To bring a spiritual fulfilment to the individual and harmony and amity to society.

Whereas denying a fact is a clear breach of truth, exaggerating, underrating, hiding and distorting are its four contradictions. We underrate out of prejudice and overrate due to infatuation. We lie because of three basic reasons: fear, selfishness and vanity. Children lie due to the fear of punishment and adults due to the fear of shame. Children lie for not wanting to share with other children what they like to keep for themselves, just as some adults do not like to fully pay their share of income-tax. Children and adults lie in order to enhance their self-importance.

Practice of truth does not merely mean not to lie, boast, conceal, misrepresent or depreciate. It also means to have a sense of duty, self-respect and obligation; trustworthiness, loyalty and responsibility; moral courage, commitment and consistency. It means to be reasonable, fair-minded and considerate. Practice of truth covers the whole gamut of ethics. It is, indeed, a lifelong process, a lifelong effort.

As truth is infinite, no one can have the last word about it. No religion has an exclusive authority to represent truth. Untruth is behind the claim of truth which rejects investigation. Untruth is behind all beliefs and ideologies that do not tolerate the plurality of opinion. A truth expressed in a scripture is an experience of its author that came to him as a revelation in his search for wisdom, and which continues to endure due to its collective relevance. Its main purpose is to serve and enlighten humanity.

The Buddha said that he was not teaching truth but about truth. The spirit of yoga is expressed in the saying "a revealed truth is only a part of the truth," for there is a lot to be learned by the individual in his search, a long way to go in the limitless land of self-discovery.

MEANING OF PHILOSOPHY

Our lives are shaped by two basic forces. One is the need to preserve the vehicle of consciousness, the physical body conditioned by its primordial instincts, or the force of self-preservation. The other is the need to be fulfilled through a sense of purpose, meaning, relatedness in various roles, a sense of belonging, or the force of self-extension, a corollary to self-preservation.

When the mind is less cultivated, life functions through physical instincts, and motivation is directly related to their fulfilment by material incentive and security, and the exercise of the power of one's ego over weaker egos, or by submission to stronger egos. However, as material security does not necessarily create self-confidence, there remains the anxiety of not having enough or losing what one has. As ego-sensation in relationship, characterised by self-interest and possessiveness, does not give the fulfilment one longs for, it is difficult to get over the feeling of so many empty pockets in life.

It is these empty pockets or insecurities that conceive philosophy and religion. Life is woven around myths because people seem to need them for their ever-shifting sentimental identity and emotional release, philosophical or religious direction to a good, ethical life not being enough. We like to live in light and shadow, sometimes to feel free under the sun and see ourselves as we are and things as they are, but mostly we soak in the moods of our elongated egos and want to be comforted in the shadows of the make-belief.

We need superstars like Krishna and Jesus, not as they really were on this earth but in our own idealised versions, in order to seek help and be comforted when buffeted by the vagaries and afflictions of life and failed illusions of our own making.

There are two basic purposes of philosophy. One is to improve the quality of motivation, so that there is a better capacity to relate, reconstruct and improve self-expression in conduct, action, evaluation of goals and make effort for their realisation. The other is to develop an insight into life, a deeper comprehension of things, an ability to determine what one really wants and needs, and a capacity to absorb the essence of knowledge rather than merely remain on the level of dialectics or the sensation of intellect by induction and deduction.

Philosophy, thus, is a vision of life through a better motivation and understanding, the Sanskrit word for philosophy being *darshana* or vision, just as the Greek meaning is love (*philos*) of wisdom (*sophia*).

ROLE OF PSYCHOLOGY

Whereas the purpose of philosophy is to give inspiration, idealism and direction, the role of psychology is to improve self-knowledge and give an understanding of how the mind works. Basically, it means a rational knowledge (*logos*) of the inner mind (*psyche*). In Sanskrit, the word for psychology is *manovigyana* or verifiable knowledge (*vigyana*) of the mind (*manas*).

In spite of the theological connotation of our soul (*psyche* also means soul) being pure, immortal, an image of God, the Greek and the modern meaning indicates to an individuality of consciousness, both in its material and spiritual qualities, expressing itself through tangible instincts and longings and, in the process, being covered by layers of mental patterns acquired through sense-experience and thinking.

Thus, psychology is not merely knowing how the mind works in the subconscious level in order to understand our behaviour, character moulds, instinctive reflexes and emotional conflicts; its purpose is to give a better understanding of our spiritual longings, an ability to sift the true from the false as to beliefs, inclinations and affirmations, and try to sublimate the negative with the help of the positive (*pratipaksha bhavana*). In yoga psychology, it is not enough to know the underlying causes of one's conflicts, but imperative it is to provide a regimen for the reorientation of attitude and action to resolve them.

Philosophy and psychology are interrelated, and their purpose is to search for the truth of our being, both in its material and spiritual facets. Their purpose is assimilation of knowledge in order to make the best use of it, and to enhance the depth and clarity of our relationships and, therefore, identities. The goal is not merely a better understanding of life and motivation, but to find spiritual security and fulfilment, deepen the experience of inner harmony and improve our character.

All search presupposes a want, and all wants are due to a feeling of isolation. On the physical level, not sensing the body enough by oneself, there arises the need for sense-experience in contact with sense-objects. On the mental level, the inadequacy of perception leads to a search for knowledge, ratiocination, investigation, discovery, invention. On the emotional level, the insufficiency of self-love leads to greater dimensions of love in relationship to others. On the spiritual level, the inadequacy of identity and a lack of fulfilment and security within the family and among friends give rise to religion and notions about God.

In trying to make up for this insufficiency we impose our egos on each other in friendship, in family and social relationship. Since everyone is doing the same and no one likes the selfishness of the other, there is mutual dissatisfaction. Out of this arises a sense of isolation. Isolation is due to a lack of understanding, and a lack of understanding is because of self-importance. Being isolated one feeds on self-pity and stews in unhappiness.

INTERRESPONSE OF CONSCIOUSNESS

Consciousness is individual and group-oriented, and it can function only through relatedness, directly or by the memory of it. The individuality of consciousness is sustained only by its ability to interrespond, just as the validity of truth is in its capacity to verify itself, the Latin word for truth being *veritas* or that which is verifiable, and the Sanskrit word is *sat* or that which truly or verifiably exists, not in the siesta of a hot summer day! There is nothing called an isolated truth, or an absolute or ultimate truth. The transcendental nature of truth means only that anything we know to be true is subject to improvement, endlessly, for truth is infinite.

Philosophical posturing as to an unseen God being the only reality (*Brahma satyam*) and the tangible world, with which one has perforce to cope, being an illusion (*jagat mithya*) is not only conducive to hypocrisy but makes people irresponsible, indolent and irrational. When thin air becomes an unaccountable reality and the visible is thought to be unreal, instead of coming to grips with life, one becomes an escapist and unproductive (except reproductionally) and tends to exist on the subsistence level alone.

Likewise, the creation being God's *lila* (play) makes one a fatalist and blurs the line between good and evil, and what takes over is not divine inspiration but the peasant's cunning. Sayings like "God does not play the roulette" or "one cannot know the mind of God" is not convincing either and makes a cruel mockery of divine wisdom, when the history of humanity is fractured by genocide, plague (it wiped out one-third of the population of Europe in the fourteenth century), famine and holocaust.

Personally, I prefer the definition of (indefinable) God as a transcendental and immanent source of our being expressed, however limitedly, through the consciousness of spiritual values, rather than an unconscionably incompetent or powerless divine ruler. We are what we make ourselves to be. Spiritual effort, character-building, prayers (*purushartha*) serve like a lens through which the rays of the sun equally dispersed on all, like the immanence of God, are focussed to gather strength to help us move forward. In the ups and downs of life that is all we can do. Some lenses being more powerful due to will and endeavour are more effective, and those of us who are weaker have to find peace and harmony by coming to terms with the possible, having done our best.

In the interresponse of life, as the individual consciousness tries to fulfil itself, finds its reality through the relativity of experience, it is generally frustrated in the process. Out of this arises a need for transcendence, a need to reach out into the beyond, into the infinite, a need to be free from structured ideas.

SECURITY OF EGO

Life functions in this seeming contradiction of dependence on relatedness and yet needing to rise above this dependence in order to experience the ever-elusive fullness of our being, for we are both a material product and also children of the infinite spirit. Thus, within the individuality of consciousness there is the built-in urge to dissolve individuality, just as in the atom the cohesive force coexists with the decohesive force.

Being incomplete, the individual needs to be whole through a series of relatedness in the family, religion, regional culture and tradition, which leads to the acquisition of layers of personality. The Latin word *persona* comes from the Etruscan *phersu*, meaning a mask. To act out the different roles we get involved in, we constantly put on so many masks over our elusive soul. Who can really say, deep down within, what one truly is? As to the sky-scraping claims about the human being created in the image of God and the soul being ever pure and blissful, the best that can be said is that they do serve a useful, inspiring and motivational purpose.

Life begins with imitation and, consciously or unconsciously, we keep trying to acquire better kinds of *persona*—sometimes getting stuck with one for a long time—in order to discard an old and less-satisfying one. To be gratified, we try to conform to the object of gratification through a process of possessing and being possessed. Thus, the need for the security of the ego is at the base of all relatedness.

The security of the ego is sought in the easiest way, such as on the material base of property and income with which relationships are formed, sometimes even bought, but the real security comes from the security of unselfish love and understanding, and it means to sublimate our egos. Thus, the discipline and education of the self is a primary concern of philosophy. Without self-discipline and self-confidence, two cornerstones of character, there can be no inner security, and self-confidence comes only through loving and practising and gaining experience of what one believes in. Formation of values means to see a little more clearly, feel a little more deeply and learn a little more comprehensively, so that one can be more secure and fulfilled.

IMMORTALITY OF SOUL

The consciousness of individuality or the ego-self leads to attachment to those objects that sustain such consciousness, such as the body and the artifacts that make it happy, and this attachment is extended into the beyond through notions of immortality and such states of existence in afterlife that would (God willing!) be just heavenly.

Immortality of soul, a direct product of attachment to our individual self, serves two concrete purposes as a premise of belief. Instruments of religion such as temples, holy places, prayers, acquiring virtue to merit such immortality, soften the rough edges of life, provide a place to seek peace, serve as an ethical restraint in society, and give security through spiritual identity and hope. The other purpose, consciously or unconsciously, gives incentive to be remembered after death. Didn't Baruch Spinoza say that the "author of a tome on humility takes care of putting his name on the first folio" and don't we build statues of our idols the world over? But out of this incentive comes leadership, flower arts, literature and architecture, and out of moral convictions are formed cultural moulds and national identities. It is the attachment to one's beliefs, even if they are altruistic and idealistic, that makes their propagation and, therefore, civilisation possible.

As material success leaves still a part of oneself unfulfilled, and so does the exercise of power as a leader, or seeking happiness through human love or good deeds, one is led to ask: Is there anything in life that would give the fulfilment one misses? Out of this inquiry is born spiritual search, very often leading to a momentarily blissful escape into pretty illusions about what is beyond tangible reality, such as "eternal bliss" (*sic*, one could get sick of it!) and glorious salvation from every known and unknown demon.

Yet, this spiritual search alone, in and through the tangible, that enables the experience of a deeper peace, inner harmony, purity of heart, sublimity of soul, or whatever one might call it, and out of such inspiration evolve clarity of vision, a wholesome maturity, a nobler character, a truer wisdom, a better capacity to cope with life. This search begins in every little thing that is done, in every little duty on every level of relationship, in the understanding and direction of every desire and aspiration, and does not end until the last day of life. There can be only bursts of enlightenment or sudden encounters with truths about which a long search had already been going on subconsciously, but there is nothing called an ultimate enlightenment. God or truth being infinite, attaining God-realisation or self-realisation in one's lifetime is a relative goal of seeking spiritual progress at best, even if thought to be a pinnacle of attainment, and it also serves as a canonical hat for the purpose of institutional hagiolatry.

In all search there is the extension of the experience of the known into the unknown in order to expand the dimensions of the known and encounter truths that were never known. Science does so through hypothesis, and if it cannot prove itself it is discarded for a new hypothesis. Philosophy does so through speculation, and if a theory does not work out a new theory is geared to a desired result. Religion does so through faith, and if it does not give the believer inner peace and spiritual strength, two of its touchstones, there is something wrong with that faith.

If you discard the known in order not to extend the conditioning of the known and wait for the unknown to reveal itself, it is more likely that you will be sitting forever and remain the same fool, and what guarantee is there that what you call the awareness of reality is not a state of your own mind? That is why it is all the more necessary not to commit the same escapist errors that conduce to the deficiency of the known. Otherwise, there will be no end to the illusions about the unknown.

WHAT IS MORE IMPORTANT?

When I came to New York for the first time in 1961, I was told by my host, the late John Olin Murrey, then a senior Vice-President of the Macy's, "In America we have a dictum that if you have not succeeded in your career by the time you are 40, then you are a failure." Competitiveness, one of the western ethos, has indeed led to rapid material progress in the West, but it has also exacted a high price in cardiovascular tension, psychological stress and family alienation.

There are two types of success, the outer and the inner, and one needs a balance of the both. For one's peace of mind and happiness and also of the family, inner success is more important than an overriding concern in not to miss the career bus. It means to be a decent person: compassionate, understanding and honest, reliable, patient and trustworthy, caring, loving and modest, selfless, loyal and pure-hearted. The purpose of outer success is after all to be happy and self-confident and make others happy. Its relevance, therefore, depends on the inner success.

However, it is good to be reminded of the fact that only one person in 10 has leadership qualities in any field of achievement. How are the rest of the nine to come to terms with not being able to succeed or rise to the top in a career? Is that not a cause for frustration among 90 percent of those who happen to be egged on by ambitious parents or wives to be equal to the 10 percent?

Some of us are born talented and the rest are less so. Some are ambitious enough to stretch their talents and the rest are easy-going even to find out if they have potential talents or not. Some are alert to look for and grasp opportunities and astute enough to exploit circumstances energetically, whereas others being lackadaisical fall by the roadside. Some have initiative, enterprise and perseverance, all necessary to get ahead in life, and others do not.

As the term itself indicates, without motivation one remains stagnant, but it is necessary to examine the nature of motivation and come to terms with what is possible and necessary for a useful life and for one's happiness, and in being supportive to others and contributive to society, of which we are a part for better or worse.

To reshape our motivation and ethos, it is good to be reminded of a few pithy sayings that evolved out of the minds of some seekers of truth, to each of which I have added a one-sentence commentary.

"The path is more important than the goal," for if the path is noble, so will be the goal.

"Walking is more important than reaching," for if you learn how to walk sensibly and know where you are going, there you will surely be arriving.

"Doing is more important than achieving," for if you act intelligently and diligently, the result will certainly be rewarding.

"Means are more important than the end," for the consequences of the means will be harvested as well in the end.

"Being is more important than professing," for if your example is good, your words will surely be more reassuring.

"Learning is more important than scholarship," for if you absorb the lessons of life carefully, you will indeed avoid many errors in human relationship.

"Duty is more important than renunciation," for you must first of all have something significant to renounce, whereas there will always be duties to fulfil in any circumstance of life.

"Obligations are more important than rights," for only after carrying out your obligations conscientiously, have you the right to claim your rights.

"Not offending others and not taking offence are more important than forgiving," for by not causing trouble to others and make them react, or by not making yourself vulnerable, you would not need to sit on the throne of forgiving.

"Being interested wholeheartedly and unselfishly in what you do and expecting a good result is more important than disinterested action regardless of result," for how can you improve your action without giving the best of yourself and learning from the result if it has been appropriately and efficiently done or not?

"Loving your friends is more important than loving your enemies," for it is your friends that care for and make it possible for you to love them, and your enemies give a damn whether you do so or not.

"Loving God is more important than fearing him," for fear invariably casts a pall over love and love is a greater liberating force to free us from errors than fear.

UNIVERSAL SPIRIT OF YOGA

In the Autumn 1988 issue of *Spectrum*, I found it quite interesting that the chairman of the British Wheel of Yoga, Pat Chittananda, was trying to initiate a dialogue with the Christian clergy to promote an understanding of what yoga is about. What is surprising, however, is that in a progressive country like Britain it should start so late.

As early as in 1960, as a secretary of the late Swami Sivananda, the founder of the Divine Life Society in Rishikesh, India, I was present when the Catholic archbishop of Agra came to him to enquire about the spiritual goals of yoga. That was two years before the Second Vetican Council began. It is known among the Jesuits that their former superior general, Pedro

Arrupe, practised yoga. In 1963, Thomas Merton, who was then a director of the Trappist monastery in Gethsemane, Kentucky, and already a famous author of Christian literature, invited me to give classes there not only of yoga philosophy but also of *asanas*.

Later, in 1968, I gave courses on Gyana Yoga at the Salvador University in Buenos Aires under its Jesuit rector Father Quiles. Since then I have done so in many other Catholic universities in both the Americas. That is why I find it so odd that in Britain Pat has still to say in the Chairman's Letter that "yoga is not evil" or that no one is "trying to convert anyone to Hinduism".

Yogic View of Religion: The fact is that, if you are secure in the moorings of your own religion, no one can take it away from you or convert you into another, and it is very odd that this anxiety should arise in a religion famous for its proselytising zeal and then try to deny others what it itself wishes to pursue.

Yoga is, of course, not a particular religion mainly because it is not bound to any obligatory dogma, such as Jesus Christ being the *only* begotten son of God, but it does respect the beliefs of those who worship him as a divine incarnation just as the Hindus believe Rama and Krishna to be so. In yoga, religion is a very private and personal concern of faith. What it tries to promote is a broadminded vision of one's personal choice.

To those who practise yoga, life itself becomes a living experience of religion, both in its highest spiritual and literal sense, for *re-ligare*, the Latin root for religion, means a continuous process of re-integration of the human nature with its potentially divine counterpart. Whatever means is useful to realise this goal, not in an afterlife, about which one can only speculate, but during one's lifetime, can be called practice of yoga. One who is deeply committed to spiritual ideals while not believing in any particular godhead is, indeed, a better religious person than a believer lacking in moral qualities.

Religion as a tribal identity is among the most primitive instincts of man because of ignorance, fear and insecurity, and can be dangerously divisive in a backward society. However, the general idea of religion is to unite the masses by an allegiance to a common divinity through identical beliefs, rituals and cultural habits. The yogic ideal of union (*yuj*), as also of *re-ligare*, retying, evolved because of the insatiable human hunger for perfect love, peace and truth, indicating to a spiritual source of one's being, a spark of God within, by a conscious unity with which it was believed that life could be made happier. The idea of this possibility also indicates to the fact that no one can want something of which one has no conscious or primordially unconscious experience.

Human and Divine Nature: As truth is self-evident, from universal experience we know that our origins are in both matter and spirit which coexist in a state of interrelatedness. Energy in a pulsating and interacting form being the basis of matter, we are a product of the nature's law of evolution. Having evolved from lower forms of life, our body and mind are subject to the law of cohesion and decohesion, adaptive mutation, recombination, development and extinction of the form.

Early in human existence, a short lifespan made a high birthrate necessary, uncertain food supply induced greed, the need to hunt for food made violence imperative, physical weakness before a stronger opponent conduced to cunningness. It is only since nine thousand years, since the agricultural revolution, when collective living became a necessity, that moral codes began to serve, albeit not too successfully, as a restraining factor on the nature's neutral law of the bigger fish eating the smaller fish, or the survival of the fittest, or the ten percent of the more efficient among us having more rights than the ninety percent of the less capable, which we are still adhering to under the veneer of civilised norms of society.

However, being unhappy with natural laws, we became aware of a potential spiritual source of our being some three thousand years ago, when Vedanta philosophy spoke of man to be basically divine and also, at about the same time, the Old Testament declared that God created man in his own image. As identity has to be upward in order to give security and make evolution possible, harping on our monkey image is hardly helpful, and this clarion call to measure up to a divine image became the highest motivation that morality bestowed, rather than merely providing a balance of mutual self-interest.

It was among the most intelligent philosophical devices that helped to civilise society, and it had to come from the mouth of God in order to be acceptable to the primitive mind in awe and fearful of the supernatural, and also to inspire the more refined minds to raise themselves to their spiritual source. This image of God, or the Vedantic concept of man being potentially divine, in spite of his enormous capacity for wickedness, was no myth or an invention either, but a self-evident truth as we all know that our peace and happiness lie in the restraint and sublimation of the ego, love of truth and compassion, in goodness and purity of heart, and not in their contradiction. This is a basic ideal of yoga.

BASIC UNITIES

Unity of Life: Not only are the problems of suffering, selfishness and aggression similar everywhere, but also the need for justice, love and security. There cannot be a greater motivation for social justice than the ideal of not treating others as one would not like to be treated by others, the basis of Judeo-Christian ethics, and there cannot be a better inspiration for it than the recognition of the presence of God in everyone, as in Vedanta philosophy. In the midst of the self-evident inequality in every aspect of life, holding on to this belief in a common, spiritually-uniting factor is the best way to promote the civilising urges in society.

There is also a basic relatedness between man and nature, in spite of the occasionally adversary relationship. When nature is destructive and not beneficial, man has to control it to the extent necessary, such as by building dams and digging canals, but if he overexploits nature, the basic unity is disturbed and his welfare suffers. Sometimes nature is harmonious and sometimes not, such as in the case of overpopulation and epidemics. Nature by itself does not have a perfect intelligence, as man himself is an unfinished product, but behind this deficiency in creation there is a moving force of transcending imperfection. So, the intelligence of man and nature has to be mutually adaptive. Instead of conquering, man needs cooperation with nature.

Unity of Knowledge and Faith: Overcoming ignorance is a primary goal of yoga: ignorance of human nature and the spiritual make-up of our being, about life ridden by insecurity and attachment, about differing cultures due to dissimilar habits and appearance, about the universe we live in with many illusions and superstitions. It is ignorance that makes us deny the world as an illusion to avoid an unpleasant reality and seek comfort in the foggy bottom of speculation, and it is also ignorance that causes infatuation with what is inherently imperfect.

In yoga there is no antagonism between faith and reason, and their integration is a basic goal. Faith is the sunlight that lifts the mist of ignorance. Faith is the fountain of inspiration to search for truth, and reason is a disciplined effort to make such a search enlightening. There is neither blind faith nor dry intellection in yoga. No spiritual search is possible without inspiration, and the fountain of faith cannot irrigate the field of life well without the aqueduct of reason.

Reconciliation of the material and the spiritual, or man and God, is another goal of yoga. Out of a transcendental source, of which we know very little as yet, sprang this universe, and through a long process of evolution out of it rose man, and in him slowly awoke the need to know the ultimate origin of his origins. Thus, he sketched in the pages of his scriptures what he understood to be his source, the multihued imageries of God, reflecting the evolution of his own mind with its need for protection, emotional fulfilment and search for a meaning in life, and the clearer and purer his mind became the brighter the light of his inner spirit shone through it.

Unity of Creeds: In this process, man devised codes of conduct for his material security, and he wrote and recited prayers to improve his self-image through a higher identity and also for his protection. Thus, he organised religions with three basic components: rituals for group identity and personal sanctity; mythology to bring some colour to his rather dull life and also to explain a metaphysical meaning by interesting stories for simple minds; and philosophy to motivate, inspire and direct individual and collective life.

The last one helped him to define a sense of right and wrong, the four guiding principles of what is right being: 1) that which promotes harmony and unity, 2) that which helps to be creative and progressive, 3) that which seeks justice and welfare for all, relating one's own interests with that of the others, and 4) that which does not need to be concealed or be secretive about. The wrong is in their contradiction.

It is ignorance that makes us suspicious of each other's religion, and it is ignorance that confuses religion to be social customs and habits of prayer, rather than different ways of looking at and reaching out to the same spiritual source and destination. Yoga regards religions to be like different rivers rising from and flowing into the same ocean with different names, rising at first as vapour, then forming into clouds, becoming springs and snows in the mountains, then flowing as streams and swelling with rains as rivers to take on the characteristics of the lands they flow over, but ultimately to merge into the same ocean from which they rose.

Unity of Paths: A medieval sage of India, Appaya Dikshita, asked God for forgiveness for the three errors he made in the course of his devotional practices: to give him a name and a form who cannot be defined or limited to any concept or form; to localise him in a house of worship who is everywhere; and to praise him who does not need nor is susceptible to any praise like human beings. Yet he did so, the sage said, because his limited mind could not think of the infinite, because he needed a sacred place where he could forget the blemished world, and that in order not to be vain and proud he needed to attribute all glory to his divine father. This is the universal spirit of yoga.

Yoga being union, all its paths are intertwined, although we may be more involved with one particular path than the others. We cannot separate the search for truth in our understanding of life, in our thinking and conduct (Gyana Yoga) from the need to sublimate our passions and emotions through selfless love and devotion (Bhakti Yoga), nor from the need to look within, understand our mind and seek unity with God (Raja Yoga), nor from doing our duty with the love of the ideal of service (Karma Yoga). Hatha Yoga is not only a part of Raja Yoga but is useful also to the others by keeping the body healthy. What objection can Christianity have to all this?

WHO REALLY IS A YOGI?

By definition, of course, one who practises yoga is a yogi. But who really is a yogi? In India, the image of a yogi is generally of a man sitting in lotus posture, in deep meditation, bare-bodied, even if high up in the Himalayas. He seems to have no possession at all. The idea is that he has withdrawn from the world, is impervious to heat and cold, has absolute domination over his mind, breath and body, and is seemingly in a continuous state of transcendental consciousness (*samadhi*), or union with God (*Ishwara*) as Patanjali would say. But what good is he to his fellow-beings? His followers would claim that he is helping the entire humankind by his meditation. But where is the evidence? After all, the first qualification of truth (in Latin *veritas*) is verification.

In the West, if someone twists his body in various postures (*asanas*) and does certain breathing exercises (*pranayamas*) regularly, he can claim himself to be a yogi, just because he practises two of the aspects of Hatha Yoga. But Hatha Yoga is only a minor branch of yoga, even though all-important in the West, and Hatha Yogis in India are generally not highly regarded, mainly because most of them tend to be overconscious of their bodies and are rather ignorant of the spiritual side of yoga. There is surely nothing derogatory about Hatha Yoga, as long as one does not lose the sight of the higher goals that an optimum condition of physical and mental health may help to attain. But there are many Hatha Yogis who, in spite of their lifelong practice, fall sick due to the factors of heredity and lifestyle.

The meaning of the word yoga, of course, is 'union'. A more significant translation would be 'integration'. It means an integration of the body, mind and soul, bringing the three aspects of the human being into a state of balance. The term body indicates physical nature, dominated by earthly instincts.

What is meant by mind is rational intelligence and by soul unselfish, idealistic aspiration to realise higher values. Yoga also means unity of heart and mind, or faith and reason, faith that is love of an ideal and reason a search to know its reality. It is a folly to separate the two.

Patanjali interprets yoga as a controlled state of mind in the second *sutra* of his Raja Yoga, to be acquired through meditation, but urges ethical and spiritual disciplines (*yama* and *niyama*) as the first two steps because, without a practical application of noble ideals, meditation will at best be a relaxing experience through a mild form of self-hypnosis or just an exercise in wool-gathering.

Many traditional books define yoga as "union of man with God." But who knows what God is? For any two entities to unite spiritually, one must know the other very well on a tangible, understandable level. Since we do not know what God is, and what is learned about God from anywhere is only half of the truth, the other half having to be completed by each one for oneself, it is better to begin by working on ourselves.

The highest value of yoga is in the integration of the two sides of our nature, human and spiritual. The fact that a liar does not want to be lied to, a hater to be hated, a violent person to be treated violently, that one finds peace in forgiveness rather than by vengeance, shows that we do have a spiritual side. The sublimation of the human nature by awakening the dormant soul within is the basic goal of a yogi. He starts with bringing his thought, word and deed in a straight line, for any yogic integration begins with integrity.

FIVE INTEGRITIES

The five integrities that a yogi should seek to perfect are:

1) *Integrity of thought* means to be honest with oneself and not indulge in wishful thinking. It means to search for truth by evidence, rather than a dumb acceptance of what is said just

because it suits oneself to do so. It is to measure the validity of a theory by its consequence through its implementation, and testing on a collective basis over a long period of time, for truth is not merely a claim verified but it is a principle of common security and welfare.

It is said that "Dreams are private myths and myths are public dreams," both being necessary to communicate between the known and the unknown, between individual and public psyche and the reality of human nature. The weaving of myths around and about God is inevitable due to man's psychological inadequacy and dependence, but as long as they do not mislead people by encouraging irrationality and are done in good taste, they serve a useful purpose. However, the yogi should search his heart to find out if he really believes in what he reads and professes.

2) *Integrity of feeling* means not to indulge in sentimentalism, which simply is a form of self-love, either about God or in a human relationship. It is to deepen sentiments by the purity of devotion. Even on a human level, a better definition of love is that it is a form of devotion for the finest qualities and values in a person one loves. Then, the basic requirement of measuring one's feelings by deeds has to be met. When the heart moves, the hands also should move.

3) *Integrity of speech* indicates not merely to desist from lying blatantly but not to exaggerate, undermine, misrepresent, manipulate or distort facts to suit one's convenience. It is to refrain from saying something one does not really mean. It is not to be a panegyrist without conviction or perform for the gallery for self-enhancement. It means the supreme importance of keeping one's word. It is to avoid dripping with fat by flattering a vainglorious person, for a yogi should not indulge in buttering up others or allow their vanity to be tickled by it.

4) *Integrity of action* is to be constructive in deed and avoid harming others either thoughtlessly or deliberately due to

vindictiveness. It means to have a sense of duty and carry it out intelligently and responsibly. It is to have the spirit of service and selflessness in helping someone in need, without making him feel like an object of charity.

5) *Integrity of conduct* begins with the Biblical injunction of not to treat others as one would not oneself like to be treated. It is to respect the rights of others before thinking about one's own prerogatives. It needs boundless patience and tolerance and a profound understanding of the generally complex human nature.

These five integrities are the basis of a yogic life, because it is only integrity with oneself and with others that makes integration with God viable at all. The greatness of a culture is directly relevant to the average level of honesty of its people, just as an abiding honesty and selflessness are the shining qualities of a yogi. Duplicity cannot sully his generous heart, and his tolerance for the defects of others is due to his deep compassion, while his inner detachment makes his sense of responsibility all the more effective.

OTHER QUALITIES OF CHARACTER

Just as simple peasants cannot distinguish between intelligence and cunning or between dignity and vanity, the spiritually primitive cannot differentiate between tolerance and indifference or detachment and imperviousness to responsibility. The yogi does not live an unconcerned life but is full of concern for the welfare of those he cares for and is responsible to, because he is highly conscientious. He is never impersonal, since his religion begins with the assumption of personal responsibility in whatever he does, and his ears are surely sensitive to the call of duty. He never says that he is carrying out God's will, because he is not conceited enough to think that he has a private telephone line to God, but prays for guidance and strength to do what must be done to the best of his ability and in the light of his understanding, and with the help of God, but knowing well that it is he alone who must bear the responsibility for his deeds. He knows that it is imperative to come to grips with the realities of life and avoids being a philosophical sculptor whose material is fog!

A true yogi is not image-conscious and does not have the distressing habit of performing for others as a spiritual person, for a self-serving image, carefully polished up, can be mercilessly contradicted by one's deeds that will inevitably reflect upon it. One of the main reasons for not progressing on the path of yoga is the predilection to self-delusion. It is easy to fool oneself by pretty lies and, if indulged in long enough and if there are sycophants around to cater to one's vainglory, there is little to prevent oneself from being addicted to it.

A yogi should not be inclined to a false sense of modesty either and ought to avoid the habit of an elaborate display of humility to impress others. Vanity and arrogance are the twin companions of renown and power, even if they are dressed up in a dubious gesture of modesty, or in a theatrical claim of fulfilling God's mission or being dragged upon to do so by the urging of others.

There are two levels of progress in a person's life, the outer and the inner. Outer progress is a product of ambition and will and an insatiable hunger for achievement and wanting to be famous. It is a result of initiative, daring and tireless perseverance, as well as the capacity to exploit the circumstances to one's best advantage and the ability to harness other people's talents and employ them for self-enhancement. It is the result of a burning and consuming longing for success in what one craves for.

The inner progress consists in the cultivation of a pristine conscience, in painstaking and arduous crafting of ideals to be guided by in the sublimation of human nature, and to make oneself useful to others and in sharing the best one has. For such a person life is what he does with it, making the best use of his inner resources and grasping every opportunity to widen the horizons of his mind by learning in whatever ways he can, by cleansing his heart through selfless service, by refinement of his passions and sentiments through love of God and of those he can relate with. To him the saying that "life is transitory" means that it is all the more the reason to grasp well and make the best use of the moment, rather than drift about in lethargic detachment. To him life is far too precious and the focus of human relationship too short-lived as to be sullied by little grudges, meanness and animus.

WHO NEEDS A GURU?

No one is good enough to be another's spiritual master in an absolute sense—as a guide surely, but respecting the autonomy of the disciple. One should try to learn from those who have a superior quality of knowledge, worthwhile for application. The greatest teacher is God within, our innermost conscience, which has to be awakened through spiritual aspiration and, if we are lucky enough, with the help of a few we can relate to due to the chemistry of spirit, affinity of ideals.

Is a guru absolutely necessary? I would say no. Most great teachers did not have any. Ramakrishna, Ramana Maharshi, Aurobindo and Sivananda did not have a guru in the traditional sense. Totapuri's contact with and initiation of Ramakrishna were informal. Vishwananda saw Sivananda in a *dharmashala* (inn) opposite the old post office of Rishikesh only for a few days (they never met again), and his token act of initiating Sivananda into monkhood (*sannyasa*), on 1 June 1924, was only symbolically meaningful. Aurobindo's encounter with a teacher, when a professor at Baroda College, was casual. Ramana Maharshi did not have a guru. Neither was initiated as a monk. They were self-made gurus. The real meaning of a guru is a specially personal and long-lasting spiritual bond with a disciple. Few indeed are lucky to have it. To have masses of disciples is a contradiction of this meaning.

DEFINITIONS OF GURU

The two most commonly-accepted interpretations of the word guru are "one who removes the darkness of (spiritual) ignorance" and "one who clears the obstacles on the (spiritual) path". As the Buddha says, the teachers can only show the ways for the disciples to choose from and walk along.

In India, the head of an *ashram* is called a guru, equivalent to an abbot in a Catholic monastery. A guru is also one who gives a mantra or *sannyasa* initiation. These are institutional and general definitions of the term guru. There need not be an incompatibility between the general and personal meanings, but the more general the term becomes, obviously the less personal its significance is.

That no spiritual progress is possible without a guru and that there is no need for a guru at all are equally ridiculous assertions. To have an honest and efficient teacher is a great help, but to be an unquestioning spiritual slave of another is to deny oneself personal responsibility. A glass is, of course, useful when it is empty, denoting humility of spirit and receptivity, but one should also have the choice of emptying what is let to be put in, if unsuitable.

It is not necessarily true that when the *chela* (disciple) is ready the guru will appear. Even supposing the disciple is ready, it is not sure that the guru will appear by himself. Instead of waiting forever, the *chela* should seek out a suitable teacher to learn from.

To learn simple arithmetic one has to go to a primary school first, then for algebra, geometry and more of arithmetic to a high school, and for higher maths to a university. One cannot master advanced mathematics right from the beginning all alone. Then, with a basic grounding, the erstwhile student progresses with personal research, while not losing a special bond if it did develop with a teacher. Looking back, my first five years with Swami Sivananda were most valuable for gaining maturity of perspective.

One should choose such teachings that, first of all, make sense in order to find out its usefulness by practical application. The purpose is to learn as best as one can, select the best and ignore the rest. That is what I did. The bottom line is not to be a hypocrite and pretend to follow and prattle something one does not honestly believe in. It is as simple as that.

GURU IS NO GOD

Along with Swami Venkatesananda, I happened to be in the last batch who had the benefit of learning from Swami Sivananda's class-talks. Thereafter, other senior monks did the teaching. We also learned from his books. What we learned most was, however, from the way he expressed his thoughts casually, from his attitude, his behaviour, the way he made decisions, his patience, tolerance, discretion, his forbearance of the foibles of others.

Meeting Jiddu Krishnamurti years ago, I was nonplussed at his obduracy in rejecting gurus and dismissing out of hand the ochre robe. He had a point, of course, there being so many sullied models swishing around in silken *gerua* (ochre) habits and, specially in India, knowing such theatrical hyperbole that connotes the role of a guru. However, leaving aside bad examples, including irrationally-dictatorial gurus, there are genuine swamis and decent gurus who never use their designations with a capital letter metaphorically.

To say that a guru is a visible god is to belittle the vision of the divine. People are, first of all and after all, human beings. After a lifelong effort at self-improvement and often with the advantage of being born with less of imperfection, there can be shining examples of integrity, compassion, selflessness and pure-heartedness. It does not mean that they are perfect and incapable of an occasional error of judgment or conduct due to the force of circumstances. That is why it is fair to say that saints actually live in heaven (an idealised vision of what they ought to be) and that they are made on earth by their disciples and institutions.

The double-consciousness of a *jivanmukta* (liberated soul while alive), that is, being in tune with God within and acting outwardly like others, as it is claimed, is rubbish, because one cannot be a saint inside and cut corners or behave otherwise externally. One should not only desist from doing what is wrong but ought not to be seen doing what can be considered improper. Then, again, why the fiat about liberation? From what? From imperfection? From the cycle of birth and death? Is it not complaining too much for being fed up with life? One cannot understand something in order to cope with while rejecting it, and given the chance one would indeed choose the imperfect known in preference to the Elysian unknown, for the simple reason that consciousness is geared to the tangible.

There are people, of course, who are inclined to be dependent, and some with a special need for a father-figure. For them a charismatic guru comes handy, although falling into wrong hands it can be very harmful. A real guru helps the disciple to stand on his or her mental, emotional and spiritual feet. A real guru does not brag about, or cause to be bragged about, as a self-realised or God-realised soul for the simple reason that these are mythical terms, self-realisation or God-realisation being an infinite process and cannot be worn as a celestial order. A real guru is also happy to see his disciple surpass him spiritually and as a teacher. Now you should know who really is a guru, a very difficult role to fulfil.

Chapter Two

THE PATH OF KNOWLEDGE

PHILOSOPHY AND PRACTICE OF GYANA YOGA

Gyana Yoga is one of the four major branches of yoga, the others being Bhakti, Raja and Karma, whereas Hatha Yoga is an auxiliary to Raja Yoga. If the earlier parts of the Vedas—*Samhitas, Brahmanas* and *Aranyakas*—could be called the Old Testament of India, the Upanishads, together with the *Bhagavad Gita,* are the New Testament.

The path of Gyana Yoga evolved about three thousand years ago. Its foundations are in the metaphysical philosophy of the Upanishads, which are also called Vedanta or the concluding (*anta*) parts of the Vedas. The Sanskrit word for knowledge is *gyana*, also spelt *jnana* but pronounced with the sound *ga* (as in go) with a slightly nasal sound of *gna*. The word knowledge comes from the Latin *gnoscere* (to know) which is derived from the Greek *gnosis*.

The purpose of Gyana Yoga is the realisation of one's spiritual potentialities and liberation or freedom from illusion, delusion, superimposition, untruth, fear, uncertainty, anxiety. Aristotle said that we all have an inherent right to knowledge, the right to know the truth. The New Testament says that truth shall make one free. The Upanishads say, *satyam, gyanam, anantam Brahma* or the supreme spirit is infinite truth and knowledge.

The second most important of human rights, after the right to life, *i.e.,* protection under the rule of law and the right to survive through the right to work, is the right to knowledge. It means not only the availability of universal education but the freedom to explore, know and express the truth after due verification by facts, and their relevance in the best light of one's understanding, so that people can be better informed and protected from exploitation by untruth, manipulated information and religious and ideological demagogy.

A society remains backward and impoverished because of its addiction to lie to itself and declare truth by fiat, confuse knowledge through regimented information such as under totalitarian governments, befuddle faith through blind conformity and abuse liberty through irresponsible licence. It is the controlled manipulation of knowledge, whether by the state or by a theocratic authority, that impedes the material, moral and spiritual progress of a nation.

A remarkable saying is: The main obstacle to knowledge, on a personal level, is the insolent ego and the main corruptor of faith is passionate dogmatism.

The purpose of knowledge is to know oneself so that the ego can be educated, desires controlled and passions sublimated. It is to know each other for improving mutual relationship through sharing of values and discipline of irrational expectation. It is to know the nature of the world and the universe we live in, so as to be free from the ignorance of our surroundings and, therefore, superstition. It is to learn a vocation to be economically independent and contribute to society, to deepen one's spiritual and cultural values in the process of trying to be a better person. It is to strive collectively to create a more compassionate, just and civilised society.

Even though it is said that Gyana Yoga is practised mainly by meditation on selected verses of the Upanishads and on *maha vakyas* or great sayings of related scriptures, it is actually a lifelong process of cultivating a philosophy of life and its application under different circumstances, requiring a lot of wisdom through experience, idealism and strength of character.

It is a common fallacy to think that techniques and daily routine alone, such as getting up before dawn, sitting in a cross-legged posture, closing the eyes and meditating on some mystic symbols, repeating a secret mantra, chanting hymns from the scriptures and doing some *asanas* and *pranayamas*, comprise the whole practice of yoga. These are only disciplinary means to a way of life guided by a state of mind that is shaped and reshaped through profound thinking and understanding of spiritual values in the anvil of personal experience.

The real practice of yoga consists in what you make of your life, how you think, feel, behave and relate, how you handle your emotions, passions and prejudices, how you cultivate a broad-minded, unbiased vision, what does God or the spirit of your being mean to you, how fulfilling are your relationships and, as such, how you form your overall perspective and, in the process, cultivate yourself.

The term self-realisation covers the gamut of all these, including the realisation of one's higher self which, according to Judeo-Christian credo, is called the 'image of God' consisting of infinite spiritual potentialities identical with the supreme goodness attributed to God. I prefer not to capitalise the letter 's' in the word self simply because we know so little even of our little self and avoid indulging in the bombastics about the higher self, while yet recognising the universal experience of the flow of the purest of emotions from this spiritual source.

God-realisation and self-realisation are relative terms indicating a lifelong quest which does not cease until the last day of one's life. Human nature being what it is can never be totally free from its residual dross even in a highly evolved soul. The idealised versions of a self-realised or liberated soul on earth are to show respect for saintly persons or for the creation of an institutional hierarchy.

FOURFOLD DISCIPLINES

Shankaracharya, the eighth-century Vedantin, sets down some basic requirements for a Gyana Yogi in his *Vivekachudamani*, which are also elaborated by other teachers as *sadhana chatushtaya* or fourfold spiritual disciplines. They are, of course, not the only ones for or exclusive to Gyana Yogis.

1) *Viveka* or cultivation of a discerning intelligence: To think by facts, not indulging in emotional fantasies. To try to know the nature of reality by uniting the perception of the external with the understanding of one's relationship with it through an inward search for its relevance. It is to know the nature of *maya* or the illusion experienced when under the spell of infatuation or being a slave of attachment, passions and desires.

Viveka should make one free from the myth about *maya* as well which projects the world as an illusion, in itself an irresponsible attitude born of unresolved frustration and discontentment on account of one's foolish attachment caused by self-love. The world is not an illusion but an empirical, even if changing, reality. Just because something is subject to change does not make it illusory. The illusion, or the avoidance of it, consists in one's attitude, perception of relevance and relationship to life.

Examples: Money as a token of acquiring material objects is not an illusion, nor are the objects illusory in themselves. It is hypocritical to deny their reality. Illusion is in the idea that money can buy friendship or love, although gratitude it can, or that material objects can make one happy, even if they do make life easier. The chemical property of the liquid in a £ 50 bottle of perfume is surely not an illusion. Its molecular reality is undeniable. The illusion is in a silly girl's imagining that the use of it will make her physically desirable enough for the eventual purpose of landing a prince charming.

One would be a liar to say that a house, to buy which someone has worked hard for years, is an illusion. Its reality to give protection against elements and material security by the title of ownership is obvious and necessary. But, just as one does not live by bread alone, one is not happy with a material reality by itself. Behind this external reality there is an inner reality which one seeks to relate with, for we are both matter and spirit. It is the reality of having a home which consists in a psychological experience of love and care, a sense of belonging to each other through sharing of values, understanding and support, an inner meaning of a home behind the external ownership of a house.

As such, whereas it will be irresponsible to deny the reality of a house by indulging in such inanity as 'snake-in-the-rope' analogy*, it will be even more irresponsible to neglect the nurturing of the greater reality of a home, wherever or with whomever or amidst whatever surrounding one lives, even if that be only a temporary home.

2) *Vairagya* or dispassion is acquired by the application of *viveka* in one's daily life. It does not mean a lack of interest or involvement. It means to free oneself from dependence on others at all levels, but mainly emotionally as in an ego-ridden, possessive relationship. It means to deepen one's spiritual love through the sublimation of physical passions.

The philosophy of *vairagya* consists in non-expectation while being unselfishly involved in the welfare of those one loves. It is not a moribund state of mind, the negative goal of

---

* A Vedantic saying about the illusory perception of the world as one would presume a rope lying on the ground to be a snake. One has to be rather dim and unduly apprehensive for such an assumption.

which is to be alive to nothing, avoid responsibility and vegetate in the dusk between life and death.

The goal of *vairagya* is to avoid mistakes by loss of judgment in a blindly attached relationship. Its purpose is to understand, educate and purify passions and desires, and acquire mastery over them for a better direction of one's life. The *Brihadaranyaka Upanishad* says: "The spirit of man consists of desire. As is his desire, so is his resolve. As is his resolve, so is his deed. As is his deed, so is his fate. If a man regulates his desire properly, he can lead himself to a desirable destiny."

The ideal is to have a measure of control over one's life. It means: Do not be resigned to presumptuous, ununderstood karmas of a past life which cannot be verified anyhow, do not be a victim of an unseen fate, do not be like a dry leaf tossed about by the gusts of other people's attitudes, do not be weak. The *Mahabharata* says, "to be weak is a great sin".

Vairagya should neither be mistaken for a state of egolessness. However much one tries, one cannot be free from the ego. You can only suppress it, hide it. To be unselfish and unassuming is a virtue, but to be egoless is not a desirable goal. The ego, or the consciousness of one's individuality, is imperative to making a choice, in order to be personally responsible. Also, a person with a listless ego can be a victim of another's strong ego and, thus, be easily manipulable and exploitable.

It is understandable though how uncomfortable one can get in the company of self-important persons, especially if they happen to be stupid. The ideal is to educate, refine and sublimate the ego, not to throw one's weight around and be obnoxious, not to be vain and conceited, for there is a lot to learn and much to improve in oneself. To be modest ought to be a natural virtue. Ignorance and dumbness combined with pretension and vainglory are malodorous ingredients for repugnance.

3) *Shat-sampatti* or the sixfold virtues to cultivate are:

i) *Shama* or tranquillity is acquired through the practice of detachment, patience, tolerance and understanding of human nature, meditation on the qualities of inner peace and freedom, and by recognising and correcting the causes of restlessness which are basically due to an excess of the ego, too many desires, uncontrolled passions such as anger and infatuation, and an absence of love due to one's selfishness.

ii) *Dama* is self-control, not through repression or guilt-complex, but by the love of the ideal behind as to why one should sublimate a negative instinct such as resentment because one is hurt more by it than the person resented. It is done by the substitution of a higher emotion through loving and helping those who need our love and attention, and by the practice of charity of heart. Patanjali calls this substitution process *pratipaksha bhavana* or a counterposing of feelings.

iii) *Titiksha* does not mean foolish austerity but signifies endurance of adverse conditions without complaining, after one has tried unsuccessfully, to change them. Reinhold Niebuhr speaks eloquently of this ideal: "God, grant me the serenity to accept the things I cannot change, courage to change the things I can, and the wisdom to know the difference." It also means self-denial to strengthen will power and physical endurance to toughen the body and mind.

iv) *Uparati* is aspiring for an inner satisfaction with the help of a higher desire in the process of overcoming a lower desire such as sensual passion through spiritual love, a desire to be famous by a desire for selfless service. It is also a form of substitution.

v) *Shraddha* or faith is cultivated, not by conformity or blind acceptance of a credo, but by a careful examination of the premises and motivation of one's beliefs, *i.e.,* if they are a manner of hoping for what is convenient or wishful thinking, or if they represent a true love of the ideal on which one's faith is focussed. When faith is love, it means to search for the true nature of the object of faith. It means practice of the spiritual qualities represented by such an object of faith, the person of Jesus to a Christian for example.

vi) *Samadhana* is resolution of doubts and inner contradictions through study and contemplation. It also means strengthening of resolve to do one's best in what should be done and commitment to ideals, with a mind free from fanaticism.

WHAT IS LIBERATION?

4) *Mumukshutwa* is the last of the four sets of disciplines given by Shankaracharya. Some commentators translate this term as a 'burning longing for liberation'. It is not to be misunderstood, however, as an escape from the 'cycle of birth and death' as the goal is superficially thought of by many Hindus, or as some Christians seeking salvation in order to avoid eternal damnation in the hell, because given the choice one is more likely to choose reincarnating into a state of existence known to oneself rather than opting for what is an unverified promise of a heavenly sojourn for ever.

As of now, personally it matters little to me as to what happens after death. In order to believe in an afterlife or be afraid of death one has to be sufficiently attached to the present life. If there is a reincarnation, as the Upanishads and also Pythagoras and Plato believed, it makes little difference because the conscious mind is not carried over to the next so as to remember the past motivation for striving for a better life.

Eternal heaven or hell, or being hurled into an animal birth, are not convincing enough for a rational mind, for even the most imperfect judge would not be so drastic in judging so a person on the dock in front of him. The soul, on the death of the body, being dissolved in the universal spirit would be ideal, like the symbolic doll made of salt dissolved itself as it started to swim in the ocean in search of its origin. But no one can be sure of one's preference at the moment of death, if a choice were possible. It is unrealistic to underestimate attachment to life.

What is more important is the tangible kind of liberation one should seek in this life, the only one we know enough to cope with, to take measure of and handle with sufficient care, so as not to hurt others and ourselves, to make the best of what we have, within potentially and without circumstantially. Thus, *mumukshutwa* can be interpreted as a longing to be free from the defects of human nature each day of one's life, rather than waiting for liberation or salvation on death.

Mumukshutwa is spiritual aspiration through a life devoted to 1) understanding, restraint and sublimation of mundane desires and passions, 2) integrity, honesty and straightforwardness, 3) compassion, generosity of heart, selfless service and love of one's fellow-beings, 4) education, discipline and refinement of the ego, and 5) commitment to such basic values as accountability, duty, trustworthiness, constancy, loyalty, responsibility, reliability and moral courage. The true meaning of *mumukshutwa* is to be free from the contradiction of these ideals in our character. It is, indeed, a lifelong process and demands attention everyday.

In a similar category of interpretation *mumukshutwa* can be defined as a longing for liberation from twelve *kleshas* or causes of human suffering: 1) *ahamkara*, ego, 2) *swartha*, selfishness, 3) *darpa*, arrogance, 4) *mada*, intoxication by pride, 5) *moha*, infatuation, 6) *kama*, lust, 7) *krodha*, anger, 8) *lobha*, greed, 9) *matsarya*, jealousy, 10) *irsha*, envy, 11) *dwesha*, hate, and 12) *dambha*, hypocrisy.

Far from being a dry intellectual pursuit, Gyana Yoga is a practical philosophy of life.

Gyana is a mental vision formed through a search for reality and strengthened by its application in daily life. It includes faith and devotion, mental discipline and meditation that inspired the teachings of Bhakti and Raja Yogas. The basic line, however, is liberation from *avidya* or ignorance and *maya* or illusion due to the ignorance of reality. *Vidya* or knowledge of reality in following the path of truth as per one's best understanding, however, is the primary concern of Gyana Yoga.

Transcendental knowledge is its goal, but it should not be taken to mean jumping out of one's mind into an airy state of blissful loftiness. The term is indicative of an ever-widening dimension of knowledge. As knowledge is infinite, any revelation is subject to a better revelation, any transcendental knowledge is geared to a greater transcendence. To transcend something you must know well what you are transcending. As knowledge, in order to express itself, has to be defined, there can always be a better definition. As such, Gyana Yoga is free from dogmatism characteristic to revealed religions.

The first step to Gyana is the awareness that one does not know enough. The *Kena Upanishad* says: "He who knows not [that he] knows not, knows not. He who knows [that he] knows not, knows." The second step is to find its validity by application, so that affirmations like 'reality is Brahman' or 'that thou art' do not remain figments of imagination. It is more important to know the truth of 'what am I' and start working on oneself from that level than jump into an ineffable 'that thou art'.

Like perfection, love, faith and devotion, truth has to be ever progressive and subject to verification in order to be acceptable as truth rather than an opinion. The Latin word for truth is *veritas* and the Sanskrit *satya* (truth) comes from *sat* or that which exists. Whether God as a deity exists or not is not a question of truth but of faith, and the reality of faith is in the truth of its consequence, *i.e.*, if the believer has spiritual strength and security and, therefore, peace and freedom from fear and anxiety.

WHAT IS GOD?

In Gyana Yoga, personal God such as the heavenly father is regarded as an idealised and visionary form of the universal spirit, not physical but spiritual, shaped and reshaped by the individual's devotional aspiration, which is again conditioned by one's cultural and historical background. As such, it is not imperative to a Gyana Yogi to believe in a personal deity but in the infinite spirit sustaining life at all levels, from the structuring of matter through energy to the expression of such spiritual qualities as peace and love, integrity and purity of heart, that are consciously or unconsciously longed for in human existence.

Most religions presuppose a supernatural creator, omnipotent and omniscient, to psychologically help in the process of survival and sustain hope that life can be happier herein and, due to attachment to the herein, in the hereafter. The Vedic religion, by observing the elemental forces of nature, created supernatural entities behind them. In Gyana Yoga, these elemental forces were fused into a transcendental spiritual force, calling it Brahman or the universal spirit, not a person, not a deity, not a creator but a creative, sustaining, illuminating and dissolving principle.

By observation we know that a life-giving principle enables continuity of existence, for example the seed of a tree becoming another tree, as it is with the animals and the humans, that it substantiates matter through energy, living beings through the vital force and the universe, including our earth, through a cosmic force whether one calls it a combination of the electromagnetic, gravitational and the cohesive and decohesive forces.

In an earlier age, before the evolution of Gyana Yoga, the instinct of fear and the desire to be protected and happy created sacrificial rituals in order to propitiate the elemental forces of nature. To promote a wholesome outlook, Gyana Yoga postulated that there is a superior force behind natural forces, that the universe is the body of this spiritual force or God, that all life is sacred, for there is God in all, that if you love God you love nature, love animals and love human beings. This postulation of divine immanence, while yet being transcendental, is a unique contribution of Gyana Yoga to the spiritual culture of humanity.

The diffidence to and fear of the supernatural gave place to optimism and love of idealism. Antagonism among the worshippers of different religious deities was sought to be dissolved by making these gods various expressions of the same spiritual essence as per the differing predilections in the cultural backgrounds of the people to express their devotion and aspiration, rather than subordinate or annul them under a supremely dictatorial God.

Gyana Yoga speaks of *prakriti* as the material force in creation, making evolution possible through interaction and competition, elimination and assimilation. Behind *prakriti*, out of which the body and mind are formed with instincts and passions, is *purusha* or the spiritual force expressing itself by love and truth, purity and selflessness, harmony and peace, in human consciousness.

This spiritual force is the essence of the individual soul that is identical with the infinite spirit. For example, if the sun is the source of light, the content of the individual soul can be compared to a spark of it in a state of embodiment. The physical body is the vehicle, within it is the mind containing instincts, memories and a discerning intelligence, and within the mind is hidden the spiritual spark giving it the light of perception and life to the body. The mind is like a lampshade. The cleaner the lampshade the clearer the expression of the light.

WHAT IS DESTINY?

The interaction of the material and spiritual forces shapes human destiny. When the spiritual force has a better sway over the material force, there is harmony and life is happier. When the material force dominates the spiritual force, there is conflict with its consequent suffering. In a state of fusion of these two forces the infinite spirit is transcendent and, thus, impartial and beyond good and evil.

Without the interaction of these two forces emerging from a transcendental source, consciousness cannot be evaluative. *Prakriti* or nature by itself is neither moral nor immoral, such as in the suffering brought about by an earthquake to both the good and the wicked alike and, thus, cannot be called an act of God but a consequence of an evolutionary process in nature.

Our responsibility to both these forces in awakening and tapping the spiritual and controlling and utilising the natural, within and without, makes us the hewer of our destiny, although there is always an element of the unknown which Gyana Yoga tries to explain by the philosophy of karma. Unlike in many religions, the infinite spirit, God of the Upanishads, does not reward or punish. One reaches out to it through holy aspiration and draws strength and inspiration for one's deeds. It is the individual who rewards and punishes himself through his deeds.

The philosophy of karma is a rationalisation of destiny as a substitute to the presumption about God's will and nihilistic pessimism about the unfairness of life, such as the circumstance of birth, inequality of opportunity, difference in intelligence, inborn talents and character traits, the instances of some of those trying to live honestly losing and some of the wicked winning. It tries to answer the question why life is so unequal and full of vagaries.

There is nothing dogmatic about the theory of karma, as also with the other basic philosophical positions in yoga, but an attempt is made to promote an understanding of the nature of life. If it helps, fine. If it does not, search more and find your own solution.

As attachment to life causes notions about afterlife and as reward and punishment determine the nature of afterlife in heaven or hell, the idea of one life alone makes divine justice brutal and amnesty brought about by repentance only rather farcical. The philosophy of karma and the inevitable reincarnation is an attempt, however imperfect, to make life fairer.

Love of life is inherent in all and leads to attachment to our existence, and this attachment to notions of immortality. Immortality presupposes life after death. As desire for a life free from trouble assumes experience of happiness, and as no happiness can be sustained as such without the polarity of experience, a state of permanent bliss is an irrational expectation.

As everything in creation is subject to change, the Upanishads presume heaven and hell to be as impermanent as the earth, and are for a temporary sojourn only for the virtuous and the wicked, respectively. Symbolically they ought to be regarded as a part of life's experience right here on earth.

The predilection to reincarnation on earth is an acknowledgement of the preference of the known rather than the unknown, if one is given the choice, although the Upanishads speculate about many planes of existence of higher and lower levels of evolution. Such an idea is surely not impossible considering that in the galaxy of our solar system alone there are a hundred to two hundred thousand million stars.

If a medium-size star like our sun can have an earth among its nine planets with a life-supporting environment, there could be millions of others among the billions of galaxies.

Ultimately, Gyana Yoga presumes, when the human being attains an optimum level of spiritual evolution and when all earthly desires are satiated and sublimated, there remains only the longing of the pure essence of the soul to merge itself into its origin, the infinite, eternal, universal and transcendental spirit. The embodied spirit finally returns to its source. The doll made of salt loses its embodiment in the salt of the ocean.

PATHS ARE INTERRELATED

As in other yogas, Gyana requires guidance, ethical conduct and self-discipline. First is through study and contemplation. It is an individual search, although with the help of teachers, but spiritual dependence on any external authority is not encouraged and only guidance sought in order to improve one's discernment. Ultimately, anyhow, all learning is through personal experience.

Ethical conduct needs an adequate sense of right and wrong developed by study and contemplation, and substantiated by practical experience and the evaluation of the results of one's actions. Self-discipline is best acquired through inspiration of the ideal behind the act of discipline. If you want something for your good, you have to love the goal with your heart and soul.

It is a mistaken idea that Gyana Yoga is devoid of emotion, for knowledge and devotion, which is a higher form of emotion, are two sides of the same coin. The two cannot be separated. Just as Gyana is not merely an intellectual vision, Bhakti is neither a flux of emotionalism. Through devotion comes peace and through knowledge strength, through devotion grace and through knowledge wisdom.

Brahman, while not being a deity but infinite spirit, is grace that is love and light that is knowledge. Knowledge is born in the heart through spiritual aspiration, not in the head. Reason or *yukti* (literally, uniting) is learned in the head through intellectual discipline and Gyana or wisdom is awakened in the heart as a result of absorbing the essence of knowledge through the practice of spiritual ideals.

In Gyana Yoga, God is neither one nor many but transcendental and universal spirit. The infinite cannot be particularised as one, or even absolute (*ab*, from, *solvere*, free) because the absoluteness of the absolute is dependent on the non-absolute and, thus, cannot be 'free from' or truly absolute. There are no greater or lesser gods but better and lesser understanding of spiritual values and, therefore, of God.

The immanence of the transcendental spirit gave birth to morality which Gyana Yoga does not consider as social norms but as a basic respect for life expressed through disciplines like, as per Patanjali's rules codified many centuries later, non-violence (*ahimsa*), truthfulness (*satya*), chastity (*brahmacharya*), non-stealing or honesty (*asteya*) and non-covetousness (*aparigraha*).

Teachings of the scriptures are called threads (*sutra*) with which one has to weave one's own garment of realisation. Illusions are not outside but in our own mind. The changing nature of the material world does not make it unreal, just as one's ideation about the reality of Brahman does not make God any more real in life but the practice of spiritual values attributed to him.

Gyana Yoga respects saints and prophets and acknowledges their role in the guidance of humanity. It insists on the autonomy of the individual spirit and personal responsibility for spiritual progress. Whereas God's grace and the unique role of the personal deity, such as Jesus Christ for the

Christians and Krishna for the Vaishnavite Hindus, are imperative in Bhakti Yoga, they are not basic to Gyana Yoga.

Ethical conduct is meant to give a concrete expression to knowledge, devotion and meditation. It is a common imperative to all yogas, as also self-denial and self-discipline in order to gain inner strength. Without integrity and mental clarity (Gyana), love and compassion (Bhakti), one-pointed and balanced mind (Raja) and righteous and selfless conduct (Karma) no branch of yoga can be of great significance.*

THE SPIRIT OF THE UPANISHADS

The fulfilment of a sense of belonging is one of the deeper human needs. In all civilisations, the questions about our origin and the purpose of existence have troubled thinking minds in search of an inner security and the reason for being alive. Some forty thousand years ago, man began to express his relatedness to life around through his cave paintings and, much earlier, his feelings by blowing into his bamboo flute. Nine thousand years ago, agricultural communities were already living on the banks of the Euphrates, Tigris, Jordan, Nile and the Yellow river. In ancient India, some 6,000 years ago agricultural communities were thriving in the region of the five rivers (*pancha apas*, from which the name Punjab is derived).

Rains and floods, so necessary for agriculture, gave man a sense of relatedness to nature. His primitive mind was frightened by natural forces: lightning, thunder, storm, earthquake, death. Man's constant companion was fear, even as it is today in a reasonable form. His life was and still is violent, because he has evolved from the brute forces of nature.

We are individual capsules of thousands of millions of cells, each with a limited and similar intelligence of its own,

* Excerpts from class-talks given at Saint Vincent's monastery in Mill Hill, London, between June 1 and 7, 1991, during a spiritual retreat.

bearing the imprint of not only our physical forms and susceptibility to disease but also emotional and character patterns, transforming and evolving, adapting and mutating in relationship to environment through their own momentum as well as by our individual effort.

The idea that man originated from a divine being came much later to help him overcome his brutish nature by a higher sense of identity, for identity serves its purpose, to give security and fulfilment, only when directed upward. However, those who devised such an identity extended their own imperfect nature by making the creator, being disgusted with his creation, which was after all his work, try to liquidate his creatures by deluge (Genesis). Man transferred his insecurity and jealousy by making God demand that no other gods be adored before him and threaten that if idols were worshipped, not only will such a worshipper be punished but his children and their children as well, revealing man's vengeful character (the first two of the Ten Commandments), and his distressing egolatry *(Bhagavad Gita).*

The clever among men exploited man's fear for survival by inventing a series of rites to propitiate supernatural entities called gods behind natural forces which threatened him, thereby creating a caste for commiseration between men and gods. The murderous nature of man expressed itself through human sacrifice, of those whom he did not like or was envious of. A little improvement in his relationship to the supernatural we note in the sacrifice of the bull in Sumer, or the horse in ancient India (*Ashwamedha Yagna*), or the ram in Judea.

In Vedic India, some 3,800 years ago, poets began to sing hymns in praise of entities behind natural forces, because man was awed and frightened by them, such as by lightning (Indra) as well as needed them for agriculture (Varuna) and survival (Vayu and Agni). Man's relationship to Jehova was not very different either, being afraid of and needing him as well for protection. All these responses show that we have evolved from the forces of nature, reflecting the violence of storm and the gentleness of breeze, domination of the powerful and the submission of the weak.

More than 3,200 years ago, astute and intelligent leaders like Moses tried to unify these forces into a supremely powerful creator, demanding the highest from his chosen people (sic) a moral obedience, which would make them deserving of God's love, and therefore protection, by overcoming their passions (again the forces of nature) to which they might succumb by not living up to the goodness of God in whose image they were created, although Moses did not explain how God could be as vengeful as man himself.

From the gods we needed power because being powerful we could survive better, we needed wisdom because being ignorant our life was full of fears. Thus, Zeus became the powerful leader of the Greek gods and, to a lesser extent, Indra of the Hindu gods. Jehova became the only true God for the Jews rejecting all other gods, as Allah for the Moslems, and the Christ the sole incarnation of God for the Christians.

MYSTICAL VISION

In the later Vedic period, about the time of Solomon, the Upanishads tried to unify all the Hindu gods into a mystical, eternal, all-pervasive, infinite spirit called Brahman who, by becoming all, not rejecting any, made religious prejudice irrelevant, and it did not matter by what name it was called. It did not solve social prejudice, of course, but an attempt was made at theological tolerance. The transformation of a primordial and transcendental spiritual essence as the universe by its creative principle (*brahma*) and its sustenance by its cosmic mind (*hiranyagarbha*) through the laws of nature (*prakriti*) was a unique idea originating in the Upanishads, although it was not explained how could a perfect essence become an imperfect creation.

A product of this mystical vision was the Buḍdha who, 2,500 years ago, thought that love among people was more important than what one thought about God. He taught that love was the water which put out the fire of hate, and said that when one's house was on fire one did not ask who caused the fire but tried to put it out. So, indeed, it is pointless to dispute about God when there is so much suffering in life but more important it is to find ways to overcome it by spiritual effort.

Two thousand years ago, a great reformer arose in a Hellenised Jewish Society, to whom God was love and his justice was tempered by mercy. Jesus made loving God meaningful by loving one's neighbours, and returning good for evil as a way of overcoming the vengeful human nature. He appealed to the good in us and, like the Buddha, taught that the retribution of evil can only perpetuate evil, and the way out of it was to step out and do the opposite.

The Vedic immanence of God by sensing which we can soften somewhat the coarseness of life, the Jewish ideal of not treating others as one would not like to be treated, the Buddhist compassion, the Christian charity and the Moslem brotherhood did not free the mind from intolerance, of course, but as a positive influence helped to civilise society.

A mystical vision of the "tree of life" rises in the Upanishads and later in the *Bhagavad Gita,* a tree which has roots in heaven and the trunk, branches, leaves and fruits on earth, the latter being our earthly existence conditioned by material surroundings, while yet drawing its sap from the roots projected into our divine identity.

The Upanishads speak of our bodies as a part of the universe, our minds as sparks of the cosmic intelligence trapped in their opaque jackets of matter, and our souls as droplets of the infinite spiritual essence expressing itself through truth and love, beauty and goodness, however limited their understanding be in our finite minds, but they make morality meaningful and provide a healing grace to life.

The Upanishads underrate rituals and glorify Gyana or wisdom which is meaningful only when applied on a tangible level in human relationship. They do not edify suffering but the means to overcome it through renunciation of attachment and pride, and by truth, love and self-discipline. They ask for the worship of Brahman by the practice of three ideals: *rita* which is a sum total of righteousness, truth, faith and divine law, *yagna* or sacrifice of ignorance and selfishness, and *tyaga* or renunciation of passion, vanity and slavery to the sense-objects.

Sacrifice is not a diminishing act but a creative process, because knowledge frees us to be creative whilst ignorance and selfishness make us limited. By renouncing attachment and pride, passion and vanity, we learn to love truly and relate better with others. Seeking truth we improve our understanding of life and can deal with its problems without being affected by *maya* or illusion, a product of perception without wisdom or perception distorted by passion and attachment, and refrain from the illusion of regarding the world as an illusion.

ALL-PERVASIVE SPIRIT

The *Chhandogya Upanishad* gives an all-pervasive vision of God and man's relatedness to him, which is a typical *elan* in Gyana Yoga:

The infinite spirit
Is above and below,
To the east and to the west,
To the north and to the south;
Truly, it is the whole universe.

Then comes the teaching in the same Upanishad about dissolving our isolated egos:

I am above and below, I am
To the east and the west,
To the north and to the south;
Truly, I am this whole universe.

After this message of the relatedness of the human spirit to the transcendental and yet immanent infinite spirit, a vision of our destiny is given in the *Mundaka Upanishad*:

As rivers flowing forward
Find their home in the ocean,
Leaving name and form behind,
So does man, released
From name and form,
Draw near the divine spirit
Which is beyond the beyond.

This inseparability of the immanence and transcendence of God is a special contribution of the Upanishads to the philosophical and religious search of humanity. The all-pervasiveness of *Isha* (Lord or God) is narrated in the *Isha Upanishad*:

The unmoving one
Is swifter than thought;
The gods (luminous intellects)
Cannot get hold of it,
As it speeds ahead of them.
It moves and moves not,
It is far (for the ignorant)
And yet near (to the wise);
It is within the whole universe
And yet beyond it.

The Upanishads speak of God interchangeably as *purusha* (supreme being), *brahman* (infinite spirit) and *paramatman* (supreme soul), while maintaining that such a being is formless, all-pervasive and transcendent, of which the soul or the spirit of man is a part, not a part of the partless spirit but like the formless space within a jar (*ghatakasha*) taking the form of the jar and apparently being in a state of separateness from the formless space around it, the human vehicle as the body, mind and personality being the jar.

The many visions or ideas about God can be compared to the colours of a rainbow, as man tries to find his real self through many cultures, religious posturing and spiritual aspiration, refracting the white light of his inner spirit in the many hues of his mind. Although they apparently clash with each other when set apart, ultimately they come from the same source, the white light.

This is the spirit of the Upanishads which shone for a while in ancient India. To negate this universal vision and make God a tribal deity is to use religion as a divisive and obscurant force, which we often do, rather than a uniting and illuminating influence in life, which its Latin root *re-ligare* (reunite) literally means. Religion becomes an opiate when it sets apart God from the world and makes him a means of escape from suffering that is a part of life. This does not solve the problems that cause suffering but anesthetises one to it.

The obvious reality is that man has not found the happiness he seeks and, in the process of seeking it, has created a God of his imagination. If the imagination is primitive and merely to serve the need for protection, the bones of his fear and prejudice rattle in the closets of his scriptures. If his imagination widens and soars as spiritual aspiration, he finds the reality of peace and fulfilment, and tries to make the world a better place to live in, to the extend he is capable of, by the expression of his higher self. Thus, the meaning of life is realised individually as to what we want to make of it and are capable of effectuating. The Upanishads ask us to shape it by three means:

Through loving devotion (*bhakti*) to what is noble or to spiritual ideals, the supreme symbol of which is God, without a threat of having to be accountable to a deity and grovel for mercy, and without emotional theatrics.

Through contemplative understanding (*gyana*) of what such ideals mean in the depth of our feelings rather than through an intellectual effort, in a pure heart rather than by doctrinaire dialectics.

We make such an understanding of our love meaningful for what we adore spiritually, in the way we act (*karma*) and get along and work with others, in how we love those who are dear to us, how we hope and manage our desires, how we cope with adversity that may cross our path, and how we pick ourselves up from the consequences of our errors, our minds and feelings temporarily bruised but the spirit remaining unsullied.

THE VISION OF VEDANTA

Is there a meaning to our existence? It is for the individual to make one. By itself there is none, considering the massive, brutal forces, and the consequent suffering, through which life has evolved. In the march of civilisation we have tried to tame our animal nature, and refine our sensibilities to widen the awareness of what we are and wish to be, and what is around. Through such an interaction we seem to seek out a purpose, create a motivation, for being alive. The bottom line is love of life.

The invention of agriculture nearly ten thousand years ago, having forced us to live in communities, led to initial experiments in what should be our behaviour pattern, for the sake of social harmony and creativity. Out of it evolved notions of justice through retribution and reward.

Even earlier, the struggle for survival created an inherent insecurity in our mindset, and initiated the role of shamans who gave the sick herbal and mineral extracts, and did magical incantations to cast off the evil eye by imagining and invoking supernatural forces. Millennia rolled on.

From insecurity came fear, and from fear the need to be saved. Thus came about the idea of salvation. Few thought that it was cruel to be damned by the original sin of a mythical ancestor, that was neither comprehensible nor fair, and then be offered the grail of salvation!

Since human relationship was not all that pretty, the cloud of unhappiness, not being emotionally fulfilled adequately, drifted in and out of our consciousness. Thus, fear and unhappiness became the parents of religion, and tribal identity for group security its jealous mistress.

Attachment to life as we know, to our body and the objects of pleasure to make it happy, led to the notions of afterlife minus the miseries. The urge for happiness and to avoid suffering being inherent, there rose the visions of paradise and fantasies of eternal bliss.

Few bothered to think that the intensity of experience wanes through continuity, and that any psychological experience is possible at all by its relativity to the residual memory of its opposite. It was easier to be spaced out in transdimensional fog than to come into grips with tangible reality requiring personal responsibility.

Being tired of the bipolar swings from excitement to ennui, the fatigue of the spirit gave birth to the idea of going beyond the mind, rising above duality, merging in the infinite spirit.

Since we did not want those we disliked on earth to be around in paradise, and were too weak to punish those who had harmed us, we invented an appropriate place like hell for them to be roasted in!

As civilisation evolved, the angst of existence produced some real philosophers—not the stereotype wool-gatherers—who sought answers to the quirks of life from within, asking the reason why, observing and learning from experience, trying to free the mind from superstition and ignorance.

FAITH AND REASON

Much earlier had formed the second oldest profession, to which in a way I happen to belong, that of the priests, the successors of shamans (the spirit inevitably takes a back seat behind flesh). They tried to cope with a vastly numerous and rather superstitious clientele, by seeking guidance from above, in their fertile minds communicating with heavenly deities.

Brahmanas, or the intermediaries between Brahma the creator and his imperfectly-created beings, crafted *karma-kanda* in the Vedas, or ritualistic duties to absolve sin and, therefore, punishment, and ensure heavenly existence in after-life, and to keep themselves employed meanwhile!

The rishis or philosophers devised *gyana-kanda,* or moral duties inspired by the knowledge of spiritual identity among fellow-beings, and search for reality behind appearance. They sought the roots of spirit inside human nature through some basic observations: that truth gave security, unselfish love fulfilment, and purity of heart peace. They found that it was a universal experience.

Hebrew prophets like Moses, Samuel, Isaiah, Micah and others, having earlier discovered (if you don't like the subversively-honest word 'invented') God, as he came to be regarded in Western and Islamic societies, laid out what conduct should be on the platform of Ten Commandments. They sought guidance from above by the fulcrum of faith to interpret what God said through Moses in the Torah, although other authors also contributed to it after him.

Hellenic philosophers like Socrates, Plato, Aristotle, Pythagoras and others sought direction from within in the fountain of reason and spirited dialogue, thereby enabling personal search and consensus.

Both did so by commitment to ideals they loved, the former through obedience and the latter by reason. The former had the motivation of heaven, and the fear of hell. The latter had the satisfaction of the search for truth, and in being fair to all citizens alike (ignoring the slaves).

The imperative of commandment is obedience, and the tool of obedience, in the common mind, fear. The imperative of reason is mutual welfare, and the tool of discipline the love of the reason why, or inspiration, rather than manipulating the emotions of fear and unhappiness, which religion did.

Religion found the individual to be weak-minded, indecisive, selfish and prone to avoid responsibility. It provided the alternative as submission to God's will (as if you had a direct line of communication), while obeying his commandments as the scripture dictated. The celebration of the suffering of Job, of the virtuous, not questioning God's wisdom, became the test of faith.

Human nature being more emotional than rational, more lazy to work on itself than getting emotional about a deity to appeal to for a way out, religion succeeded and the philosophers failed. You have only to look at the clientele.

Few bothered to think that Job's case was exceptional in being rewarded in this life itself. To the suffering individual, the incomprehension of a divine mind becomes meaningless, as does the promissory note of reward in the intangible afterlife.

Suffering by itself corrupts and promotes servility, unless one specifically tries to learn from it before getting benumbed. The proclamation of its virtue also comes handy in offsetting the possibility of a revolution by the masses against the minority of the privileged classes, thus safeguarding their hypocritically much-maligned filthy lucre.

For some, like Job, faith is acceptance of fate ordained by God. For the vast majority faith is just a hope. For only a few faith is commitment to the ideals that the deity ought to inspire: purity of heart, selfless love and integrity; devotion, discernment and dispassion; loyalty, fairness and duty; responsibility, humility and accountability.

Belief is a bridge between the known and the unknown. It begins with a provisional acceptance requiring a search in order to encounter the reality of its premise. If you accept nothing, you find nothing. If you accept something and do nothing to find its truth, you remain stupid! If the search is fruitful, the element of doubt inherent in belief disappears. Then you no longer say "I believe that it is so" but calmly state "I *know* that it is so, and yet I have a lot more to know about it."

Belief by itself means a possibility, even plausibility. If you stretch it too far, it enters the realm of wishful thinking, if not hypocrisy.

CONSCIENCE

Devising the role model of God is fundamental to evolution, as identity serves both the needs for security and upliftment from a deficient state of being. Imagine the shock to self-importance if one is identified with the monkey! Imagine, again, the sanity of chest-thumping for being created equally in the image of God, or the *jivatma* (individual soul) being identical with the *paramatma* (supreme soul), when at every step the inequality of life contradicts it. The easy way out is to blame it on *agyana* (ignorance) or the original sin.

The presumption, however, provided the seeds of human rights and adult franchise, which took nearly three thousand years to germinate, apart from individual spiritual aspiration since much earlier, that gave birth to conscience. The sanctity of life is the basis of democracy.

Conscience is a product of a sense of guilt in giving vent to lower passions, in the process of surviving at the expense of weaker individuals. It is evolutionary in nature, and mainly formed by education and cultural influence. No one is born with a God-given conscience for making a choice.

The raw human nature on its own has no conscience, and actuates itself by the rule of mother nature (*prakriti*): that might makes right, that the fittest ought to survive at the expense of the weaklings, that cheating is inevitable if one can get away with it.

The human spirit, originating in *purusha* (infinite spirit), however, feels suffocated by such a rule, and seeks peace by countering it through self-restraint, self-denial, compassion and fairness to all.

The human nature being a contradiction unto itself, due to the interaction of *purusha* and *prakriti*, falls for the palliative provided by religion that the creator's wisdom is ineffable, that if you cannot overcame suffering, you have to bear the burden gracefully.

Few bother to see the contradiction of how can the supreme being be all-powerful and yet indifferent to the prevalence of injustice, be all-merciful and yet unable or unwilling to prevent suffering brought about by war, famine, holocaust, Gulag, genocide and pestilence.

Thus, arises the philosophy, religion's palliatives apart, that life is what you are able to make of it, tapping the potentials from within, and making use of the opportunities around, venturing out and seeking them, to the best of your ability. Only then can you learn from the quirks of fate. Only by experimenting any premise of knowledge in real life that you know its reality.

ORIGIN OF VEDANTA

Like the Old Testament, the Vedas speak of the story of a people who called themselves *arya* (in Sanskrit the word means noble). The Vedas are the earliest religious literature extant that have shaped the Hindu view of life. The word is derived from the root *vid*, to know. About the time of Abraham, some 3,700 years ago, the Aryans came from the north-west to the 'land of five rivers,' *pancha apas*, from which the name of the province Punjab is derived. They found an already-existing civilisation in the Indus valley in what is now Pakistan. Its roots may have existed earlier in Sumeria.

The Aryan tribes got partially absorbed by it, willy nilly, and extended themselves into the Gangetic plains and the Himalayas within a few centuries. They were fascinated by nature, and had already composed many exquisite odes expressing their relationship with the universe. These formed the early part of the Vedas, and were called *Samhita*. The Aryans recited the odes as a part of their religious practice.

By the time of the early Hebrew prophets, nearly 3,000 years ago, the philosophers among the Aryans started composing the Upanishads. These came to be known as *Vedanta*, and formed the fourth part of the Vedas, the second and the third parts being *Brahmana* and *Aranyaka*, consisting of rituals and social codes, respectively. The word *anta* means conclusion, as well as culmination, of the Vedic teachings.

In Vedanta, the sages variously expressed the soaring of the human spirit in search of its identity. Most of the authors of the Upanishads—consisting of succinct philosophical treatises—were anonymous, although some like Yagnyavalkya and Aitareya identified themselves. Krishna Dwaipayana Vyasa reflected the teachings in his *Brahma-sutra* and, in the name of Krishna, in the *Bhagavad Gita*. So did other subsequent philosophers like Gaudapada, Shankara and Ramanuja, giving different facets to Vedanta, some erudite in treating the nature of existence, and some sculpted in fog in stretching the doctrine of *maya* or illusion!

Vedanta is also known as Gyana Yoga, or the path of knowledge. The Greek word for knowledge *gnosis* may have come from *gyana*, just as from *gnosis* the Latin *gnoscere*, to know. Although Vedanta philosophy has its roots in the Upanishads, it has a constantly evolving and adapting leitmotif, like any other philosophy, or for that matter religion, to be meaningful to life.

SPIRITUAL GOAL

The awareness of one's ignorance is the first step to knowledge. The second step is, after learning a premise of knowledge, to apply it in action. One does not know so much by reading and contemplating but by doing, through which alone knowledge improves and becomes useful. Whatever the merits of the awareness of or being one with the infinite, it has done no good to the world!

Knowledge has two sides: 1) empirical, and 2) the pertinence of what is perceived empirically. The Sanskrit root for truth is *sat*, or that which exists, just as the Latin for truth is *veritas*, or that which is verifiable. The pertinence of the verifiable has an infinite possibility of widening its understanding and applicability. Empirical chemistry or physics, for example, has an endless relevance to improving the quality of life, as through a proper vocation the shaping of perspective.

The purpose of knowledge is to give us a bearing, thus a measure of security, and direction for a sense of purpose and creativity, thus fulfilment. The goal of knowledge is to enlighten the mind, free it from *avidya*, or ignorance. From ignorance is born fear, anxiety, superstition, prejudice. As such, ignorance is the worst pollutant. From fear comes intolerance, and from intolerance injustice and violence.

The philosophy of Vedanta is to regard the world as a stage, in which the actors play out a morality play (*lila*), just as in ancient Greece the actors put on different masks to act out their roles. The word personality comes from Etruscan *phersu*, meaning a mask. Acting out the roles we give ourselves is to fulfil life, not bear with but try to overcome suffering and be happy, happiness (*ananda*) being the innate nature of the spirit, embodied in an inadequate vehicle, living in an imperfect world.

Freedom of the soul (individual, pure consciousness, or *chit*) from material bondage is the spiritual goal, and its merger in the transcendental spirit (*Brahman*) the common destiny. This freedom is attained through devotion to one's inner spirit (*atman*) or that which represents spiritual values, understanding of the various truths of existence, and a life of self-discipline and self-improvement. It is the presence of soul that makes progress possible.

Life suffers when it is led by the blind force of impulses and mundane desires. The purpose of Vedanta philosophy is to understand, educate and sublimate them. It is done by the cultivation of a moral sense and its application in daily life by the practice of some basic ideals, not as commandments but as guidelines to cherish:

* *Chitta-suddhi,* or purity of heart: to be free from hate, malice, resentment, vengeance, avarice, wickedness, and imputing bad motives to others.

* *Daya*, or compassion: a feeling heart, spontaneous kindness, being considerate of the needs of others, with matching deeds.

* *Satya*, or integrity: of feeling or depth of sentiment, rather than sentimentalism, of thinking, of expression through speech and action, not hurting, and honesty to oneself and others.

* *Tyaga,* or self-abnegation: not to be selfish, thinking of the welfare of others before one's own, not to be possessive or a slave of desires, practising detachment, overcoming infatuation.

* *Dama,* or self-discipline: sublimation of passions, of lust by selfless love, of anger by patience and tolerance, of greed by self-restraint.

* *Viveka,* or discernment: to know the difference between right and wrong by measuring the consequence, if constructive not destructive, unifying not divisive, healing not hurting, authentic not deceitful.

* *Vinaya,* or humility: purification of the ego by practising modesty, knowing that there is a lot to learn and to improve oneself.

* *Mumukshutva,* or spiritual aspiration: a longing to be free from bondage, or dependence, attachment, character deficiencies.

PHILOSOPHICAL POSTULATES

The philosophy of Vedanta evolved as a positive unifying force of reconciliation among diverging concepts of God in ancient India. Its other purpose was to make religion (*dharma*) a practical way of life by the performance of one's duty (*dharma*) based on righteousness (*dharma*). To the Sanskrit word for religion, Vedanta added the same for duty and righteousness, *dhri* being the root, meaning that which supports.

By the vision of monism, making God a transcendental, all-pervading spirit, rather than a singular, all-important and the only valid deity as in monotheism, it took away the inherent sting of intolerance and iconoclasm. Judaism, Christianity and Islam have a lot to learn from it, as all religions should from the best in each other.

The broad perspective of Vedanta is expressed in the following way.

* Brahman or the infinite spirit is not a deity or a substance that can be confined within a conceptual image, but is the spiritual essence in creation while being transcendental.

Thus, polytheistic differences were submerged by the vision that what people call God is but a spiritual form of one's devotion, sacred love and holy aspiration. It comes into shape in the process of trying to relate to the transcendental spirit.

That is why the *Bhagavad Gita* says that God comes to the devotee in the form of his or her seeking. The *Kena Upanishad* points out that the *devas* or the elemental forces of nature have no power of their own but are able to function on account of the supreme spirit (Brahman) within them.

* Even though Brahman cannot be defined, the human spirit can relate to the indefinable through spiritual ideals like love and truth, but qualified by the adjectives to rise above qualification: 1) infinite, to expand them constantly; 2) eternal, to provide the security of permanency; 3) universal, to have the relevancy among all, irrespective of religious and cultural background; and 4) transcendental, in order to realise them better ever more.

* The mantra *Isha vasyam idam sarvam* in the *Isha Upanishad*, that all is pervaded by the infinite spirit, created for the first time in human consciousness a sense of sanctity for all forms of life, not only for the humankind, and not merely confined to one's own tribes, but respect for animals and nature as well, which has only recently penetrated western thinking through the institutions for the prevention of cruelty against animals (even if they are eaten to satisfy greed!), and ecological responsibility.

* The three monotheistic religions, Judaism, Christianity and Islam, uphold God as the transcendental, commanding creator, but the Brahman of Vedanta, while being transcendental does not have a dictating role. Being the essence of the universe, as energy in matter, *prakriti* or the neutral natural force makes evolution possible through the interaction of atoms (*anu*) and so also its dissolution. Being the essence as *purusha* or spiritual force, it gives birth to individual

consciousness, evolving as conscience and shaping moral values.

RECONCILIATION AND UNITY

This vision of the all-pervasiveness of spirit shaped some basic ideals of tolerance, reconciliation and unity.

* Vedanta sought to reconcile religious antagonism by the epigraphic comparison of various faiths in search of God as vapours rising from the ocean and becoming clouds, then by coming into contact with the mountains and forming as springs and streams, they began to flow and joined together as rivers, then coursed through different lands, and acquired their characteristics, but only to meet their ultimate destination by merging into the ocean from where they had sprung.

Thus, in spite of religious differences and cultural habits, Vedanta postulated that humanity's origin and destiny are the same. Or, the simile of a multihued garland of flowers, each one different, but a common, running thread of the universal spirit holistically uniting them.

* Vedanta spoke of the identity of this spirit as the essence of the individual soul, like a spark of light being identical with the sun, or a drop of water with the ocean. Thus, all members of humanity having a common spiritual heritage should try to rise above religious dogmatism and extend the law of "thou shalt not kill" beyond their tribal and national groups and live without warfare.

* The light of the spirit is equally luminous in every soul (an echo of the Biblical ethos that God created all human beings equally in his own image), but expresses itself in different degrees of transparency through one's conscience due to the shades of opacity or impurity of the covering sheaths, the various layers of the mind, or fails to. Uncovering the light within, and expressing it through spiritual values in relationship is the goal of life.

* No one should be coerced into following a dictated path of faith, but each should grow according to the law of one's own evolution as per personal inspiration, choice and effort. Just as there are many paths leading to the summit of a mountain, the role of the teachers is only to show them and provide the expertise of their own experience, but it is the individual who has to do the climbing and arriving at the peak of self-realisation (it is better not to be bombastic by capitalising the 's').

* The ultimate goal is the merger of the individual soul in the transcendental consciousness. This is illustrated by the simile of a doll made up of salt which wanted to know where it came from and, thus, entering the ocean began to swim in search of its origin. The more it swam the less became its form, which finally disappeared, but not its essence which became one with its source, the ocean.

The mystical vision of God, not referring to a deity, is given in Vedanta in the words *sat-chit-ananda*, reflecting the ultimate longing for the reality of truth (*sat*), its ever-widening comprehension (*chit*), and realisation as supreme love (*ananda*).

The deity is meant to serve the need of a limited mind to focus on, but is a superimposition, and no one should be dogmatic about its supremacy.

OTHERWORLDLINESS

There is a running thread of otherworldliness throughout Indian spiritual literature. It has caused a structural weakness in the mindset of the people raised on it, thwarting inventiveness, creativity, initiative. There have been occasional flashes of excellence in mathematics, such as in the invention of the decimal before the common era, and in metallurgy, as in the case of the 1,700 year-old iron pillar still unoxidised in the complex of Qutab Minar in Delhi.

However, one hardly sees any contribution to science and engineering, let alone social engineering, to improve the quality of life. There is nothing like the creativity of the early-medieval China, or the late medieval Europe. This lack of concern for material things has been commented upon by some Macedonians who came to India with Alexander the Great. He took with him to Babylon two Indian gymnosophists, ascetic philosophers who hardly wore any clothing.

Later, the chroniclers Al Beruni and Ibn Batuta in the courts of the Turko-Afghan invaders, in the tenth-eleventh and thirteenth centuries, respectively, made similar comments, in addition to rating the Indians as irrational, unlike the Chinese.

Yet, in Chanakya's *Arthashastra* one finds a deep insight into realpolitik, and so also about social values based on moral principles to cope with the foibles of human nature in the *Mahabharata*, *Ramayana* and the *Panchatantra* (all BCE), and later in the *Puranas*. But one cannot avoid the deep-rooted antipathy to the world in the Indian religious lore. Anything rejected remains misunderstood.

Christianity had the same tendency until it became a state religion in the fourth century. Since then it has paid only lip-service to, and assiduously ignored, the otherworldliness in the teachings of Jesus.

In India, there was nothing like the age of reason which unfolded in the UK, France and the USA some 250 years ago, with the rediscovery of the Hellenic homocentric ideals of the rule of reason, fairness to and autonomy of the individual, and blending into them the theocentric Christian humanism.

The age of reason was, of course, blinkered within the tribal identities of their innovators. The Americans did not condescend to respect the basic human rights of the native Indians in their own land, let alone consider citizenship, and contemptuously treated the Negro slaves as beasts of burden.

The British and the French excluded, in the same way, the denizens of their colonies from the age of reason. The white man's burden became an egregiously self-righteous euphemism for the white man's greed. It took nearly 200 years for the intellectuals in the western democracies to recognise thc selective morality of their ancestors, or the uncivilised equation in signs such as "Chinese and dogs are not allowed" at the entrance of the park facing Shanghai's Bund.

The Indians never bothered to cultivate a sense of history. Without the knowledge of the past, one cannot understand how the present came about and, therefore, fails to correct its deficiencies, nor can one apply to the present those measures that had proved themselves in the past, for projection into the future. When reality is sought in the thin air, and the tangible world hypocritically dismissed as unreal, stagnation takes over, and detachment becomes synonymous with indifference and irresponsibility!

MAYA AND ADVAITA

The doctrine of *maya* is a later accretion to Vedanta philosophy, denoting the illusory nature of existence. The original teachings do not underrate the importance of the world as *dharma-kshetra*, or a field of righteous duty. *Maya* indicates the nature of the mind fooling itself by its craving and attachment, and forgetting the inner reality behind appearance, such as happiness being in the possession of material wealth and experience of sensual pleasure. Happiness is, indeed, in a state of harmony with oneself and with others.

Maya denotes the temporary nature of life's experience, in the sense that no infatuation or sorrow lasts forever, and warns that if the mind conjures up fantasies in a relationship, it should be prepared for disillusionment. Not to be carried away by wishful thinking and passions, not to suffer on account of injured vanity, not to be swayed by pride and prejudice, to be balanced in success and failure, pleasure and pain, is what the doctrine of *maya* tries to teach.

The thread of unity, *advaita* or non-duality, is emphasised in recognition of bickering selfishness in human nature, and its aggressiveness causing so much division and suffering. It is meant to remind us that the *atman*, or what the Bible says the image of God, is identical in all. This assumption is to provide the basis to our moral values. *Advaita* is not meant to create a dull uniformity of perception, or disregard the fact that it is the interaction within multiplicity that makes progress possible.

The ontology of Gaudapada and other philosophers of his ilk that the *jivatma* (individual soul) and the *paramatma* (supreme soul) are one and the same (indivisible, *advaita*) drags down the transcendence of Brahman. Identical in its content, maybe, but to say *aham-brahmasmi* (I am Brahman), or that the spark of light is the same as the sun, smacks of pompous irrationality, when you consider one's human nature contradicting such a bombast sooner or later! What relevancy does it have to real life?

The relevancy of Vedanta is to take the best of its adaptable postulations to make the journey through life more agreeable, meaningful, creative, enlightening and fulfilling, rising above religious differences. Its basic message that life should be lived by spiritual values rather than rituals or devotional exercises was astonishingly farsighted, and is even more valid today than it was nearly three thousand years ago.

Chapter Three

THE INTEGRAL PATH

FIRST STEPS IN RAJA YOGA

Raja Yoga originated in northern India some 2,300 years ago, although the system came to be known by that name many centuries later. Patanjali classified, and expressed in his own way, the already-existing teachings into eight interrelated parts and called them Ashtanga Yoga, or the yoga with eight limbs. In his 194 spare aphorisms (*sutras*), he laid down a moral foundation by the ten disciplines of *yama* and *niyama*. Then stressed the importance of mastery over postures (*asana*) for meditation and regulation of breath (*pranayama*), and curiously enough not Hatha Yoga on the whole, although since many centuries earlier some forms of it, without the name yoga, were evidently practised. To be fair to him, he may not have known the benefit of the wide-ranging postures and breathing exercises like *kapalabhati* (also a purificatory *kriya*) on physical health, or would have been turned off by some weird practices of the ascetics, the same way as Gautama Buddha who was said to have observed, "I do not have to twist my body into knots to attain illumination."

Patanjali emphasised the path of meditation (*samyama*) through a combined practice of withdrawing attention from the memory of sense-objects to conduce to a state of abstraction (*pratyahara*) in order to concentrate on (*dharana*) and be absorbed in one's spiritual ideal (*dhyana*). He spoke of the highest goal to be the individual soul's union (yoga) with the supreme soul (*Ishwara*), attainable in a transcendental state, having summed up all the former practices together (*samadhi*).

The oldest of the yogas is Gyana Yoga, or the path of Vedanta, which evolved between 2,800 and 3,000, years ago, although modern Indian scholars tend to push back the period by about 500 years, basing their hypothesis on some archeological digs found in recent years in the area of Dwaraka, in northwestern India, the ancient capital of Krishna's kingdom. The philosopher-king, later worshipped as an *avatara*, taught to Arjuna a synthesis of many yogas, which was recorded in the *Bhagavad Gita* in a dramatised setting of a battlefield sermon by Krishna Dwaipayana Vyasa, giving importance to fulfilling one's duty through selfless action, or Karma Yoga, as the highest *dharma* (religion), and also combining with devotion, cultivation of virtues and meditation.

Ritualistic practices were universal in ancient India, became even more prominent in the age of the Puranas, the first thousand years of the Christian era, and continue to dominate the village life of today, human nature being very dependent and emotional rather than self-confident and rational. The path of meditation remained exclusive among a minority seeking spiritual progress and self-knowledge. Ancient in origin, Hatha Yoga as a system was outlined about 700 years ago in northern India by Swatmarama, a disciple of Gorakhnath, the founder of an ascetic sect. Popular in the West, it is practised by a fewer number of people, percentagewise, in India. In its complete and extended form, it is a stepping stone to Kundalini Yoga rather than Raja Yoga, the current contention notwithstanding.

Even if more comprehensive, Raja Yoga is not a royal (raja) path any more than the three other main branches of yoga: Gyana, Bhakti and Karma. The four paths are interrelated and differ only to suit individual temperament, while each being indispensable to the other. Without discernment devotion can become merely emotionalism, and without devotion discernment a dry intellection. Without selfless service meditation can become an escapism, and without an inner balance and clarity of perspective through meditation service can become an exercise of the self-righteous ego. Likewise, the eight branches of Raja Yoga are intertwined. Actually, they are seven parts to be practised together, *samadhi* or the eighth being a culmination of the seventh, *dhyana*, rather than a practice by itself.

The first two consist of basic ideals to guide one's life, five restraints (*yama*) and five rules for observance (*niyama*). The following two are for physical and mental discipline through steadiness of posture (*asana*) and breath-control (*pranayama*), both to facilitate meditation. The next three, *pratyahara*, *dharana* and *dhyana*, as defined before, are to submerge mental waves to acquire harmony, a better understanding of oneself, purify character blemishes and sublimate passions by *pratipaksha bhavana* or affirmative contemplation on their opposite positive qualities, and finally to seek spiritual unity.

GUIDELINES FOR MEDITATION

Although rather overrated in western yoga circles, Patanjali made a unique contribution to self-improvement by the method of replacing what is negative through the practice of its positive counterpart, that is, instead of harping on what one should not do, by meditating on and doing what one ought to. The mind being a field of energy needs a channel to express itself. Denying a negative instinct, its energy is repressed and, thus, complexes are formed. By giving it a better kind of motivation, its energy is channelled in a constructive way. Patanjali's insight into the nature of the mind laid a foundation to future psychological investigation; and his work is probably the earliest of its kind on the subject.

The purpose of *pratyahara* is to make the mind abstract by a counter-feeding process. When the senses are withdrawn as one begins the practice of meditation, the mind immediately starts to feed on its memories, wandering from one to another. A memory is sustained as long as the I is involved in it. It is impossible to think of something without being a participant in it, such as you would not remember a billboard on a highway without being interested in what it advertised. So, one of the best methods of *pratyahara* may be practised as follows:

Sit in a comfortable posture, with the back, shoulders and neck straight without being rigid. Relax the mind by feeling detached. Do not think that you have to meditate on anything, nor have to stop thinking or make the mind blank. Forget yourself. Breathe spontaneously, just being gently conscious of the coolness of the inflowing breath (*puraka prana*) deep inside the head, and the warmth of the outflowing breath (*rechaka prana*) inside the nostrils. This is to absorb the mind in a subtle physical feeling. It should be continuous. From time to time, repeat mentally 'shanti' or peace while inhaling and 'mukti' or freedom while exhaling, in order to guide a psychological feeling of an inner calm, a profound peacefulness, and a deep sense of release from all that is negative.

When a thought drifts in, say to it "I am not interested in you, I am absorbed in peace". Then gently refocus the mind on the practice. The thought will drift away, lacking your attention. Thoughts will continue to move in and out, of course. Do not resist them but bring the mind back again and again to your practice. As Patanjali says, the key to success is *abhyasa*, continuous practice. The counter-feeding process, replacing wandering, weightier thoughts with subtle, lighter feelings, is called *pratyahara*.

After five minutes, pause for a while, unfocussing the mind, breathing freely, keeping the eyes closed. Then begin the next step, *dharana*. One of the best forms of it is concentrating on a slow and clear pronunciation of a mantra mentally, with or without synchronising with breathing. If the mantra is 'Soham', repeat slowly 'So' (the infinite spirit) while inhaling, and 'ham' (I am one with, *not* I am, for it is ridiculous for a drop of water to call itself the ocean), while exhaling. Continue the repetition for five minutes in deep concentration, feeling that this sense of oneness fills your heart with sublime love with every inflow of the breath and you are being enveloped by it with every outflow. Then pause for a minute or two, the mind relaxed, unfocussed, breathing spontaneously.

Now you may begin *dhyana*, the purpose of which is to be absorbed in the ideal of the mantra just repeated. There are different kinds of mantras. The word mantra means to consciously (*manas*) engrave (*trada*) in the subconscious a feeling of one's spiritual identity through continuous repetition of a sound-form, such as in the case of an *ishta* (from Ishwara) mantra. If you have repeated 'Soham' (I am one with the infinite spirit), or 'Om Namah Shivaya' (I consecrate myself to the auspicious Lord), or 'Om Namo Narayanaya' (to the Lord who sustains me), or 'Om Jesus', now begin the contemplative part or *dhyana* with the help of the following three phrases.

Repeat mentally "My body is your temple" a few times, slowly. Then feel the flow of a harmonious energy coursing through the body, giving it strength, health, a sense of well being, feeling as if you are inside a house of worship. Likewise, repeat "My mind is your altar" and visualise a clear sky, an expansive altar of the infinite spirit, feeling that such is your mind, free from impurity, profoundly peaceful. Then repeat "My soul is where you reside" and visualise in your heart a sphere of light, or a yellow lotus, or an image relative to the mantra, as a symbol of pure love, uplifting you, filling you with the warmth of a spiritual presence. Thus, *dhyana* is a process of absorbing the ideal of meditation. It may be done for five to ten minutes and can be alternated with *japa* or repetition of mantra.

When the help of contemplation is not needed to maintain the awareness of spiritual unity, without crossing of thoughts or body-consciousness, it is called *samadhi*, the eighth step, or summing up (*sama*) and transcending (*adhi*) the three previous steps in *samyama*.

PSYCHOLOGY OF VIOLENCE

The five *yamas* are: 1) *ahimsa* or non-violence; 2) *satya* or truthfulness; 3) *brahmacharya* or chastity, the literal meaning being godly (*brahma*) conduct (*achara*); 4) *asteya* or honesty, literally non-stealing , and 5) *aparigraha* or non-covetousness, including refraining from adultery.

The five *niyamas* are: 1) *saucha* or physical cleanliness and mental purity; 2) *santosha* or contentment by cultivating inner harmony through the education and sublimation of the ego and control of desires; 3) *tapas* or endurance of adverse conditions without complaining as well as sensible austerity; 4) *swadhyaya* or self-education by study and practice of useful teachings; and 5) *Ishwara* (God) *pranidhana* (dedication to) or spiritual aspiration.

In this article I shall dwell at length on the importance of the first *yama* or non-violence, as in the history of humanity no other century has been so accursed by violence as the twentieth. The instinct of violence is the product of the nature's law of the strong exercising power over the weak and the weak seeking vengeance. On the individual level, three factors coming together make violence possible: 1) genetical predisposition or which is inherited from generally one of the parents; 2) the family, social and cultural environment in which one is raised and lives; and 3) the immediate or triggering factor of provocation.

Violence is both an impulsive act and a brew cooking in the mind and leading to verbal abuse and harmful action. The first cause is resentment or a strong dislike making one intolerant. The second cause behind the first is the insecure and unfulfilled ego, leading to loss of self-control. One cannot cure rancour by trying to love the person resented but by treating the cause, the insecure ego, through the practice of detachment, non-expectation and understanding of why the relationship went sour. Then the ego has to be educated and fulfilled in a wholesome way by being considerate, caring and helpful to those who need you, first of all, rather than the person who has harmed you.

Violence is possible only when oriented to an object or a person. Crashing crockery is a result of getting mad at oneself. Most of us like or dislike a person, not so much due to the individual's values but to the extent our self-interest is served or denied and egos fulfilled or troubled, by identifying the good or bad in ourselves. The opposite of violence is love, but one cannot order someone to love another just for the sake of loving. To love is to be less self-centred, which means to learn to be compassionate, patient and tolerant. Improving a relationship means respecting and sharing of each other's values. Love can blossom only in an unselfish heart.

Violence is inborn because of our prehistoric past, when survival was dependent on killing. After hunger and the urge for procreation, aggression is the third most powerful instinct, followed by fear. On the animal plane, violence is a product of fear, just as fanaticism is a reaction to insecurity. Like most instincts, violence is an emotional experience and expression, such as procreation through passion, hate through anger, avarice by jealousy. The higher emotions are experienced as devotion and selfless love and expressed through caring, helping and serving. As life is evolutionary, higher emotions are inborn like the lower emotions but in different stages of dormancy and dependent on external influence for their development, together with self-effort. As both are in conflict with each other, the development of the higher emotions needs the aid of meditation. The following exercise may be helpful in sublimating the instinct of violence.

After practising the first three steps given in the guidelines of meditation, the fourth may be done in the following way. Repeat mentally, while feeling the coolness of the inflowing breath inside the head, "Peace is my real nature" and feeling the warmth of the outflowing breath inside the nostrils "not conflict". After repeating so four or five times, breathe spontaneously and feel that with every inflow subtle impressions of peace are gathering in the inner recesses of the mind, while untying and emptying the knots of conflicts with every outflowing breath. Then repeat "Love is my real nature", "not resentment", and follow the same process. Then "Strength is my real nature", "not weakness". "Patience is my real nature", "not impatience". "Tolerance is my real nature", "not intolerance". "Happiness is my real nature", "not unhappiness".

Pause for a couple of minutes, unfocusing the mind. Now, inhaling repeat "Peace" and exhaling "only peace", four or five times. Likewise, "Love", "spiritual love". "Strength", "mental strength". "Patience", "gentle patience". "Tolerance", "loving kindness". "Happiness", "inner fullness". Conclude by breathing freely for a few minutes, feeling peaceful and restful.

TRUTHFULNESS AND CHASTITY

The second *yama* is fundamental to self-confidence, for *satya* or truthfulness means security and strength. We are weak because we are neither honest with ourselves nor with others. Truthfulness has many facets. One has to start with oneself. It is not quite easy to deceive one's superiors, very difficult to deceive one's subordinates, and most easy is self-deception—so goes a saying. Honesty with oneself is the first step to self-improvement. Without integrity in a relationship there cannot be any trust and without trust no stability. Without credibility there cannot be mutual respect and without the respect of others one cannot have self-esteem. Lack of self-esteem is a basic cause of depression and self-destructiveness.

Truthfulness is not synonymous with tactlessness but tactlessness and stupidity are. Thoughtfulness is imperative to the usefulness of truth. A measure of truth is in its constructiveness, just as the mark of untruth is in its destructiveness. That which promotes harmony and peace is the criterion of truth. Unity is its goal, not division. It is truth that makes the mind free from fear. The nature of its independence makes one free from anxiety, for truth stands by itself without the support of a second truth, whereas untruth stays in a state of perpetual dependence on a chain of lies. Truth is neither hard nor soft but neutral. Hardness is in the intention of the person who uses truth to hurt another, or in the unwillingness of oneself to accept an unpleasant fact.

Untruth is due to the fear of a loss of reputation, to which one loses claim by being a hypocrite. It is also due to selfishness, such as hiding one's gain, trying not to pay the full share of income-tax, for example. Its other cause is vanity which makes one lie in order to exaggerate self-importance. Practice of truth should always be relative to love and conducive to harmony. It means to be unselfish and to cultivate humility of spirit, for there is a lot to learn and a great deal to improve.

Brahmacharya or chastity as a restraint of sexual passion is directly related to responsibility, faithfulness and integrity. Sexuality is a primordial means for the survival of the species. There is nothing to be ashamed about it, for we wil' not be here without it. The feeling of shame or squeamishness, although can be exaggerated due to religious and cultural hang-up, is ingrained in the human consciousness. It is because we are both body and spirit. Physical in nature, sexuality as a means of sense-gratification is to make oneself self-confident as a body, to be agreeable for its acceptance, partly for survival and partly for being loved as a person. However, as a spirit our longing to be fulfilled is bottomless, and the finite means of the senses simply cannot keep up to their promises, and thus the veiled disappointment, the squeamishness, the hang-up.

The body, however, is not the person one relates to but a vehicle, and what is lovable and unlovable are really the qualities of the person inside the vehicle. Thus, sexual passion by itself is not satisfactory, much less fulfilling, without mutual harmony of the qualities of two persons related. By itself it is neither holy nor unholy but like energy its nature is dependent on how it is used and the consequences it produces. Being physical, it is limited in its capacity to give the psychological fulfilment the soul seeks and, therefore, the need for decency, refinement, responsibility, understanding, care and concern for the person within the body, to make the relationship more meaningful. Otherwise, it is a relationship of possessing an object for ego-gratification through the senses. However, since the person is not an object, insecurity is inevitable in such a relationship, with jealousy as its companion.

Like the physical body, sexual passion is neither pure nor impure but how one keeps it. Like the body needing to be washed, sexual passion needs to be cleansed by unselfish love. It is lying, deceiving, hiding, lacking in feeling, callousness and irresponsibility that makes it impure. In yoga circles in India, as indeed in the Hindu culture generally, sexuality is regarded more pathologically and hypocritically while extolling celibacy, as *brahmacharya* is interpreted in a narrow sense, rather than as a sublimation of passion through deeper emotions of loving kindness and affection, the universal experience being when the mind is drawn closer to the spirit the less it needs to be gratified by the senses. As in the case of non-violence, similarly paraphrased affirmative meditation will be helpful.

HONESTY AND NON-COVETOUSNESS

There is no greater morality than identifying one's welfare and rights with that of the others. This is the basis of *asteya* or honesty or not depriving others of what belongs to them. Social justice is promoted by the right to work and an equitable share of the benefit of productivity as per one's capacity, but providing an adequate means of subsistence with dignity. Stealing out of necessity cannot be justified because it means violating another's right to keep what he or she has earned or inherited. In the case of concentration of wealth among a minority, it is up to a civilised legal process to close the gap of disparity such as by death duty and wealth levy. A crime should be regarded as a crime, whatever the cause, and the individual should be accountable first of all, while society should take the necessary measures to treat the cause.

Access to education is a universal right but has to be geared to the individual's intelligence and vocational talent. Whereas the ideal of compassion should assure survival with dignity, human beings should not be regarded as objects of charity. Protection of the ignorant and the less talented from being exploited by the astute and the more efficient is the ideal of *asteya*, but it also means educating the ignorant and create opportunities to express people's talents. Better distribution of wealth by itself does not solve the problem of stealing but moral education and a better way of investing riches in order to generate wealth by productivity, because without productivity by incentive and good management, distributed wealth will disappear soon and poverty will be universalised. Selfishness is the root cause of stealing, deceiving and exploiting—all that is to be refrained in *asteya* by educating and sublimating egoism.

The morality of non-covetousness, *aparigraha*, is work ethic, that is, one must earn the right to have what one desires. *Apara* means 'of another' and *agraha* 'to crave for'. Thus, *aparigraha* is craving for what belongs to another. Envy arises in an empty mind unwilling to educate and apply itself to useful effort. It simmers in a lazy nature hankering for gain without honest labour, in a wicked heart resenting the success of others. Desires like horses need control and direction. They have to be understood and motivated with the ideals of creativity, relating material progress with self-improvement. Desires have to be measured by one's capacity and the effort needed to realise them, while considering if they are worthwhile.

Such a person will not be covetous of the success of others. Purity of heart, right motivation and corresponding effort, not expecting something for which one has not worked, are the means to counter covetousness. Envy and jealousy are primitive instincts that need a lot of education. To be aware of one's deficiency is the first requisite, but to progress one must love its positive counterpart and practise it. Ethics is not limited to the five *yamas*. "Do not treat others as you yourself would not want to be treated" is the basis of morality.

CLEANLINESS, CONTENTMENT, FORTITUDE

Saucha is both physical cleanliness and mental purity. It also means keeping one's surroundings clean. It is to bathe daily in a hot climate and on alternate days in cold weather. Cleanliness has a direct influence over the mind. Mental *saucha* is thinking positively. When a negative thought about a person arises, it should be countered by remembering an act of helpfulness he or she might have done in the past. In rare cases, when it is impossible to find a positive remembrance of a person who has treated you badly over a long period of time and when resentment thereof keeps welling up, immediately think of someone you love and respect. It is also necessary to avoid external negative influence. Meditation, including affirmative contemplation, helps to purify the mind.

Santosha is a state of contentment which is acquired by replacing a lower desire by a higher one, such as a desire for a material object by a wish to learn and do something useful. One has to know the difference between a need and a want. Needs are physical and mental, in order to keep the body nourished, healthy and protected, and the mind occupied with interesting things to do and learn. Wants are mainly a product of external stimuli. The difference between a need and a want is that if you can do without something and yet desire it, it is a want, and if you cannot reasonably do without it, it is a need. The reason behind want after meeting one's basic needs is a desire to be happy, but happiness is an inner fulfilment that comes by making others happy.

Santosha is also a personal satisfaction in doing something one likes to do. It is in learning well what one loves to learn, such as music, visual arts, cooking, carpentry, literature, history, geography, astronomy, or whatever helps you to integrate with life. It is in self-expression through creative effort, such as in serving a worthy cause. It is a state of inner calm that comes after one has done the best in what is needed to be done. It is not enough that one prays for the good of others but in what way one contributes to it. An ego-centric person cannot have *santosha*, nor is it derived by ego massage by one's lackeys. Finally, it is in coming to terms with oneself and the rest of the world. Total happiness cannot last long, and such a goal is not only irrational but unethical in the sense that when there is so much suffering around, one has no right to be exclusively happy.

Tıpas should not be understood in the narrow sense of physical austerity. It is not mortification of the body but self-discipline, patience, tolerance, not complaining, self-abnegation. It is bearing with fortitude adverse conditions that could not be avoided after having tried to overcome them. It is to toughen the body and mind by not being over protective against heat and cold. As Swami Sivananda used to say, bearing insult and injury is an exacting form of *tapas*. It is to be balanced in pleasure and pain.

SELF-EDUCATION AND SPIRITUAL ASPIRATION

Swadhyaya is self-education, not only by the study of scriptures as the term is narrowly interpreted, but of any useful literature that is helpful to self-knowledge and understanding of life around. It is to guide (*ducere*), to teach (*docere*) and to learn (*discere*) by oneself (*swa*) through studying (*dhyaya*) great works. No knowledge is possible without a desire to know, by focussing attention to and loving the subject, thereby conducing to receptivity. Knowledge does not merely mean gathering of facts but the perception of their relevance which produces ideas for understanding. In Greek *idein* means to see mentally.

An isolated idea is an opinion, but when it is tested in a collective experience by different individuals arriving at approximately the same conclusion, it acquires the characteristic of knowledge that can be made use of by all. The purpose of *swadhyaya* is to search for truth by oneself with the help of such ideals that have been realised by the search of others and expressed in their works. It is said that a revealed truth is only a part of the truth and the rest of it one has to find by oneself.

Ishwara-pranidhana is dedication or offering oneself (*pranidhana*) to God (*Ishwara*). It simply means to have spiritual aspiration, which is first of all wanting to be a better person—decent, honest, caring, selfless, pure-hearted, compassionate, free from prejudice, patient, tolerant, loving, helpful, creative, harmonious. Dedication to God consists in the realisation of these values and expressing them in our conduct, rather than how and how long we pray and worship. This is, indeed, the bottom line of God-realisation. Prayer is a movement of heart to progress spiritually, no matter how it is directed, but fundamentally in relationship to what we do, rather than a petitioning process to a deity somewhere up in the sky.

Some teachers interpret *Ishwara-pranidhana* to be self-surrender to God or to divine will, but one has to understand what that really means. No one can for sure say what is divine will other than in a manner of accepting what seems to be one's destiny after having tried to shape it as best as possible in the light of understanding what one wants out of life, or accepting stoically an adverse condition after trying to avert it, or a bereavement for example. Fatalism and irresponsibility go together and are not synonymous to self-surrender to God.

Life is a long journey to awaken our spiritual consciousness and express it in how we live. We are born with partially formed, innocent-seeming nature. Our rudimentary characteristics come into focus early in life and begin to develop, both in good and bad ways, as per the influence of our surroundings and self-actuation. No one is born like a blank page but with something already written on it, call it genetical imprint, personal karma, or God's design, or whatever. Then our parents write on it their share, as do some close relatives, schools, the church, the society around. Then we start our own writing and keep rewriting, editing and reediting, as long as we live.

Human nature has an infinite capacity of adaptation, inclusive of genes. Just imagine a Jewish infant and an Arab infant, after being born in a maternity ward, separated and misplaced, then taken home by the Arab and the Jewish mothers *vice versa*, and the Jewish child growing up in an Arab home and in an Arab culture, and the Arab child *vice versa.* Then imagine the relevance of the Jewish blood and Arab blood as to the qualities of character. Don't we make a fool of ourselves by making such a fuss about royal blood and commoner's blood? In spite of genetical inheritance, we are what we see, hear and read, where we live, learn and grow up, and above all we are what we want to be and not to be. I have known an Indian nuclear scientist in New York. His grandfather was an illiterate farmer and father a semi-literate greengrocer in a village near Hyderabad, who as a boy managed to get out of his surroundings.

A spiritual satisfaction psychologically induced by meditation or by the realisation of a worthy goal is temporary in nature. To be long-lasting, it has to be the result of moral values realised over a long period of time. However, only a congenital idiot can be forever satisfied or happy. Peace and self-confidence are a result of fulfilment achieved through a commitment to worthy ideals. It is self-centredness that prevents learning from and correcting one's errors. The primary concern of yoga, as in the steps taught by Patanjali, is to try to cure this chronic malaise of human nature manifest in various forms. Only the pure-hearted can call themselves real yogis. In such a heart alone can peace and love grow and truth and wisdom flower.

Chapter Four

HOW TO MEDITATE

MEDITATION: A PROCESS OF UNDERSTANDING AND ENRICHING LIFE

The practice of yoga begins in a spiritual sense with trying to integrate the various aspects of one's personality: the emotional with the rational, the instinctive with the intuitive, the material with the spiritual.

The student of yoga, instead of being a helpless victim of circumstances or other people's attitudes, tries to shape his or her life through meditation, or through cultivating self-generated impressions in the subconscious.

Yoga means union or integration, that is to say, union of the conscious mind with the subconscious, which leads to a better understanding of oneself and of each other. It is essentially a process of self-realisation. In a religious sense it means union of man with God. In metaphysical terms, it is union of the primordial unconscious with the superconscious, and of the microcosm with the macrocosm.

GENERAL PATTERN

Everyone is born with a distinct, innate background, characterised by the particular, inborn impressions of the instincts of self-preservation and self-extension. This is termed the individuality of the primordial unconscious, or *antar chitta*. This level of consciousness is apparent even when an infant is six months old, as every mother knows well how different each of her children is, right from early childhood.

As the infant begins to respond to the external world, another level of consciousness is formed. It is called *vahir chitta* or the subconscious, in which the experience of the objects, through the means of the senses, is particularised as memories. This process goes on until death.

Whereas the innate impressions, *samskaras,* faintly influence the general pattern of our aptitudes, the subconscious impressions that we receive, beginning through the relationship with mother, father and other immediate relatives, keep on shaping our lives as we change from childhood into youth. The world around us, circumstances, friends, our studies, the news media and the many commercial embellishments, determine a substantial part of our character.

Whereas it is not always possible to change our circumstances or the disposition of others, it *is* within our power to cultivate our will, a philosophy of life and to adapt *our* disposition to others and to circumstances.

I-CONSCIOUSNESS

In order to practise meditation one should have an understanding of the self.

I-consciousness or the ego is the propelling agent in life. The self projects outwardly through instincts and inwardly through reflection. When the I is involved in mundane things, it is called materialistic. When the I functions through spiritual virtue it is called idealistic.

Mundane or spiritual, the I functions through a state of conditioning. The instinctive aspect of our consciousness, while preserving the particularity of our being, involves us in a world of bondage. The spiritual aspect, through idealism, discipline and sublimation, gives us a sense of harmony, peace, unity and yet freedom.

In its positive aspect, the I is like Lucifer the angel; in its negative aspect, it is like Lucifer the devil.

A participatory consciousness such as the I, functions through movement. Movement is caused by desire, and it is meaningful when there is a goal to be attained. As movement is the nature of consciousness, the movement, that is, desire loses its motive power once the desire is fulfilled; then the desired object becomes less interesting.

FULFILMENT

Thus, the I-consciousness fulfils itself through a series of temporary desires. From the mundane to the spiritual, from dependence on the external embellishment to the integrity of character, from conflict within to harmony in relationship to others, the I-consciousness evolves.

One's state of mind is in accordance with the nature of the identity one fulfils within oneself. When it is sought through the possession of material things, one tends to get disappointed, because, for example, money cannot buy true friendship. It is in the strength of character, capacity to love and understand, it is in the discipline of the selfish nature that the sense of belonging is fulfilled.

No one needs to be convinced of one's material nature. We are continuously influenced by the objects of the senses through enjoyment in attainment, or frustration in failure. But what is greatly needed is self-confidence in the experience of the spiritual reality within ourselves.

Anything in existence is tangible only on the basis of duality, such as the experience of joy being conditioned by the experience of sorrow. Both are a part of life and should be taken in their stride as they come and go, that is, one should neither be swept overboard by happiness nor be crushed by depression.

Lofty ideals expressed through symbolic words like God, eternal truth, pure love, indicate how inadequate life is, how insecure is one's identity in the relativity of experience. The validity of these ideals lies in their ability to lift one's spirit through a sense of the spiritual, of duty, of honour, and also by a feeling for, and understanding of, other human beings.

The thoughts given here would provide some specific themes for contemplation. However, mere contemplation is not meditation. Abstraction of thought, concentration, affirmation of ideals and their experience, all put together, constitute meditation.

MEDITATION TECHNIQUES

The following are a few of the suggested techniques:

Sit with your back, neck and head straight, without being rigid. You do not have to sit cross-legged, but the spine should be relatively straight. A slack spine or drooping head means mental sloth, and feeling merely restful or being drowsy does not mean meditation. Awareness, being wakeful inwardly, is the basis of meditation.

The first step is to cultivate a feeling of mental calm. Thoughts cannot be controlled without giving the mind a feeling to dwell on. In fact, thought-control is not implied at all, but the *substitution of thought by a feeling*.

The eyes are closed, and you feel totally at peace, with yourself and the rest of the world. The mind will, of course, wander, but you tell yourself that the thoughts that pass in your mind are merely superficial superimpositions on the vastness of your being, not confined within a form, not tied down by the identity of a name, representing the body-mind-ego principle, that is, the personality.

DETACHMENT

The spirit within is not bound by the limits of a personality. You feel as if you are someone different, *a detached witnessing agent,* not involved in the thought-process, represented by the participation of the ego. You feel that you are like the sky in which the clouds pass by, without affecting the sky itself, and that *you* are that limitless sky, in which thoughts come and go without affecting you.

This is called the process of abstraction, *pratyahara*. Remember, thoughts function only through the agency of the ego, the participator in memory: "I did this, I went there, that person did such a thing to me, I enjoyed, I suffered." As long as the ego is *not* relatively detached, you do not understand your mind well. You must, therefore, tell yourself: "I am not this body, not this mind, not this ego, but the all-encompassing, infinite spirit, in which the thoughts of someone else (as it were) come and go."

There is another theme: Imagine a vast ocean, without any shores visible. Immensely deep and profoundly calm underneath, on the surface of which waves are rising and falling. You are this vast, deep ocean, and the waves, your thoughts, are only a fraction, a superficial surface of your being. They do not affect your depth.

RHYTHMIC BREATHING

As you contemplate thus, all the time you consciously sense the movement of the breath, *prana,* within your nostrils. The breathing is rhythmic, not too long, not too short; approximately, three to five seconds to inhale and the same length of time to exhale.

From time to time, stop the contemplation process, but keep the mind absorbed in experiencing the breath. When you inhale, feel the cool air in the nerves above and behind the palate, deep within the head; then try to extend the feeling, a sensation in the nerves, inside the top of the head, associating it with the idea of mental calm.

When exhaling, feel the warmth of the breath within the lower nostrils with a sense of expansiveness and diffusion. Breath and mind *(prana* and *manas)* are closely related. As you experience the breath, the suggestion—before, during or immediately after—becomes more receptive to the mind.

Then, there is the process of spiritual identity, while experiencing the movement of the breath within.

We are creatures of suggestion, and are affected on the basis of the ego by whatever the life around tells us to be or not to be. Our egos also function similarly, based on the memory of sense-experience and ego-fulfilment. Thus, we have a strong sense of division and selfishness.

One now counteracts this state of mind by a series of suggestions. As you inhale, experiencing the breath, feel the thought that "the cosmic spiritual essence, permeating everything, and representing the source of life inside all things, is merging with the individual spiritual essence within me." While exhaling, *vice versa*. Rising above the consciousness of the body and the play of the ego through the name-form-identity process, you feel that you are united in spirit with all, rising above infatuation and hate, possessiveness and retribution.

RELAXATION

From time to time just relax. Stretch your legs, move the shoulders, take a few deep breaths, and sit peacefully for a while. Then resume the experience of the *prana* (breath) and the process of identity.

After some time, when you have a measure of the experience of mental abstraction *(pratyahara),* peacefully watch the movement of thoughts; all the time telling yourself that you are merely a witness, not a participant. This is called *sakshi bhava,* or witnessing attitude. In the course of time, through this you will be able to understand yourself better, sort out the complexes and, through subsequent steps in meditation, such as affirmation and experience of ideals *(dhyana),* begin to reeducate your own mind. This is helped a great deal by the steps in concentration *(dharana).**

---

* Excerpts from a lecture given at Coxton Hall in London on 15 August 1973.

A GUIDE TO MEDITATION

In the West, the word meditation means a concentrated state of mind in serious reflection. The Latin root of the word meditation *mederi* means "to heal". It is an effort to heal the afflictions of the mind, the hurt ego, by trying to understand the cause of the problem and finding a way to solve it, that is, by knowing what countermeasures to take. To meditate is to deepen a state of understanding.

In the East, however, meditation does not mean thinking at all but fixing the mind in a spiritual ideal, to be one with it, or the thought-process dissolving in the consciousness of it. According to Zen Buddhism, meditation does not involve any concept but is an awareness of an inner silence. As per Patanjali, meditation is a combination of three steps: *pratyahara* or abstraction or withdrawal of the mind from the sense-objects or attention to their memory; *dharana* or concentration; and *dhyana* or contemplation which, however, is not a thought-process but an absorption of the feeling of oneness with the ideal.

Awareness of an inner silence is not something easy to achieve. It can be confused with a state of dullness or being soporific, which is not the purpose of meditation. To meditate does not mean to have a good rest while sitting pretty, and silence is not productive without spiritual aspiration. On the other hand, few have the capacity to think clearly, and too much of mental exercise could lead to tension and confusion.

In Bhakti Yoga, meditation is visualisation of the image of a chosen deity, together with mental repetition of a relevant mantra. For the Vedantin it is to contemplate on the meaning of selected verses from the Upanishads or similar scriptures. For the Catholics, it is saying the rosary, based on mantras like "Our Father which art in heaven," or "Hail Mary, full of grace." For them meditation also consists in feeling close to Jesus after receiving communion and retiring to a quiet place, and feel the idea of transubstantiation of the Eucharist.

St. Albert the Great, the teacher of St. Thomas Aquinas, observed that meditation for philosophers is a process of perfecting a thought, and for devotees of their love of God. Prayers said in silence as a dedication of oneself to God can also be called meditation, because it means turning the mind inward to one's spiritual source, leading to peace and inner fulfilment.

For the Hindus, repetition of a mantra, with or without a rosary, but with a feeling of spiritual oneness is meditation. A common Buddhist meditation consists in repeating the mantras: *Buddham sharanam gachchhami, dhammam sharanam gachchhami, sangham sharanam gachchhami* (I proceed remembering the Buddha, the righteous path and the welfare of my community). The Tibetans base their meditation on the mantra *Om mani padme hum* (I am Om, the jewel in the lotus of my heart). For Moslems, meditation is called *zikr* or repetition of selected names of God from the Koran, generally with a rosary. Feeling the breath, which is a technique in *pratyahara*, is an exercise in Zen meditation (the word Zen is derived from *dhyana* or meditation), as also counting from one to 20 or more, over and over again.

WHY MEDITATE?

The two basic goals of meditation are: 1) Spiritual renewal, or the feeling of oneness with a higher source of life, no matter whether one calls it the infinite and eternal spirit, transcendental and yet immanent in everything, or a divine being called God, or supreme truth, from which flow peace, wisdom and strength. 2) Through introversion, acquiring a deep state of peace, to search for the basic truths of life, to separate reality from illusion, to discard illusory ideas about illusion itself, to acquire a clear understanding of reality rather than confusing it with a foggy thoughtless state. The first is relatively easier through devotion and a sincere dedication. The second needs a long practice, to acquire philosophical maturity.

Peace of mind is a product of the first goal, which helps in understanding the problems one faces. An expanded state of consciousness enables one to loosen the psychological tightness of attachment and rise above petty reactions by the realisation that there is more to life than snobbery caused by the insecure ego and resentment by wounded vanity. A sense of elevation and oneness with a spiritual source helps to sublimate gross passions and acquire emotional maturity. The identity of oneself with the essence of one's being strengthens the will to act according to what one should and should not do, after having made appropriate decisions.

Clarity of mind, which is a part of the second goal, helps to cultivate a sense of right and wrong, a basic purpose of education and a litmus test of any culture. The Greek root, *charassein,* of the word character means "to engrave," and its Sanskrit word, *charitra*, means "to cultivate." To engrave or to cultivate cherished ideals is what meditation is for, practised in a state of peace and clarity of mind, instilling a love of truth, of what one wishes to be, by sowing the seeds of suggestion through a deep feeling of devotion and dedication.

Purity of heart or freedom from resentment, hate, prejudice and negative thinking is another objective of meditation. Although it is said that repetition of a mantra helps to cleanse and enlighten the mind, there is no evidence that the mental sound-form does so, but the faith in it and the sincerity to direct one's life by the ideals behind. Thus, it is wrong to say that mantras are meaningless sound-forms. It is also advisable to discard the myth that no progress in meditation or spiritual life is possible without an initiation by a guru, although a worthy teacher is a help. As the Buddha says:

"By oneself alone is one purified,
Purity and impurity depending on oneself,
As no one can purify another.
By oneself one must walk the path;
The teacher merely shows the way."

WHAT IS REQUIRED TO MEDITATE?

The injunction "let your whole life be an act of meditation," is nonsense, first because it is impossible and, secondly, because its value is diluted. Meditation is a specific act by itself, to be practised regularly. Then it is a process, in order to guide one's life for the act to be meaningful. Meditation, to be effective, should inspire a philosophy to guide one's life or a code of conduct to practise. That is why Patanjali's Raja Yoga begins with two sets of ethics and regulations, *yama* and *niyama*. Practical idealism is the first requirement in meditation, so as not to make it a hypocritical act, but to support it by a philosophy guiding one's attitude, motivation, action and relationship.

The second requisite is a suitable place to meditate, clean and peaceful, wherein to create the right kind of atmosphere by keeping a symbol like Om on an altar with flowers and, when meditating, lighting a candle and mild incense, if desired.

The third is the right kind of posture, whether sitting cross-legged, if comfortable, or in a straight-back and firm chair, while keeping the neck, shoulders and back straight, without being rigid, so as to remain alert by breathing adequately (oxygen helps to maintain lucidity). For most of the people, even in India, the lotus posture *(padmasana)* is symbolic rather than practical, for one can meditate only when the mind is free from self-inflicted pain in the legs and hips; nor does it make any sense to let them go numb. The position of the arms should be relaxed by keeping the palms facing up in the lap, one over the other, or the hands should be on the knees with the palms up or down but fingers loose and relaxed, with the tips of the index finger and thumb gently touching. If sitting in a chair, the feet should be together on the floor, with equal weight.

The fourth is cultivating a relaxed disposition before beginning the practice of meditation. There should be no fighting with thoughts or trying to stop the mind, as it were, or even a desire to achieve anything at all, for it is not an ego-trip or climbing the ladder of success, but an effortless feeling of a deep, inner poise and faith in, and love for, what one wishes to do: a quiet, absorbing predisposition to the ideal of the act.

With a relaxed mind one may begin with the awareness of an abiding, expanding relatedness to all that is around, to the whole universe, and to the transcendent and immanent spiritual source, which is also the essence of one's inner being or soul. There should be a feeling of absorption and envelopment by a deep, inner peace. No doubt thoughts will come and go, but not to be distracted by a thought means not identifying with it, because a thought is sustained by the self's involvement with it. When a thought comes, one may gently tell oneself "I am not interested but detached and in peace." To begin meditation, it is necessary to compose oneself in this way for a few minutes.

The fifth requisite is called techniques that constitute the main practice of meditation. They are of several kinds, depending on religious or monastic or ashram traditions. For example, in some Catholic monasteries there are little books of meditation consisting of a thought for each day of the year, gleaned from the scriptures, which is memorised and contemplated upon in solitude, while mentally repeating the phrases from time to time to guide the meditation. In the chapel, meditation is done differently, when a monk reads aloud passages from sacred writings and his brethren sit with heads bent, eyes closed and fingers crossed, deeply concentrating on what is read.

It will, however, be appropriate to give some basic steps to an integral form of meditation, combining some practices in *pratyahara, dharana* and *dhyana*. The suitability of techniques varies from person to person and the choice should be from what is available in books or through a teacher. However, it should be remembered that, just as the mark of good journalism is accuracy and the evidence of a serious research, so also the mark of a good teaching is clarity and precision.

HOW TO MEDITATE?

After a few minutes of relaxation as described in how to cultivate a predisposition, gradually absorb the breath in the mind, that is, be aware of the coolness of the inflowing *prana* deep inside the head, in the nerve cells, and the warmth of the outflowing *prana* inside the lower nostrils, while breathing spontaneously. There is no need to breathe deliberately slowly, for the concentration in feeling the breath will automatically make it slow and find its own rhythm. The important thing is to have a sense of being filled with peace and to feel free from all tension and bondage. The practice may be continued for, say, 10 minutes.

The purpose of this form of *pratyahara* is a conscious experience of the *prana*, the external form of which is the breath and the internal source the soul. The Latin root, *spirare,* of the word respiration means "to breathe," and is derived from the word *spiritus,* the soul's essence that gives life to the body through the vital principle, *prana*. By experiencing the breath through its coolness and warmth, one becomes aware of its source within by a sense of immense peace *(shanti)* and freedom *(mukti),* the two psychological forms of expression of the spirit within.

After a month of practice, the first stage can be prolonged by continuing to feel only the coolness deep inside the head even when exhaling, and ignoring the warmth of the outgoing *prana*, and renewing the cool feeling with the help of each inward breath. The psychological experience of this exercise is a state of fullness which can be guided by repeating the word *paripurnam* or its English equivalent "spiritual fullness," from time to time. This may be done for five minutes or more, depending on the ability to maintain attention.

Any practice in a prolonged state, especially in the beginning, loses its depth. Thus, after 10 or 15 minutes, detach the mind from the breath, keep the eyes closed and feel restful for a minute or two. One may also loosen up the shoulders, neck and the legs, if there is tension.

REPETITION OF MANTRA

The second part of meditation, which is an aspect of internal *dharana* (concentration), consists of *japa* or repetition of a mantra, and can be combined with *dhyana* (contemplation). A mantra is a sound-form representing a basic spiritual ideal, such as uniting with the infinite spirit *(Om)*, or transcendental truth, knowledge, infinity *(satyam, gyanam, anantam)*, or a personal deity like Shiva or Vishnu or Buddha or Christ. A mantra can also be an affirmation of an ideal, such as *Soham* (I am one with the infinite) or *Hari Om Tat Sat* (the Lord is the infinite spirit, that is the truth). The two well known Hebrew mantras are *Adonai* (my Lord) and *Elohim* (the all-powerful Lord of all).

A mantra should not be considered a magic formula, for there is no magic in yoga. Continuous repetition of a sound-form helps to tap mental energy and focus it into the subconscious in order to plant and stimulate a spiritual ideal therein. This is the basic purpose of *japa*. To call it transcendental meditation is to indulge in hyperbole. There are various kinds of mantras but for *japa* its shorter forms are recommended, such as *Om* or *Soham*, or a slightly longer form as *Hari Om* or *Hari Om Tat Sat*.

According to the voluminous Sanskrit-English dictionary by Sir Monier-Williams (Oxford University Press), the word mantra means, among other definitions, "to concentrate with", drawing its roots *man* from *manas* or mind or, more specifically, the conscious aspect of the mind, and *tra* from possibly *trada* (see under *tra*) or that which "pierces" or as per my inference that which "engraves". Thus, mantra is a sound-form to "consciously engrave" in the subconscious a spiritual ideal of identity. *Trada* also means that which "opens up", thus inferentially "one's spiritual consciousness". Remotely, the root *tra* can also be traced to *tras* (see under *tra*) which means "to shine", thus inferentially the "spirit within illuminating."

The mind is a field of energy. Energy pulsates through a principle or structure of movement. The mind moves by the pulsation of memory, latching on to one and then to another. Thus, the energy of the mind is dispersed. The purpose of repeating a sound-form continuously is to make the mind move in a tight circle, thus tapping its energy. Simultaneously, the sentiment of love for the spiritual ideal behind should be felt deeply within.

One may begin the second part of meditation by refocusing the mind in the breath, trying to be absorbed in it, as before, for a minute or two. Then start the mental intonation of the mantra *Om,* slowly and concentrating deeply, along with the inflowing breath, feeling its coolness, and again with the outflowing, feeling the warmth. The process should be continuous for several minutes. Then have a short pause, detaching the mind and experiencing an inner silence, and after which repeat the practice. Continue for a total of 10 minutes in the first month and then extend by another five minutes or so.

DHARANA AND DHYANA

The psychological counterpart of this exercise, to be contemplated alternately, consists in feeling a subtle, sacred presence within: in the body giving it health or physical well-being, in the mind enlightening it with understanding and wiping out the shadows of negativity, and in the heart or the soul awakening spiritual aspiration. The last means loving "God with all your heart and with all your soul," in the words of Jesus. These guiding sentiments are relative to the repetition of *Om,* which can be directed in between *japa*.

If the mantra is *Soham,* the sound *So* (infinite spirit) should be mentally intoned with the inflowing breath and *ham* (I am one with) with the outflowing, in the same way as with *Om*. The sentiment or the contemplative part may be based on the affirmation: "I am one with the eternal, infinite spirit within and around. The self in me is of the spiritual nature of my soul, rather than a product of physical instincts and personality traits. The self in me is purified by this communion with my soul, the essence of which is the same as the infinite, transcendental spirit of God."

For a devout Christian the mantra can be *Jesus Christ*. Although it is not essential to synchronise the repetition of a mantra with the breath, the feeling of a harmonious rhythm can be developed by doing so, as if the mantra is floating in and out, permeating and enveloping oneself. Examples: repeat *Hari Om* inhaling and *Tat Sat* exhaling; or *Jesus* inhaling, *Christ* exhaling; or for those of the Jewish faith, *Adonai* inhaling, *Elohim* exhaling. While doing *japa* the mind should be deeply concentrated in intoning silently the mantra with a feeling of love for the ideal. Combining this *dharana* (concentration) with *dhyana* (contemplation relative to the mantra) is done in the following way:

If the mantra is *Jesus Christ,* or *Adonai-Elohim,* repeat the words for five minutes, then unfocus the mind breathing spontaneously for a minute or two, and begin the contemplative part for five minutes or so. This is done with the help of three phrases. In the case of *Jesus Christ* or a Vishnu mantra like *Om Namo Narayanaya,* the image of the deity may be visualised in the mind, or in the case of *Adonai-Elohim* a sphere of light as a symbol, but it is not easy and can be considered optional.

This combined form of *dharana* and *dhyana* may be practised for five minutes each and then extended to an equal amount of time or a total of 20 minutes, or as long as one wishes.

The idea of sticking to one mantra only is to accustom the mind to its sound pattern, in order to engrave its grooves in the subconscious, as it were. The choice may be made by oneself. Experience will tell, given enough time, if a mantra is suitable to one's psychological make-up through a sense of harmony with it, or not. There is no rule that a mantra cannot be changed if the mind resists it.

The preference of receiving initiation from a guru is personal but there is no dogma that to repeat a mantra one has to be initiated into it. Sensible teachers try to find out the psychological inclination of the student before giving a mantra, rather than perfunctorily superimpose one with a dubious understanding that the former can know what is appropriate for the latter just by sensing the vibrations. My teacher, the late Swami Sivananda, never urged anyone to receive mantra-initiation but, if someone came to him for it, he generally inquired about the preference, as to how a spiritual identity is sought, before giving an appropriate mantra.

Whereas a mantra should not be treated frivolously by revealing it to just anybody, to make a top secret of it is rather silly. All mantras can be found in books.

AFFIRMATIONS IN MEDITATION

After the practice of the second part a short pause is necessary, keeping the eyes closed and feeling detached and restful. If there is tension, move the shoulders and the head a little. Breathe freely for a minute or two and then refocus the mind in the breath to begin the third part of this integral meditation, all of it being a combination of *pratyahara, dharana* and *dhyana*. This last part is a process of seeding the subconscious with some basic affirmations, relative to their opposite traits which are common to human nature.

The mind is a complex organism susceptible to influence. No one is born like a blank page on which the parents and others write what is good or bad. We are all born with innate propensities of character, even though in a rudimentary state, but each as a distinct individual. Then the first few years are highly impressionable, marking the subconscious indelibly through parental influence. Afterwards, in adolescence and later years, we keep on marking the formative mind by the influence of our surroundings and by our own positive endeavour or falling into bad habits, as well as by being susceptible to wholesome or negative influence of individuals we closely come into contact with.

The purpose of the following part of meditation is self-educative, as to what should be our nature and should not be, the "reality" being what we need for our security and happiness. One may make a list of affirmations as per individual preference and necessity, and memorise them. However, they should be few and short. The following six affirmations are recommended.

While inhaling and feeling the breath, mentally repeat slowly and with a deep conviction "Peace is my real nature" and while exhaling "Not conflict". Repeat the phrase three or four times each, then try to absorb the meaning in silence for about a minute, breathing spontaneously. Then continue with "Love is my real nature," "Not resentment"; "Truth is my real nature," "Not untruth"; "Happiness is my real nature," "Not unhapiness"; "Strength is my real nature," "Not weakness"; "Freedom is my real nature," "Not bondage."

Then give a short pause, breathing freely and feeling detached. Begin again, fixing the mind in the breath, and repeat three or four times each, inhaling "Peace" and exhaling "Only peace"; "Love", "Spiritual love"; "Truth", "Only truth"; "Happiness", "Inner fullness"; "Strength", "Mental strength"; "Freedom", "Spiritual freedom". Then conclude with a pause of at least three minutes, breathing freely.

The best time to meditate is in the morning, but only if one wakes up fresh. Otherwise, an appropriate hour should be chosen, but not immediately after a meal. This session of meditation will take from 45 minutes to one hour. In the beginning one may shorten it to 20 to 30 minutes and, after sufficient practice, prolong up to one hour. For most people a long meditation is not useful and may even build up tension. The quality is more important than the length of it.

MORE WAYS OF MEDITATION

The purpose of yoga is mind control.

There are two ways of doing this: through some techniques of meditation and by a psychological process of self-education. Both are interrelated and should be combined. The following six techniques may be tried and some of them chosen for regular practice according to the individual's compatibility.

1. Fix the mind in the breath, feeling the coolness deep inside the head while inhaling and the warmth inside the lower nostrils while exhaling. Repeat mentally "peace" or "harmony" inhaling, and "freedom" or "liberation" exhaling. The idea is to feel peaceful and free from conflict and anxiety.

2. Breathe alternately, as in *nadi sodhana pranayama*, that is, inhaling through the left nostril and exhaling through the right, and inhaling again through the right and exhaling through the left, and follow the same technique as in the first. The thumb and the ring finger are used to hold the nose. Practise for one month. Then add to it retention of breath after inhaling, for a few seconds or as long as one can comfortably,

while repeating mentally "inner strength". An alternate form of autosuggestion can be "will" while inhaling, "spiritual strength" retaining and "harmony" exhaling. Concentration on or feeling the breath is important. While retaining, concentrate on the heartbeat.

3. Breathe freely, that is, not concentrating on the breath but visualising a green field (a symbol of the sub-conscious), surrounded by a circular horizon of dark-green trees (the unconscious). Above is a light-blue, clear sky (the spiritual origin of life). Imagine a gentle breeze blowing from above and smoothening the green grass (the conflicts in the subconscious) and then penetrating into the dark-green woods beyond. Repeat mentally "peace" inhaling, "only peace" exhaling and, likewise, "love", "only love"; "freedom", "spiritual freedom". There is no need to retain the breath.

4. Visualise an ocean, with a circular horizon, deep blue in colour, a symbol of life. The sky above is clear and light-blue, the infinite spirit, the source of life. The ocean is full of gently rolling waves, which are individual souls and you are one of them, moving in harmony with one another, as you feel the gentle rhythm of your breath. Say to yourself: "I am in peace with myself and in peace with the world," "the essence of my soul is the same as that of all souls."

5. Keep a candle on level with the eyes at a distance of one metre. Concentrate on the candle-flame for a few seconds, then close the eyes and visualise it as a sphere of light within the head. Contemplate on harmony, peace, fullness and inner strength, repeating the words from time to time with the inflowing and outflowing breath. Open the eyes to concentrate on the flame again and repeat the process.

6. Fix the mind on the breath as in the first exercise and practise the following six affirmations by repeating them half-a-dozen times each, alternating with a deep feeling of the absorption of their meaning, while breathing spontaneously,

without concentration. After one month, add retention, with repetition of the relevant affirmation and concentration on the heartbeat.

a. Inhale peace, retaining repeat "profound harmony" and exhale conflict.
b. Inhale love, retaining repeat "spiritual fullness" and exhale resentment or ill-feeling. Likewise:
c. Generosity, charity of heart, selfishness.
d. Understanding, patience, intolerance.
e. Honesty, truth, insincerity.
f. Compassion, selfless love, attachment.

One may formulate other autosuggestions as per the need of the moment. Each of these exercises can be done for a few minutes, sitting in a comfortable posture with closed eyes, but with the back, shoulders and neck straight without being rigid. When tension builds up or the quality of meditation becomes shallow, discontinue and resume the next day. A session of half an hour daily, preferably in the morning before breakfast or in the evening before dinner, is recommended. It can be prolonged and done in the morning and evening as per the individual's inclination. Motivation, quality and regularity are important. As Patanjali says, practice is the key to success.

Chapter Five

OUR MIND AND SELF-EDUCATION

We can know our mind by observing our desires and tendencies, and our reaction to challenge, when the security of the ego is threatened. Our inclinations, choices as to books, magazines, TV programmes, places of entertainment and friends give a general indication to our nature. We also know about the kind of insecurity and lack of fulfilment by observing our intolerance, nagging, vituperation, harping on mistakes made by others, nursing of resentment over the years.

To observe the mind well one has to be impartial, that is, egoless. It is as if observing someone else's mind as a silent witness, not getting involved in self-justification, nor self-condemnation, but as a patient, kindly and understanding friend trying to help, pointing out that unhappiness is caused by selfishness and self-aggrandisement, dissatisfaction by superficiality and frivolity, anxiety by attachment and insecurity of the ego. It is a method called *sakshi bhava*. Self-observation and analysis should not be overdone but, in order to overcome the fear of one's negative shadow, one has to face and come to terms with oneself, from time to time.

The state of the mind is dependent on the state of the I, as it projects itself in the process of its survival and fulfilment, through the archetypal and recent background of race, religion, culture, social influence and education, and gathers experience by interaction, thereby forming layers upon layers of memory, one's happiness or unhappiness always depending on how the I has been treated.

Consciously or unconsciously one envies those who are successful in their profession due to their motivation, intelligence, endeavour and, above all, being more alert and, therefore, capable of learning, more astute to process and make use of knowledge, and more strong-willed to get where they wish to be. One also admires those who have been able to realise some spiritual ideals and gathered a measure of peace and happiness.

However given the choice, one is likely to pursue material success first and, failing or not being fulfilled by it, would turn to spiritual values. The reason is that one is oriented more empirically than philosophically, as survival is a greater priority than one's need to be happy through a philosophically-induced or religiously-consoled state of mind. One is hardly aware of being related to a spiritual origin from which flow security and happiness, security by faith and happiness by doing something useful and loving the good of others.

Since the infinite spirit is immanent in all, the experience of a sacred presence within by meditation and as a bonding link to those we can identify with by a loving relationship of caring, sharing and understanding, is the only way to lighten the weight of selfishness and loosen the strain of pride and vanity. This can never be done by meditation alone but by identifying the good of oneself with that of those we live and work with.

SELF-EDUCATION

The following guidelines for self-education may be useful:

Watch your thoughts. When you find yourself thinking badly of someone, immediately remember the good the person had done to you before. Then think of someone you love. This is one way of overcoming negative thinking.

Avoid the sin of generalised aspersion. The individual alone is responsible for his or her guilt or fault. To accuse an entire race or nation for individual misdeeds and deficiencies is uncivilised.

Watch your behaviour. If you are lying, remind yourself to be truthful and then make the correction, because trustworthiness is more important than a dubious advantage of the moment.

If you are angry, *ask yourself to be patient* and then explain to the person your problem and what you expect, saying that you would expect the same from yourself.

When you attempt to pass the blame to others, *correct yourself* and accept your share of responsibility. Otherwise, you will never learn.

When you think of another as a sexual object *ask yourself if you really love and care for the person*. Then be reminded that it is the human qualities that determine the durability of happiness in a relationship, not the passion of the moment, nor the physical attraction.

The following ways of coping with our problems through self-education may be tried:

1. Identify the basic problem rather than generalise and say that you are smothered by so many problems, which is a mental trick for not having to deal with one, because the mind knows that it cannot solve all of them at the same time.

2. After identifying a problem, such as unhappiness or frustration or anger or intolerance, locate the main cause. You will find that most probably it is self-centredness or egoism or selfishness, whichever way you look at it.

3. Then identify some of the lateral causes flowing from the basic cause. For example, in the case of unhappiness, they could be: a) self-pity, b) too many expectations, c) too much attachment or possessiveness, d) self-importance, and e) lack of spiritual goals.

4. Match each of them with a counterpart to practise specifically in the following way, which is called the *pratipaksha* method in Raja Yoga.

a) Think more of others than of your own problems, be considerate, listen more and be helpful.

b) Expect more from yourself than from others, expect only when you deserve, expect only after making it quite clear as to what you expect in a given situation, and expect after taking into account the limitations of human nature.

c) Excessive attachment or possessiveness is caused by the insecurity of one's love. Therefore, it is necessary to think of the good of someone you love rather than your loving. Understand that such a good is best achieved the way the loved person wants it to be rather than on your own terms. Ask yourself if you are doing anything good or merely proclaiming your love, and if you are concerned about drawing the attention of others to the good you are doing. Unselfishness overcomes the insecurity of love and lessens attachment or possessiveness.

d) If you are vain, know that there is a lot to learn because you do not know enough. If you wish to be regarded well, you have a lot to improve your nature. Control self-justification and indirect self-praise as well as eulogising your children or spouse to others.

e) Write down in bold letters on separate cards and keep them only where you can see them, in order to be reminded of some worthy goals such as: Be Just, Love Mercy, Do not Be False, Be Unselfish, Control Passion, Be Modest, Think Positively.

Even if these may sound rather old-fashioned, they have a timeless value. The Buddha says: "Do not accept a teaching just because it is given by your teacher, but find out if it is valid in your own experience, and only then accept it." All these steps are arduous and need a lot of faith, discernment, patience and practice. But who has ever progressed and achieved anything worthy without toil?

Chapter Six

THOUGHTS TO PONDER

Most of us are creatures of beliefs that are convenient to justify our desires and longings, allay the basic fears and uncertainties, and fulfill a sense of belonging. Their usefulness is to the extent they help to make us better human beings and bring a deeper meaning to our being alive.

Lofty words like altruism, transcendental truth, God, eternal love are only indicative of how inadequate our life is and how insecure our identity in relationship. Their ability to lift our spirit is in their translation as duty, honour, feeling for and understanding of each other.

Philosophy is meant to form principles and shape criteria. If you have no principles then you have no philosophy.

Religion is meant to promote spiritual fellowship among people, not merely within a particular faith. This is possible only through an understanding heart and freedom from prejudice. The bigot can never be religious, much less spiritual.

Justice is meant to promote respect for the rule of law, and a law can be respected only when it gives equal legal protection to all, while striving to promote mutual responsibility for social security and welfare.

Moral norms are not merely social habits but spiritual ligaments in the body of society and represent not just the outlines of social behaviour but are meant to appeal to the better side of human nature. They are not merely to hold people together through a balance of self-interest but to sustain spiritual responsibility to each other.

People should ask themselves the following basic questions:

How can you expect respect from others if you have no self-respect in your own eyes?

How can you have self-respect if you lie, deceive and act as a coward and a weakling, if you are arrogant, vain and selfish?

How can you have peace of mind if you are self-centered and have no basic integrity of character?

How can you be happy if you are a slave of passion and keep being attached to those who do not really care for you?

How can you expect the love of others if you are selfish and full of yourself?

How can you expect success if you do not work hard and try to acquire the necessary talents to get what you want?

How can you have inner harmony if you have no devotion to spiritual ideals?

What worth is all the effort to keep yourself and your family in material comfort if you have failed to find harmony in your heart and give peace and love to your family and friends?

Spiritual life does not consist in singing the glory of God and chanting mantras but in the practice of integrity, compassion, fulfilling of duties and obligations, acceptance of personal responsibility, selfless service for a common cause that does not enhance the ego of anyone in particular, and in the sublimation of passions.

A tree can remain standing in spite of stormy weather only if it has deep roots. Likewise, the tree of life can be stable only through the deep roots of actions motivated by love, a sense of justice tempered by compassion and understanding, and unselfish support of those you care for when they are in need.

The tree of life can have many branches of knowledge and many leaves of prayers, but without its deep roots it will fall down with its branches and leaves when the storm comes.

Chapter Seven
JUST FOR TODAY

Resolve to yourself:

Just for today I will try to live through only this day, putting down the load of the past and worry about the future.

Just for today I will try to adjust myself to life as it unfolds, my work, my family, the circumstances as they come, and try not to be upset if they do not conform to my desires, but accept them as they are, while gently talking over if there could be a better way of getting things done.

Just for today I will exercise my body and read something to improve and stimulate my mind and lift my spirit.

Just for today I will seek out my soul in meditation and feel its inner calm and expansiveness and, thus, transcend little conflicts and pettiness that life is heir to.

Just for today I will try to be kind to everyone I meet or work or live with.

Just for today I will try to rise above resentment if and when it raises its ugly head, by thinking of the good I received, even as a painful lesson, from someone I am resentful of.

Just for today I will try to be attentive and helpful to someone who needs my attention and help.

Just for today I will try to hold my temper, even displeasure, if and when provoked, and by cool indifference put off the offender.

Just for today I will not tense up thinking of someone who had hurt my ego but like a duck shake off the droplets of the egos of others sprayed over me.

Just for today I will refrain from criticising or speaking ill of others, reminding myself that I have so many deficiencies to overcome.

Just for today I will desist from being a coward and be true to my principles.

Just for today I will speak less about myself and listen more to what others have to say.

Just for today I will try to be a little less selfish and find a way to do a generous deed.

Just for today I will try not to feel sorry for myself and think of how may I alleviate the suffering of another.

Just for today I will try not to be self-important and recognise the merits of others.

Just for today I will programme the day and set out things to be done and when avoiding the two big pests, indecision and hurry.

Just for today I will be unafraid to be happy and enjoy what is good, beautiful and graceful, and with the sunshine of the positive melt the fog of the negative.

Just for today I will try to love those I can, drawing from the infinite love that God is.

Just for today I will tell myself that there are two days I should not worry about, yesterday with its mistakes and aches and tomorrow with its uncertainties and apprehensions, but live this today as well as I can, as mindful of my duties as I can be and as committed to my ideals as the inner spirit guides me along.

Just for today I will try to practise any or more of the above as best as I can.

For yesterday has gone forever and over which I have no control, and while all the regrets in my heart cannot make it any better the only good it can teach me is not to repeat the same errors.

For tomorrow the sun will rise and it will be just another day, but over which I have no control either, and I shall take it in my stride as it dawns and until then I shall not worry about it, unborn as it is.

That leaves only today, and it is surely enough to fill my plate, for one can deal with one day at a time only and foolish it is to refight yesterday's battle and try to tilt against tomorrow's rolling of the windmill.

*So, let me live one day at a time only.**

* Adapted and enlarged by Swami Shivapremananda from an anonymous text published in a Bulletin of the Faith House at New Brighton, Merseyside, England.

Chapter Eight

THE MYSTIQUE OF CHANTS

There are three principal reasons for chants: to feel, express and relate. Life is ruled by instincts and emotions. Reason helps to understand and direct their expression. Instincts are basically for self-preservation and emotions are for relating, both with the tangible and the intangible.

The human being is a body and a spirit, the tangible and the intangible; functioning through physical consciousness, grasping, analysing, demanding, giving and relating on a level one can comprehend and yet reaching out into another level of subtle consciousness which one does not quite understand but which one knows to exist deep within oneself and which one tries to fulfil through a sense of the transcendental, such as in inner peace, in a higher form of love, in being a part of the infinite.

Nature expresses itself through energy forms and sound is one of the most expressive ones. Thus, there is music on earth from its very early history: leaves rustling in the breeze, brooks gurgling through beds of stones, waves breaking on the shores, wind whistling through fields. Then, on the animal level, sound becomes a means of communication and many types of expression and, on the human level, it finds its vast dimensions.

The history of chants is as old as the human being. Being conscious of nature around and feeling to be a part of it, man learned to communicate his needs among his fellow-beings through words, that is, sound forms. Then he began to feel a lift in his consciousness by expressing his emotions through songs when he was happy as well as when he felt the burden of sorrow. He sang when he had a good harvest and wanted to share his happiness with the other harvesters, and sought to relate his gratitude to nature. He also poured out his laments when he lost a dear one, so as to hold on to the memory of the departed and find some relief from sorrow and to wish the vanished soul well, which he thought must have gone to a strange and unknown world.

There must have been traditions of prayers, chants and other forms of music in the proto-Dravidian culture of the Northwestern part of the Indian subcontinent when the Aryans came there between 1800 and 1500 B.C., but hardly anything is known about these. The earliest references to Sanskrit chants can be traced back to about 1500 B.C., when the nomadic Aryans had settled down in this region of India. There were bards of tribes who sang and recited before their chieftains the compositions that came to be known as *Samhitas*, the first books of the Vedas.

ODES TO NATURE

These were in adoration of nature and expressed a fascination for natural forces, both in fear and in gratitude. The poets thought that, behind the brilliance, heat and the consuming nature of fire, there must be a supernatural power and gave it a name, Agni. Fire burnt and destroyed, and there was fear. It was also needed for cooking and providing heat when the weather was cold, and there was gratitude. The poets felt the breeze and related it to breath and life itself just as they knew storms and saw the destruction caused by them, and gave to this elemental power the name Vayu. They slaked their thirst with the waters of springs, saw the rains soften and make the land bloom and also were terrified by the force of floods, and called this natural power Varuna.

Thus were evolved the ways of relating human life to nature. Odes were composed and chanted to various nature-gods, such as those mentioned and many others. There were not yet the anthropomorphic type of gods, nor was there the monistic idea of God which came later in the age of the

Upanishads, after 1200 B.C. These were forces of nature and were worshipped as spirits with superhuman attributes.

In the course of time, these poetical compositions called *Samhitas* were put together in rhetoric and prosody with cadences, and were meant to be chanted in specific ways, especially in the Sama Veda. Subsequently, a sense of spiritual identity was further developed in the liturgy of the books called the *Brahmanas,* and when a still higher sense of belonging to the infinite arose in the Upanishads, there came a different variety of chants with greater dimensions.

The tradition of chants indicates two distinct needs in human nature, dominated by a profound sense of inadequacy throughout one's existence. These are: security and fulfilment. Physical security to start with, out of which comes the anxiety to be protected from all types of physical threats, including disease, natural calamities, economic difficulties, wars and anything that endangered one's life. Then there is the need for psychological, emotional and spiritual security.

NEED TO BE FULFILLED

The other dominant need, to be fulfilled, also begins on the physical level, such as in anything that would gratify the senses and make the body happy. Then comes the need to be fulfilled mentally such as through curiosity, search for knowledge, and the longing to be fulfilled emotionally by human love, and to be fulfilled spiritually through a sense of belonging to one's subtle source, not really knowing what it is and yet being conscious of its presence in one's life as the immanent infinite through which feelings, emotions, knowledge and life itself try to become transcendental.

This is how all the ideas of God came about, crude and fanciful, sublime and wondrous. This is how chants and hymns arose out of the consciousness of man, whining and dithyrambic, supplicant and contrite, terrified of harm and longing for truth and love—all these, all the time, indicating the two basic needs of life: wanting to be protected and to be fulfilled.

It all started quite early, with the infant crying for nourishment, the child begging the parents for this or that which will gratify it physically. The fear of parental punishment was none too soon imprinted in the child's mind and, in adult life, the fear of the tribal chief and his cohorts. Thus, there existed these two basic realities: clamouring for favours and being terrified of punishment by the physically strong. Out of this came a strange, slimy thing called flattery which was, later, to be specially reserved for God.

Parents were soon found to be not so powerful after all, either to reward or punish. The tribal chief, who had a wider authority over his followers, learnt that there was a better way to deal with the complaints he could not cope with that were brought by the people and decided to get rid of the pests currying for favours as well. This he simply did by asking his bards, who later became priests, to tell the people that there was someone else, in fact, several of them, to whom they could go with their difficulties and also hanker for favours. These were the gods and, later, the personal, monotheistic God, who fulfilled such a social need.

OTHER FACTORS

There was also the motivational factor: to raise the people to superhuman efforts in times of stress and danger through beliefs such as God being on their side to protect them and bring death and destruction upon their enemies if only everyone would do his or her best. When natural calamities visited, these became acts of God because people were not good enough and could do better, and it also helped them to bear their misfortunes stoically. So, keep praying and sing all the hymns you can.

There was yet another factor, also based on the need for security. It was the fear of death, the terror of the unknown. It shows that, as the consciousness of man evolved, increasingly he could not accept the fact of his extinction. It also shows that he knew that he was not merely a body but there was something in him that would not die. Thus, he clung to the belief that he was a soul as well. The fact of physical death he knew all too well, and he became preoccupied with what might happen to the unseen, subtle entity, his *psyche*, the Greek word for soul, his *atma*, after the body died.

Man, of course, did not know what his soul was but he knew a little about his mind and he was well aware of his body, his physical instincts. Yet he felt the presence of something subtle in him through his longing for peace, fulfilment in human love which eluded him most of the time, and in his need to be fulfilled spiritually. This he did not know how to do. However, since he knew his body well, he transferred his physical instincts and ideas of life to his soul and wanted its continuity under ideal circumstances in order to satisfy them, and such a place he called heaven.

The fear of death was, thus, due to an excessive attachment to physical existence. The fear of the unknown was, thus, actually a fear of losing the known, for one cannot really be afraid of something one does not know, just as a child would not realise that fire burns until after getting burnt. This special kind of fear of extinction, or uncertainty of the continuity of one's existence, played a dominant role in religions, gave birth to ideas about heaven and was, thus, interwoven in hymns and chants. Since no one could save man from death in the world he knew, his only recourse was to ask an all-powerful spiritual deity to bestow upon him eternal life. In the *Katha Upanishad,* life in heaven itself was considered inadequate and the ultimate destiny of man was in his merger in Brahman the infinite spirit.

This fear of death did not arise, of course, as long as life continued normally. However, the explicit fact behind chants and prayers was that, in a desperate situation, when no tangible help could be found or was not adequate, the human heart cried out for help and sought to relate itself to a source of power for support, peace and consolation. The spirit of man rose from the limited vehicle, his body and mind, and reached out to the limitless sky and tried to revive itself by relating to the universal spirit.

This is the mystique of chants, in fact, of all prayers.

ATTRIBUTES OF LIFE

Gods and goddesses are attributes of life itself, through which one seeks to relate to the infinite which the Upanishads call the impersonal, transcendental Brahman, a term representing monism, whereas the same purpose of relating to one's spiritual source by the adoration of the best qualities of life is served by the Judeo-Christian concept of personal God, which the Hindus call *Ishwara*, a term denoting monotheism, which is but an attempt to fuse all gods and goddesses together and sublimating their shortcomings, such as divine wrath and an addiction to praise and power, through the ideas of an all-encompassing love and forgiveness, the God of relentless justice becoming the God of mercy.

In fact, the concepts of God are shapes of spiritual aspirations of the individual and the group, superimposed on the infinite spirit. The purpose of chants is just that: the movement of one's heart in relating to the infinite, to one's spiritual source, in various shapes of ideals and longings.

Chants are of a religious nature, *re-ligare* or to rebind, not only in their contents but also there is a considerable significance in their cadences, intonations and rhythm in relating, integrating individual consciousness with higher levels of consciousness through which is felt an inner peace and sublimation of emotions. They even give a sense of the collective unconscious, such as in feeling one's roots in the primordial vibrations of the universe.

THE PRIMORDIAL UNCONSCIOUS

Nature itself represents the primordial unconscious, such as in the principle of cohesion in the molecular structure of an element. In the rustling of leaves, in the distant, rolling thunder, in the murmuring of a stream, in the dusk slowly sinking into night and the dawn emerging out of darkness, in so many facets of nature, there is a relatedness to unknown or little known human emotions. By humming a tune, listening to music, singing, playing a musical instrument, through devotional chants, one is expressing such a relationship.

The universe pulsates with energy, and the human consciousness is its highest form so far known, even though there is so much more to know about it. Divine consciousness, transcendental, infinite consciousness, the universal mind, are all conjectures of the basic human longing to widen the horizons of one's perception, the longing to burst out of the limitations of instincts and memories, to experience a relatedness with the cosmic whole.

Since sound is energy and energy is movement and movement is in relationship, both with the tangible and the intangible, the purpose of chants is to fulfil this basic longing. It is specially true when they represent soaring harmony in sound forms. The chants manupulate on emotions, exercise and move them, meander and lift them, attenuate and diffuse them.

In the primitive forms of chants the rhythm aspect is more prominent. Being repetitive and alliterative, rhythmic and exuberant, they release pent up emotions and bring about a hypnotic effect. There are people who go into trance by listening to or doing such chants. By themselves their spiritual value is doubtful.

Chants also serve another purpose, that of group identity, providing a collective security, just as denominational religious chants do. However, their spiritual aim is not to confine people into groups or divide them but to give a sense of unity and interrelatedness of life, of joys and sorrows, light and shadow, microcosm and macrocosm, man and God.

Chapter Nine

KNOWLEDGE THROUGH ENQUIRY

The first step to knowledge is observation. It is done in two stages: an immediate assessment, and a relatively long-term perception. For example, we know the nature of our mind, our character, by our reaction to challenge: cowardice or strength, self-importance or self-confidence. The ego is easily provoked in an insecure mind. The gut-reaction in being defensive shows the insecurity within.

One who is secure in a premise of knowledge would not enter into an argument when that premise is challenged, after making one's position known. Religious intolerance is very much indicative of the unconscious insecurity in one's own faith. You have only to see the flag-waving syndrome that yoga is not a religion. If you are secure in your belief, no one can take it away from you.

The second stage is in observing what goes on inside the mind over a period of time, say, a couple of days or a week: the occurrence of waves of resentment, daydreaming without the intention of doing anything about it, the tendency to postpone a decision, work-shirking, gossiping, making up stories, the lying habit. All these point to our character pattern, the load we carry on our feet of clay, mostly half-baked. In the furnace of life, instead of baking them well, they only seem to get singed!

We have a very short history of seeking self-knowledge, and of the universe from which we have evolved, and continue to be influenced by constantly. The quirk of the recombination of particles of energy, beginning as early as three billion years ago on this planet, through trial and error of the aeon-old evolutionary process, through the atomic interaction of chemistry and biology, we have at last become modern humans. Our brains have evolved enough to question what particles they are made of, and from what source and what for. It is good to remember that only fifty thousand years ago we were grunting savages!

Since words became visible as written language less than three thousand years ago, individual minds began to wake up, and think on a much wider scale by the stimuli of the minds of others, first expressed by laborious handwriting, then by movable types, and now on the computer screen. The more we observed, the more we shared the observation of others, and the more we learned about the nature of our mind and our character.

PSYCHOLOGY BEGAN LONG AGO

Psychology did not begin with Sigmund Freud, but some 3,500 years ago, at first through oral tradition and, nearly a thousand years later, in written form in the Vedas and the Old Testament. It began as an insight into human nature. One has only to read in the *Samhitas* (first part of the Vedas) how people sought to alleviate insecurity, and feel protected, by trying to propitiate the forces of nature through hymnal overtures. Or, Samuel warning David of God's displeasure due to the king's succumbing to his character flaws.

In the Bible, the Buddhist scriptures and the Confucian and Taoist texts, in *Ramayana, Mahabharata*, the *Panchatantra* and the *Puranas*, human nature is graphically portrayed, describing character traits and how the mind works. It was done mainly through observation, rather than investigation and analysis as in modern times. Neuro-science had to wait a long time. But the sooth-sayers, shamans and priests seem to have done their job fairly well, considering the record of the present day well-meaning shrinks, in spite of the chemical aids to treat mental illness.

The mind is a particular field of energy, also called individual consciousness, which inhabits two spheres of the gray matter known as the brain. As I do not have any training in neuro-science or modern psychology, I will keep my adumbration to the yogic points of view, as indicated in old Indian texts, but in the light of current understanding, as well as personal observation, experience and dealing with people under psychological stress.

One cannot say that something is true or real without the necessary evidence. As in any energy field, the mind has its positive and negative wave-lengths, and neutral or quiescent state. The term positive is intended to mean harmonious, and the negative conflictive. The emanation of this energy is visual, such as in facial expression and body language, and verbal. But it has a short range outside the brain, for example, two persons together saying the same thing at the same time, or one speaking what is in the other's mind at the moment.

There is no evidence of collective consciousness, although due to the cultural influence our behaviour can be predictable under specific circumstances. The atmosphere of a place is palpable, of course, as in the difference between an active and inactive church. It is due to some contributive factors like wax-burning candles, incense, sonorous chanting, and the devotional imprint of those who worship there. But to call it a collective consciousness will be a misnomer, for consciousness is individual.

In the same way, there is no collective karma. Karma is a consequence of a particular action, as well as a current one. Collective suffering due to war, or a group of people dying in an airplane accident, cannot be called a collective karma, but plain bad luck. Good or bad luck is a term for an event, the cause of which is as yet incognito. That is a more honest way of looking at it. To attribute an unverifiable cause will be dishonest.

IS THERE AN AFTER-LIFE?

Let me digress briefly into the topic of after-life, because it speaks about the nature of our mind. Since the beginning of human history, afterlife has been speculated. The Upanishads write about transition to higher planes of existence called different grades of heaven, or the lower ones of the nature of hell, as per one's meritorious or wicked deeds, only to reincarnate on this planet to resume the evolutionary process until the individual soul is merged in Brahman or the transcendental spirit.

Some texts speak of direct rebirth here on earth, after the individual consciousness has slept for a while in a disembodied state. The worst kind of speculation, and the most pagan one (read superstitious) at that, is the ultimate reward in an eternal heaven, or eternal punishment in the ultimate hell, after having waited in a limbo indefinitely for the day of final judgment.

It indicates two characteristics of the mind: the extremes of greed and vengeance. Having invented the merciful God, such an attitude becomes an oxymoron.

A mundane judge punishes a murderer with a twenty-five-year life term, subject to one-third remission for good behaviour. How can God be worse? Astrophysicists presume that out of two hundred billion stars in our galaxy, one in a hundred thousand may have a planetary system, but we do not know if there are evolved forms of life, higher or lower than that of the earth. Then there are a hundred billion galaxies of all kinds in the universe, according to the British physicist Stephen Hawking. Why are we so primitively self-important in our religious thinking?

The existence of heaven and hell is, indeed, academic. It is for the scientists to determine the nature of the universe, and the laws that govern it. What really matters to us is what we do with our life, and how we understand and cope with it. In a pure heart, with compassion and integrity, love and the warmth of feelings, decency and fair-mindedness, we experience the heaven within. By expressing them in our relationship with others, we create a similar heaven around. In their contradiction we suffer from hell, both within and without.

REINCARNATION

The same way we can deal with the subject of reincarnation. It speaks of the nature of our mind. Among Hindus, or those who practise the Hindu faith, it is almost a universal belief, just as the credence in the eternal heaven and hell among practising Jews, Christians and Islamists. However, as the individual consciousness does not carry its memory from one lifetime to the next, for all practical purposes what really counts is the life as we know it. Reincarnated or not, every life is a unique experience in itself. Why speculate about something that you cannot verify, but just on the basis of hearsay?

Yet, the theory of reincarnation is a far better postulation than any of the following:

The caprice of chance, or dumb luck, good or bad, in which free will is irrelevant. Why bother about something in which you have no say?

The will of God who knows what is best for his creation. His mind is beyond human comprehension. A divine mystery should not be probed into. So, do your best, and accept your destiny without complaint. First of all, anything that you do not understand is unhelpful, and the fiat of mystery can be used to deceive people.

During the past quarter of a century, physics and chemistry have made giant strides in comprehending the laws of the universe, of genetics and biology, unlike religion. True science is modest enough to recognise many areas of knowledge that remain to be explored. Religion has done little to improve the spiritual quality of life.

Speculation about reincarnation is an attempt to explain the *inequality* and *inequity* of life, with a logical sequence, even if unverifiable.

We are all born with a different quantum of intelligence. Like the ligaments binding the knees and the pelvic joints, we can stretch our intelligence by mental exercise only up to a point, in a limited way, not drastically. The inequality is due to our self-effort, or the lack of it, in the past lives. The same rule of recycled self-effort holds good for inborn talent in audio-visual arts, poetical and mathematical excellence, and a genius being born in unfavourable circumstances.

In a poverty-stricken family, a child grows up emotionally rich and with sound character, on account of marvellous parents, and does not grudge material deprivation. Another child grows up emotionally stunted and morally rudderless, in a wealthy family. Why this inequity of birth? An honest person tries to live a decent life of upright conduct, but runs through a series of bad luck. A wicked person, on the other hand, seems to be rewarded by fate. Is there justice in life? Reincarnation theorists try to explain this inequity by the idea of unrealised retribution and compensation of a debit or credit balance in the past life now being recuperated. The present karma, however, will have its consequence, in due course.

As we cannot relate the present with an unknown past, the philosophy of reincarnation is just a philosophy of life. It is a doctrine of *redeemable* accountability, of assuming responsibility for one's fate. It is meant to pick up the haversack, and soldier on, rather than pass the blame on to the parents, society or God for one's bad luck. It is a manner of reconciling with an unjust world, and coming to terms with fate. It is a philosophy of making God a constitutional monarch, and oneself the author of one's destiny.

Also, accountability to an invisible God after death is not a deterrent to evil deeds, and has little meaning as to shaping our actions, rather than accountability to our fellow-beings, and social institutions defined by law, and ultimately to our conscience. In the same way, the hope for a better life in the next incarnation as a result of good deeds is meaningless, since the memory of the present one will not be carried over.

The theorists of reincarnation were psychologically perspicacious. The preference of choice inclines to the known. Given an option between returning to an imperfect world which one knows, and having a passport without the certainty of getting an entry visa to heaven from St. Peter, the human mind would surely choose the former!

Personally I will be quite happy, when my body is reduced to ashes and dissolved in the sea or river (*apas*) and my last breath is mingled in the atmosphere (*vayu*), if my soul merges in the infinite spirit, its individuality gone for ever.

FIVE ASPECTS OF THE MIND

There are two main classifications of the mind according to yogic tradition. One is called the inner (*antar*) formation (*karana*), and the other five (*pancha*) sheaths (*kosha*).

In the inner format, the inmost content of our being is the I-consciousness (*aham*). In a state of identity with its spiritual source, it is known as soul (*atma*), which the Bible calls the image of God in Genesis, in which we are supposed to have been created. When identified with the body and mind, and their orientation with the world around, it is called the ego (*ahamkara*).

The yogis thought that the soul is located in the heart, as did the Christians. It was because the fluctuation of emotions is felt in the palpitation of the heart, which is but a strong muscular pump to circulate the blood. The soul can be characterised as the life-principle, as well as the spiritual side of human nature. It is an energy field within our mind and body. Gyana Yoga refers to soul as a spark of the infinite spirit in a state of embodiment (*jivatma*).

Whereas the Bible gives an exclusively divine nature to the soul as the image of God, and so do the Vedas, the Greek word for it, *psyche*, refers to the unconscious, including both its spiritual and materialistic propensities. Modern psychology and psychiatry follow this definition.

The second layer, which is mostly dormant, is the principle of transcendental wisdom, or spiritual enlightenment (*buddhi*). The title Buddha given to Gautama means the Enlightened One. Now we know, of course, that there are no layers in the brain, but it consists of billions of neurons which function through electro-chemical interaction. The word *buddhi* is also generally used for intelligence. Intuitive perception takes place both in the fields of *buddhi* and the unconscious.

The third and fourth layers are called *chitta*, or the base of consciousness (*chit*). The word *chitta* is sometimes used for the entire mind. The inner (*antar*) is the field of basic instincts or *samskaras* (deep-rooted impressions). The modern term for it is the unconscious. The outer (*vahir*) part of chitta or the fourth aspect, serves as a field of memory (*smriti*). The current term is the subconscious.

The difference between the two is that the conscious part of the mind has access to the subconscious in order to think, but not to the unconscious which serves the role of stimulating desires in the subconscious.

Our education takes place in the subconscious, primarily by registering experience through action, or laboratory experiment, or doing calculus, and secondarily by the study of books and observation. Whereas the unconscious never sleeps, the subconscious pulsates from time to time in dream (*swapna*), releasing tension caused by stress and playing games by juggling desire and anxiety. The yogis fantasised that some gurus give mantra initiation in dream to a select few.

The fifth or the outermost is known as *manas*, or the conscious level of the mind. The term *manas* is also generally used to refer to the entire mind. It functions through the senses (sight, hearing, smell, taste and touch), but with reference to the memory field for perception. Its role is to think, evaluate, select, make decisions, and will to act.

THE FIVE SHEATHS

The second classification is done by wrapping the image of God, or the spark of the infinite spirit, inside five sheaths (*pancha kosha*).

The outermost is the physical body called *anna-maya*, or that which is sustained by food (*anna*). The word *maya* (made of) should not be confused with *maayaa* (illusion). It is similar to the Christian concept of the tabernacle as a temporary habitation of the soul.

Inside it is the *prana-maya*, or the sheath made of five vital functions to keep the body alive. It does so by the following process: breathing (*prana*), assimilating nourishment (*samana*), circulating nutrition through the blood-stream (*vyana*), eliminating toxin (*apana*), and sustaining the mind (*udana*).

Within the vital sheath is *mano-maya*, or the shroud consisting of the three sub-layers of the mind: the field of instincts (unconscious), of memory (subconscious), and of thinking (conscious).

Inside the mental sheath is the dormant *vignana-maya*, or the microcosmic field containing the knowledge of macrocosm. It is presumed to contain all the laws that govern the universe. Any scientific breakthrough or discovery of what has been hetherto unknown, is attributed to this *kosha* (sheath).

The innermost sheath is called *ananda-maya*, also dormant, or soul-consciousness, or a state of blissful union with its spiritual origin, or God within. It is replete with transcendental wisdom. Within it lies spiritual intuition.

The paranormal or psychic propensity is in the unconscious layer of the *mano-maya*. The term spiritual should not be confused with the psychical. Spirituality consists in the inculcation of moral values, such as integrity and compassion, self-restraint and altruism, decency of conduct and goodness of heart, freedom from malice and humility of spirit.

The source of spirituality is in the *ananda-maya*. The spiritually-evolved mind may not have psychical visions, and the paranormally inclined may fail to meet the standards of spirituality. Both are unrelated.

Intuition has two aspects. The subconscious works by itself on a spiritual value or a scientific problem, in which the conscious mind has engaged itself for a long time. In a quiet moment, there is a sudden flash of insight. It is called intuition coming from the subconscious. However, the yogis presumed another kind of intuition arising in the *ananda-maya* or the *vignana-maya*.

Rare foresight of events through divination is said to take place in the latter. The success rate is miniscule, but the fact that it does occur gives credence to the theory that an event occurs in the astral plane before actualising itself, just as an architect draws a plan for a house before building it.

FIVE BUILDING BLOCKS

The mind is a product of five factors. The yogis presumed them as the building blocks with which the mind is formed. They are referred to as karmas, both as a consequence of action and as a process of acting.

The first is called *adrishta* (unseen) or *avyakta* (inexplicable) karma. It is said to be the residual effect of karmas done in the past life or lives, shaping our inborn nature and potentialities, and deciding the kind of household and environment we would be born in. Charles Darwin spoke of the former as inherited traits of character. At present it is called genetical inheritance from our parents and grandparents, perhaps further back.

The second is *griha* (house) karma, or the kind of household we come to, the kind of parents we have. In the first six months of infancy, and even earlier during the later period of gestation, we are indelibly influenced by the mother because of close physical and emotional contact, the father playing a secondary role.

After six months, in the next three years, the parental influence, or that of those we grow up with, is still very strong. From the third year on the child is able to vaguely remember events, and more clearly further on. The absorption process continues with diminishing indelibility through adolescence.

We grow up emotionally and characterwise in the field of *griha* karma through the security of love, and moral guidance by the forthright example of what we are asked to obey. If the feedback is negative, we grow up emotionally and morally insecure.

The third is *samaja* (society) karma, or the surroundings in which we grow up, the type of schools we go to, the kind of teachers, family members and friends we are influenced by, the kind of neighbours we associate with. The environmental factors shaping our personality help to fulfil some basic needs: the desire for approval to strengthen our sense of honour, fear of rejection or disapproval, guidance to make decisions, individual identity through role models, and group identity such as belonging to a cultural tradition.

The fourth is *swartha* (*swa* oneself, *artha* interest) karma, or action motivated by self-interest, self-indulgence, cutting corners to one's advantage, exploiting those who are vulnerable, abusing the weak, deceiving the gullible.

The fifth is *purushartha* karma, or actions motivated by spiritual (*purusha*) ideals. It is this building block that decides the transformation of our character (*charitra*). The word *charitra* means grazing (*chara*) or cultivating such traits that would help us to be ethically upright, emotionally stable and have peace of mind.

Life is what we make of it by coming to terms with our mind. It is in coming to terms with life around, the kind of relationship we have at home and place of work. In any bonding relationship, the requirements are:

Acceptance of what we and others are, and then working on ourselves by self-effort, and on our relationship with others through better communication, thereby improving mutual understanding. By sharing of ideals we learn to grow up together. Mutual respect due to common motivation gives us self-confidence. It is, indeed, a lifelong process.

INDIVIDUALITY OF CONSCIOUSNESS

Aham is the principle of the individuality of a spiritual essence called *atma,* which is intangible in the sense that it cannot be measured by an instrument but a force in itself, and because it cannot be duplicated by any material energy. Once it departs, the body or the mind cannot be revived by any means.

The physical body of the mind, the brain, being material, is sustained by matter or food as well as *prana* which is preserved both by food and the pulsation of *aham* or the I wishing to exist. The mind is not self-luminous. The pulsating I gives the motive-power to the instincts in the mind, which generate desires in relationship to objects through an outward projection, and register them inwardly as memory by experience, for later reference.

One thinks because the I is in the thought. No thought can be sustained without being interested in it. The seer and the seen coming together externally with the objects through the senses, and inwardly through memory, cause a ripple in the mind. It is called *vritti* or that which conduces the experience of pleasure and pain. When the I feels detached, the thought-process ceases momentarily, but as it relates itself through a subtle feeling of peace and harmony to a spiritual source in meditation, it is able to control the mind. As Patanjali says in the second aphorism of his *Yogasutras,* yoga is the control of mental ripples or impulses *(yogaschitta-vritti Nirodhah).*

The psychic materials of the mind are *sattva, rajas* and *tamas,* with which character is formed. It is because they are in a state of disequilibrium, *tamas* dominating *rajas* or *vice versa* and *rajas* overbearing *sattva,* the need for mind control rises, for no one does anything without a need. *Tamas* is lethargy, negativity, selfishness, self-pity, hate and depression. *Rajas* is passion, egotism, pride, vanity, ambition and restlessness. *Sattva* is peace, love, integrity, positive outlook, spiritual aspiration and inner harmony. When *sattva* dominates, *tamas* is absorbed in *rajas* and *rajas* in *sattva* and, thus, they coexist in a state of sublimation. This is the goal of yoga, the purpose of mind control.

Chapter Ten

CRITERION AND INNER BALANCE

The word criterion is derived from the Greek *krites*, to judge, meaning to "judge or assess a situation". To act well, we must judge the circumstances and form a criterion. To relate well, we should judge a person's values, character, which we are all the time doing anyhow, without saying so. Judging means to evaluate, which is fundamental to making a decision, not sitting in judgment with a condemning attitude, the purport of the saying "judge not others".

In Sanskrit, criterion is *lakshana*, an outlook, or *adarsha*, an ideal, formed by *vichara* (enquiry). *Adarsha* means towards (*aa*) a vision (*darsha*). *Chara* means to graze or masticate, that is, to think and rethink (*vi* is re). The word for science is *vigyana* or "research" through investigation. In Latin *scire* (the root for science) is to know, from *gnoscere*, a word derived from the Greek *gnosis*, very similar to an older word *gyana* or knowledge that is arrived at through a union of an outer and inner, or an empirical and evaluative perception. *Lakshana* is from *laksha* or seeing.

The word *charitra*, character, also comes from *chara*, that is, to inculcate in oneself moral values, the Greek root for character, *charassein*, to engrave, having a similar meaning. The criterion of character, for example, is formed by such qualities as:

Integrity, trustworthiness and loyalty,
Duty, honour and responsibility,
Moral courage, will and commitment,
Fidelity, discretion and fairness.

The purpose behind criterion is to cope and channel the primordial urges to survive and be happy. These energy impulses swirling in the mind can only be dealt with in three ways: by indulgence, repression or sublimation. Indiscriminate indulgence leads to error and suffering, repression to tension and complexes, and sublimation through a higher motivation to a more satisfying inner experience and self-expression. This is the criterion of discipline.

Among animals, life is a biological process through instinctive effort. They are not vain enough to give the impression of a struggle, except when fighting against odds, as humans do even when they are not really struggling due to self-importance, laziness or self-pity to dramatise survival. Just look at our habit of grumbling!

If we merely functioned through instincts like animals, we would probably be making less mistakes. Since we live by our fancies as well as instincts, fancies about ourselves and others, we are prone to suffer from mistaken judgment.

No one can live without criterion because we have to work and deal with each other, whether we like it or not. The question is if we have a good or bad judgment, as it is intimately conducive to our state of mind, harmonious or perturbed, happy or unhappy.

INSTINCT, IMPULSE, DESIRE, AMBITION

Survival is through instinct. Instinct is an impulse which becomes a desire through a thought-process trying to make survival agreeable. Any desire is oriented to personal happiness, even in the process of making others happy. Criterion is a means to satisfy this very reasonable desire to be happy.

When a desire does not have a vision beyond its immediate results, it is only an impulse for self-fulfilment and, therefore, lacks criterion. Thus, criterion is a desire with a vision to express ourselves. All actions, in order not to be impulsive and, thus, capable of causing harm, must have a criterion.

One cannot and should not be desireless in action but try to be free from selfishness, so that an action guided by a good criterion can conduce to a long-standing positive result, and also because interest in a good result will teach us how to act better in the future and be responsible for our action. Acting with indifference to result will only guarantee inefficiency.

Criterion is, therefore, not an intellectual luxury but a daily necessity. It is needed to prevent mistakes and, thus, suffering to oneself and to others. It is needed to understand the meaning of life, more than to prevent mistakes only, and to plan for a better future, to progress towards desirable goals.

The criterion behind ambition, for example, is to approximate a healthy motivation with one's untapped talents, combine intelligence with effort, and find out the limits of possibility to make life progressive and useful, while not neglecting the need for inner peace through spiritual values.

To have no ambition at all means to vegetate. Ambition is negative when it is sought to be fulfilled at the expense of others, or denying our time and attention to those we are responsible for. Ambition has a greater role than merely ego-fulfilment. It means to be more useful to one another, creative and efficient in work and, thus, successful in an undertaking. With selfish ambition no one has found happiness, nor the person without any ambition, who has only succeeded to make the mind opaque by indifference.

Since everyone likes life to be agreeable, we make fanciful assessment of a disagreeable situation in order not to face reality. We accuse others of the defects we suffer from, so as not to face them in ourselves. We like to live in a world of our fancy, all for the sake of avoiding suffering, which we cannot do anyhow through illusion, even by the illusion of regarding the world as an illusion. So, the question is not between a choice of criterion or no criterion, but between a good criterion and a bad criterion. Look at the errors of judgment our leaders make!

The birth of criterion is in the saying of Rabbi Hillel, a contemporary of Jesus Christ, who is said to have observed, "The essence of the Torah consists in not treating others as one would not like to be treated by others; the rest is a commentary." Thus, the first step is consideration for others.

DISCIPLINES TO FORM CRITERION

This means to educate, discipline and sublimate the ego expressed through selfishness, self-centredness, self-importance, self-pity and vanity.

Selfishness or meanness through the practice of generosity.

Self-centredness by consideration for and attention to others.

Self-importance by facing the fact that one has a lot to learn and improve.

Self-pity by not blaming others and recognising one's own fault.

Vanity by filling the emptiness (*vanus* means empty) through the practice of modesty and learning to be useful to others.

If one practises these ideals and also the aforesaid qualities of character, it will not be difficult to have a better judgment, the basis of which is, indeed:

Do not be false, do not be a hypocrite, and do not say with an instant reflex, "I am not false, I am not a hypocrite", since the truth will shine on the image however much it is polished by pretence.

Avoid self-justification. It does not mean that you should not defend yourself. If truth is on your side, it will speak for itself, and if you are in error, you cannot afford to justify yourself anyhow, which is a bad habit and bad manners.

The formation of criterion is helped by the following disciplines:

Do not fail to learn from your experience. There is an old saying, "The wise learn from the mistakes of others, the intelligent from their own mistakes, and the fools never learn from their errors and keep repeating them."

Make your evaluation by facts, not wishful thinking, and remember that the first premise of truth is evidence, *veritas*, verify.

Relate your choice of what you do with its long-term effect, rather than a short-term result. A quick gain by short-sighted selfishness makes a long-term loss inevitable.

Do not expect from others what you are not yourself willing to be or do, and make sure to communicate your expectation than be silent while expecting it.

Any good action with a good judgment is like a capital investment, that is, it should be able to sustain itself. It means to help one to help oneself. A good action with a bad judgment is like helping one to be dependent and irresponsible, and create a sequence of unreasonable expectations.

Anything that is secretive has a built-in possibility of deception, whether in a teaching, in an action, or in a relationship. Avoid it.

Respect the opinion, feelings and needs of others when you relate your own to theirs.

In forming a close relationship, look beyond external charm and appearance, such as if the person possesses an adequate measure of compassion (is not hard-hearted), authenticity (is not two-faced) and responsibility (can be counted on), is not too self-centred, self-important and prone to self-pity.

Have an open mind, a disposition to learn, because we do not know enough, pride and superficiality being impediments to learning.

Avoid negative thinking. When a resentful thought about someone arises, think of a good deed he or she had done to you, thus countering a negative energy ripple with a positive counterpart. Remember that resentment harms you rather than the person resented.

Try to be free from prejudice and infatuation. Both are blinding energy to be abjured: prejudice through fairness and objectivity, infatuation by reason and being mindful of character traits of the person infatuated with.

FINDING INNER PEACE

No one has found inner peace by closing the eyes and trying to forget the world, or by meditating on the fiat that God alone is real and the world unreal.

Inner peace is realised by the practice of the aforesaid guidelines. Then, be mindful of the basis of inner peace:

Lowering the level of expectation.

Managing desires you can cope with.

A sense of values as to what is more important, setting a priority of choice.

Practice of detachment, not indifference, but abjuring possessiveness, not taking yourself too seriously as to be heavy-laden with self-importance, because sooner or later someone will make you fall on your face.

Keeping the mind occupied with something interesting to learn.

Engaging yourself in some useful project, some work to do, places to go.

Recognising and accepting the limitations of circumstances and people around. Adapting, adjusting, accommodating, without losing your bearing,

Measuring what you can do with what you have within, as to capacity and motivation, and without as to circumstantial possibility.

Peace is neither exclusively within, as to being united with God, nor without, as to coming to terms with life around, but in a mixing of both.

Spiritual exercises such as loving God in prayer and meditation, repeating a mantra or affirmations as to what is our real nature in a divine relationship (*Tat twam asi, Soham*), will conduce a temporary state of elevation, peace and harmony, and possibly some inner strength. What will actually help is to keep in mind these disciplines and guiding principles in order to love and practise them and make them one's constant companions.

Spiritual exercises like techniques of concentration do not by themselves improve human nature but the sincerity behind to apply their purpose and to make us wiser and better persons.

VALIDITY OF BELIEFS

What is the ultimate cause of this cosmos with billions of expanding universes? Is there a creator, as religion claims? If so, what is his nature? Is there a great purpose, a supreme wisdom, behind creation? For the formation of criterion, these questions cannot be answered merely by scientific investigation, even if modern physics has arrived at a point of origin of the cosmos well over ten thousand million years ago, and is beginning to understand the basic material forces governing our galaxy.

The question about the creator enters the world of speculation to serve a very specific need for protection, such as by prayer to a deity, in the process of survival; a need for a moral order through a celestial commandment for social peace, when people had little access to humanitarian education; and to have strength to bear our burdens with patience and equanimity by believing in a divine wisdom setting our destiny.

The validity of such credence is in not so much if they are provable, but if they help to serve these very obvious human needs.

Any speculation to be meaningful must make life more agreeable and provide the motive-power of inspiration. Religion gives us a set of beliefs through legendary assertions. If they fail to inspire, they remain sterile. Apart from conformity to help group identity and cohesion through customs and observances, belief actually means hoping on a personal level. Hoping for anything makes sense only when it is related to what *is* with the *plausibility* of what *can be*, to make up for the deficiency. It loses meaning if the goal is too far-fetched and, thus, unattainable and if one does nothing about realising the ideal behind belief, so as to remain forever hoping. Similarly, faith means commitment to ideals representing the premise of faith, God. This is the criterion of belief and faith.

There are no revealed truths but individual perception of reality through spiritual aspiration, which must prove its validity through collective verification over a long period of time. A prophet's claim at God-given revelation was meant to make a teaching more acceptable in earlier times.

Does God exist as an entity? Are there *bodhisattwas*, heavenly beings, residing in superior planes of existence? There is no possibility of verification, but as a life-giving principle the existence of a transcendental force behind material forms of energy would be foolish to discount, for that would be like saying all that is there is what we are capable of determining with our relatively recently-acquired level of intelligence.

By observation one does not find the evidence of the rule of an omnipotent power, nor that of a transcendental wisdom. You have only to look at the amount of suffering in this world, the extensive physical misery in which a fifth of human beings exist, and the pervasive psychological unhappiness of both the rich and poor. There is evidence, however, that by believing in and attuning to a source of strength and wisdom, one finds an inner poise and guidance that was lacking before.

SPIRITUAL REALITY

By observation we know that there is a universal preference of good over evil, truth over deception, love over hate, harmony over conflict, purity over impurity, knowledge over ignorance, even if the non-preferable dominate our life due to the force of nature. This evidence indicates that above our physical nature there is a spiritual reality of our being, that it is universal and transcendent. This is the best definition of God as a tangible truth in human existence at least, not as a deity.

The foundation of wisdom is personal experience, that is, application of a speculation in a practical relationship. The principal means to evaluate an experience is reasoning, that is, relating effect with cause, action with reaction, theory with result, equal consideration of one's interests with that of others.

Some teachers decry dependence on experience due to one's tendency to be influenced by other people's experience and urge, thus, the negation of superimposition. Well and good, but one has to be really stupid to do so, giving up the personal obligation of determination through objective evaluation.

Then there is the frustration with the limited horizon of experience that gives rise to the speculation of a direct perception, abjuring personalness or any superimposition, to wait in utter stillness for the pure light of awareness to dawn. What guarantee is there that what is claimed to be so is not a shaft of perception as a result of the subconscious working unconsciously on a series of earlier speculations over a length of time?

Progress is due to searching, appraising, applying, experimenting, knowing and re-knowing, improving and learning anew through lesser results.

Experience is both empirical like heat and cold, and psychological as happiness and unhappiness. Reasoning helps to understand as to why one is happy or unhappy and, thus, serves as an instrument of choice. Determining one's security and welfare in relationship to others, and formation of motivation for desirable goals is the main purpose of reasoning and, therefore, having a criterion.

The ultimate purpose of criterion is the cultivation of conscience. To be conscientious is to be close to God. To be close to God is to develop an understanding of spiritual values and their absorption in our conscience through their application in human relationship. A well-developed sense of right and wrong, without self-righteousness, and the ability to choose the positive are the result of this absorption.

Imperfect as we are, having been created as if similar to the image of the devil than that of God, it is a long process, a long struggle of going against human nature, through education over generations and passing on the genetical character imprints. Then again through education in early life at home and school, and by personal effort at character formation do we develop our conscience and the capacity to choose.

It is, thus, silly to say that God gave us intelligence, the instrument of choice, and so we are to be blamed for the mess we have created: First of all, intelligence is genetically unequal and partly malleable by environmental influence. Responsible, of course, we are for our fate, but what a brutish start, what an enormous price to pay for the progress and happiness we long for!

Blame it on the devil for the mess in creation, who made his first appearance in the Old Testament's Book of Chronicles, which was supposed to have been written in the fourth century B.C. The Christians picked him up and have kept the holy spirit struggling against him until the return of the Christ to establish the kingdom of heaven. But when? Spare me, though, your inventive symbolism to clothe an understandable mindset of earlier times.

LOVE OF LIFE

We need to survive because we love life. In the process of survival we go through agreeable and disagreeable experiences, and the love of life makes us choose what is agreeable only. Thus, the necessity of criterion.

All forms of existence are made possible through the interaction of different forms of energy. When they are relatively harmonious, there is a prolonged cohesion. When not, there is decay, disintegration. So also in human relationship through different aspects of our nature, such as *sattwa* or goodness and harmony, *rajas*, or competitiveness and passion, and *tamas*, or inertia and negativity.

The experience of perfect love or harmony can never be continuous but interspersed with less-than-perfect sides of our nature. The question is how well can we reduce the widely-varying fluctuations by a better direction of our energies for greater creativity and balance. For this we need motivation or love of ideals, and a good judgment to fulfil them.

The most intense form of psychological suffering is caused by irrational attachment, which is actually a form of self-love. The more acute the attachment for a person the more sharp the pain on account of disappointment. It is caused by selfishness expressed in the form of possessiveness, an unwillingness to accept the fact of having crossed the point of no return. To a lesser extent this is the case of our relationship with material objects.

Selfishness is an inborn trait caused by the need to survive. When excessive, it makes our life empty, preventing the flowing in of other people's love and not having any resource to give from. The cure for selfishness is to be considerate and useful to others, restrain hypersensitiveness by tolerance and detachment, think of and listen to others more than to think and speak about oneself. These are the first steps to educate and purify the ego.

Selfless love, even if imperfect but made real through deed, gives a sense of spiritual relatedness, and this is what gives a meaning to one's life, to be happy in the happiness of others, in sharing our values, doing some useful work, in trying to be a better person.

HAPPINESS AND HARMONY

No one can experience a prolonged state of harmony within oneself, the dullness of indifference yes, but no real depth of happiness, even of momentary euphoria and temporarily profound meditation. Happiness and fulfilment are in the realisation of spiritual goals such as purity of heart and sublimation of the ego, always in relationship to the welfare of others.

Happiness is also in the widening of the horizon of one's mind through the study of the experiences of humanity that are available in the form of well-crafted literature, not blatant acclamations without the ring of truth. They help to clear and stimulate the mind and acquire a depth of understanding, conducing to a personal involvement with ideals and contentment.

Occasional disharmony will inevitably come up because there is an element of unpredictability in other people's nature, but it is up to oneself as how to handle such a situation and control one's reaction to it and, thus, not to be shaken up on account of wounded vanity. Little disappointments are to be expected, without seeking them, and accepted as a part of one's education.

Second only to attachment, irrational expectations from others, also on account of self-centredness, perturbs our peace. First of all, it is necessary to deserve before expecting anything, then look to the nature of the person from whom something is expected, before complaining of disappointment.

Satisfaction should be sought within oneself through selfless love, devotion to duty, work ethic and pursuit of understanding. It is not true that in non-expectation alone is happiness, or a desireless person is really happy, but at best resigned and indifferent, for life is an onward movement, to be better than one is, to do better than what one does. Without motivation for useful goals life becomes stagnant and dull, and an easy prey to unhappiness.

Motivation for irrational goals, such as to be free from the cycle of birth and death, or attaining the eternal life hereafter, or enjoy an ever-blissful state herein, can neither be sustained nor fulfilling, because the hereafter cannot be verified, nor its promises. In reality, one would choose what is tangibly attainable and rationally viable. Likewise, motivation for psychic powers cannot last long because the effort required is too demanding, there has to be an inborn predisposition, and the result too dubious to justify a useful purpose. Motivation sustains itself on feedback and attainability of its goal in the near future.

Religions have guided an understanding of life and its problems, projected its goals, prescribed moral codes in the name of God. They are actually structured and restructured by well-crafted teachings of intelligent, fallible men, revealing the light of their understanding of the conditions of their times, of human nature and its anxieties and hopes.

Religions reveal the story of life that shaped the identities of many peoples. We are to learn from it and reorient our criterion in the process of adapting to changing times. Scriptures represent the search for truth and the experiences of their authors. They are meant to stimulate our own search and deepen the understanding of life.

Otherwise, without the benefit of personal and collective verification of what is said to be God's revelation in the light of our own experience, religious teachings become artificial superimpositions and often conduce to hypocrisy. To progress one has to be receptive to both old and new ideas, think for oneself, form one's own criteria of values and verify their truths by practical application.

PRAKRITI AND PURUSHA

The dignity and autonomy of the individual and his or her corresponding obligations to society are the basis of civilisation. The philosophy of a nation is the cream of its culture. It is a conglomeration of ideas about life pulsating in socio-political institutions and individual and collective aspiration to improve prevalent conditions.

Criteria are formed by the institutions like the church teaching a way of life dedicated to spiritual values, universities promoting scientific research and humanitarian ideals, business organisations devoted to material welfare and gain, political and labour entities representing and protecting their constituents' interests and aspirations through consensus as in democracies, or by dictatorial imposition as in totalitarian states.

The individual's life is, however, dominated by the need for survival and coping with one's ego expressing its insecurity through all kinds of emotions: relating, imposing, submitting, seeking happiness. Human nature is expressed by the interaction of two kinds of energies, material and spiritual, the former springing from *prakriti* and the latter from *purusha*. It is a product of both the forces. We are neither images of God, nor of the devil, but a hybrid of both.

Purusha as a spark of pure light, the content of one's soul, tries to express itself through the longing for unselfish love, beauty, harmony, truth. It is, however, encased in the several layers of the mind, a product of *prakriti*, in which vibrate the primordial instincts for survival: dense, heavy, crude, choking, clashing. The pure light gets distorted. Seeking companionship with another soul and filtering through the mind, it becomes sexually oriented and expresses itself as passion between male and female, for ego-gratification, as also between friends.

The energy of *prakriti* takes over, and passion becomes possessiveness, attachment and infatuation confused as love. When rejected, it becomes hate. When encroached upon by another, it becomes jealousy. The pure light trying to focus understanding in the mind becomes distorted as a dogmatic opinion, the orientation of the ego or I-consciousness having shifted from soul to mind.

The ego is a product of both *purusha* and *prakriti*. It wants its resonance with other egos in love, knowledge, goodness, in sharing life's spiritual values. But this urge filters through the mind and gets distorted by the energies of selfishness, aggression, doubt, anxiety. Thus, the ego is in a constant need of education, because it mostly lives in the mind, and is a creature of its moods.

It is in the mind that all education takes place: by the learning and thinking process, uniting other people's experiences through study of their books with one's own experience, by seeking harmony within and identity with *purusha* or the spiritual content of the self. This reorientation alone and the consequent refinement of the mind can conduce to inner balance and harmony in relationship with others.

LOWER AND HIGHER NATURE

Vedanta says "the self is raised by the self", meaning that there are two sides to our nature, the lower needing the help of the higher. It is a constant struggle, more in those who are conscientious and less in those who vegetate by inertia, an interaction in light and shadow. The I-consciousness or the ego forgets itself when identified with and is in the light of *purusha*, is thus purified, and spontaneously acts with wisdom and harmony, expressing *buddhi*.

When identified with the mind in its two levels, the *antar chitta* or the field of *samskaras*, deep-rooted impressions, called the unconscious, and the *vahir chitta* or the field of *smriti*, perceptible memory, called the subconscious, it casts its long and often-distorted shadows. In the subconscious through memory pulsation the ego is elated and depressed, flies high excitedly in success and sulks gloomily in failure, as also in being praised and censured by others.

In the subconscious the ego becomes dogmatic, haughty, self-important, gets puffed up due to its identity with a race, religion, national culture, regional vanity, family name, educational titles, social status. Whether they have any real worth or not is not the point. The ego likes to be the king or queen in his or her own castle, the subconscious. In a raw state it is despotic. Through education it becomes a constitutional monarch. In relationship with others it is argumentative, pretentious, throws its weight around, gets delirious when massaged on the right side and vicious when scratched on the wrong.

In the unconscious the ego becomes impulsively infatuated, jealous, possessive, narcissistically passionate, neurotically depressive, resentful and hateful. In relationship with others it becomes abusive, threatening, violent, suffering from an immense insecurity. In the unconscious the ego is a creature of the primordial instincts of survival and the libido.

It is the freedom of the spirit, the freedom to learn, think, teach and express oneself, always with responsibility to others, the freedom to be a non-conformist, an atheist or monist, an idolater or monotheist, the freedom to oppose violence, dogmatism and hidebound ideologies, and search for truth, always with evidence as a guideline and never by a religious fiat, that makes society progressive, that improves the quality of life both materially and spiritually.

EDUCATION IS SALVATION

Social peace is the result of this freedom, out of which come leadership and political responsibility and wisdom. The basis of it is education, to create a moral consciousness, a personal sense of duty, obligation and accountability, a boundless curiosity to learn whatever is under and within the sky, whatever is within oneself to tap, develop, improve upon and utilise.

Personal peace, of course, depends on the education, refinement and sublimation of the ego. It is in the ability to manage our attitude and conduct, and come to terms with changing circumstances by the philosophy "even this will pass away, so balance the mind in pleasure and pain", that "we came with nothing and will depart the same way, so why make a mess of yourself in between"?

Raw human nature grows like a jungle. Life can be savage if our untutored nature is allowed to run wild. The idea of a noble savage is a throwback into the myth of being spontaneous, unhampered by over-tutoring and wanting to be free from repression on account of bad tutoring, and be blissfully irresponsible. There is nothing noble in a savage who is but spontaneously expressing his brutish nature. The value of spontaneity is in what one is spontaneous about.

Life can be cultivated like a garden if the desirable plants are tended, cultivated, and the undesirable weeds removed. Like a garden, individually and collectively, it needs constant care and renewal. Otherwise, within a few generations, the descendants of a gifted people can become like the Romans decadent and subjugated by barbarians, or like Germany being taken over by home-grown Nazis, as it was.

Education is a mental, moral, technological and cultural preparation of an individual for a better understanding and control and direction of his or her life. A just society makes this possible through a democratic means of its availability, on the basis of intelligence and aptitude, through autonomous institutions of knowledge and culture, without the control and interference of state or religion.

Education and personal experience are the father and mother of criterion. They should prepare the mind like a vast, frontierless region for hundreds of philosophers and saintly souls to guide and inspire; hundreds of scientists, architects and engineers to investigate, invent, innovate and build; statesmen and idealists to promote justice and our sense of worth; poets and musicians to recite and sing; painters and mystics to sketch the facets of life as it is and as it can be.

Education is to make our potentialities come alive to motivate and fulfil, for in a work well done, a duty well carried out, a love well sublimated, an ideal well realised lies our inner peace. A society's progress depends on the amount of investment it makes in research for the best and the brightest, and in tapping, vocationally training and making the optimum use of the human resources in the rank and file.

St. Paul said that truth should make us free, indeed from our capacity to harm ourselves and others on account of the ignorance of our spiritual resources. A prayer in the Vedas urges, "Lead me on from the unreal to the real and from darkness to light." This search for truth, to free the mind from ignorance is, after all, the goal of education.

Replacement of anarchy with order and passion by reason is the purpose of knowledge. Love of, and commitment to, the ideals that represent the object of devotion are the purpose of faith. Knowledge and faith are the two wheels of the cart we ride, knowledge that is understanding and faith that is a deep emotion for the best in ourselves. The failure of knowledge is in intellectual vanity and self-righteousness, and of faith in superstition and emotional theatre. The failure of philosophy and religion is in their incapacity to differentiate.

The highest meaning of our existence is in what we put into it. After birth we grow psychologically by receiving from others, such as the protection of love and guidance through education from our parents, if we are lucky enough, and by the help of others in later life. What makes life's journey meaningful is not whether we have received enough or not, but what we are willing to and capable of putting into it and transmit to others.

This meaning alone transcends the inevitable death of the individual, because we continue to live in the memories of those we have associated with, left our marks on, such as relatives and companions that survive, and the more gifted among us who have left their traces in arts and literature, science and technology, social reform and welfare. Even on a modest scale, the meaning of life consists in what we have meant to each other within the family and among friends, through love and understanding, care and protection, help and consolation. Life is, indeed, what we make of it.

ON EDUCATING THE EGO

The culture of a person is not so much in the knowledge of the audio-visual arts and architecture, but in his or her day-to-day behaviour. It consists in the education and sublimation of the ego. It is a lifelong process.

Some teachers write about the necessity of egolessness, and some even theatrically exhort to annihilate the ego. If you observe them closely, you will find in them an enormous ego, clothed in false gestures of humility.

It is neither possible nor wise to demolish the ego. Egolessness in the sense of not being selfish or egotistic is a virtue, of course.

The ego is a product of the individuality of consciousness. It is what motivates survival and, through ambition and competition, enables progress and achievement. In a refined state, it forms and expresses the best of criteria. In a repressed condition, it conduces to indifference and irresponsibility. In a weak-minded person, it becomes vulnerable to exploitation by stronger and cunning egos.

The mind is a field of energy. Generally speaking, it has five aspects: 1) *Ahamkara* or the consciousness of 'I am a body, mind and soul'. It is also called the ego, the *id*. 2) *Antar-chitta* or the inner mind, the stratum of the basic instincts, including the archetype, also known as the unconscious. 3) *Vahir-chitta* or the subconscious containing the stratum of memory, to which the conscious mind has access unlike to the unconscious, and where one dreams. 4) *Manas* or the thinking principle, the intellect, consciously evaluating, determining, desiring, willing. 5) *Buddhi* or the higher intelligence, generally dormant, that intuitively perceives deeper spiritual values when awakened. It is also called the superconscious or soul-consciousness.

It is *ahamkara* or the ego that makes any movement in the mind possible. In deep sleep it enables the *prana* (autonomous vital functions) to pulsate to keep the body alive. Through dreams it releases the tension of anxiety, trauma, unhappiness, desire and passion.

In the unconscious it gives impulse to the instincts. In the subconscious it is the participation of the ego that makes thinking possible. Consciously it gives zest to life by willing and acting out its wishes. In the depth of our soul it experiences the purity of heart, unselfish love, the "peace that passeth understanding".

Any energy pulsation caused by the ego can be treated only in three ways: by indulging in, by repressing and by sublimating. Through indulgence of the ripple of anger, for example, the ego becomes more aggressive. By repression it develops complexes. By sublimation of this energy through the love of the ideals of patience and tolerance, peace and understanding, the ego gets refined and becomes wholesome, in the yogic way.

Chapter Eleven

GUIDING VALUES

PEACE AND LIBERTY

By definition peace is a state of calmness, a sense of harmony, an experience of tranquillity. However, peace is essentially a consequence of a philosophy of life in which one comes to terms with oneself and the rest of the world. It is a result of how we manage our egos in relationship with each other, how we cope with our expectations and desires. Real peace is not attained through renunciation but fulfilment, if it is not to be confused with a mental opacity or indifference. It is an inner serenity cultivated through a deep understanding of life and sublimation of passions, by a sense of spiritual identity.

Peace is a product of security: spiritual, psychological and physical. Security can never be found in self-centredness but in the integrity and balance of perspective, altruism and compatibility of values within relationship. Security is in the capacity to love, in a deed meticulously performed, in a duty well carried out, in a responsibility fulfilled with painstaking care. The result is an inner spiritual satisfaction called peace.

Life is hardly static but a continuous movement, and movement is either due to the exigency of the circumstances, or ambition, or by the stimulus of desire, or a sense of deficiency. Peace is a pause, not merely to rest, but to feel the meaning in the movement of life. As such, peace is creative only when sensitive to the movement—in love and compassion, striving and aspiring, caring and understanding. If it is merely to rest, it becomes dullness when prolonged. Movement without an experience of its meaning is restlessness, peace without sensitivity is laziness.

Peace is not a virtue in itself but a vital need to recuperate from mental and emotional activity, inasmuch as one has to drink water to quench thirst. Yet, life cannot sustain on something subtle like peace, just as one cannot live on water alone. Peace is an after-effect of the fulfilment of one's spiritual goals. The individual cannot grow without struggle, and society cannot progress without challenge. If one seeks to avoid challenge, hide from the problems of life, the result can be mental inertia, insensitivity and self-centredness.

Peace, to be spiritually renewing and effective, can never be continuous, either individually or collectively. All talks about eternal or permanent peace are wishful thinking. You can be eternally peaceful only when you are dead. Whereas absence of war and subjective awareness of an underlying poise are desirable goals, individual and social ferment from time to time are nature's means of renovation and progress.

MEANS OF PEACE

Some basic means of personal peace are:

1) *Spiritual security,* such as in a religious faith, not in fanciful beliefs, but faith in the power of spiritual ideals that give strength of conviction and, therefore, self-confidence. Such a faith is totally free from dogmatism because it is a continuous search for the truth of what one believes in and loves. Belief, in order not to be a sheepish conformity or unproductive wishful thinking, has to be inspired by the love of the ideal it represents. Its realisation brings peace, even the mere fact of being involved with it.

2) *Psychological security,* such as in the understanding and discipline of desire or ambition, so that we learn to approximate our wants with capacity and effort, relate expectation with the knowledge of human nature and with what we are willing to give in a relationship, and try to live by the philosophy that doing what we believe in and love is by itself a reward enough rather than the result thereof. However, no action should be

unmindful of its result, because how else can you know if a deed has been well done?

3) *Emotional security,* such as in the health of the ego, so that we are not overburdened with a sense of the self, that there is freedom from hate and resentment, that we do not suffer from dependence on infatuated love. It is selfishness that destroys love, thus, inner fulfilment. Self-love quickly turns into self-pity, thus, one lacks peace. Love is not only caring but sharing, sharing not only of what we materially value but spiritually aspire for. In such a compatibility there is emotional security.

Some basic means of collective or social peace are:

1) *Security of justice,* or the rule of law based on fairness, which means freedom from the fear of permissive or random violence, or demagogy of one group over other groups, or exploitation of the weak by the powerful. Social peace is a result of easy access to justice, its promptness, its impartiality and effectiveness for all concerned.

2) *Economic security,* or the absence of degrading poverty and uncertainty of material subsistence. Dogmatic harping on distribution of riches quickly becomes distribution of thin air without productivity, ingenuity, work ethic and good management. These cannot be materialised out of the ideological hat but by universal education vocationally geared, encouraging talent and motivating initiative by appropriate reward.

3) *Security of rights,* by educating people to equate the rights of others with one's own, cultivating a sense of duty and responsibility, doing honest labour with efficiency, and making it evident in public service, resulting in good government and stable democratic institutions. It is a fundamental right of the

public to expect from them efficient management and integrity, without which social peace is inevitably perturbed.

MEANING OF LIBERTY

Liberty basically means freedom of the human spirit. We like to think that we are born free, but we are not. We bring with us innate, rudimentary instincts of self-preservation, therefore, selfishness and possessiveness, and self-extension, therefore, aggression and exploitation. Through education in our childhood and adult life, we learn to channel these basic instincts into creative forces. It is the nature of our spiritual self to long for the limitless inside the moorings of our earthly self. That is why we aspire for lib.rty, and do not like limited conditions.

However, freedom means expression, and the validity of expression is in what is expressed. Thus, the health of liberty depends on the quality of individuals who express themselves, so that freedom does not mean a licence to cause discord or bring out the worst in us, but encourages to give our best to society for the sake of general benefit. The reality of liberty is, indeed, in its usefulness.

The bases of liberty are: 1) individual responsibility, 2) respect for what is generally accepted as permissible, and 3) submission to the interest of the majority arrived at by a consensus.

Freedom is to deepen our experience of the quality of life, with a sense of "justice towards all and malice towards none" When the mind is free from dead habits, warping prejudices, corrosive passions and suffocating egotism, we experience the freedom of our inner spirit.

The fundamental rights of liberty are:

1) *Mental freedom,* to think freely without being bound by ideological or religious dogmas, to speak freely without the fear of reprisal, and to express freely in arts, literature and media without censorship.

2) *Social freedom,* such as to live and move and work without discrimination and make use of public utilities without apartheid.

3) *Physical freedom,* or freedom from indignity inflicted on one's person by a powerful individual, party or state, such as by physical abuse or arbitrary arrest, and from the indignity of hunger, inadequate clothing and shelter.

4) *Psychological freedom,* or the right to live without fear, either of a secret police, or of organised or random violence and expropriation of material possession by theft or decree, which means an effective rule of law in society.

5) *Spiritual freedom,* or the liberty of religious beliefs and the right to worship, including the right to be an avowed atheist or to disbelieve in an established theological or political dogma.

Like everything precious in life, liberty cannot be taken for granted. It must be nursed, sustained and protected. It is an individual and collective responsibility, a product of a moral sense. It is essentially a mark of spiritual strength. In order to be effective, it is an ideal to which people have to raise themselves. By the fiat of ideology, without checks and balances, it becomes licentiousness.

Peace and liberty are our basic spiritual rights, without which the human spirit suffocates. It is foolish to expect someone to transmit peace to oneself. It has to be cultivated within and in one's relationship with others. It is also foolish to expect lasting peace in the solitude of nature or in a sanctuary, because even there one has to cope with oneself in the long run. Likewise, the libertine has no right to liberty to harm others.

Liberty without responsibility is only conducive to chaos. There is nothing called infinite peace or total freedom in life. One can only strive to widen their dimensions in this imperfect world.*

* Based on an interview given in Channel 13 of the Television of Catholic University in Santiago, Chile.

Chapter Twelve

WHAT IS CULTURE?

The word culture is derived from the Latin root *colere* which means "to cultivate" as well as "to adore." Thus, culture is primarily cultivation of mind through love of ideals.

Just as the Latin meaning of culture is to cultivate and adore the subtle, its Sanskrit meaning of *samskriti,* is to create a sense of the whole within oneself and in society, freeing the mind from narrow concepts, prejudices and passions. Even though the purpose of culture is cultivation of mind and to acquire a deeper insight into the soul of a tradition, a people, a nation, its goal is an integral vision of life, self-knowledge and strength of character. It means to sublimate our emotions, free our lives from fears and superstitions, make us better human beings and create an active individual and social conscience.

Personal behaviour is a measuring factor of the individual's culture. How society treats its members does, indeed, determine its cultural level. Bursts of talents in arts and architecture represent the aspirations of a culture. Democratic institutions, relevancy of rights and responsibility, social justice, a collective moral sense, even commercial integrity are all pertinent to the cultural maturity of a people.

Culture is, thus, a better expression of the spirit in our existence through the vitality of a creative conscience, for without conscience there is no culture. Its five principles are:

1) Tolerance, that is, discipline of the ego, of gross passions.
2) Understanding, breadth of vision, depth of perception.
3) A feeling heart, sensitivity, compassion, refinement of emotions.
4) Sense of duty, responsibility, and spirit of service.
5) A wholesome conduct, integrity in human relationship.

INTEGRATION AND EVOLUTION

Without a desire to learn about and experience the depth of life there is no culture. Life is an experience and expression of relationship: in feelings, ideas and actions; with nature, people and spiritual values. The I seeks its security as a body through sensation and possession, as a mind by the exercise of opinion and involvement of feelings, and as a spirit through its sense of being a part of the whole in the consciousness of the infinite. As the first two bases are inadequate, one seeks fulfilment in the last, and as the last is not tangible enough, one goes back to the first two for a reassessment. The purpose of culture is, thus, an integration of the material and the spiritual.

The determining value of the term "material" is the principle of possession, because that which is concrete can be captured and, therefore, meant to be possessed and likely to be attached to. The term "spiritual" is characterised by freedom due to its subtle, interpenetrating and transcendental nature. In the same way, the term "positive" is a state of inner freedom from passions, an experience of peace, tranquillity, out of which comes fulfilment, from fulfilment happiness, from happiness a capacity to relate and in order to integrate. The term "negative" is a state of isolation of the self in justification of the ego, either through self-pity or resentment.

When a lack of fulfilment of the ego fails to awaken the mind to reason and, therefore, to think and feel and relate with a deeper understanding, it is called a state of prejudice and rejection. Thus rejecting, one becomes rejected, self-loving one begins to hate oneself unconsciously. It is the self that experiences the innate instincts through memory-oriented desires, either in preference or rejection, from which arise the love to possess and the passion to hate the dispossessor.

Introspection, devotion to spiritual ideals and discernment conduce to clarity of mind to understand the nature of things and their interrelatedness, and this comprehension helps to subdue passions, leading to inner harmony. Thus, to be positive is to be free, to be negative to be bound. Truth is positive because it is a rhythmic, symmetrical interaction of perception, in which balance is the uniting principle of the perceiver and the perceived. Love is positive, because within its fulfilling interaction there is the transcending principle which frees the individual from isolation and dependence on self-gratifying passions.

The purpose of culture is to move our life from darkness or ignorance (*tamas*) to desiring, experimenting, asserting (*rajas*), to finding, understanding, integrating (*sattva*). From mass to force and from force to balance. From inertia to movement and from movement to order. From inhibition to desire and from desire to sublimation of desire. From laziness to restlessness and from restlessness to equanimity. From mental opacity to discussion and from discussion to profound silence.

The ideal of culture is essentially the education, refinement and sublimation of the ego through self-effort. For, the searching self is the feeling self, the feeling self the knowing self, the knowing self the fulfilling self, and fulfilment is in doing what we can to the best of our understanding of one another. In such a process there is the diminishing of the gross self and better spiritual integration.

RELATIONSHIP AND CHARACTER

We are all individuals formed and reformed through relationship. Our happiness and misery are a product of relationship. However much we may talk about individualism and personal independence, our life is influenced by collective structures such as the family, place of work and the general fabric of the society we live in. Relationship means interresponse, and interresponse is communication. Most of our problems arise because we have little integrity or genuine representation in communication other than gratification of the ego-sense.

Relationship between two persons begins with the awareness of each other. We have, of course, no problem with sense-awareness, but it is the awareness of each other's feelings and needs and the willingness to care for these that enable communication to be meaningful. In relationship we throw ourselves at each other, our views, physical and emotional demands, and thus fail to communicate. In the family unit, although physically related, we fail to communicate because the gratification of our expectations, our egos, becomes more important than responding to one another's feelings, problems and needs.

Self-centredness is the basic cause of our feeling isolated, not being understood. Through selfishness we push ourselves on to, or run away from, one another and thus fail to communicate. How can we communicate when by loving we mean to gratify self-love through another person? Being concerned with the protection of our images in relationship, which is indicative of insecurity, we tend to be hypocritical. It is the lac' of character which vitiates relationship.

Strength of character never hurts another but lack of tact, which means an excessive awareness of the rightness of one's position *vis a vis* another's and, as a consequence, impatience or outright contempt through self-projection. However, self-righteousness is not strength of character. Character is not temperament either, as the Latins conveniently make out the term to be, such as when referring to the good or bad character of a person by his or her benign disposition or aggressiveness, respectively, regardless of moral values. A man of integrity is surely a man of good character, whether aggressive (*mal caracter*) or not. The criteria of character are in the following integrities:

1. Integrity of knowledge, as to what may I know and how may I know, that is, not wishful thinking.
2. Integrity of feelings, in what do I care for, in what way does someone mean anything to me. (Love is blind when one is in love with the image superimposed and, therefore, unable to see clearly).
3. Integrity of action, in what may I do and how may I act, for the reality of a relationship is measured by what is done within it.
4. Integrity of self, or the truth in the expression and functioning of our individuality.
5. Integrity of relevancy, so that the validity of a hope or expectation is in the approximation of our capacity and effort for its realisation.

DISCIPLINE AND SENSITIVITY

There are two basic factors in culture: discipline of the raw physical nature, and spiritual sensitivity. The why of discipline is based on the fact that life is expressed through energy and our egos are thrown at one another by the drives of our passions and emotions. The purpose of discipline is not repression of life's energies. Energy implies movement and discipline means direction of energies. Thus, discipline is really a process of attunement which is understanding and love of the reason why.

Attunement gives health to discipline, repression makes us hurt one another through its byproducts: intolerance, resentment, peptic ulcer and hardening of the arteries. Discipline means to cultivate a sense of integration, to be sensitive, to be aware of life, to be attentive. Without attention there is no understanding, thus no attunement, which is the purpose of discipline. One does not get attention through justification, condemnation and dogmatic conclusion. Without the ability to inspire interest within oneself, a feeling of one's relatedness to the life around, there can be no attention, thus no discipline.

Spiritual sensitivity, one of the bases of culture, is to appreciate the immanence of the transcendental spirit, the cohesive principle of life such as we know in the common longings for truth and love, security and a sense of belonging. Spiritual sensitivity implies:

1. *A creative conscience,* meaning movement of mind in the clear spring of reason, and movement of heart in the refreshing breeze of faith. However, faith does not mean an unquestioning belief in an authority or institution, for it promotes dependence and retards initiative, or encourages fanaticism, a byproduct of ignorance, fear and insecurity. Faith means wanting to know, to feel, to unite, to experience the essence of life, and conscience is a result of this movement of heart. Conscience is that which makes this movement tangible through a grasp of the reality by effective discernment, and fulfilment of responsibility by productive action.

2. *A creative will,* wanting to test one's beliefs, experiment with ideas, ideals, in the field of action so that one learns their relative validity. After all, an ideal or a dogma is useful to the extent it serves the human being, promotes commonweal and a tradition is meaningful in the sense that it gives one an identity in the present and direction into the future, not to make oneself a fossil. A dogma is meant to serve the human being, not *vice versa.* A tradition is to provide one with a scaffolding to build one's life, not to make one its prisoner. A doctrine is to give one initiative to think and act, not to encourage spiritual dependence on a religious order or its interpreters. A human being is not meant to be a sycophant of unseen deities or super-egos on earth, but a participant in the life process.

3) *Integrity in relationship* begins with the family structure. Life is emulative and the formation of a sense of

values begins in the family. If the parents cannot communicate the strength of truth or of character by their example, they have already defrauded their role of parenthood. A new life can flower best where there is mutual communication, not dark niches in the mind to be hidden from one another, where one does not use another for self-love or ego-gratification, where to love is not to make one dependent but instill dependability, security, loyalty and require these very qualities from the loved ones.

4) *A civic consciousness.* A sense of duty should not merely be confined within the family, but extended to a wider, tangible circle so that one learns to respect another's rights while protecting one's own, has a collective sense of responsibility and regard for public property as much as for one's own. This naturally means self-discipline and a sensitivity to the life around, for an enforced social or theocratic discipline without individual initiative becomes a dull, collective conformity. In such a case society loses its creative vitality through overdependence on group directive and security.

A civic consciousness is the result of the respect for the right to live. To live is to experience and express. To experience means to participate, to express to communicate. To participate means to share, to give and to receive, to be responsible and make others responsible. To communicate means to be genuine, not a fraud unto oneself and to others, to believe in what one says and to be attentive to what is said. On the animal level communication is through instincts, on the human by the interaction of reason, and on the spiritual through the purity of feelings. The purpose of culture is to give a better expression to the higher levels of our nature.

The average quality of individuals reflects on the quality of society's values. Social patterns are based on precedence and set and inspired by leadership, and leadership rises from the people. Thus, the primary concern of society should be:

1) To make people think for themselves, encourage the element of curiosity to seek and to learn, to be interested in.

2) To promote initiative by delegation of individual responsibility and creating motivation through a sense of belonging, thereby opening up creative urges.

3) To generate a sense of relevancy that all rights are pertinent to specific areas of responsibility and fulfilment of corresponding obligation, that no special group in society can dictate its interests over those of another.

It is the abdication of responsibility that leads to the loss of freedom. It is the loss of individual perspective and capacity to communicate and share and give a collective viability to such a vision that conduces to disorder, stagnation and dictatorship. It is not so much what one says or believes that matters, but what one is able to do to make culture an individual and collective experience in the institutions of society.

To put it simply, the relevancy of a person's culture is not so much in his or her knowledge of the arts but behaviour, especially to the underlings, and that of a nation, not so much in its artistical background but in the fairness of the treatment of its citizens under the rule of law, especially of its minorities.

Chapter Thirteen

HOW TO COPE WITH HUMAN NATURE

The main cause of dissatisfaction in our relationship with others is selfishness and egotism or self-importance. From selfishness comes attachment which is a form of self-love through the means of another person. From selfishness comes irresponsibility which is a lack of consideration for others. One can, of course, be selfish while yet being responsible but an inculcated sense of duty at least restrains selfishness by making one responsible.

The ego impedes attention to the opinion and sentiment of others due to the reason that one feels full of oneself or vain, which is due to lacking in real substance (the Latin root *vanus* means empty). This conduces to pretention and, therefore, being false.

Pride is also a form of egotism. It prevents learning and, thus, a self-important person remains stupid. National vainglory and pride about past greatness without relevance to the present, reverses progress and leads to national backwardness, inefficiency and, therefore, poverty.

Self-pity is a major cause of our dissatisfaction because, when something goes wrong, we tend to pass the blame to others and feel victimised, rather than take personal responsibility for what went wrong.

In addition to these, another cause of our dissatisfaction is weakness of character. It is conduced by being false both to oneself and others, the lying habit, the deceiving nature. It not only corrupts oneself but, when it becomes a national character such as manipulating information, hiding facts, unwillingness to face unpleasant realities, wishful thinking, it corrupts the nation and, as a result, the people suffer.

Shrewdness, without a basic integrity of character, is indicative of spiritual poverty, for a short-term material benefit through deceit or exploiting the weakness of the circumstances contributes to untrustworthiness of the individual and leads to public cynicism and social resentment in the long run.

Weakness of character also means lacking in loyalty and constancy, or being only a fair-weather friend and an opportunist. The root cause is selfishness. Weakness of will is due to laziness, a tendency to shirk responsibility and be dependent on others, and postpone a hard decision as long as possible, for will is a product of the experience of persevering action and action of motivating interest. Will without consideration of the others is merely obstinacy.

Cowardice is due to a lack of self-esteem, hypocrisy and self-indulgence as well as not having strong convictions. Through self-justification when something goes wrong and pretension, one remains false in the eyes of oneself and of others. Deceit is a primary cause of losing friendship. An excess of selfishness, arrogance, vanity, unreliability and irresponsibility are the other contributive factors.

TWELVE DISCIPLINES

We may give ourselves the following dozen disciplines when coping with our problems with others:

1) Do not be impulsive. You can avoid many errors of judgment and conduct.

2) Think, discern and determine the cause of the problem.

3) Decide what should be done to solve it, such as making a gesture of understanding, expressing a wish to communicate when tempers have cooled down.

4) If there is no response, think again as to what appropriate attitude should be taken such as patience with

firmness, keeping an open mind free from prejudice, not to repeat the same mistake again which caused the problem, and then go your own way while respecting the right of the other person also to do so.

5) Reduce your expectation and accept the limitation of human nature as you yourself know in your case, and adapt different ways of relating anew with those you can.

6) Do not forget to fulfil your obligations to others before expecting others to do so, and also make it clear what is required in a mutual relationship, life being a two-way street. If there is no success, go your own way and have as little to do as possible with irresponsible persons.

7) Through contemplation and meditation generate inner peace and a sense of belonging to the spirit of God within, sublimating the ego and dependence on others.

8) Express this inner poise in your relationship through patience and understanding.

9) Have some useful interests to occupy the mind such as in the world of books, learning about different cultures and their historical development, geography, literature, biographies and languages.

10) Learn work ethic and something creative to do, not only to keep the mind occupied but to gain self-confidence and a sense of being useful, and express this security in your relationship with others.

11) Do not look backward and lament over a lost friendship, for there are others who need your attention, understanding, sympathy and friendship. Lamenting is anyhow a useless sentiment. When the line of no return is crossed in a relationship, nature automatically sunders it. Accept the reality gracefully and do not lose your dignity.

12) Keep the body active through some form of physical exercise, including brisk walks, not only for physical health but

also to make your thinking less rigid and more lucid through better breathing, so that you could have a clearer perspective and relate yourself better with others.

Friendship of mutual convenience can never be deep, satisfactory and long-lasting. It is only in the compatibility of attitude and values such as integrity, care, helpfulness, freedom from prejudice and unselfish love that true friendship endures.

Chapter Fourteen

THE BUDDHA'S WAY

Just as Jesus was born a Jew and died a Jew, the Buddha was born a Hindu and died a Hindu. Just as Jesus tried to reform Judaism, the Buddha tried to reform Hinduism. Paul formed a religion around Jesus the Christ. Sariputra and Maudgalyana formed a religion around Gautama the Buddha. Jesus said to Peter, "You are the rock on which I shall found my church," but the word he used for church in Greek translation is *kyrios* or God, meaning relationship to God. There is no evidence that the Buddha intended to found a religion but he termed his teachings as the Middle Way, avoiding the extremes of rituals and asceticism.

His teachings are based on four facts of life:

a) Suffering exists and is inevitable to human experience. One should learn to prevent it as far as possible, rather than meekly accept it.

b) Ignorance is its main cause, especially ignorance of the human nature, ignorance that happiness is found through desire for power and sense-enjoyment as well as attachment.

c) There are ways to avoid suffering, and it is mainly through understanding of life and its application to attain a balance of experience.

d) This balance is achieved through the practice of the Middle Way or the Eightfold Path. It consists of:

1) Positive thinking.

2) Speaking the truth.

3) Constructive action.

4) Right conduct.

5) Sane disposition or attitude to life.

6) Intelligent effort, for self-betterment and general welfare.

7) Honest occupation, in which no deceit or lying or harm to any creature is involved.

8) Effective meditation or spiritual aspiration, not indulging in psychic experience or mysteries.

The above is not a literal translation from the *Tripitaka*, but my interpretive rendition. In the spirit of yoga, the Buddha says: Do not accept a teaching unless it is in accord with your reasoning. Do not accept it merely because it is sanctioned by usage, custom or tradition.

The Buddha says:

No one is noble by birth,
No one is ignoble by birth.
One is noble by one's own deeds,
One is ignoble by one's own deeds.
By oneself is evil done,
By oneself is one defiled.
By oneself is evil avoided,
By oneself alone is one purified.
Purity and impurity depend on oneself,
No one can purify another.
By oneself one must walk the path,
Teachers merely show the way.

For the students of yoga it is good to imbibe this spirit of Vedanta philosophy, although the Buddha does not identify the above lines as such.

Chapter Fifteen

YOGA AND CHRISTIANITY

There are dozens of parallel ideals in Christianity and yoga. Christianity started as a universal (*katholikos*, the Greek word for universal) religion, but the two words are oxymoron, contradictory in terms, because no religion can be universal.

Idea is a Greek word, adapted to other European languages, which means to see, or having a conceptual vision.

Ideal is to make that concept real by its realisation through inspiration, acting upon it and by the consequent experience of its meaning. Ideal is perfecting an idea in the process of its fulfilment or embodiment.

The popular idea that a practical person is less idealistic and an idealistic person is rather impractical is silly. If an ideal is unattainable and, thus, not meant to be attained, there is no point in having it, in the first place. It jumps logic.

The moving spirit in doing something worthy is, similarly, the ideal behind that gives the inspiration. An ideal is the goal of an idea, a standard of perfection.

A thought-form is the body of knowledge. An ideal is the essence of that knowledge. To have an ideal is to realise the value of a particular knowledge, its purpose behind. It means the search for the reality of an idea by the practice of it and to make it real.

The Sanskrit word for ideal is *adarsha* which means towards (*a*) a vision (*darsha*), or the aspiration to realise a goal. *Drik* means direction, *drishta* vista and *darshana* philosophy. Thus, in Sanskrit philosophy means a conceptual vision.

Religion in practice serves the purpose of tribal identities, linking emotionally the flock (read folk) to the supernatural, for protection and succour through common rituals and hymns of adoration, in common languages. This identity of liturgy and moral codes, spilling over into social habits, provides group security.

Thus, sets of dogmas, or rules of belief, are inevitable in any religion, to keep the flock in line, to conserve tribal identity for the sake of group security. Even at the dawn of the third millennium, for the vast majority of people, this seems to be the case.

Yoga, on the other hand, is not a particular religion, but a philosophy of life guided by spiritual values, a state of mind, freely chosen and individually formed. Thus, it has no set dogmas but universal moral ideals and holy aspiration. It has the same goal, a spiritual union, as the word religion literally indicates, *re-ligare*, to reunite oneself with one's divine source.

There are dozens of parallel ideals in Christianity and yoga. One should not exaggerate external differences between dualism (Christianity) and monism (Gyana Yoga), but seek common ground, such as in the saying of Jesus "My Father and I are one" and Bhakti Yoga's vision of God as the Father of all humanity, just as the Christ said "You are the children of God".

As long as the individual consciousness is in a state of evolution to find its unity with its origin, the universal spirit or God, there is duality. When there is the final merger of the former in the latter, there being no more the vehicle of individuality, the goal of monism is realised.

There are three basic ideals common to yoga and Christianity.

First, Christianity envisages a spiritual origin of humankind and the whole of the creation itself. Yoga also perceives a common spiritual origin of life (*purusha*) that becomes the universe, while being transcendental, by the pulsation (*spandana*) of its material energy (*prakriti*), of creation, sustenance and dissolution, and finds its heightened expression on the human level.

There is no difference between the biblical and yogic view in this regard, if one ignores the literary image of God making man out of clay and breathing life into him.

Secondly, in yoga and Christianity, it is the presence of the spirit within the individual consciousness, inside the human frame, that enables evolution. In yoga it is called *jivatma* (individual soul) identical with *paramatma* (supreme soul). In the Old Testament it is the image of God (Genesis), and in the New Testament the Kingdom of God within.

Soul-consciousness or *atma-gyana* in yoga and Christ-consciousness in Christianity are expressed through higher emotions as selfless love and goodness of heart amidst the powerful survival and libidinal instincts, the higher nature appealing to the lower.

The law of substitution is paramount to overcome anything that hinders one's happiness and progress. It is done by the awakening of soul-consciousness. In order to be successful in desisting from what is wrong, it is not enough to keep within the circle of the admonition of what should not be done. One has to come out of that circle by the impetus of what should be done and be involved with it.

Repression distorts the mind and sublimation alone clears it and gives inspiration for creativity. The mind being a field of energy can be treated only in three ways: either repress it by the fear of punishment, or indulge in it hedonistically, or sublimate it with the help of the positive.

In Christianity the appeal is to the higher nature, such as in the injunction of returning good against evil, not seeking vengeance, not following the rule of taking an eye for an eye, tooth for a tooth, but to purify the heart through love and forgiveness.

In yoga the appeal is the same, such as in the words of the Buddha, "Hatred does not cease by the retribution of hatred but by the response of love."

IMMANENCE OF GOD

The third ideal is the immanence of God or the universal spirit. It means that life can be improved, that human nature could evolve through seeking and fulfilling of a spiritual presence within (image of God) and respecting its existence on the level of humankind at least.

That God created all people equally can have any meaning only on the basis of the commonness of his presence in all souls. Nothing else is equal in life. On the basis of the recognition of this common spiritual element can there be the preservation of human dignity and the possibility of forming a just society.

Apart from providing a balance of mutual interest, all ethical principles or moral laws are based on the recognition of this common spiritual presence. In modern democracies, the system of universal franchise is based on this principle, without the spiritual prefix.

Some Christians find it difficult to accept the immanence of God because of their orientation of his exclusive existence in heaven. Being in the universe is a threat to his diminution, who is transcendental. But God is not a material being whose immanence as spirit does not affect its transcendence, just as space everywhere remains the same even if being within the roofs and walls structured on the ground.

When Jesus says to seek the kingdom of God, it means to find a spiritual meaning in life, to practise such ideals as truth and love that represent the image of him within. To seek and serve it more than anything else is the Christian way.

In yoga the presence of God as universal spirit is explained on five levels:

1. In matter as a cohesive principle or energy that gives substance to it.
2. In all living organism, including vegetation, as a life principle.
3. In the animal forms of life as individual minds conditioned by life-supporting instincts.
4. In the higher forms of life, such as on the human level, as the power of reason and determination.
5. In an evolved human level as soul-consciousness through spiritual aspiration and moral idealism.

It is because of God's transcendental nature that there is no limit to the understanding of truth and the feeling of love even on the human level.

A common ground about the vision of God in yoga and Christianity can be found in the words of the Christ to the Samaritan woman at the well: "God is spirit and those who worship him must worship in spirit and in truth." (John IV:24)

By worshipping in spirit Jesus probably meant through spiritual aspiration, and in truth by a life of truthful conduct and in accordance to the teachings in the Torah.

In yoga God as spirit can be defined by five mystical terms:

1. Universal, therefore immanent or present everywhere.

2. Infinite, thus without a form or being limited spatially, or confined to a house of worship or place of pilgrimage or heaven.

3. Eternal, thus not being bound by time, or subject to change through the influence of time.

4. Transcendental, that which alone, as a principle, helps the evolution of consciousness and, thus, our perception of truth and love, laws and ideals, in an ever-expansive way.

5. Inner light, that which enlightens the mind with reason and wisdom, and elevates it by holy aspiration.

TANGIBLE VALUES

However, these mystical qualities attributed to God cannot have sufficient meaning without some tangible means of realisation. Thus, the five paths leading to him are:

1. Truth which is determined by evidence, consequence, and the principles of equality such as in common good, liberation (truth shall set you free), and independence (it does not need any support).

2. Love and devotion for spiritual ideals in a general sense, and regard and affection for the loved ones on a personal level.

3. Beauty, which means sublimation of lower passions to experience the depth of pure love, of grace and harmony, to refine our perception of the outer reality and expression of the inner spirit.

4. Goodness, or purity of heart, which is trying to be free from resentment and hate, prejudice and pettiness, wickedness and fanaticism.

5. Justice, or fairness to all, identifying our interests with those of others, not treating others as we would not like to be treated.

In Christianity these values are overwhelmingly present. The essence of the teachings of Jesus can be said as: "Love God (or spiritual ideals) with all your heart, love your neighbour as yourself, and do not be a hypocrite." Peace and love, forgiveness and renunciation of worldliness, are the cornerstones of Christianity.

The basis of yoga can be said to consist in:

1. Dedication to, or faith in, or love of spiritual values such as integrity and compassion, altruism and duty,

responsibility and loyalty, self-improvement and humility of spirit. That is the real meaning of loving God. Emotionalism is not love but devotion and dedication.

2. Basing upon them, to develop a keen sense of right and wrong, and guide one's conduct accordingly. The basics are simple: to harm is wrong, to heal right; action conducing disharmony is wrong, promoting peace is right; to cheat is wrong, to be honest is right; to be crooked is wrong, to be straightforward is right.

3. To consider life as a gift of God rather than a punishment, as something precious to make it useful and creative, to make others happy and, in the process, be happy.

4. Our journey through life can be made comfortable through faith and knowledge. These are the two wheels on which life moves. If they are well made and kept in a good condition, the jolts on the way that are inevitable can be better absorbed and, thus, less will be our suffering.

Faith means a deeper sense of values and love of ideals through which one matures emotionally and gains a measure of freedom from human bondage.

Knowledge is to liberate the mind from superstition and fear through the search for reality and a better understanding of the life around, the universe we live in. It also pertains to our inner nature, of the psychological layers of our being, through which to free the mind from prejudice and fanaticism, and the ignorance of our spiritual roots.

5. The most fundamental of all is the sublimation of our earthly nature. It means disciplining and overcoming common human weaknesses: selfishness, pride and vanity; anger, hate and jealousy; deceit, greed and envy; covetousness, lust and aggressiveness; hypocrisy, deviousness and backbiting.

CONCLUSION

The yogic way of life consists less in doing the postures (*asanas*) and breathing exercises (*pranayamas*), or dietetic preferences, but more on our effort at self-improvement, Karma Yoga or selfless service, and to have inner strength and harmony through meditation.

In the Christian way, Jesus speaks about it as: Do not pray in the market place so that others can see you, but in your room so that God can hear what is in your heart. Ask not God for mundane things, for he knows what is good for you, but ask him what he wants of you.

It simply means base your life on spiritual ideals and overcome your weaknesses. Carry the cross (at least a measure of self-abnegation) and follow me (be inspired by his example to do what is right as best as you can and in the best light of your understanding).

Life is what we make of it, with our inner resources, with self-effort, and in relationship to the circumstances, which are, in part, our own creation, with an element of the unknown. In Christianity it is called God's will, in yoga the consequence of a past, unseen karma.

What we are is the result of what we have tried to be or did not try to be, and what we are doing now or failing to do.

We are true or false to God in direct relationship to if we are true or false, just or unjust, kind or unkind to each other.

In the yogic spirit, worship of spiritual ideals is the worship of God as spirit, without form, which the individual can as well do through the conceptual form of Jesus or, as in the Hebrew tradition, Adonai-Elohim, a supreme father-like mystical figure in heaven.

Prayer is a movement of heart through the feeling of spiritual love. It is an inner communion. The real meaning of it is the movement of our life through deed, inspired by that love.

Christian beliefs, such as in its mythology, will largely remain empty if the above ideals, which pulsate in the teachings of Jesus, do not find an adequate expression in a Christian's life.

The British author, G.K. Chesterton, said that Christianity has not failed; it has simply not been practised, having found it too difficult to do so. I do not entirely subscribe to this view.

Christianity has had a violent past, quite contrary to the spirit of its initiator. It is still a narrow-minded religion, rather than *katholikos*. Yet, there can be no denial of the fact that the Western civilisation is founded on Christian values, with deep roots in the Old Testament and the enlightened ideas of the Hellenic civilisation, which were revived in the age of reason at the end of the eighteenth century.

Yogic ideals went to sleep in India centuries ago. In the middle of the nineteenth century Raja Ram Mohan Roy initiated the revival process, which is still ongoing. As in any civilisation, birth, flowering of growth, decay and phasing out are followed by rebirth, and rebirth needs adaptation, according to the needs of the age and cultural environment.

As such, both the East and the West can learn from each other, without losing their roots.

Chapter Sixteen

YOGA, GOD AND RELIGION

WHAT YOGA MEANS

Yoga is first of all self-discipline. A state of oneness with one's spiritual source comes much later, which is a goal. As the root *yuj* or yoke suggests, it is to discipline the mind with the love of spiritual ideals, and direct one's effort towards their realisation. It is only then that 'union', its purpose, becomes meaningful.

A person sitting cross-legged, with eyes closed, high up on a mountaintop (good for taking a photograph), is only a romantic idea to unite oneself with God, or whatever that word might mean. Mostly, it is an escapism leading to mental atrophy.

Discipline is not an imposition of will, or mind over body, neither is it repression on account of fear, but a process of learning (the Latin root *discere* means to learn, not impose), inspired by the love of the reason why.

Yoga as physical culture, consisting mainly of *asana* and *pranayama*, is only a minor aspect of it. They are good for physical health, but has little influence over the mind, in the sense of self-discipline. They do relax the nervous system, of course, and for a short while the mind stays peaceful. By themselves they do not conduce peace of mind.

Yoga is a state of mind, a way of life that seeks to integrate the material and spiritual aspects of it, unite faith with reason, refine emotions with devotion, discipline and sublimate raw instincts through moral values, improve human relationship by ethical conduct, cultivate equanimity in pleasure and pain, success and failure, and seek out wider dimensions of life.

Various techniques of meditation play a great role in self-cultivation. Meditation on peace and freedom, and on one's spiritual identity are the most important themes. It is done in combination with the experience of breath, and also with the litany of a mantra. Affirmation of phrases is meant to cut grooves in the subconscious to motivate attitude and action.

ETHICS IS THE BEDROCK

To be more honest, decent and useful, to appreciate more the happier moments, and take in stride the unhappy ones without bitterness and complaint, is the yogic way. To be mindful of the present, and optimistically look forward to the future, is the yogic way.

The mind of a practitioner of yoga should have wide open windows, so that the fresh breeze of knowledge sought out from multiple sources may flow in, to clear the cobwebs of bias and bigotry, sectarian dogmatism and malice, self-absorption and egolatry.

Just by practising *asana* and *pranayama* one does not become a yogi. It indicates a high level of evolution through spiritual aspiration, self-control and selfless service. In the West the words 'yoga' and 'yogi' are generally debased due to vanity, lack of knowledge and commercial motivation.

To live as best as we can, to think and act positively, and consider life a blessing rather than a burden to grumble about, not to be judgmental about the faults of others, oneself not being free from them, to have charity of heart, not to be stingy of feelings for others, is the yogic way.

Not to be dogmatic about anything, to learn the relativity of things in determining what is more important and what is less, to know when enough is enough, never to think to be a possessor of truth, to know that its understanding can always be better, never to lose the capacity of wondering and learning anew, is the yogic way.

WHAT GOD MEANS

The idea of God as an anthropomorphic supreme being high up in the heaven does not fascinate me. I do not need him sitting in judgment over me, dishing out reward and punishment. Accountability to an invisible deity beyond the tangibility of time is spurious, and has not helped anyone to be a better person. Accountability to be meaningful has to be to one's fellow beings, and to one's own conscience.

Belief in an original sin is likewise meaningless, since one cannot relate to it as to when it occurred for no fault of oneself. Neither do I need to be saved, for no one is threatening me. It seems ridiculous that I am damned for no fault of mine, and then being offered the holy grail of salvation, but only if I believe in the saviour. The Hebrew name of Jesus *Yehoshua* means 'Yaweh saves thee'.

Salvation means that I have to save myself from my own errors, from the deficiencies of my character, everyday of my life. 'By the grace and help of God' means through faith in the spiritual resources within me, and by my own self-effort.

Life eternal does not fascinate me either, for the life as I know it and have to cope with is plateful enough! What happens after death is a speculation that is a waste of time. I have a strong suspicion that the notion of immortality is a consequence of our attachment to the body and all that is required to sustain and keep it comfortable.

Heaven and hell are here, within and without, in the state of my mind and the circumstances around. In peace and understanding, with compassion and kindness in my heart, with integrity and decency in my conduct with others, with a clear conscience and freedom from resentment and prejudice, I am in heaven. In their contradiction I am in hell.

Why speculate about something which you cannot verify? Imagine a transmigrating Chinese encountering a Caucasianlooking deity sitting on a throne in heaven, or *vice versa*, or a European Christian finding a middle-eastern, Semitic-looking Jesus Christ!

A rational vision of God, although contradicting the word 'theos' itself, is the universal spirit which is eternal, infinite and transcendental. This formless spiritual essence of the ever-changing universe is called eternal for not being a captive of time, and thus changeless.

It is infinite for surpassing space, universal as the immanent force giving life to all the forces in existence. It is transcendental for rising above and beyond them all, and through such a magnetic pull making evolution possible. No one can deny the existence of the various patterns of energy out of which has evolved life as we know it, and no sane person can say that this is all there is to know.

A MENTAL IMAGE

Personalised God as father in heaven, loving and benevolent, is an idealised, mystical form created by one's devotion and aspiration to relate to the infinite spirit when desparately needing a spiritual help. It is a mental image shaped by one's cultural environment and tradition. It also serves a need for spiritual fulfilment when disappointed in life.

It is more honest to say that the human being created God in his or her image, rather than God creating us in his image. God being jealous of a rival, or vengeful, or propitiable by praise and unquestioning submission to his will speaks more of our human nature as it is, and yet being merciful and forgiving and full of goodness as we ought to be.

The atheist is a person who does not believe in a particular heavenly deity. In reality, however, no one can truly be an atheist, if God means the essence of all spiritual values, in an ever-widening sense. No one can deny the fact that we are happy with the positive and unhappy with the negative. We are happy when there is peace in our heart, and are in peace with each other. In compassion, integrity, being responsible and helpful to one another we are happy.

The word 'atheist' is a stick to beat with those who do not agree to a limited vision of a heavenly deity devised by scriptures, and thus to be apprehensive about for not being God-fearing, and as such an unsafe company.

Out of an original energy particle, as it began to vibrate, emerged this universe, and out of its forces evolved the human consciousness to invent the images of God, with all kinds of fantasies, a god that will not fail us, a god who will not stop loving us, an almighty who will protect us because we need to survive, and also because we need a role model to evolve and be fulfilled.

The image of God in which we are supposed to have been created (Genesis I:27) is an ideal, not a reality, meant to shape our moral and spiritual values, our conscience, with constantly-evolving understanding. Thus, God to me is a supreme symbol of my conscience in the best light of my comprehension, always humbly expectant that it can be clearer, fairer, purer.

My soul is a spark of the infinite spirit in a state of embodiment. The same spark twinkles as myriads of God's light in the souls of humanity, awaiting individual discovery and realisation.

WHAT RELIGION MEANS

It is said that in a polite company one should not talk about religion or politics, because of the tendency to get emotional about such topics. Whether we practise a religion or not, we are tagged by an immediately identifiable one, such as by our name. Religion has always shaped social habits and customs, as well as a moral code of conduct defining a way of life. I cannot deny that I was born a Brahmin even though I despise the Hindu caste system by birth alone.

As the word 'religion' indicates, *re-ligare* in Latin means to retie or reunite us, imperfect and therefore unfulfilled as we are, with our mythically perfect creator, and thus regain Elysium. In its enlightened form religion can inspire the deepest longings in a pure heart: unselfish love, compassion, fellowship, altruism, moral sense, duty, responsibility, integrity.

Yet, in an unenlightened mind it can be a dangerous instrument to manipulate the primitive instincts of fear and insecurity, the need to survive being a primal cry. When the source of security provided by religion through a god, or a messiah like Jesus, or a set of beliefs is challenged, fear born of ignorance takes over. Fear begets intolerance, and intolerance violence.

No religion has been more responsible in shedding blood in the name of one almighty God than the three monotheistic ones: Christianity in the middle ages, Islam all throughout, and Judaism in its inception immediately after Moses. The partition of India after the British rule was forced by the sword of Islam to carve out Pakistan or 'the land of the pure', with inevitable retaliation.

Religion tried to improve the human being by making God the measure of his or her destiny. It generally failed in this by manipulating one's fear and insecurity by a supernatural promise of reward and threat of punishment on the basis of a mandated rule of conduct. The fear of an intangible hell in an afterlife does not prevent crime, nor does the embellishment of an unseen heaven promote good behaviour.

Religion would have had a better result if it had inspired us to be decent and make our life agreeable here by appealing to our better instincts, making us responsible to others, and live as best as we can, rather than emphasise emotional fervour for a mythical deity, and salvation through him or by his delegate or messiah like the Christ in the hereafter.

The age of reason at the end of the eighteenth century and humanism in the nineteenth tried to make the human being the measure of all things, taking into account our material needs, and sought to promote social justice through collective responsibility, but without God as a model.

This effort also failed because of the assumption that people behave best and work better in a collective role rather than primarily out of self-interest. Modern democracies are devised with a combination of the both.

The bottom line of the relevancy of religion is ethical inspiration. Its role has been since time immemorial, from the time human beings learned to live together since the invention of agriculture some nine thousand years ago. It began as shamanism to provide succour to physical ailment by herbal remedies, and to psychic ills through incantation and the flair of magic which the medicine man or the shaman did in a combined role.

With the progress of civilisation, religious and spiritual successors of the shaman continue to fulfil this psychic need, apart from moral guidance, but basically a need for inner security. The more the self-confidence the less the relevancy of religion, but for the vast majority of people the psychic need will continue to be there, and therefore the successors of the shamans, the religious and spiritual teachers, will carry on the second oldest profession in the world.

Anyone who loves and practises honesty, kindness and unselfishness, duty, honour and responsibility, sublimation of passions, moral courage and modesty, is a 'religious' person in the sense of *re-ligare*, whether he or she goes to a church or not, believes in God or not, does any devotional act or not. Real devotion consists in how we relate and are committed to those who are close to us, how we carry out an act of service with love and care.

Chapter Seventeen

THE PLAY OF THE THREE GUNAS

Nearly three thousand years ago, Vedanta philosophy speculated that the universe is composed of threc *gunas* or categories of energy representing the primordial forces of nature, *prakriti*, the pulsation (*spandana*) of which is the basic principle of creation.

These energy forms are classified as:

1) *Tamas*. Elemental matter, particles of dust and their condensed forms like planets. It pulsates as cohesive and decohesive energy. By itself it has no light. Its quality is opacity.

2) *Rajas*. It is matter in a state of combustion or fire, emanating energy in the form of light, motion, expansion, attraction (gravity), magnetism, as in our solar system. Its quality is power.

3) *Sattwa*. It consists of invisible, subtle matter called *akasha*, ether, pervading the seemingly empty space. Its quality is balance.

Sattwa is the initiating principle of all the elemental forces, *rajas* represents their creativity, evolution and multiplicity, and *tamas* their density and decay or the reabsorbing process.

The three *gunas* do not exist independently. They are in different degrees of interaction, one predominating over the other.

In the vast space, millions of light years across, *sattwa* is beginning to manifest matter and a universe is coming into being, *rajas* and *tamas* remaining in latent energy form. In another part, *rajas* is dominant, combining, multiplying, expanding and evolving the elements, and culminating them as human beings in our earth, as far as we know, or as the Hindu legend speculates, eventually as gods, far more evolved than us.

In this predominance of *rajas*, *sattwa* and *tamas* coexist with a lesser force.

Yet in another part of space, *tamas* or the decaying and reabsorbing process is predominant, such as in a dwarf star. The end of a universe is called *pralaya* or dissolution.

THE SOURCE

The legend *Brahman* is the source of everything, which the mind cannot grasp, but in order to identify the original atom, if you wish, a name (*Brahman* or the Great Being) is given to say that it is beyond any name to qualify any entity. Out of it is born *Hiranyagarbha* or the 'golden womb'.

From *Hiranyagarbha*, in each universe is born *Ishwara*, the presiding being with its three aspects: the creative (*Brahma*), the sustaining (*Vishnu*) and the reabsorbing (*Shiva*). From these three combined forces, *purusha* or the as-yet-dormant spiritual energy, and *prakriti* or the material form of energy are born. The term *purusha* also refers sometimes to a supreme being (*paramatma*).

Out of *Hiranyagarbha sattwa, rajas* and *tamas* are born. Ancient yogic minds speculated that, after thousands of billions of years, *sattwa*, *rajas* and *tamas* will fuse together, when all the universes will disappear. That end of all existence is called *maha-pralaya* or great dissolution. Then, after an infinity of time span, there will be another beginning of another megacycle of existence.

Coming back to our planet, which has evolved from the cosmic dust or atoms (*anu*) and become dense matter (*sthula*), the manifestation of *sattwa*, *rajas* and *tamas* is reversed. Here the existence began with the predominance of *tamas*, whilst *rajas* and *sattwa* remaining latent.

The universe is ruled by the law of *prakriti*, which from the human point of view has no criterion. The stronger atom absorbs the weaker, one nucleus combines with another, then divides and recoalesces as various forms of matter. Out of such particles of cosmic dust, countless organisms and sentient forms of life are evolved, constantly adapting to the surrounding forces of nature. In their survival process, masses of them have disappeared, as per the law of the survival of the fittest.

At last, from micro-organism, plant life, lower and higher forms of animal life, the cleverest of the animal species, the humankind, has evolved. When did the soul, the spiritual content of our being, as we identify it, awake in our consciousness? Was it when *sattwa* expressed itself as altruistic love?

THE SOUL

The yogic insight recognises this aspect of *purusha* as soul (*jivatma*) on the human and animal level as well, as the spiritual content of individual consciousness. Out of the pulsation of soul, pure felicity in altruistic love (*ananda*) is born, as also transcendental wisdom (*chit*) and the consciousness of a deathless state of existence (*sat*). Out of the soul's pulsation, a basic moral sense is evolved with the help of education and spiritual aspiration.

Why is it said that *prakriti* has no criterion? Because such dubious acts of God as earthquake and hurricane are but undiscerning neutral forces of nature. Those who happen to be on the spot, deserving or undeserving, do suffer with poetic indifference of nature. From *tamas* or dense inert matter surged the pulsation of *rajas* in the form of tectonic and atmospheric forces, *sattwa* remaining latent and expressing serenity for a while before sunrise and after sunset and when nature is in peace.

Purusha, the spirit within, expresses itself as *sattwa* in the human consciousness, and urges that it is not moral that the law of *prakriti*, the bigger fish having the right to eat the smaller, should prevail among people. Even if human nature is a product of *prakriti*, the pulsation of *purusha* within makes us struggle against our baser instincts.

TAMASIC NATURE

In the vast majority of people *tamas* prevails, and *sattwa* and *rajas* remain dormant. It expresses itself as lethargy, a dull state of mind, lack of curiosity and initiative. However, *tamas* can be quite active in their lower appetites, such as in eating, drinking, copulating and sleeping much. Such people have to be led, being indecisive, and are fit mainly for manual labour. Only through education, *rajas* and *sattwa* can be activated in them.

Tamas exudes in negative thinking, conniving, wishing to harm others but without the guts to do so, and waiting for the opportunity to strike when no personal risk is involved. The *tamasic* people run after worldly pleasure if available gratis, or are envious of those who have them. Their character is subterranean. They prefer to be hidden enemies. They are basically selfish and irresponsible due to being self-centred.

Dishonesty is natural to the *tamasic*. They like to daydream without any sense of reality or willingness to realise their spurious ambition. They are quick to criticise, find fault and tend to be destructive. They are possessive as long as it costs them nothing.

No one is, however, entirely *tamasic* without the occasional, weak ripples of *rajas* and *sattwa*. When a person is called very *tamasic*, what is meant is the preponderance of that quality. The same is true when one is considered *rajasic* or *sattwic*. All the three qualities coexist in all of us in different degrees of manifestation.

RAJASIC NATURE

Rajas represents outgoing nature. When *rajas* predominates, one becomes energetic, ambitious, is willing to make effort to fulfil worldly desires, is curious enough to expand the horizons of knowledge, is courageous and does not shy away from risks, is partly generous and partly selfish, vain, proud and aggressive, and sometimes violent when challenged. The *rajasic* type can be shamelessly egolatrous and spontaneously self-important, is generally creative but can be destructive when opposed.

Soldier type is the *rajasic* person, whereas the *tamasic* is the tenant-peasant kind. The *rajasic* provide the business, political and bureaucratic leadership. They can excel in generalship but not necessarily as wise rulers. One can recognise them as open enemies. They are dominating and possessive whilst willing to pay the price required. They have the A-type personality. *Sattwa* and *tamas* are latent in them.

The ego is a dominant trait in the *rajasic*. That is why they can be quite offensive sometimes. Without ego no leadership is possible, for it provides the motive-power. When the ego is educated by the *sattwic* quality of consideration of the interest, feelings and opinion of others, it becomes inoffensive and serves as a positive, creative force. The *rajasic* are proud whilst being clever, whereas the *tamasic* are self-important whilst being stupid.

Among the majority of the *rajasic* people and the relative minority of the *tamasic*, sometimes *sattwa* surfaces fleetingly. The *sattwic* type, or in whom *sattwa* predominates, are very few indeed.

SATTWIC NATURE

The *sattwic* are pure-hearted, free from resentment, incapable of hating others, decent, honest and generous without being calculative. Truthfulness is natural to them, whilst being careful not to cause trouble to or hurt others. Their benevolence is substantiated by altruism, and not merely expressed in attitude. They are kind-hearted, fair-minded, compassionate, patient and tolerant without being indifferent. Their modesty is genuine, they are free from any kind of pretention, especially from pretending to be humble.

The *sattwic* people tend to be rather gullible and, therefore, cannot provide business or political leadership which requires manipulation. They are never dogmatic. Ruthlessness that is required in business and politics is contrary to their nature. They have a keen insight into the nature of things but their unwillingness to face and tendency to underrate a negative reality makes them somewhat gullible.

The predominantly *sattwic* kind can be excellent educationists, scientists and administrators when autonomous or not being politically dictated. The philosopher-king being a myth, the *sattwic* type can be at best persuasive and impartial constitutional monarchs or heads of state. Being selfless, they can be worthy servants of humanity. Being wise and modest, they can be inspiring spiritual teachers.

The *sattwic* kind are rare among prominent gurus or heads of religious institutions, any role of organisational leadership being subject to the manipulation of the circumstantial exigencies. It is also irrational to expect those with the preponderance of *sattwa* to be entirely free from occasional bouts of *rajas* and *tamas*, human nature being never perfect.

Selfishness and the uneducated ego are the main causes of suffering. They arise from *tamas*. As all of us wish to be happy and avoid suffering through mistakes, it is to our interest to educate and purify the *tamas* in us by cultivating *rajasic* initiative, enterprise, work ethic, perseverance and creative self-effort. One cannot jump to *sattwa* from a *tamasic* state but has to ascend through *rajas*. The belief that repeating the divine name alone will purify *tamas* is a myth.

Human nature needs a lifelong education. Self-improvement needs a mix of *rajas* and *sattwa*. The body needs the discipline of Hatha Yoga or any other form of physical exercise. The mind needs the discipline of Raja Yoga and the heart of Bhakti Yoga. Selfishness in us needs the discipline of Karma Yoga and our spiritual aspiration of Gyana Yoga.*

---

* This article is adapted from a seminar conducted by Swami Shivapremananda on 7th March 1999 at his Sivananda Yoga-Vedanta Centre in Montevideo, Uruguay.

Chapter Eighteen

RUMINATIONS

[Editor's note: The following sayings have been translated by Swamiji from his original work in Spanish 'Ventana del Alma', now in its sixth edition, which consists of excerpts from his class-talks given in recent years at his Yoga-Vedanta Centres in Buenos Aires, Montevideo and Santiago, in South America.]

KNOWLEDGE AND SPIRITUALITY

Knowledge can be taught but spirituality is a personal responsibility and is cultivated by oneself alone, because no one can impart it to another or trigger it by a magic touch, as it were. A sudden flash of knowledge is the result of a long search, a long preparation, a long struggle, a long wait, the soul's energies gathering into an unlit ball of fire that explodes at a particular moment and rarely through the instrumentality of a long-expected initiation. But the light fades in the course of time and has to be nursed back to brightness from time to time through self-effort.

Integrity, compassion, selflessness, purity of heart, freedom from malice and hate, prejudice and wicked thinking, sublimation of passions and humility of spirit are the essential definitions of spirituality, or who is a spiritual person, much more than asceticism and prayerfulness.

No one can measure anther's spirituality, and appearance can be very deceptive. A husband can be most charming to guests and friends, but you have to ask his wife what he actually is at home. So also, a guru can have a very holy appearance in public, but you have to ask his personal attendants what he really is in private.

Ignorance is the worst pollutant of all. From ignorance comes insecurity, from insecurity fear, from fear intolerance, from intolerance fanaticism, and from fanaticism violence and destructiveness.

Knowledge is not the determining factor of a person's culture but behaviour. One can be very knowledgeable in the fine arts, for example, but unthinkingly tactless and exuberantly immodest.

Commonsense is surely a misnomer. It is rather uncommon among people.

The fact that women generally have more commonsense than men is due to their nurturing role, the practical nesting instincts in rearing their defenceless offspring, expressing as coumonsense.

The inability to understand the difference between the desirable and the possible leads to bad decisions, as does failing to approximate ambition with the talent and effort required.

If the conscience is clear there is no need to justify oneself; if not, it will be hard to successfully do so.

The tendency to deceive others leads to deceiving oneself through self-justification.

TRUTH

A revealed truth is only a part of the truth, an insight that comes through spiritual aspiration and deep meditation of a highly-evolved soul, that is claimed in the scriptures as revelation from God but in effect a personal realisation of its author. The rest of it, or other dimensions of truth, one has to find out by oneself. Ultimately, truth is infinite and universal. Our search for truth is a spiritual journey which is very personal, very private, and full of trials and errors.

It is ridiculous to speak of God-given truths and wave the banner of divine revelation. It is better to speak about self-evident truths.

The Buddha said that he was not revealing truth but speaking about truth.

Sat (in Sanskrit) means that which exists, really is, and not an assumption. *Satya*, or that which is based on an existence, has two aspects, the material and the spiritual. The material reality of a house is meant to provide security and the spiritual reality fulfilment through love, integrity, supportiveness and a sense of belonging among those who make a home within it.

To speak of material existence as an illusion is not only irresponsible but utterly hypocritical.

We need truth first of all for security. Integrity in a relationship is the basis of security.

Universality of truth is another aspect, for the sake of its pertinence to all, even if it differs in degrees, as for example the truth of a medical product like aspirin is to alleviate pain even if it is to a greater or lesser extent individually.

Yet another aspect of truth is its transcendental nature, that it can still be better: a level of perfection of love, of justice, of understanding leading to a greater level of perfection. That is why truth is called infinite.

Infinity is, however, without focus. In order to substantiate its spirit there have to be definable principles to be guided by. To say that truth is pathless is as silly as to call this universe an illusion.

Freedom is the consequence of truth, to set the mind free from anxiety, just as bondage is the outcome of untruth.

Independence is the nature of truth, that it can stand on its own, just as dependence is the result of untruth, one lie needing a series of lies to prop up the original and the following ones.

No one can reveal us the truth but only speak about it in the light of one's realisation. Psychic experiences have nothing to do with spirituality or realisation of truth.

Self-realised or God-realised souls are institutional creations like saints, no doubt highly evolved, but to claim that they are perfect beings is to go against evidence.

WHO ARE WE?

The content of our soul is transcendental love and truth, beauty and goodness, peace and harmony, purity of heart and clarity of wisdom, that the universal spirit within us reflects in our consciousness. Thus, the individuality of the consciousness of the spirit within can be called a soul, and the content of it the universal spirit. As such, if God is the ocean, a drop of it is a soul; if God is the sun, a spark of the light of it is a soul.

We are a contradiction unto ourselves. We are both spirit and matter, light and shadow. The pure light of our soul is veiled by many layers of our personality, revealing it in various hues and according to their transparencies, sometimes obscuring it, sometimes shining a facet of it through. We are in this world to cleanse these layers, not deny them by fiat, to harmonise and sublimate them with the help of our inner light, not repress and make them atrophied.

Until the day we die, we will be both spirit and body, the mind serving as a bridge between the two. We are happy when the consciousness is closer to the spirit, in and through and beyond our relationship with others. We are unhappy when it suffocates inside the ego in the relativity of its negative feedback from others.

We cannot understand the world if we reject and curse it. To regard this world as an illusion is like brushing the dirt under the carpet, not cleaning it.

We cannot learn from the mistake of a past life, granting a belief in reincarnation, because the memory of the mistakes is not carried over to the present one, but can only learn from what we do now and what we remember.

TREE OF LIFE

All of us on this earth are different from each other, just as each leaf is different from the other while belonging to the same tree. Thus, individually apart, we all belong to the common tree of our species, drawing the psychological sap from the same mixed source of creation, from the reservoir of good and evil, positive and negative. God and devil coexist within us.

Our fears and anxieties, hopes and disappointments, desires and frustrations, all have a common streak in each of us. They well up from the same primordial psyche that is being shaped and reshaped, refined and tarnished, anchored and let adrift for a while by the forces of history, with religions and ideologies serving as handmaidens, popping up a litany of ideas, some intelligent and some pure bromide, as to who we are, what we want to be, where we have come from and where we want to go.

If you ask me where I have come from, all I can honestly say is from my mother's womb.

Each of us should grow according to the law of our own spiritual growth through personal effort in the light of our best understanding. The human being is not like a clod of earth to be kneaded into a shape by the *diktat* of an ideology, religious or political, neither by a guru nor a messiah. One can only inspire the heart and mind by the purity of idealism and clarity of reason, so that the individual may learn to choose, be personally responsible and walk his or her own path, and society may do likewise by consensus. Guidance by all means, imposition never.

Freedom of thought is a basic right to be encouraged. No one has the right to impose on others a straitjacketed belief or ideology. But one should learn that every right is imperative to an obligation, liberty to responsibility, personal freedom to self-discipline, individual choice to consideration for others.

The scriptures of religions represent the vision of their authors trying to ensure tribal identities, their minds reflecting the shape of values and thinking of their times, their souls searching for common spiritual roots. Yogic texts such as the Vedas, the *Bhagavad Gita,* do not escape the play of light and shadow, as in the latter Krishna threatening to hurl the sinners to hell, or in the former the author of an Upanishad praying for a fair-skinned son (the Aryan invaders having already mixed with the brown-skinned locals)!

Wishful thinking does not even elude Patanjali, such as the yogi attaining omniscience and omnipotence (so much for modesty!), or speaking of *siddhis* or occult powers making the body as light as a feather or as heavy as a mountain (what for?) in the *Yogasutras*. The pathetic syndrome of eternal bliss (too much of it might unhinge you) or the world being a figment of imagination (*maya*) only shows how escapist the mind can be and its reluctance to come into grips with a hard reality. Life is what you make of it.

ROOTS ABOVE, BRANCHES BELOW

In the following free-rendering of the opening verses of Chapter XV of the *Bhagavad Gita* by Sir Edwin Arnold in his *Song Celestial*, Krishna speaks of the symbolic tree of life:

"Men call the *ashwattha*, the banyan tree,
which hath its boughs beneath,
its roots above, the ever-holy tree..."

"If ye knew well the teaching of the tree,
what its shape saith, and whence it springs,
and then how it must end,
and all the ills of it..."

"New growths upspringing to that happier sky,
which they who reach shall have no day to die...
for to him come they from passions

and from dreams who break away,
who part the bonds constraining them to flesh."

HEAVEN AND HELL

Heaven and hell are within each of us and in our surroundings. When truth and love, goodness and kindness reign in our relationship with each other, at home and in the community, we experience heaven and the presence of God. When justice and commonweal, understanding and tolerance, clarity of reason and purity of devotion rule our lives, we are indeed in heaven and in the company of God. In their contradiction we are in hell, both within and without, suffering the absence of God.

In work ethic, in the aftertaste of a duty well carried out, an obligation well fulfilled, we experience heaven. In nourishing and tending carefully a loving relationship, in the inspiration of trying to realise a spiritual ideal, we are in heaven. Whereas, when our hearts are ruled by passion and prejudice, and contort with resentment and malice, we are in hell. When our heads simmer with anger and nerves tense up with bitterness, when words and looks are used as daggers, and actions plotted and executed to harm each other, we are in hell.

Eternal heaven and hell are wishful thinking. The roots of *satchidananda* (pure being-awareness-felicity) in our souls give an elusive awareness (*chit*) of an eternally-existing (*sat*) of heaven (*ananda*) within us. Did not Jesus say, "the kingdom of God is within you"? But due to our attachment to physical existence we like to make heaven an abode of happy denizens enjoying forever rivers of milk and honey. How cloying that can be! Might as well throw in a few *houris* and their masculine counterparts.

DESTINY

Destiny is what you have within and without, tapping inner resources, potentialities, and making the best use of the circumstances. Thus, destiny is in a large measure what we do with what we have, notwithstanding an element of the incognito. Destiny is not sitting around and saying that it is my karma as to what little I have and how I suffer, but through self-effort trying to overcome suffering, deficiencies, and better yourself and the circumstances. It is only after doing so, accept with fortitude what cannot be overcome. You do not know what is your destiny without trying to find out what it can be by self-effort.

Get hold of the first opportunity for anything good that comes by. Do not wait for a better one to appear the next time, for there may not be a next time. Be alert, have initiative, keep looking for opportunities. If you have found a friend or a teacher of integrity, do not let that person move away through your selfishness or indifference, but sustain such a friendship by sharing the best in you.

POVERTY AND SUFFERING

Suffering by itself does not purify. Otherwise the majority of us would be saints. Only when we are willing to correct the cause of suffering can we learn from it. By sharing the suffering of those while helping to alleviate it, we purify ourselves. When suffering is prolonged, we become anaesthetised to it and, therefore, cannot learn from it. Overcoming suffering is an obligatory goal, and only when suffering cannot be avoided should we accept it stoically.

Poverty is degrading and dependence demeaning. Economic freedom is the first freedom because it gives one the freedom of choice, autonomy. Money is not the root cause of all evil but attachment to it can lead to many problems. Poverty and wealth can both be bondages from which we should try to free ourselves. It is not true that the poor will sail to heaven through the eye of the needle of misfortune and the rich will stay behind with the camels.

Believing is not conforming. Generally speaking, believing means hoping in relationship to what is plausible. But if we do not try to realise our hopes with diligent effort, we will be forever hoping. Without searching, testing, substantiating, we cannot know what we are asked to believe to be true or not. We can really accept, assimilate, what we know. Thus, to know we must search.

It is sad to see that those who claim to have a revelation through meditation cut corners, lacking in integrity, and indulge in 'spiritual' theatre. There being so much unhappiness in life, spiritual teachers should never be merchants in human misery but be all the more responsible due to the gullibility of people. There is an old Indian saying, "the ochre robe hides a lot of dirt." It should never be worn as a mark of 'swamihood' light-heartedly.

SPIRITUAL DISCIPLINE

Emotionalism in Bhakti Yoga experienced by singing devotional chants and odes by itself does not purify the heart, although they can be momentarily uplifting, nor do long hours of saying the rosary mechanically, nor getting up before dawn to practise concentration and meditation as per Raja Yoga, nor contemplation on the *mahavakyas* (great affirmations) and metaphysical themes of the Upanishads as per Gyana Yoga.

They are helpful only when combined with a spiritual discipline that consists in leading a life of ethical idealism and altruism, watchfulness over one's motives and trying to be free from hypocrisy and egotism, passion and prejudice. Spiritual life is more a process as to how we think and express ourselves in attitude and conduct, sense of values and corresponding action, rather than consisting of devotional acts by themselves. Without a moral basis spiritual exercises are like pouring water in a leaking pot.

If anything goes wrong, you are at least fifty percent to blame. So, accept your share, learn from your mistakes, do not pass on the blame to others and wallow in self-pity. Not only does it weaken yourself but makes others dislike you.

Worse than feeling sorry for yourself is to let people feel sorry for you. Keep your suffering to yourself. Others have enough of their own load.

Those teachers who tastelessly brag about performing 'egodectomy' on their disciples have themselves an enormous ego to answer for.

If politics is the art of the possible and philosophy of the impossible (some sayings can really be stupid), why bother about philosophy at all? The purpose of philosophy, any philosophy, is to motivate and guide the individual and society towards recognisable goals, to fulfil needs and aspirations.

As an itinerant teacher, I feel like a rolling stone gathering no moss. I fail to understand why should stones gather moss at all. I rather like them smooth and clean!

To be emotional and demonstrative in public, even boys and girls spooning in the open, is the mark of a poor breeding. Emotions and intimacies should be strictly private.

Appreciative exclamations like 'smashing', 'terrific' are indicative of society's fascination with violence. Exuberant greetings to a casual acquaintance like "how wonderful" or "marvellous to see you" (wouldn't have given a damn if that person lived or died five minutes ago or after) speak of superficiality and addiction to hypocrisy.

Saints are made on earth but they actually live in heaven. Haven't you heard the joke? Two women met in a park. One remarked, "My husband is an angel." The other replied somberly, "You are very lucky, mine is still alive!"

In my sixty years of observation I have found that a spiritual teacher is really great if he practises some fifty percent of what he teaches. For most of them it is only ten percent.

In a religious institution when titles, social standing and material riches of others become a major consideration for treatment, its integrity is compromised proportionately.

REALITY AND APPEARANCE

In 1964, I was on a Vienna-Zurich overnight express. My companions in the compartment were two rather prosaic men for the upper berths, and on the lower was an Austrian actress in her early thirties with finely-chiselled features, who was gushing forth to make small talk with charming effect. As I said *Gute Nacht*, I saw her powdering her nose with a vanity mirror and wondered whom she was trying to impress other than her insecure self. She would have looked naturally pretty without the affirmation of obvious make-up.

As I woke up in the morning nearing Zurich, the men had left and the lady cheerily greeted *Guten Morgen*, sitting near and looking out the window. Her face was a sight! The paint on the plucked-out edge of the right brow had raised itself into an askance accent and the eyeshadow had stretched on to the right temple like a kitten's paw. The false eyelashes were slightly askew and the washed blue of her irises looked more faded in the morning light. She suddenly got up and said, "You mustn't look at me until I have done my toilet" and left for the washroom at the end of the corridor.

I asked myself if a Vedantin, dismissing airily her previous evening's appearance as an illusion while trying to uphold the reality of Brahman in his mental fog, would have thought the same way of that morning's empirical reality of her looks?

Jawaharlal Nehru and John Kennedy, both endowed with good looks and sparkling intelligence, both married to beautiful women and having risen to the apogee of their political career, complained that life was unfair to them. From my observation and personal experience I know that, barring some twenty-six percent of humanity (according to a United Nations report) who live in abject poverty and go hungry, life treats us generally more fairly and kindly than most of us deserve. We should count our blessings before complaining.

Some years ago, reading about the suspension of the Swiss Jesuit Hans Kueng from teaching Catholic theology at the Tuebingen University by the Roman Curia, I remembered the saying of Mark Twain, "A man is admitted to the Church for what he believes and expelled from it for what he knows!"

Once I knew a prominent spiritual teacher who greeted visitors with exaggerated gestures of humility and yet was fond of saying what an expert he was in doing 'egodectomy' on others. One has to have an enormous ego to excise the egos of others. Endowed with many virtues, he was also a paragon of vanity. In all of us, light and shadow shimmer and hide in our nature.

PAST AND PRESENT

A knowledge of our past, our roots, is essential to understand the problems of the present, to know how our societies have been shaped, even deformed, by the institutions, philosophies, religious myths, attitude and thinking habit inherited from the past. The evaluation of the good and bad harvest of the seeds sown in the past should have a direct bearing on deciding what kind of harvest we would like to have in the future.

The relevancy of the past is to learn from its errors rather than being proud of something which is no longer valid, such as "those yon glory days of the empire" or the "wonder that was India". Instead, we should try to make our tomorrow better than today with the help of such ideals that have helped the evolution of our civilisation.

In interpreting the mindset of the past the mentality of the present projects itself to suit its self-interest. Those who indulge in the delirium of past greatness which is no longer there, show the decadence of their character and their unwillingness to face what is unpleasant in the present, and are at best expressing a primitive urge for survival. Unless they are shaken up from such a torpid frivolity, their society will have no better future.

The individual's character is first of all a genetical product of his or her immediate ancestors and their influence in early life, whose genes themselves were shaped by the strengths and weaknesses of the society in which they grew up, either struggled to reform themselves by personal effort or by the force of circumstances, or simply did not care and were thus swept to being what they became by the raw instincts of survival. This lesson should never be forgotten by the present generation, and the individual must decide what to be and what not to be.

Evolution is not a continuous process. Through one or two centuries of effort, civilisations burst out in different regions, then declined into decay and slumbered for a long time, some died out and some were reborn in other shapes. Millennia ago in Assyria and Egypt it became possible to see speech rather than hear it by the invention of writing. The vision of the infinite spirit as God without form, being immanent in all, whilst yet transcendental, that dawned three thousand years ago in India, still sustains tolerance of all faiths in Hinduism.

The seeds of civilisation sown in the classical age in Greece still dominate western culture. The invention of movable printing blocks eleven hundred years ago in China gave universal access to learning. Decentralisation of Church education through Protestant reformation made industrial revolution possible. Recognition of the common spiritual dignity (image of God) in all gave birth to human rights and democracy.

IDEALS TO CHERISH

An open-mindedness, that is, a readiness to learn what life is about, the nature of the universe, to know our mind and its deceptive ways, to separate illusion from reality, to think by facts rather than self-serving presumption, are ideals to cherish.

To be aware of one's and society's deficiencies and to believe in the capacity to change, to take personal responsibility and never pass on the blame to others, to have an obligation to search for evidence to support anything that is claimed to be true, are ideals to cherish.

To know that envy and avarice are corroding acids to be cleansed by self-effort to achieve what is envied and, if lacking the capacity for it, to strive for other areas of achievement, to relate one's own good with common good, are ideals to cherish.

When the mindset that encourages the pathology that ours is the best society, the best nation of all, the only true religion or God, the ultimate leader or guru, from that moment the decline of such a presumed status sets in, even if it seems optimum as to one's preference in comparison to other options.

I would like to quote here a wise and fair saying of Pope Paul VI, "There are other ways to God than the Christian path, but for Christians it is the best way."

Repentance is not synonymous with contriteness alone but its reality consists in acts of recompense that should follow as a result.

To love one's enemy is only a psychological process of overcoming hate and desire for revenge. Retaliation when one is stronger than the opponent and cowardice when weaker are intrinsic to nature. That being so, loving one's enemy is not to be regarded as a virtue but to purify one's heart of malice and resentment. In reality, you can love your enemy only when he or she lets you, and if so, the enemy is no longer an enemy.

There is nothing divine in pardoning someone who has offended you. When something goes wrong in a relationship, at least fifty percent of the fault lies with oneself for causing the provocation or not taking precaution to let a situation go out of hand. Such being the case and having accepted your part of responsibility, what is there to pardon? Self-importance is at the base of being offended.

When weakness becomes synonymous with goodness hypocrisy prevails.

When personal opinion becomes public policy on the level of leadership unfairness prevails.

Goodness does not come naturally but is a result of education and conscious effort, such as being honest when there is the opportunity to be dishonest, not to think negatively, not to be self-centred.

The insecure individual seeks security through group identity. Group identity means being different from other groups that do not look like us, thus creating the *us* and *them* mentality. When the *us* becomes insecure due to social anomalies like unemployment and inflation, hating *them* serves as the demagogue's instrument to bring out the worst in ethnic or national majority groups.

The more the ignorance of others the more we are apprehensive of them. Fear makes us insecure, and insecurity conduces intolerance. Intolerance sickens to fanaticism, and fanaticism leads to violence. Thus, fear is the mother of violence, oppression and injustice, and ignorance their grandmother.

For society's ills we always need some scapegoat, some group to blame, while ignoring that such ills are a result of the inherent deficiencies of our own culture and poor leadership, for which we are individually and collectively responsible. Instead of trying to correct them on personal and leadership level by educational effort and better policy direction, we like to create foreign devils.

When it comes to prejudice, majority opinion cannot only be unjust but destructive. Intelligent leadership alone can appeal to the better instincts in human nature and prevent society to harm itself.

The habitual stereotype of the ugly image that we impose on a racial or religious minority speaks of an intrinsic weakness of our cultural and religious background. The more honest we are the better we can come to terms with and overcome our deficiencies and the less we will need minority or external enemy groups to blame.

Distortion of truth comes from the imperative of blind obedience to laws given in the name of God or otherwise by superegos, rather than exercising one's free will to seek truth within or outside the laws which religion or political ideology devised to have power over people.

SHAPING OF CONSCIOUSNESS

"Then even nothingness was not, nor existence.
There was no air then, nor the heavens beyond it.
Who covered it? Where was it? In whose keeping?
Was there then cosmic water, in depths unfathomed?
But, after all, who knows, and who can say,
Whence it all came, and how creation happened?
The gods themselves are later than creation.
So who knows truly whence it has arisen?"

(*Rig Veda*, X, 129, translated by A.L. Basham)

An unmanifest, transcendental force became the original *anu* (atom). Then, "the one became many" (*Rig Veda*). The many interacting gave birth to the universe, the immensity of which we have only come to know this century. It is the pervasiveness of this transcendental force that makes the existence of matter possible through energy that science has learned to measure. Its interaction in atoms, fusing and dividing, enables the cycles of existence, *Purusha* through *prakriti* becoming *vishwa* or the transcendental spirit through primordial force becoming the universe. In the process the spirit does not change.

The spirit in a state of embodiment through the individuality of consciousness or the principle of becoming is called soul, shaping matter into body and mind to reside in, and express itself through the five *pranas* and five senses and a series of identities, thus forming a personality to wrap around.

Originally our soul (individuality of consciousness) must have been oriented to its content, the transcendental yet immanent spirit. That is why our insatiable hunger for love and truth, the longing to transcend the relativity of their experience. In a state of balance the mind experiences the spirit through the subtle emanation of spiritual qualities such as peace and harmony, unselfish love and fulfilment, purity and goodness, truth and enlightenment.

The common experience of individual consciousness is through its orientation to *antar chitta*, the inner mind or the unconscious, to sustain and protect the body and extend it to the next generation. Thus the ego is under the impulse of primordial instincts surging from the inner mind.

Then the ego is oriented to *vahir chitta* or the subconscious or the field of experience above the unconscious, where it determines its welfare through a sense of right and wrong, avoiding errors caused by impulses, and developing personality traits. It is here the education of the ego takes place, the shaping of consciousness.

Then again the ego is consciously active in its orientation to *manas*, the determining and choosing aspect of the mind, always functioning in relationship to the subconscious, planting suggestions in it, sifting through a flood of influence from the surroundings, checking and restraining impulses surging from the unconscious.

At times happy and at times unhappy through its identities with what is around, sometimes worked up and sometimes pensive in the subconscious, the ego seeks repose in sleep but cannot altogether escape its experiences that swirl irrationally in dreams. Then in deep sleep it comes close to the spirit and remains for a while in opaque peace.

In meditation the ego seeks out its spiritual identity when *buddhi* or soul-consciousness reflects in its awareness, at first as peace becoming deeper and deeper, then in a state of transcendental oneness. For a while it is no longer aware of itself, nor its vehicles, the body and mind, nor its surroundings. Coming out of such a deep meditation, the ego feels thoroughly cleansed, is at peace with itself and the rest of the world, until its identities emerge from the mind and envelop it anew.

The saga of the ego is played out in the mind and expressed in philosophy and religion, arts and literature, architecture and science. The instinct of survival of its vehicle and the need for protection gave birth to religion, seeking individual and group security. Identical beliefs and resultant customs communicated through identical languages make individuals secure within the group. Thus is expressed identical aspiration forming the mindset of a culture.

Yet the ego is not really happy with all that. Happy for a while, of course, in the fulfilment of its desires, but not quite long until fatigue takes over through the ups and downs in its journey. Then wisdom filters in for those who have tried to educate and sublimate it and resignation rues in those who did not.

Thus, the ego as a liberated soul seeks to dissolve in the infinite spirit for those who have risen above their desires when it discards the body. For those who did not, the ego as a bound soul paints in myriad hues the imagery of afterlife, reincarnation, meeting God in heaven or the devil in hell or whatever, until the time of death.

Rest in peace while you live, for life is burdensome enough to add preoccupation with the afterlife. If you try to sort out what is herein and make a good job of it with yourself and others, the hereafter will sort itself out when it is time to go.

WE ARE WHAT WE MAKE OURSELVES TO BE

As we like to improve and renew an object we associate with, such as a house, so should we try to improve and renew a close relationship. As we need to wash and bathe, so does our character need constant purification.

More than the influence of the genes, people leave the mark of their character in those they closely associate with: their strength and weaknesses, integrity and deceit, courage and cowardice, selflessness and egotism, responsibility and carelessness, trustworthiness and unreliability.

Before departing, when death would separate one another, we should leave our mark of pleasant and warm memories of love and care, understanding and support, guidance and dependability. That is what people feel grateful about, not so much material inheritance.

As life is impermanent, as things of the world are transitory, it is all the more important that one should make the best use of all that is good, be wholeheartedly involved in the evolution of both ourselves and the society we live in, because there is not much time to lose by being unconcerned, careless, irresponsible and selfish, indulging in the fantasy about the unreality of the world.

Instead of worrying about the problems of life, it is better to worry about doing something useful.

Love of God is actually a love of spiritual ideals. God-realisation is a process of realising them.

Fear of God is ridiculous in whatever way one might interpret it, for fear by itself is a cowering instinct and, therefore, negative. You cannot love someone you fear.

Common opinion is not necessarily common sense, just as common sense is not that common at all.

Apart from learning a vocation, education means helping to develop oneself, to tap and develop all that is best within, and make use of the best around, as per the circumstances. Education is to motivate, inspire, discipline and guide.

A true scholar should be eclectically erudite and polymathic in his or her interests.

What people presume to be God is what religious leaders in the past have chosen to make of him, and they themselves choose to make of him. Whatever the vision, it has served and does help to provide the psychological prop for strength, solace and hope in moments of despair.

That humankind was made in the image of God means that we should aspire for the realisation of and measure up to highest spiritual ideals, as progress is possible only through identity with role models. However, what I find unconscionable is, having botched the job, God decided to liquidate his creation *en masse* by deluge. He failed again in spite of those saved in the Noah's ark from the result we see.

God created the universe in six days, and the great work fatigued him so much that he needed to rest on the seventh day. If one observes the conditions in this world, he seems to be still resting!

When God evicted Adam and Eve from heaven with spare fig leaves, Adam turned to Eve and said, "Look, what has happened to us." Eve responded, "But, darling, we have each other." Adam said Oh! and kept quiet.

Cause and effect are in a state of coexistence, maintained by the constancy of change, such as a cause leading to its effect and the effect, adapting to circumstances, transforming into a cause for a further effect.

Existence of anything is a consequence of an underlying essence, just as matter is to energy. Only the essence that is not a substance can be eternal, not its expressive individual form such as a field of consciousness or a soul or an idea of the essence itself. Immortality of the soul pertains to its essence, not its form, for when the individuality disappears, so does the soul. Can it be that the idea of the spiritual essence being eternal, call it God or whatever, is an offshoot of attachment to the individuality of consciousness, faced with the fact that what it tangibly deals with is transitory?

LIFE IS PRECIOUS

Life is too precious and the focus of human relationship too transitory to be sullied by little grudges and pettiness.

The main reason for incompetence is self-centredness, either in a state of foggy satisfaction with oneself, or being too preoccupied with self-interest and personal problems, so that the mind is oblivious of others and incapable of having initiative. Another major reason for incompetence is that one thinks too much of oneself and is predisposed to self-delusion and, therefore, incapable of learning by clear observation and objective assessment.

Nothing hurts a nation more than a topsy-turvy view of reality, both on the spiritual and secular levels of leadership, which inevitably infiltrates into people's mentality. You can see the harm done by ideologues and those who boast about past greatness.

A person's character is measured not by how peace-loving or amiable he or she is but by trustworthiness, integrity, moral courage, responsibility and a sense of duty.

[Speaking about a close friend] What I liked about him was his unpretentious nature and that he was not a glory-hopper. [In the *ashram*] He was too honest to be a court panegyrist and never performed for the galleries for self-enhancement. He was level-headed enough in not to be afflicted by the peculiar disease of saving humanity, for it is a posture of arrogance in itself and betrays a shallowness of mind. He never fell for god-incarnates and regarded them as paragons of vanity. It was distasteful to him to indulge in such glorification by fiat, since history can have perspective only after a sufficient lapse of time, and biographies are misnomers, anyhow, if bereft of the evidence of serious research and balanced scrutiny.

The bodyguards of half-truths and untruths are often employed to protect the reality of a person sought to be seen in a better light in history.

Vanity and arrogance are twin companions of renown and power, even if they are deodorised and dressed up in presentable forms.

Some swamis are like performing holy men and little else; so also some holy women.

[Writing to a devoted student about to be married] I wish you and your future husband all the blessings that life can offer in the process of building two lives together, because marriage is like a career (whereas a mistress or a lover is only a hobby), in the sense that you put so much into it: commitment, loyalty, patience, understanding, forbearance of each other's deficiencies, sharing of mutual values and also interests. Above all, it is a journey into the unknown, which can be successful and rewarding only if both try to be better human beings and stay spiritually intertwined in fair and adverse weather, knowing well that they love and, therefore, can count on each other for comfort and support. Best of luck and God bless.

As physicists know, there is no basic order in the universe, even though the physical laws of nature have an orderliness within a limited time-space dimension such as in the trajectory of a comet. However, as to the fate of humanity, the predictable coexists with the unpredictable. The will of God or divine plan is a speculative palliative to bear with equanimity adverse conditions.

You may not know what God looks like but would surely know what he sounds like as he thunders in the scriptures.

After searching for God all my life I found peace in the definition that he is after all a form of my devotion to spiritual ideals which I should try to improve all the time.

The visions of a culture narcotised by the fantasies of a glorious past, cannot serve a useful purpose when they are irrelevant to the present.

Hypocrisy is an inevitable companion of an exaggerated sense of tradition, family and religion. A common fault of a backward society is to be pompous, if not ridiculous, about old-fashioned ideas while not living up to them.

If you dig enough into the lives of those who thump their chest about moral majority, you are likely to find a lot of dirt. People generally are halfway decent, that is, upto the way others would let them, and that is good enough, moral enough, for me. They do not shout about virtue or morality.

One of the purposes of literature is that it serves as a catalyst to pent-up emotions and the thinking of the reader.

A primary requirement of fiction is to make illusions convincing, just as a major role of religion is to make God credible.

If design lacks a balance between aesthetics and usefulness, it becomes a bore.

The rules of engineering are functional reliability, durability and structural integrity.

According to the Indian tradition of performing arts, the ten emotions expressed are: romantic love, heroism, abhorrence, anger, merriment, terror, wonder, compassion, fatherly affection and holy peace.

The seven facets of our inner being are:

1) The individuality of consciousness through which the ego functions.

2) Its vague orientation to a spiritual source, expressed through an inherent hope for selfless love, truth, peace, goodness, purity of heart.

3) Its longing for knowledge, although mostly dormant, of the nature of our being and the life around, which make psychology and physical sciences possible.

4) Its strong subjection to primordial instincts of survival and procreation.

5) Its tendency to dwell most of the time in the field of memory, in the subconscious, remembering, desiring, resenting, daydreaming.

6) Its coping with the circumstances and problems by thinking, evaluating, choosing, deciding and willing.

7) Its necessity to act in the process of survival and wanting to be happy, and learn from experience, however imperfectly.

Education of the ego, which functions through different levels of consciousness, is basic to avoid suffering.

Instincts function through emotions, inducing action and thereby experience, resulting in memory. It is in the memory field the ego learns to educate itself by improving motivation and avoiding errors.

Memory is a result of attention or focus, and focus of interest. Intention is the result of loving an ideal, leading to its realisation through action. Motivation is determined by the premise: truth gives security in a relationship, resulting in trustworthiness and gaining self-confidence by being trustworthy.

Since we do not like to suffer, nor look forward to dying, why not regard life to be precious, meanwhile?

GUIDELINES FOR EVALUATION

You love a person truly if you can honestly say that, given the chance to start all over again, say in another life, you would choose the same father and mother, husband or wife, son or daughter, brother or sister, guru or disciple, without any qualification. If the response is hesitant, that love is rather deficient.

You cannot love a person without liking him or her. Liking depends on qualities like the goodness of heart, an unassuming and caring nature. These two and sharing of values like integrity, trust, loyalty, constancy and responsibility serve as a bonding agent in a loving relationship.

You can measure a loving relationship by the level of:

Acceptance. Do you still reject the loved one in your heart because of some aspects of his or her past? Acceptance enables communication.

Communication. Does your heart still have some dark recesses you find difficult or are still afraid to speak about? Do you speak freely to each other? Communication improves understanding.

Understanding. It is important to know the depth of feeling and thinking of someone you love as an individual, in his or her own right, rather than in the light of your own involvement or expectation. Understanding helps in the sharing of values, which leads to trust.

Trustworthiness. Can you blindly trust each other? It is the compatibility of values that holds a relationship together. Without mutual trust there is no love. Trust inspires respect.

Respect. If there is nothing to adore, there is no love. That is what makes commitment possible. It is not idealising, but some proven qualities of character like fidelity, purity of heart and integrity.

Made of clay as we all are, it is this spiritual aspiration that helps in the making of better human beings.

Close friends regard each other somewhat better than oneself. It is an honest feeling.

Soul mates or spiritual companionship fulfils oneself psychologically more than loving God by the means of a religion.

It is essential to mutually speak of difficulties in relationship before the ego can destroy it.

Marital love is compared to wine. If based only on passion, like a cheap wine, it quickly turns into vinegar. If based on sharing of ideals, like a good wine, it becomes richer with time.

Never say no one is perfect. It shows your unwillingness to correct yourself.

Never say we are all responsible. It shows your avoidance of personal responsibility.

If you say that you accept full responsibility, immediately define what you are going to do to correct the mistake.

Think positively. Make it a habit. It is even taught to astronauts and combat pilots.

Focus on the positive aspects in a relationship and stop feeding the negative side.

Never take anyone or anything for granted. All relationship needs renewal.

Life is a two-way street. Forget about loving someone without expecting the other to learn to love. Otherwise, it is a fantasy in your head. Loving is mutually teaching each other to love.

Selfless service means you serve a good cause for a spiritual fulfilment on a personal level. There is nothing wrong in it.

In anything you do, you should be fully interested in its result. Otherwise how would you know if you have done something right and if you can do still better?

You need not run after someone to communicate who shuns you. Practise detachment.

Anxiety and insecurity are due to a lack of love. Lack of love is due to an excess of selfishness.

Identify the nature of anxiety or insecurity, determine the cause and treat it. Get involved in doing something useful. Be interested in others.

Self-confidence is a product of the experience of doing something right. To do anything well you need motivation. Without loving what you wish to do, you would not learn to do it well. Interest causes intention, intention action and action experience. Experience strengthens will.

When you say that you have no will power to do what you wish to, it means that you do not strongly love to do what you wish to. No one has learned to swim without wetting one's feet.

Lack of love in childhood causes resentment. Overcome resentment by detachment and understanding. If you have not received love, it is all the more imperative that you do not deny your love to those who need it.

It is good to remember five abnegations for self-education:

Selfishness by unselfish deeds.

Self-centredness by attention to others.

Self-pity by taking personal responsibility.

Vanity by remembering that there is a lot to learn, a lot to improve.

Pride by recognising merits in others and humility of spirit.

The amorphous emotion called love is substantiated by concern for the welfare of the loved one, helpful deed, responsibility to, loyalty and fidelity, commitment and constancy.

Faith in God means dedication and commitment to spiritual ideals, his image, in which we are supposed to have been created. It is not emotionalism.

Belief is a bridge that connects the known with the unknown, projecting from the premise of the known what is possible and plausible. Without trying to realise its ideal, it is only wishful thinking.

Belief as a hope is meaningless if nothing is done to realise it, for you will be hoping forever. To sustain belief there has to be a measure of experience, such as of peace and inner strength in God's love. It means to be grateful for the blessings in your life.

SELFISHNESS AND SELF-IMPORTANCE

The two metaphorical legs on which people seem to walk are selfishness and self-importance. These two human deficiencies are a natural byproduct of the need to survive physically and psychologically. We all need to look after ourselves and defend our position and self-interest. In the process, however, we forget that we survive better by being mutually considerate and supportive, caring and understanding.

The saying of the great Rabbi Hillel, a contemporary of Jesus Christ, is most appropriate:

"If I am not for myself,
who will be for me?

If I am only for myself,
who am I?
If not now, when?"

Being selfish, we feel isolated, because no one really likes a selfish person. It is enough to carry one's own load of selfishness, rather than being imposed upon by another's. Selfishness and self-importance can be traced to be the two basic causes of psychological suffering. Being disliked and isolated, we become unhappy. Lacking the nourishment of love, we fall back into self-love and self-pity.

A selfish person becomes automatically irresponsible, failing to think of others but habituated to think only of oneself. Responsibility is an acquired rule of conduct, as also a sense of duty, which help to restrain selfishness to some extent. Without them the human spirit remains very primitive. Irresponsibility leads to being distrusted, and distrust to a lack of self-esteem, which conduces insecurity and unhappiness.

The me-first syndrome, learning to love oneself, guarantees one to be selfish rather than gain self-esteem, for which it is justified. First of all, you have to have something lovable in you to love yourself. Loving oneself does not need any urging. We all are intrinsically prone to love ourselves.

Self-esteem is a result of self-effort to cultivate qualities to be proud of without being vain about them. Self-esteem without substance is merely vanity. *Vanus* means emptiness. If you have substance, you are not vain, inflated.

We should all be good to ourselves, of course, but not forgetting those who are around, whom we are responsible to. It is a truism, indeed, that those who live for others are happier than those who live only for themselves. It is such a motivation that steers the mental focus from one's petty problems and makes life more meaningful.

Do not fall for such sayings that you can find happiness only within or in God alone, for no real happiness can be found without, in this material world. Happiness is neither entirely within, nor without alone. It is both within and without. It is in an inner state of harmony attained through a harmonious relationship with others, in coming to terms with oneself in the process of managing one's desires, trying to be a better person.

Happiness is in an action efficiently executed with dedication and commitment. It is in a loving relationship fathomlessly deepened with unselfish devotion, in a duty fully accomplished, a responsibility well met, an obligation well fulfilled. It is not in closing the eyes and getting blissed out for a while. It is in trying to overcome a deficiency like intolerance by patience and understanding, resentment by detachment and forgiveness, prejudice by fairness and objectivity.

The fat ego, specially when lacking the physical and mental strength to defend oneself, becomes the target of other people's aggression by unnecessarily getting into an argument with a stronger ego. This leads to self-pity, thinking that others are to blame and one is but a victim, which further weakens oneself.

Selfishness with irresponsibility, self-importance with ingratitude, cowardly nature with laziness, and hypocrisy with character debility, all conduce to an unhappy life.

Selfishness being a product of the instinct of survival is physical in nature, whereas the ego or self-importance is an offshoot of the need to survive psychologically, or as a mental entity capable of knowing and deciding. It is inevitable that life has to move on these two metaphorical legs.

Foolish, indeed, is the teaching to cut them off, to destroy selfishness, to pulverise the ego. If you are foolish enough to try to do so, others will walk all over you and you will be a victim of stronger egos. They need to be disciplined, educated and guided, psychologically purified and sublimated.

A self-reliant person, thus, becomes less selfish. Being secure in an area of knowledge, there is no need to get into an argument. Being self-confident, one does not throw one's weight around. Avoiding wishful thinking and evaluating by facts, one learns to be fair and realistic.

There is great wisdom in the Talmudic saying that the essence of the Torah consists in treating others as one would like to be treated by. Do so, however, after being sure how others would like to be treated, not on your own terms alone.

CHARACTER, HONOUR, PATRIOTISM

A person of character is one who has moral principles, such as integrity, trustworthiness and courage, an adequate sense of duty, responsibility and honour, and the will to act. Will without ethical values is merely obstinacy, which is a sign of lacking in character, for it consists in being considerate of others. It is generally the weak who are obstinate.

A civilised society is known by its sense of justice tempered by compassion; individual and collective responsibility; the way the public is treated by the authorities; the state of maintenance of public property, and the individual's respect for it; the status of the minorities and that of women; religious, political and cultural freedom; and constant effort to better itself.

Passion is neither faith, nor knowledge, nor can it convey understanding, but only passion and fanaticism.

Infatuation is not love, but an irrational form of self-love. So also, blind faith is infatuation with a self-serving belief, a self-centred emotionalism, and leads at best to fatalism,and at worst to fanaticism and violence.

The honour of a person is in being honourable. When honour and vanity become synonymous in a person, he becomes ridiculous, and by posturing about his country, he makes it look ridiculous as well.

Honour and integrity are synonymous, and their companions are trustworthiness, duty and responsibility.

Patriotism should arise from hope rather than pride, hope for the realisation of such ideals that make one's country lovable.

A patriot is a person who represents the virtues of his country rather than its ugly side; lacking in ethics and responsibility, the tendency to blame other countries for its problems, being pretentious of an imagined glorious past while being backward in the present, wishing to be prosperous while being lazy. A patriot should try to be a better person, rather than feel good about himself. Samuel Johnson said that patriotism is the last refuge of the scoundrel.

Einstein said that nationalism is the worst form of a virus that a nation can be infected with. Nationalism tries to cover up its fear and insecurity by fanatical ideas of greatness which is assaulted by imaginary devils, its problems caused by foreigners; cover up its inferiority complex about its culture by the supposed threat of corruption through foreign ideologies, political or religious. It is a complex like maintaining racial purity.

To love a country you do not have to beat your breast. If you love a person, you do not make a show of it, but do something useful for him or her. So also, if you love a country, ask yourself what you are doing for its good, or if you are a good example of it.

The image of a country is seen through its main institutions, such as the character and intelligence of its parliamentarians, of the executive arm from the President and

Prime Minister down to the lower levels of the bureaucrats, of the impartiality and the independence of its judiciary, and the standard and integrity of its media. A country is respected for the values these institutions represent and defend.

If religion does not inspire a boundless concern for human welfare, compassionate justice, personal responsibility, duty, and an eternally-awestruck search for truth, it is little more than superstitious emotionalism and generally-ignored moral commandments.

You can force obedience out of fear that your neighbours will disapprove of an unbecoming conduct, for there is hardly any credence of hell-fire, but you cannot force the heart by dogmas. Since religion is mainly a question of feelings, and as feelings cannot be forced, they can only be inspired by love of ideals to fulfil one's emotional needs.

The awe for and dependence on authority ingrained in early childhood are fine-tuned and transfered to an almighty deity in adulthood, instead of inspiring reverence for life around, and learning to be self-confident, self-reliant and take responsibility for our fate.

The point of any myth is in its usefulness to inspire the search for the unknown, widen the dimension of the known, and to strengthen the human spirit.

The choice of what may I do today and how may I do that as well as I can today, changes our tomorrow. If we expect things to happen, life will surely continue monotonously.

Part Two

UNDERSTANDING OF REALITY

Reality has two aspects, the spiritual and material, or what can be and what is: our inherent if unconscious longing for selfless love and truth, and the actuality of our selfishness and lack of integrity. To overcome the negative with the positive, untruth by truth, hate by love, rancour by forgiveness is the spiritual utopia of humanity, even if reciprocity is found to be the most effective law that rules society. However, the individual and society have failed to find peace by it. Tit for tat excites the ego but saddens the soul.

We learn to evaluate and choose through a sense of right and wrong. Without it the moral development of the individual is incomplete. The sense of right and wrong is born out of the love of spiritual ideals, and is more than a social more for mutual self-interest. It is a product of cultural influence and education, of course, but is learned mainly by one's own effort. The problem is how the individual's psyche has been marked, favourably or unfavourably, by parental influence from infancy to adolescence, in addition to genetical predisposition.

The worst way to treat reality is to make it amorphous, such as the ineffability of Brahman or of a divine determinism, if there be any. The search for truth to be successful must have a well defined set of values to experiment with in real life, to know their truth. However, through such a process, when one arrives at the door of what seems to be a perfect truth, of goodness or justice for example, a new door opens up farther on, revealing a greater horizon, for the nature of truth is essentially eternal.

Political and socio-economic philosophers have sought to perfect their theories as to what an equitable society should be through the profession of, say, dialectical materialism as in the case of communism, and of nationalist fascism with racist overtones, since the early part of the twentieth century, but only to end up as disastrous experiments. The social democrats, also since about that time, have been trying to soften the hard-heartedness of capitalism by making their theories more workable, but having results only in the developed and productive societies.

Capitalism took into consideration a basic truth tapped by Adam Smith that only through the manipulation of greed, albeit with a minimum of regulatory restraint, a society could be made prosperous. It could be done by the equation of initiative and industry with profit-motive and social advancement, thereby opening up the vast energies of the fittest to compete in a free market of enterprise. The social democrats tried to counter this by getting the state involved in the competition as well, and providing a safety net for the weaker sections of society.

The religious, or rather spiritual philosophers, tried to provide a counterbalance by their theories of commitment to the ideals of social justice through compassion, on the basis of the credo that we are our brother's and sister's keepers. It was, of course, inspired by the speculation that we were all universally related to each other through the image of God, but had to be limited for practical reasons to tribal (read national) groups.

This theory was workable only in efficiently-managed, productive societies, but had to be diluted for an obvious reason. Human nature being what it is, charity without a corresponding obligation becomes liable to exploitation to the hilt, and the recipient's dependence perpetuates itself. You have only to see how the social democrats are vying with each other to veer to the centre of their socio-political spectrum.

The scientists kept their faith in the hypothetical search for reality, but had the integrity to discard an unviable hypothesis and try new ones to arrive at their truth. The motive-power of truth is security, reliability of its premise, and its inexorable imperative is evidence, for the nature of truth is measured by its consequence and universal applicability.

Some speculative philosophers, however, presumed that reality was beyond this world, which they dismissed as illusory, but only to remain fogbound and unproductive through the centuries, and were prone to be hypocritical due to the duplicity of human nature, like the paragons of morality in Victorian England.

Altruism is the basis of morality, but can sustain itself only through mutual helpfulness. Love can and should be selfless, but the fountain of this emotion is bound to dry up without reciprocal nourishment. The investment of love enhances future security, such as that of the parents in their children, serving as an insurance for their old age. In prosperous societies, social security takes care of that, of course, but only to some extent, for in times of need the aged would only turn to their children, and they would reciprocate, even if some of them uncaringly, depending on the kind of relationship they had with their parents.

Reciprocity helps survival, but the weak inevitably suffers at the hand of the strong. If the weak pardons the aggression or the despisal of the strong, it is out of weakness. The primary duty of the weak is to try to be strong, and of the youth to be responsible for their future, and not be dependent on others.

Friendship signifies affection, reliability, trust, solidarity and generosity, but only when they are mutual, for hardly any relationship is sustainable for long without the mutuality of self-interest, even though we do not like to be gross about it. There is nothing wrong to be ashamed of self-serving values, for they are a corollary to surviving more agreeably, altruism, love, decency, goodness being a part of mutual fulfilment.

MYTHS

Myths, as a cornerstone of religion, provide a romantic notion about the origin of our being in an insecure world. Myths about our divine roots give us the strength to overcome the deficiencies in our human nature. Myths about an almighty God attempt at propping up our powerless existence.

Myths about a merciful God are meant to console the distressed, although failing to answer for the overwhelming misery in which the vast majority lives. Is not compassion a healing balm that we need for each other to see us through suffering? Does it not help to soften our hard-heartedness caused by selfishness? The role model helps to bear our burden with fortitude.

The myth of a just God motivates us to create institutions of justice and fair play, stick by the rules, get together to struggle against injustice, even if justice does not have its sway from heaven. The myth about justice to be meted out in heaven serves as an anodyne to the powerless victims, although the only way to treat crime is the visibility of law-enforcement and the swiftness of a just reprisal.

The myth of God begetting a son and have him sacrificed at the altar of humankind's sinfulness, so that by believing in him people could be saved from eternal damnation, has inspired proselytizing zeal through nearly two millennia, and has brought solace to the downtrodden converts. But what about the four-fifths of humanity that do not believe in him? Don't they deserve salvation by following other paths for redemption?

It is really we who ought to save ourselves from our own errors, with or without divine inspiration or help, through self-confidence. Why inject, first of all, the idea of being damned, push us into the sea, and then throw the lifeline of salvation? Tapping our spiritual resources, or if you like from God within, or focussing our energies to the infinite source of power, should we not try to better ourselves?

Is there an infinite source of power? No doubt about it, observing the universe, a raw physical force, the earth going around the sun at 30 km a second, the sun whirling within the Milky Way at 350 km a second, and the Milky Way itself speeding outward at 600 km a second. (See *Wrinkles in Time* by George Smoot and Keay Davidson.) There is nothing divine about it. From the atomic dust of this universe, from the particles of energy that became dust, we have become human, and from those particles have evolved our mind to qualify the divine.

What is divine, after all? That which calms our mind, enlightens it, fulfils us emotionally, uplifts our spirit, we call divine. That which perturbs, confuses, degrades and makes us unhappy, we call undivine. It is in the state of consciousness the divine and undivine are conceptualised.

Myths also serve as a pep talk, reassure, and give hope. It does not matter if history proves them to be true or not. The declared myth of Krishna, in the *Bhagavad Gita*, reincarnating as an avatara to reestablish *dharma*, or righteous rule, made a mockery of itself when the Hindu religion and culture were assaulted and degraded repeatedly by the iconoclastic waves of Muslim invasion over hundreds of years.

Why religion claims that we have spiritual roots? Very simple. We have only to observe our experience and test it on a universal platform: our preference for the positive.

The highest purpose of myths is to widen the dimension of the known by projecting our search into the unknown from the premises of the possibilities and plausibilities to encounter new truths, to enrich our existence. Myths are not merely to serve as palliatives to suffer the deficiencies of the known and hope for the best in the unknown, but just the contrary.

The need for the supernatural cannot be dismissed out of hand. Its primary origin is in the need to survive, human existence being riddled with insecurity and inadequacy. The myth of an omnipotent God, even if all the evidence is to the contrary, serves this purpose. Without hope one loses the will to struggle.

It is only the supremely self-confident, well secure in one's mental and spiritual moorings, who does not need a God to appeal to, to face up to challenge and misfortune courageously and stoically. The vast majority needs an omnipotent being to beseech to, compensate for one's powerlessness by drawing strength from.

Then there is another need for any social framework to be cohesive through a role model representing spiritual and ethical ideals in order to be mutually responsible, and accountable to a common divine forum, and fulfilled emotionally as an individual.

PEACE

Peace as an overriding instrument of policy or peace at any price has led to more wars than prevented one. Non-violence and passive resistance as a policy against an armed opponent are tolerated only in a democratic society, not under a totalitarian government. Mahatma Gandhi could not have survived under Hitler or Stalin, nor under Mussolini or Franco. Even the transfer of power by Britain to India in 1947, against strong opposition of the Liberal and Conservative parties, led by Winston Churchill, was possible because of war fatigue and impoverishment of Britain after the Second World War.

It is still my conviction, in spite of the evidence to the contrary in the Kenyan and South African experience of gaining empowerment, that non-violent struggle against tyranny is the only civilised form of achieving justice, because violence brutalises the perpetrator and the heavily-armed oppressor against whom it is directed, and leads to a spiral of reprisal.

It is also my conviction that people of the cloth should keep out of politics and try to influence social issues by their moral and spiritual support, as well as for the universal human rights, the religious vocation being the celebration of the best in humanity and not personal salvation which should come last.

It is my conviction as well that what two adults do in the privacy of his or her bedroom for birth control is their concern alone. The priest and the politician should keep out of their bedrooms.

I have observed with horror the statistics of over one-thousand-a-day backyard abortions in Argentina, a country of 37 millions, where the termination of pregnancy even by rape and incest is illegal, and where nearly a third of the patients of the maternity ward of some hospitals are victims of botched abortion. In Chile, where the laws are the same, I was told by a famous gynecologist of Santiago that the statistics are even higher in that country of 15 millions.

The hard question is whether an adult female has less right than a fetus sustained in her body before it develops its nervous system around twelve weeks? Again, the priest and the politician should keep out of her bedroom.

A MISCELLANY OF MUSINGS

In children, continuing through adulthood, lying is first of all an exciting experience in the sense of self-inflation, to feel important before others. Then there are two other factors: on account of selfishness to hoard, such as a child denying having candies in order not to share with another child, or not declaring fully one's income tax; and out of fear to save one's skin, such as punishment from the elders, or social disapproval to maintain reputation or peace at home.

You have heard of lingual diarrhoea, but have you asked if it is a result of the constipation of ideas?

I have observed that the Anglo-Saxon sense of humour has a scatological character and the Latin's tend to be rather salacious.

From the beginning of humankind, the female has been treated as the property of the male, to serve him as a sex object, bearer of his progeny and as a low-cost domestic. Her biological role in childbearing and rearing has made her emotionally vulnerable and concerned about the security of the nest.

As a result, her gumption leans more to the practical side of life than the male's. As a result also, the male is less capable of forgiving the female's infidelity because of the violation of his property right in his unconscious, whereas the female is able to do so with relative forgiveness, as long as she is sure of her partner's emotional bond to provide the security of the nest, whether she has any children or not. When she loses this security, divorce ensues.

Desirelessness is another name of apathy or laziness. A higher desire is always necessary to rise above a lesser desire and to overcome indifference.

Indifference can easily be confused as tolerance. When in a position to retaliate, desisting from it is called tolerance.

To be a renunciate you have to have something to renounce in the first place.

Even if the original impression subsequently bears out more often than not, it can go hopelessly wrong.

Instant likes and dislikes can frequently be a self-echo. We like those in whom we see our aspirations and dislike those reflecting our weaknesses.

FAITH AND REASON

There is no inherent conflict between faith and reason. Blind faith spawns ignorance. If a church requires unquestioning obedience to its injunctions or dogmas, it is meant to make sure of its authority over its adherents, strengthen its institutional power and group identity. But as education becomes universal, its purpose being freedom from ignorance and make people think for themselves, such an attitude becomes counterproductive.

Reason is a goddess in her own right, as much as faith is. In fact, they are twin goddesses, psychically related. Without the discipline of reason, faith becomes at best emotionalism and at worst superstition. Without the inspiration and commitment of faith, reason becomes a dry intellection at best and an ego trip at worst.

Faith is of course an emotion, not emotionalism which is a sensation of the ego loving not the object of faith but its role in doing so. In its pure form faith is devotion. It is actually a love of the ideals that the object of faith, God or whatever, represents and the commitment to realise them. Just as the reality of love consists in what one does for the welfare of the loved person, the truth of faith is in the motivation for and consequent realisation of the ideals behind.

Thus, the word faith can be defined as a fountain of inspiration providing the motivation for the search for truth, leading to an infinite process of its realisation.

Reason protects faith from being blind, for integrity is the basis of reason.

The value of reason is not merely to be reasonable to one another, but not to be arbitrary and dogmatic. It begins with the empirical verification of a manifest substance, for truth is *veritas*. It is not only a responsibility but duty, in being honest with oneself and as a result with others. Such a verification is easy.

Then the real search begins. What causes a substance in a particular form to appear? Is there a subtle substance, E conducing MC^2? It has to be real, the demonstration of the components of which is the purpose of science, MC^2 leading to the understanding of E.

But what does the empirical substance, life as we know it, with all the complicated facets of human character, mean to us? This search for a meaning leads to infinite possibilities of understanding ourselves and others, our origin, actuality and destiny. That is the purpose of philosophy and its instrument is reason through the love of wisdom. That is why the nineteenth-century German philosopher Gotthold Lessing said, "If God had two gifts in his two hands, one the ultimate truth and the other the search for truth, he would ask for the latter."

What religion calls truth revealed by God is actually a product of such a search, the individual seeker gaining an insight to one's existence. If it endures the test of time and has a universal bearing, it acquires the epithet of a God-given law.

Even if in some Vedantic teaching it is said that there are some questions which cannot be answered by the intellect, just as Christianity says that one cannot know the mind of God, there is no question under the sun that cannot be satisfactorily explained. One can only say that, as of now, I have not found an answer to it, that science has not been able to solve the problem as yet, but the future holds infinite possibilities of knowledge.

OBITER DICTA

No one really believes in anything of which one has no direct experience. Beliefs arc a projection of possibilities on the basis of relevant antecedence.

Beliefs generally mean hoping for something which is to one's advantage. As figments of imagination they serve no purpose, except to be seen well by those who share similar figments.

The relevancy of any belief measures to the extent one is motivated to do something about it. Hoping without self-effort to realise the object of hope leads to daydreaming and being hopelessly stagnant.

In any belief there is an element of doubt which can be overcome by testing its plausibility through practical means. If its reality is confirmed, it is no longer called a belief but knowledge.

Knowledge gained by practical experience gives self-assurance, not belief which is only meant to motivate.

Knowledge does not bar the possibility of a better adaptation in the light of a deeper experience gained in the process.

This prevents knowledge from being dogmatic, just as belief motivating oneself to search for its reality keeps one free from dogmatism.

If an unverifiable substance is embraced as reality and the empirical is dismissed as an illusion, irresponsibility, lethargy, and both material and moral backwardness stalk the land.

Resignation undermines will and personal responsibility.

To consider what is available to be good enough for want of having nothing better is the stepping stone to strive for something better.

From personal experience and observation I have found that the components of human nature are a product of, approximately one-third each:

1) Genetical inheritance or karmic backlog if you wish to fancy that way.
2) Parental influence in early childhood, together with the environmental factors in later life.
3) Subsequent self-effort to better oneself, or worsen the negative traits by indulging them.

However, whatever the self-effort, genetical roots cannot be totally eradicated, even though genes are malleable, nor indeed parental influence, especially of the mother, absorbed during the first two years.

To put it another way, we are a composite of five karmas. The believer in karma automatically presupposes previous births. Karma is both a consequence of unrealised actions in the preceding life and actions done in the present, bearing a consequence in the future. Whatever the tradition says, meeting the consequence of past actions with present actions shapes our destiny. To put it in an unorthodox way, we are a product of:

1) *Adrishta* or unseen karma from the past life which brought us into this world deserving our parents.
2) *Griha* or that of our home, mainly of the parents who influence us indelibly in early childhood.
3) *Samaja* or that of society in which we are raised, influencing our adolescence mainly and partially through adulthood causing us to act.
4) *Swartha* or selfish actions done consciously and unconsciously.
5) *Purushartha* or spiritually-motivated actions.

Chapter Nineteen

SIX SYSTEMS OF INDIAN PHILOSOPHY

As in any living entity, human or animal, the primary need is survival. Unlike animals, survival on the human level can be made more agreeable with a meaningful purpose and a better understanding of oneself and the world around, rather than by the blind force of instincts. All societies reflect the strengths and weaknesses of the philosophies, religious or secular, that shaped them.

Indian philosophy is divided into two broad groups, orthodox (*astika*) and heterodox (*nastika*), the former accepting the authority of the Vedas and the latter not. The orthodox schools are called *shad-darshana* or six systems of philosophy devised by the aphoristic teachings of their authors and subject to endless interpretation. The Sanskrit word for philosophy *darshana* means a visionary perspective. They are:

1) Nyaya of Gotama or Gautama, the word *nyaya* meaning method or system or logic.

2) Vaisheshika of Kanada. The word means specific, from *vishesha* or special.

3) Sankhya of Kapila, the word meaning enumeration or discerning perception.

4) Yoga of Patanjali, consisting of eight interrelating steps more in the nature of spiritual disciplines with the exception of two physical practices, namely, *asana* and *pranayama*.

5) Mimamsa of Jaimini. The word means investigation or reflection.

6) Vedanta of Badarayana Vyasa as in his *Brahma Sutras* on the basis of the Upanishads. The word *anta* means end or the final part of the Vedas or the culmination of its teachings.

The heterodox group not accepting the authority of the Vedas are that of 1) Charvaka, 2) Bauddha and 3) Jaina philosophies.

The Vedas are the earliest Indian literature that have greatly influenced the evolution of the nation's philosophies. They have two traditions, ritualistic and philosophical, or that of *karma* meaning performance of rituals and *gyana* meaning speculation into the nature of reality as to the cause and purpose of existence.

Knowledge has two sides, empirical, and that which is relative to what does a material reality mean to oneself as well as its general significance, with an infinite possibility of widening understanding.

RELEVANCY OF IDEAS

The Mimamsa system created a philosophy to justify rituals and the Vedanta philosophy speculated about the reality behind existence. These two systems are called Purva or Karma Mimamsa and Uttara or Gyana Mimamsa, respectively.

Sankhya, Yoga, Nyaya and Vaisheshika formulated their philosophies in accordance to life's experience and observation.

Mimamsa and Sankhya do not believe in God as the creator. Accepting the authority of the Vedas by the six systems generally means belief in an afterlife, which in turn means belief in an eternal moral order determining good and evil. Deeds relative to them set the fate of humanity in an afterlife, together with reincarnation on this earth, while explaining the inequality and vagary of justice in our current existence.

Anything that is not empirical is speculation, even if these philosophies take for granted the verity of the Vedic teachings without much argument. However, the role of speculation is to find new realities by projecting into the unknown what a known reality might mean, but which can be honestly called a new reality only when it can be verified empirically.

If God exists or not is not a philosophical problem or if there is a creator, but what does God mean and if there is a criterion behind creation. By observation one does not find a criterion as to the universal wellbeing of humanity or even animals. If the criterion of a divine intelligence is posited to be incomprehensible to the human mind, it is meaningless or irrelevant to the latter if it experiences nothing better than what it does, just as an atomic particle being able to pass through the wall is irrelevant to a person who cannot pass through it, or a carpet being a mountainous territory for a microbe is irrelevant to a person walking over its flatness.

All the six systems take refuge in the law of karma in the Vedas in search of a rule of moral order in the universe and making oneself the author of one's destiny and explaining the difference of intelligence and inborn aptitudes as well as the circumstance of birth and achievement, without however answering why a soul has to get involved in a material body in the first place and then having to go through all that hassle in order to get liberated. Neither do these philosophies recognise that a moral criterion is a result of the mind being exposed to ethical ideals over generations.

In Nyaya and Vaisheshika systems moral laws are under the control and guidance of God, he being the ultimate dispenser of the human fate (as in Judeo-Christian theology), whereas in Sankhya and Mimamsa (as well as in the Bauddha and Jaina philosophies) they are autonomous and have nothing to do with the will of God. In Vedanta, God being an immanent spirit has no will of his own, like unmanifest electricity in the atmosphere waiting to be generated by the motor of human endeavour.

KARMA PHILOSOPHY

As all the six systems believe in the karma theory, it is better to examine its pertinence, although none bothers to explain it in depth but take it for granted on the authority of the Vedas. The purpose of karma philosophy, far from being fatalistic, makes one responsible, individually and collectively, as to the direction of life. Bhishma, the grandfather of Arjuna the reluctant hero of the Mahabharata war, says: "Personal effort is what matters above all. Belief in fate makes one dull." (Shantiparva in *Mahabharata*)

The karma theory automatically presupposes a previous and afterlife. Karma is of two kinds generally: 1) *Arabdha* or *Prarabdha* or that which is already bearing fruit, such as in the circumstance of birth and inborn qualities of character and aptitudes, and 2) *Anarabdha* or that which is yet to bear fruit. The latter has two subdivisions: a) *Praktana* or *Sanchita* or the force of accumulated actions as a driving power behind the individual's instincts, both constructive and destructive and, thus, creating new karmas, and b) *Kriyamana* or *Agami* or *Sanchiyamana*, or action done by one's will or desire, both positive and negative, which is influenced by external factors, examples and teachings, and done by personal choice, in turn creating new karmas to bear fruit later on.

In all karmas it is the motivation that determines the intensity of their retribution, such as in the difference between a premeditated and impulsive act of violence.

With or without a supreme deity's involvement, belief in an eternal moral order, to participate in which is one's responsibility in the best light of one's understanding, makes the acceptance of glaring inequality and injustice plausible and, therefore, self-effort meaningful, unless one is content with the ideal of doing what is appropriate whilst coping with life. In this case, if the result is not conducive to the motivation, it means to learn from failure and reorganise action and find a better way of dealing with the circumstances, irrespective of the theory of karma being real or merely speculative.

Harping on detached or unselfish action is indicative of a disgust with the utter selfishness of human nature and an unrealistic way of looking at it, because in any involvement, necessary to create motivation and, therefore, efficiency and creativity in action, there is bound to be a small measure of attachment. Without it no real love or excelling work is possible, whereas the ideal is not to be dependent on love, not to be infantile in expectation, and accept failure with equanimity, pause a while, learn from mistakes and reorient motivation and action.

RELIGION AND PHILOSOPHY

Religion is an instrument that experiments with sentiment and faith, just as philosophy does with speculation and reasoning, and both have their pertinency in finding personal and social peace, security and happiness. Unless they influence the manner of living, they remain sterile.

Religion, rising above myths and rituals, even though they serve as means of group identity, provides a way of finding peace within through a unity of the body, mind and spirit. Philosophy, rising above intellectual curiosity, serves as the basis of social structure and inspirer of civilisation, creating a system of ideals with which to motivate and guide one's life.

Life suffers when it is led by the force of blind impulses and mundane desires. The purpose of philosophy is to understand, educate and sublimate them. The bottom line of Indian philosophy is given in the four observations of the Buddha, although an excessive preoccupation with suffering and getting out of the cycle of rebirth is rather a negative way of looking at life, instead of making it agreeably creative, making unselfish love the fountain of happiness, which will invalidate the rejection of the world by the neurosis of nirvana or the eternal bliss syndrome.

The Buddha observes that 1) there is suffering, 2) there are causes for suffering, 3) that suffering can be overcome, and 4) that there is a way to overcome it. It is a very valid observation, and his eightfold path to overcome suffering is superb. It consists in:

1) Positive thinking, 2) a truthful life, 3) constructive action or work, 4) right conduct in relationship to others, 5) a sane disposition or attitude to life, 6) intelligent effort for self-improvement and general welfare, 7) honest livelihood, in which no deceit or cruelty or violence is involved, and 8) effective meditation to realise one's spiritual aspiration.

A moral sense is the highest goal of religion, a moral life its greatest practice, and a moral criterion is the best definition of spirituality. Prayer, meditation and devotional practices are only the means to its realisation, as per the following definition, if spirituality is not to be a cloud-cuckoo inanity or a holy-holy theatre. It consists of:

1) Purity of heart or that which is free from the ill effects of hate, malice, resentment, vengeance, avarice, wickedness and imputing bad motives to others.

2) Unselfish love, spontaneous compassion and kindness to and consideration of others through matching deeds.

3) Integrity of feeling or depth of sentiment rather than sentimentalism, of thinking, of expression through speech and action, and honesty to oneself and to others.

4) Sublimation of passions and worldly desires.

5) Sublimation of the ego or humility of spirit or genuine modesty, cutting out any theatrical gesture.

QUEST FOR TRUTH

Any search begins with a hypothetical acceptance of the existence of the object of search. The role of speculation is to make use of imagination and reasoning in order to find new truths. The foundation of speculation is a prior experience of an unsatisfactory reality, and the main instruments are inspiration and reasoning so as not to be carried away by daydreaming. The Nyaya, Vaisheshika and Sankhya (as also the Charvaka, Bauddha and Jaina) schools accept this position. The Mimamsa and Vedanta systems do not regard human experience and reasoning to be adequate instruments to correct answers as to if there is a supreme ruler or creator but rely on the testimony of the Vedas, just as the Jewish and Islamic religions do on the testimony of their prophets and the Christians of Jesus and the Apostles.

Except the Charvaka School, the six systems of philosophy (as also the Bauddha and Jaina) accept fate or *bhagya* as a collective consequence of one's actions in past lives and which can be overcome in the present one if self-effort is strong enough. The world is regarded as a stage in which human one acts out a morality play and the purpose of which is to overcome suffering and be happy, happiness being the innate nature of the spirit embodied in an inadequate vehicle and living in an imperfect world.

Freedom of the soul from material bondage is the spiritual goal common to all the six systems (as also in the Bauddha and Jaina philosophies), and its merger in the transcendental spirit as in the Vedanta, or its eternal existence in a state of freedom as in the Sankhya, is the common destiny.

This freedom is attained through knowledge of the various truths of existence in deep meditation, while awakening one's identity with the infinite spirit or God, the pattern of meditation varying according to different paths, and by leading a life of self-discipline and self-improvement as enjoined, for example, by Patanjali in his *Yoga Sutras:*

Practice of five *yamas* or the disciplines of non-violence, truthfulness, chastity, and getting rid of material greed and covetousness. Observance of five *niyamas* or cultivating the good habits of physical and mental cleanliness, contentment, fortitude, self-improvement through study, and dedication to God or to spiritual ideals.

Without prolonged meditation on one's relatedness to a higher power there can be no strength for their practice. Without profound meditation on some sacred teachings there can be no understanding to the problems of life and the capacity to overcome them. It is a lifelong objective. Its difficulty is noted in the Sanskrit saying: "I know what is right but have little inclination to follow it, and I know what is wrong but am too weak to desist from it," or in the saying of Jesus Christ, "the spirit is willing but the flesh is weak."

In none of the Indian philosophies repression of the baser impulses of human nature is indicated but their education and sublimation, specially in the Yoga system by meditation on and practice of their opposite counterparts. Life is regarded as transitory and, therefore, pleasure and pain, success and failure, are to be taken in their stride, not losing the sight of higher values by pleasure and success, and not being overwhelmed by pain and failure.

The earth is regarded in the *Vishnu Purana* as a mere speck of existence together with fourteen planes of more or less-evolved variety, comprising one unit among thousands of millions of others, each alternately coming into form (*shrishti*) in the course of billions of years and being withdrawn into the void (*pralaya*) likewise, and each presided over by a supreme deity, Brahma (not Brahman), one day of whom is said to be equal to 432 millions of years of the earthlings (the Hindus love zeros). This overwhelming vision of the vastness of the universe and the insignificance of the human being in it may have contributed to the otherworldliness or disregard for material things in India's philosophical systems (except Charvaka's).

With the exception of Vedanta philosophy, the rest of the six are dated by some scholars as belonging to the period after Buddha and a couple of centuries before Christ. Excluding the Buddhists, Indians generally have been remarkably negligent of record-keeping, and thus lacked a sense of history and the capacity to come to grips with reality, and be inventive and innovative. Vedanta and Yoga are the most important systems that have shaped subsequent Indian thought and to a much lesser extent the Sankhya. The remaining three hardly had any impact.

NYAYA PHILOSOPHY

Gotama or Gautama the founder of the Nyaya School laid down a procedure of arriving at the knowledge of oneself and the universe, the ultimate aim of which, he said, was the liberation of one's soul from bondage and suffering. This procedure has four parts: 1) epistemology of the process and grounds of knowledge, 2) knowledge of the physical universe, 3) of the individual soul and the means of its liberation, and 4) of God.

The means of knowledge are: 1) perception (*pratyaksha*), 2) inference (*anumana*), 3) comparison (*upamana*), and 4) testimony (*shabda*).

The objects of knowledge to be studied and understood are divided into 12 parts: 1) soul (*atma*), 2) body (*sharira*), 3) five senses (*indriyas*), 4) what they relate to (*artha*), 5) process of cognition (*buddhi*), 6) mind as the seat of perception (*manas*), 7) activity (*pravritti*), both positive and negative, in its three forms, mental, vocal and physical, 8) problems of mind (*dosha*, literally defect), 9) rebirth caused by good and bad actions (*punarjanma*), 10) experience of emotions caused by mental and physical activity (*phala*), 11) suffering (*duhkha*), and 12) liberation from suffering (*apavarga*).

Gautama (not to be confused with Gautama the Buddha) bases his philosophy on logical realism up to some extent and lays down a systematic way of looking at things. The nature of the mind is probed into. Realism means that objects exist independently of the mind, although ideas and feelings relative to them rise and fall variously in different minds. The Nyaya philosophy emphasizes a critical perception and logical reflection rather than faith, scriptural testimony or intuition, while acknowledging the need for testimony. The highest goal is liberation of soul through the knowledge of reality, both in their material and spiritual aspects. However, Gautama dangles reality, like his peers, for whatever it might mean to the individual's perception.

The first step is to differentiate between valid and invalid knowledge, such as the sun being stationary and the earth going around it, rather than the sight of the sun's movement around the earth. So also with other valid and invalid modes of perception, such as apprehension causing the sight of a rope appearing as a snake but, by dominating fear, on a closer scrutiny it turns out to be only a rope. In a more complex way, it is one's prejudice that distorts the perception of the qualities of a man, leading to an invalid opinion, but an impartial observation of his actions enables the definition of his character, leading to valid knowledge.

Perception is both ordinary (*laukika*) and extraordinary (*alaukika*), such as through the senses of an object, and awareness of a transcendental force in a state of meditation, imbuing the mind with profound peace. Nyaya (as also Vaisheshika) speaks of the six organs of knowledge, namely, the five senses (external) and the mind (internal). The mind perceives by cognition, desire, aversion, will and the experience of pleasure and pain. It is atomic (subtle) in nature and not made of gross elements like the sense-organs, but works as a coordinating instrument of every type of perception.

Alaukika perception is of three kinds. The first is the universal bearing of the characterisation of masculine and feminine traits, for example, present in different men and women, or an individual's desire to be treated fairly, irrespective of social background and habit. The second is an overall perception in combination of various qualities of an object, such as the hardness of a burning piece of sandalwood, its heat, fragrance, colour and the pleasant sensation its smoke creates in a room, a perception that is possible only through an approximation to what is pleasant, as opposed to an unpleasant feeling generated by a foul-smelling smoke from a piece of dung. The third is the intuitive perception of a reality in a highly-evolved mind with a limitless range as to the meaning of life, of God, of truth and love. This intuitive vision is a result of a prolonged logical search in deep thinking.

OTHER MEANS OF KNOWLEDGE

Inference (*anumana*) is relating a plausible knowledge to an already-existing knowledge, such as one's mortality, that one day one would surely die, is related to the knowledge that all living beings die. Relating cause and effect both ways is the role of *anumana*. Nyaya philosophy sets down an elaborate discipline of logic to arrive at valid inference.

After perception and inference, the third way of deriving knowledge is by comparison (*upamana*) based on a given description of an object or quality for the perception of another object or quality. One who has never seen a violoncello, for example, will have no problem imagining what it may look like by being told that it is a very large violin with a deeper sound. The knowledge of the quality of love is arrived at by comparing the dimension of understanding, support, confidence and deed that love denotes between two persons.

The fourth base of knowledge is by the acceptance of a testimony (*shabda*, literally spoken word) of someone who has a greater access to knowledge. A student of physics, for example, accepts the testimony of a scientist that two atoms of hydrogen and one of oxygen are the constituent of water, even though the atoms are invisible to the eye. On the basis of such a testimony the student then investigates more about the nature of water, such as heavy or light, hard or soft, of what kind of minerals it contains, etc.

Testimony has three premises : 1) trust, such as in the word of the engineer who has built the room one is sitting in that its roof would not collapse over one's head, 2) understanding well what is read in a scripture, and 3) by applying a teaching in one's life to know if it is valid for oneself or not. Nyaya philosophy divides testimony into two kinds: 1) *laukika* or secular, such as of a witness in a law court, and 2) *vaidika* or divinely-inspired statements in the Vedas, in which all the six systems put their trust rather naively, while emphasizing the importance of their correct interpretation, as do indeed the followers of the Old and New Testaments.

The Nyaya system views the universe as a composition of four elements, namely, earth, water, fire and air, and three subtle substances, *akasha* or ether, *kala* or time, and *dik* or space, which are speculated as infinite and eternal. Souls are, however, of a non-material kind and deathless. In a state of embodiment, they are subject to desire, will, likes and dislikes, pleasure and pain. Souls are infinite numerically and ubiquitous. They are different from the body and mind, although giving life to them. In a disembodied state a soul has no consciousness, but regains consciousness through reincarnation and once again becomes subject to desire and feeling. When it attains its final release, it becomes a pure substance.

The purpose of life is the liberation of soul from the cycle of birth and death, a common and rather doleful litany in all the six systems. This is done through the knowledge of various truths that are relevant to life as enunciated in the scriptures.

This knowledge is acquired by their study (*shravana*, literally hearing), reasoning as to their significance (*manana*) and deep meditation (*nididhyasana*). The *Nyaya Sutras* of Gautama refers to God as the original cause of creation, sustenance and dissolution of the universe. Its attitude is quite theistic, in the sense that all events have a bearing to the will of God who is full of compassion, but it fails to explain why he does not alleviate the suffering caused by those not following his moral order in spite of being merciful, nor his unwillingness to control their actions conducing it.

Creation is made of eternally-existing material atoms in their subtle, invisible form, in conjunction with space, time, ether, minds as atomic particles of intelligence, and souls. God is the prime ruler of everything who sets down the order of interaction of the constituent elements in the universe, including souls in their state of involution. The subsequent liberation of souls is achieved by following the divinely-inspired teachings in the Vedas and striving for perfection by doing appropriate karmas, while going through a series of reincarnation. Such is the bottom line of Nyaya philosophy.

VAISHESHIKA PHILOSOPHY

The goal of Vaisheshika philosophy, the liberation of soul or the inner consciousness from bondage, is the same as that of the Nyaya system. Like the founders of the other systems, little is known about Kanada other than that he was an ascetic and was also called Uluka. His work *Vaisheshika Sutras* is divided into 10 chapters, each consisting of two sections. This philosophy has served as a source of rumination of some other Indian philosophers as well.

In this system, epistemology or the grounds and process of arriving at knowledge is divided into seven categories: 1) substance (*dravya*), 2) quality (*guna*), 3) action (*karma*),

4) generality (*samanya*), 5) particularity (*vishesha*), 6) inherence (*samavaya*), and 7) absence of being (*abhava*).

Substance is the foundation of all knowledge. Similar to the Nyaya system, it is subdivided into nine elements: 1) earth, 2) water, 3) fire, 4) air, 5) ether, 6) time, 7) space, 8) soul and 9) mind. The first five are physical, each characterised by one or more particular qualities perceived by one or more of the five senses, inclusive of ether, which is said to be perceived by sound (when it interacts on air).

The first four elements have two aspects, gross and subtle, the former consisting of visible parts and the latter of indivisible atoms, the former destructible and, therefore, temporary and the latter not and, thus, eternal. Ether has no parts and, therefore, has only the atomic, eternal aspect. Space and time are similar and perceived by inference, such as here and there, near and far, and of past, present and future, respectively. All the three are all-pervasive unlike earth, water, fire and air.

The soul is an eternal substance and is the basis of consciousness, giving light to the mind. It is of two kinds, individual (*jivatma*) and supreme (*paramatma*), the former numerous and the latter one alone and transcendental, the former going through a series of reincarnation and the latter not being the creator of the universe, but unlike the Vedantic perception they are not the same in essence. Both are all-pervasive, the former mentally perceived in various states of consciousness and the latter inferred as the original cause of everything. The mind is composed of subtle atomic particles and, therefore, cannot be perceived through the senses but its existence is inferred through the internal phenomena of feeling, thinking and willing, and the co-ordination of what is perceived externally in the shape of ideas.

The universe is created by the supreme soul out of the atomic particles of the nine above-mentioned elements. As the atoms have no independent consciousness of their own, their interaction and direction are subject to the ultimate intelligence of *paramatma* or God, out of which evolve the laws of the universe and of action and reaction.

CATEGORICAL IMPERATIVES

Perception is qualitative, and all elemental relativities in order to be cognitive are perforce subject to qualitative experience. Thus, Kanada categorises them (therefore the name *vaisheshika* or categorical imperatives) into 24 kinds, namely: colour (*rupa*,), taste (*rasa*), smell (*gandha*), touch (*sparsha*), sound (*shabda*), number (*sankhya*), magnitude (*parimana*), distinctness (*prithaktwa*), conjunction (*samyoga*), disjunction (*vibhaga*), remoteness (*paratwa*), nearness (*aparatwa*), intelligence (*buddhi*), pleasure (*sukha*), pain (*duhkha*), desire (*ichchha*), aversion (*dwesha*), effort (*prayatna*), heaviness (*gurutwa*), fluidity (*dravatwa*), affection (*sneha*), tendency (*samskara*), merit (*dharma*), and demerit (*adharma*). These qualities can again be subdivided *ad infinitum*, such as different kinds of meritorious and unmeritorious actions propelled by various tendencies, or sounds grouped into that of musical instruments, and of consonants and vowels such as in a mantra.

Actions denote movement, and movement is in relationship. They take place in the following manner. Innate instincts surge from the unconscious into the subconscious and form as desires according to the orientation through external stimuli, then get a focus by conscious volition or willing, which in turn leads to physical deeds. Thus, one may observe the flow of instincts and desires, and by meditation on higher ideals sublimate and reorient them into more positive actions, leading to reformation of character.

Vaisheshika philosophy searches for the universal nature of human experience within the distinctive forms of individual perception and action. All parts, while being different, are interrelated, the running thread of the whole uniting the particularities of existence, like the universal need for love and protection permeating all sorts of characters, both good and bad.

Whereas all the elemental forms of substance, including the qualities of nature, constitute the nature of being, Kanada recognises the reality of non-being or void and goes through a process of differentiating the nature of existence and non-existence.

In spite of the atomic constitution of the universe, its coming into form and dissolving into the formless, this philosophy upholds an eternal moral order dispensed by the supreme being, and does not recognise the blind force of nature. The universe is ultimately governed by the transcendental wisdom of this Godhead, with sufficient autonomy of self-expression of innumerable souls inhabiting it, both in positive and negative ways, and thus determining the fate of humanity.

The Vaisheshika system gives a theistic view of life, believing in a supreme intelligence while taking into account a realistic perception of the elemental universe, out of which human nature is born and in which the individual soul is trapped. The idea of God is basically transcendental and separate from souls and also the atomic universe they inhabit, although all is dependent on and governed by this supreme, unknowable being.

SANKHYA PHILOSOPHY

The Sankhya system may be characterised as dualistic realism. The eternal plurality of souls may have given it the name *sankhya* (numbers). It has deep roots in the Vedas from which its founder Kapila drew his inspiration. However, he did not uphold the existence of God, probably like Buddha thinking that it cannot be proved. A larger version of the *Sankhya Sutras* is believed to be lost, as also the commentaries of Kapila's two succeeding disciples. However, several expositions of his teachings have been written. Like the Nyaya and Vaisheshika, Sankhya philosophy seeks to liberate the individual soul from bondage and consequent suffering. Through a process of metaphysical enumeration (*sankhya*), it seeks to know the two ultimate realities, namely, spirit and matter, or *purusha* and *prakriti*, which exist eternally independent of each other, although the original interaction of *purusha* on *prakriti* enabled the latter's manifestation.

Purusha as the transcendental spirit resides as pure consciousness in the body, mind and the senses, which are products of *prakriti*, whilst being different from them. *Prakriti* is the ultimate material force and cause of the universe which is constantly changing, unlike the unchanging, perceiving, luminous spirit.

The three main qualities (*gunas*) governing the primal force of nature are positive or cohesive vibration of upliftment and balance (*sattwa*), positive-negative or cohesive-decohesive dynamism or movement of energy (*rajas*), and negative or decaying, static heaviness of inertia (*tamas*). Like three intertwined chords in a rope, they exist in everything in creation, one more vibrant or dormant than the other, and interacting in various degrees on each other. All material objects are products of these three *gunas,* and life goes through their experience in a state of happiness and fulfilment, by the sensation of pleasure and pain, and the lassitude of indifference and avoidance of responsibility.

Cause and effect cannot be separated, as it is evident that a manifest effect such as oil is already inherent in the seed, its cause, both being identical. As such, the material universe cannot have a spiritual cause, but a subtle source of unmanifest matter (slumbering *prakriti*), when the three *gunas* existed in a state of fusion. The starting point of the universe was in the conjunction of the transcendental spirit and the original, unmanifest atom (matter) which erupted in the formation of the universe.

COMPOSITION OF THE UNIVERSE

This conjunction gave birth to *mahat* (literally the great) or cosmic mind as the driving force behind *prakriti*, awakening it from its primordial slumber. However, *mahat* is not *purusha*. As numerous souls (*purushas*) pulsated in the universe in a state of embodiment, *mahat* reflected in individual consciousness as *buddhi* or intellect. Out of *buddhi* arose the sense of being or the ego (*ahamkara*), echoing Descartes, as it were, "by beginning to think I became aware of being something." Thus surged the feelings (*abhimana*) of what I am and what is mine.

The pulsation of the I created the five organs of knowledge (*gyana-indriyas*), the five organs of action (*karma-indriyas*) and the mind (*manas*). From *ahamkara* also rose the five subtle potentialities of perception (*tanmatras*), namely, sound, touch, colour, taste and smell, and their five elemental counterparts, namely, ether, air, fire, water and earth (*pancha-bhutas*), respectively. Thus, along with and rising from *prakriti*, the seven principles of *mahat* (inclusive of *buddhi*), *ahamkara* and five *tanmatras*, their five material counterparts (*pancha-bhutas*), the five organs of knowledge, the five organs of action, and the mind constitute the components of the entire creation.

It must be remembered that nearly 2,500 years ago there were no scientific instruments to measure the particles in creation. Kapila, along with the other sages of his time, could only observe externally and internally the nature of existence. Together with Kanada, Kapila's perception and categorisation of the attributes, each doing so in his own way, seem to be remarkable. There was no knowledge of psychology in their time as we now understand the mind to function, but a deep insight is reflected on human nature in the great works of the *Mahabharata*, the *Ramayana*, the *Puranas* and the *Panchatantra*.

However, the *purusha* is different and unaffected by all the attributes of *prakriti*, although ultimately giving light and life to them to function. As in Vedanta philosophy, it is the eternal, infinite spirit within the multiplicity of pure consciousness, behind the vehicles such as the ego, the mind, the senses, which are all components of the elemental universe. Happiness and sorrow, pleasure and pain, success and failure, do not affect the soul but belong to the mind and the body. Freedom from suffering lies in one's capacity, through deep meditation and purification of the ego, to distinguish the *purusha* within one's material vehicle.

Classical Sankhya discounts one, central and supreme *purusha* as God to create and guide the universe, although along with the slumbering *prakriti*, *purusha* existed before their interaction as neither one nor many. The dualistic realism of Sankhya comes out of the observation of the play of material consciousness in one's mind, propelled by the ego, and also the elemental consciousness in nature, whilst yet trying to be aware of an unaffected and distinctive spiritual consciousness as a reality (*purusha*) within oneself.

Prakriti and *purusha* are both eternal principles, each being an ultimate cause in itself. In its multiple facets, *prakriti* is constantly changing, whereas *purusha* in its infinite plurality is unchanging and unaffected as pure consciousness. The goal of life is to rise above the bondage of *prakriti* by being aware of the pure, eternally-free consciousness of *purusha*.

YOGA PHILOSOPHY

More than any other, the Yoga system of Patanjali is widely known in the West and in India, but the difference is that in the western countries its physical aspect has a greater appeal such as through *asana* and *pranayama*, and in India a yogi is regarded to be one who has mastery over his or her mind, as well as the body, but above all whose goal is a spiritual union (yoga) with *Ishwara* or God through deep meditation.

In a way Patanjali can be regarded as the ancient father of psychology, because in no other earlier literature of its kind and not until 2,000 years later in the West, the nature of the mind has been probed into as in his *Yoga Sutras*. The primary objective of his system is mind-control. As in Sankhya, the inner self is a free spirit within the gross body with a mind that veils its pure consciousness, but unlike Kapila, Patanjali speaks of the union of the individual soul with God as the highest goal of life.

The understanding of the nature of the mind is closely related to the Sankhya system. The *chitta* or the inner mind is composed of the three primordial qualities of nature, namely, *sattwa*, *rajas* and *tamas* (their definition is given earlier under Sankhya philosophy), and one's mental state depends on the preponderance of one or the other of these qualities. With *tamas* prevailing it is lethargic, depressive, dull and negative; with *rajas* it is restless, passionate, ambitious and full of desires; and with *sattwa* it is one-pointed, harmonious, clear-headed and positively disposed.

The five causes of mental suffering, namely, ignorance, egoism, desire, aversion and fear, are described and the methods to overcome them through meditation given. The nature of right and wrong perception is differentiated, as also the states of waking, dreaming and deep sleep, and the conscious, subconscious and unconscious layers of the mind described.

Patanjali was probably the first teacher after Buddha and before Christ, the period he was likely to have lived in northern India, and one of the rare ones ever since or before, who taught that the best way to overcome a negative emotion such as hate is by meditating on its counterpart, love, and applying its positive force in relationship. This he called *pratipaksha-bhavana* or counterposing of attitude. It is not enough to know what one should not do, but after having taken into account what one should not do, it is important to get out of the circle of the "don'ts" and apply oneself to doing what one ought to. It is only thereby that the negative "muscles" of the mind, as it were, can be atrophied by not paying attention to and thus not using them, and, instead, by using the unrepressed mental energies in the practice of spiritual ideals the positive "muscles" can be strengthened.

Patanjali did not call his system a philosophy, although later on it was incorporated into the *shad-darshana* or six systems of philosophy. It was called *ashtanga-yoga* or eightfold yoga (*ashta* eight, *anga* limb) or a way of life to attain spiritual union (*yoga*). To him *darshana* or philosophy did not mean a mental vision, as the term implies, or an intellectual pursuit as generally is the case with western philosophers, Spinoza being an exception, but a pursuit of self-knowledge for self-perfection.

FOUNDATION OF YOGA

Being a spiritual philosopher, Patanjali laid down five ethical disciplines (*yamas*) and five rules to observe (*niyamas*) to start with, because he recognised that moral principles constituted the foundation of any useful or a decent way of living. Practice of self-restraint is basic to any civilised manner of living. So, he emphasised the restraint of: 1) aggressive impulses (*ahimsa*) conducing to an understanding, if not loving, relationship with one another and, thus, refraining from any form of injury; 2) of untruth to promote security through integrity and also peace of mind (*satya*); 3) of lustful urges to deepen sentiment and create a spiritual sense of belonging (*brahmacharya*); 4) of selfishness to uphold fairness and the ethics of not depriving others of what belongs to them (*asteya*);

and 5) of covetousness indicating that one has no right to desire what one is not willing to work for or does not have the talent to achieve (*aparigraha*). These he called the basic *yamas*.

The *niyamas* are the rules: 1) to keep the body and mind clean (*saucha*) because cleanliness, both physical and mental, is indeed next to godliness; 2) to practise the ideal of being content after having done one's duty and accept a situation that cannot be changed after trying one's best to change it (*santosha*); 3) to strengthen the body and develop will power through physical and mental endurance (*tapas*); 4) to educate oneself by study and learning the lessons of life from experience (*swadhyaya*); and 5) to dedicate oneself to God or be committed to spiritual ideals (*Ishwara-pranidhana*).

After taking care of the moral high ground, Patanjali asks us to prepare the body for the practice of meditation. This is done through steadiness of posture (*asana*) and can be extended to a more adequate form of Hatha Yoga, although he does not say so, for keeping the body healthy and free from tension. To prepare the mind for meditation he asks us to practise *pranayama*, because the state of mind and breath is closely related, so that instead of an agitated mind making the breath irregular, by regulating the breath one learns to steady the mind.

Then follows the three steps of meditation: 1) by withdrawing the senses from external objects and the mind from their memory through methods of abstraction (*pratyahara*); 2) by concentration on a fixed point, externally or internally or both, such as by gazing on a symbol with eyes open and visualising it mentally with eyes closed (*dharana*); and 3) by contemplation on the ideal of one's spiritual unity with the help of a phrase or a mantra such as "I am one with thee" or Soham (*dhyana*).

When the *chitta* or the inner mind is purified through meditative exercises and a level of *sattwa* or harmonious equilibrium in it is attained, one is prepared for *samadhi* or experiencing elevated degrees of oneness with God, the highest kind, *nirvikalpa*, being in a state of total freedom from all the lower levels of consciousness, including a temporary dissolution of the I.

To Patanjali God is the supreme being, eternal and all-pervasive, omnipotent and omniscient. Devotion to God, in whatever way one might seek him, is the highest means of meditation, and through which the heart is purified and the intellect enlightened. By recognising the deep-seated need for protection from a higher power and providing a methodical system of practising moral ideals and exercises of meditation, Patanjali made his *ashtanga-yoga* more appealing and applicable in daily life than the Sankhya and some other systems. That, indeed, is the reason for his popularity.

MIMAMSA PHILOSOPHY

Of the six schools, Jaimini's Mimamsa is probably the least known, except possibly in the Brahminical or priestly circles. Its purpose was to justify Vedic rituals and explain their significance through a philosophy of life revolving around religious duties. Curiously enough, Jaimini does not see the need for a central Godhead from whom the creation is supposed to originate. Matter is believed to be eternal, although constantly undergoing transformation, and subject to a spontaneous and autonomous moral order, as also an infinite number of souls involved in it and passing through a series of reincarnation according to their desires translated into karmas (actions).

Ṛitualistic and ethical duties, as enjoined by the Vedas, are to be observed not so much for heavenly rewards but for the sake of duty (*dharma*). There are many planes of existence, the higher or heavenly ones and the lower ones as well. According to some interpreter, the Vedic deities oblated to in the rituals are not persons but states of consciousness to which one tries to relate by the performance of rites, to purify the mind and free it from suffering. Rituals also conduce self-control and a sense of obligation to society to uphold a collective moral order, as directed by the Vedic scriptures.

In the absence of God, spiritual ideals take the form of *devas* or luminous beings inhabiting the heavens where the liberated souls migrate eventually after death, and do not have to reincarnate again in the lower planes such as this earth. On the foundation of Jaimini's *Mimamsa Sutras,* other commentators developed their own theories, such as the soul having no active consciousness by itself but only in a state of embodiment, and that liberation is an ultimate oblivion or transcendence of consciousness, rather than the experience of heavenly bliss.

The word *mimamsa* means solution of a philosophical problem through reflection, although not much evidence of it is found in this system. It is divided into three sections: theory of knowledge, metaphysics, and ethics and theology.

Knowledge is of two kinds, perceptual and non-perceptual. An object is perceived through the senses and the mind interprets its nature in the light of a relevant, past knowledge. Non-perceptual knowledge is dependent on faith in what one wants to believe in, to motivate life. Such knowledge is obtained from the testimony of the Vedas, although Jaimini does so selectively.

There are two types of testimony, personal and impersonal. Life basically functions on personal faith in relationship, because no one can be peaceful by being suspicious of everyone else. Such a faith is of course subject to the experience of trustworthiness in a relationship. Similarly, faith in scriptural injunction is a product of its application in practical life and experiencing its beneficial effect psychologically, such as through inner strength and peace.

The Mimamsa metaphysics believes in the immortality of soul, either involved or disinvolved, and in an eternally-existing universe composed of numerous worlds, heavenly as well as hellish, swarming with concomitant denizens. Although performance of duty for duty's sake is emphasized, one cannot escape the feeling that rituals are a means to upward mobility through transmigration and avoidance of suffering, apart from their socially-cohesive benefit. But rituals alone are not enough without obeying the guidelines of the law of karma.

Thus, Mimamsa metaphysics is both pluralistic and realistic, while not being entirely empirical due to its belief in what the Vedas say in comforting the human heart by heavenly hopes. It recognises the potential energy trapped in *bhuta* (matter) and *shabda* (sound of word), and the possibility of untapping it by burning the sacred fire and chanting of mantras, which are a part of the Vedic rites, to create a psychic effect and hopefully help in the soul's transmigration.

Theology in Mimamsa is interrelated with ethics. *Dharma* is both a religion in the name of performing rituals enjoined by the Vedas as well as a righteous life led by their criteria as to what is right and wrong. The highest good consists in the control of passions and refraining from harming others. Some interpreters contend that the heavenly deities are not worshipped but the moral and spiritual *shakti* (force) attributed to them is made a part of one's life by the psychic power of rites. The main good that came out of Mimamsa philosophy is that since people love ceremonies they ought to know more about what the rites stand for.

VEDANTA PHILOSOPHY

As the name implies, Vedanta philosophy is derived from the concluding part (*anta*, end) of the Vedas, consisting of the Upanishads, written about a thousand years before Christ. Badarayana (also known as Krishna Dwaipayana) Vyasa interpreted their teachings in his *Brahma Sutras*. He was said to have lived during that time and was the author of the *Bhagavad Gita* as well. Of all the six systems and even more than the Ashtanga (later known as Raja) Yoga of Patanjali, Vedanta has influenced Indian thinking all-pervasively, unbeknownst to the average person. It not only laid down the basis of Gyana Yoga but provided the inspiration to Bhakti Yoga and Karma Yoga as well. Other than Vyasa, its chief interpreters were Shankara and Ramanuja.

In the history of civilisation no other philosophy has expressed such a positive, unifying spirit of reconciliation. The tolerant attitude to other people's faiths in Hinduism is directly due to Vedantic teachings. By the philosophy of *monism*, making God a transcendental and all-pervasive spirit, rather than a singular, all-important and the only valid deity as in *monotheism*, it took away the inherent sting of intolerance and iconoclasm.

As in most religions and philosophies, their interpreters transplanting their own ideas through the centuries, Vedanta has been understood in different ways, even negatively by hypocritically making the world an illusion. However, its immensely broad vision can be perceived in the following way

VISION OF GOD

1) Brahman or the supreme being is not a deity or a substance that can be confined within a conceptual image, even by the term 'one alone' but an all-pervasive spiritual presence while being transcendental. Thus, polytheistic differences were submerged by the philosophy that what people call God is but a spiritual vision of the individual's devotion, sacred love and holy aspiration. They come into shape in the process of trying to relate to the transcendental spirit. That is why it is said in the *Bhagavad Gita* that God comes to the devotee in the form one seeks him. The *Kena Upanishad* points out that all the

elemental forces of nature *(devas)* have no powers of their own but are able to function only on account of the supreme spirit.

2) Even though God cannot be defined, the human spirit can relate to the indefinable through spiritual ideals but qualified by the adjectives: a) infinite, to expand them constantly; b) eternal, to make them long lasting; c) universal, to have their relevancy among all, irrespective of religious and cultural backgrounds; and d) transcendental, in order to realise them better ever more.

3) The mantra *Ishavasyam idam sarvam* in the *Isha Upanishad*, that the infinite spirit pervades all that which moves and moves not, created for the first time in human consciousness a sense of sanctity for all forms of life, not only for the humankind, and not merely limited to one's own tribes, but respect for the animals and nature as well, which has only recently penetrated western consciousness through the institutions for the prevention of cruelty against animals (even if they are eaten to satisfy greed!) and ecological responsibility.

4) In the three monotheistic religions, Judaism, Christianity and Islam, God is the transcendental creator, but in the Vedanta philosophy Brahman or the supreme spirit, while being transcendental is immanent in the universe, which can be defined in its five levels of manifestation as

a) *Anu-spandana* (vibration of atom or energy), holding together and disintegrating matter.

b) Cyclical rhythm (*ritu*) of life in the birth of a plant, its growth as a tree, its seeding process, decaying and death, and continuing the cycle again through the seed.

c) Instinctive mind (*chitta*) in the animal plane, and also in the neutral laws of nature (*prakriti*) making evolution possible.

d) Discerning intelligence (*viveka*) on the human level creating a sense of right and wrong and the karmic laws of cause and effect.

e) Intuitive soul-consciousness (*atma-gyana*) which ultimately dawns in a highly-evolved mind, such as in a state of superconsciousness (*samadhi*).

RECONCILIATION AND UNITY

This vision of God's immanence shaped some basic philosophical positions in the following way:

1) Vedanta sought to reconcile religious antagonism by the epigraphic comparison of various faiths in search of God as vapours rising from the ocean and becoming clouds, and by coming into contact with the mountains forming as streams and joining together as rivers, then flowing through different lands and acquiring their characteristics, but ultimately merging into the same ocean from where they sprung. Thus, in spite of religious differences and cultural habits, humanity's origin and destiny are the same. Or, the simile of a multihued garland of flowers, each one different, but a common, running thread of the universal spirit holistically uniting them.

2) Echoing the epigraph in the Old Testament, of the human being created in the image of God, Vedanta speaks of the identity of the transcendental spirit as the essence of the individual soul, like a spark of light being identical with the sun or a drop of water with the ocean. Thus, all members of humanity having a common spiritual heritage should try to rise above religious dogmatism and extend the law "thou shalt not kill" beyond their tribal and national groups and live without warfare.

3) The light of God is equally luminous within every soul but expressed in different degrees of brightness or dullness through one's conscience due to the opacity or impurity of the *koshas* (sheaths), such as the various layers of the mind that

cover it. Uncovering that light within and its expression through truth and love in relationship is the goal of us all.

4) No one should be coerced into following a dictated path of faith, but each should grow according to the law of one's own evolution as per personal inspiration, choice and effort. Just as there are many paths leading to the summit of a mountain, the role of the teachers is only to show them and provide the expertise of their own experience, but it is the individual who has to do the climbing and arriving at the peak of God-realisation.

5) The ultimate goal is the merger of the individual soul in the infinite spirit. It means the dissolution of the individuality of consciousness but not the disappearance of its essence. This is illustrated by the simile of a doll made up of salt who wanted to know where it came from and, thus, entering the ocean began to swim in search of its identity. The more it swam the less became its form, which finally disappeared but not its essence which became one with its origin, the ocean.

CONCLUSION

Such is the unique spirit of Vedanta. Its mystical vision of God is given in the words *sat-chit-ananda*, reflecting our longing for the reality of truth (*sat*), its comprehension (*chit*) and realisation as supreme love (*ananda*). Thus, God is ultimately transcendental truth and supreme love.

Vedanta does not emphasise *maya* or the illusory nature of the universe, although some commentators do, but speaks of how the mind can fool itself by its craving and attachment, and forget the inner reality behind what appears to be, such as happiness being in the possession of material wealth and experience of sensual pleasure, rather than within oneself and in one's relationship with others. Happiness is, indeed, in a state of harmony acquired through the fulfilment of spiritual ideals. Understanding of *maya* also means that the solid reality of the earth should not obscure the subtle reality of the infinite, invisible atoms giving form to it.

The theory of *maya* is intimately related to the temporary nature of life's experiences. No infatuation or sorrow lasts forever. The more the mind conjures up its fantasies in a relationship, the greater the disillusionment. Not to be carried away by wishful thinking and passions that the flesh is heir to, not to suffer unnecessarily on account of injured vanity, not to be swayed by pride and prejudice, to be balanced in success and failure, is what the theory of *maya* tries to teach.

The running thread of unity, *adwaita* or non-duality, is emphasized in recognition of bickering selfishness in human nature and its aggressiveness causing so much division and suffering. *Adwaita* does not intend to create a dull uniformity of perception or disregard the fact that it is the interaction within multiplicity that makes progress possible. To understand Vedanta one should seek the overall picture that emerges out of the various Upanishads, rather than get bogged down in Shankara's Advaita Vedanta.

The relevancy of any philosophy is to make the journey through life more agreeable, meaningful, creative, enlightening and fulfilling. The urge to look up to an ideal, a role model, is fundamental to evolution, and the vision of God is the highest point of reference to trace our upward identity. This has been expressed in a surpassing, universal spirit in the Vedanta system. In spite of its various unprovable speculations portraying the peculiarities of human imagination and psychological need, the basic projections of its teachings were astonishingly far-sighted and are as valid today, or even more so, than they were some three thousand years ago.

Chapter Twenty

THOUGHTS FOR THE MONTH

The following sayings were compiled from various sources, many of them from the class-talks of Swami Shivapremanandaji, founder-president of the Sivananda Yoga-Vedanta Centre of Argentina in Buenos Aires.

PRACTICAL SPIRITUALITY

All the preoccupation about God is actually preoccupation about one's own security.

Lifc is what you make with it, worthwhile or a mess!

It is not so much important when one is born or when one dies, but what is done in between.

Remembrance aside, grieve not for one who is dead, but care for those who are left behind if they need you.

To live in the hearts of those who love you is to continue living after you are gone.

What more immortality may one seek than in deeds well done, in a life well lived, in relationships well nourished, after one is gone?

Humanity is the greatest of all virtues. It is a mixture of the understanding of and unselfish feelings for others, with matching deeds.

Devotion to truth is the highest form of adoration of God.

The best thing you can say to yourself before going to sleep is: I have not been unjust, I have not hurt others, I have not lied, I have done my duty.

The moment you think or say that you are loving someone so much, immediately ask yourself what you are doing for him or her.

If you are not capable of doing something you wish to, do something that you can.

The longest journey is the journey inward.

A wise man said: I have never met a person who has given me so much trouble as myself.

It is not so much that in the height of achievement or in the accompanying benefit you succeed, but in doing the best in whatever you are capable of doing.

Nothing speaks better than action, specially when it is done before being urged.

Without a sense of humour life becomes heavier than it ought to be. The best form of it is laughing at yourself, and the worst is at the expense of others.

Selfishness, arrogance, vanity, deviousness and intolerance are the five most effective means of making yourself detested.

The more you try to pretend the less you are likely to get away with it.

Learn to count your blessings before complaining about what you lack.

The merit of the sense of individuality is not to impose it on others.

Everything new gives a new life under the sun. Do not lose the sense of curiosity.

You start aging psychologically when you begin to lose the sense of curiosity and become indifferent.

Indifference, unless the situation demands it, is not only unjust to others but deepens your ignorance.

There must be willing effort in order to achieve anything, and also the willingness to innovate, improvise and initiate new moves, and take calculated risks.

If you let the first opportunity go by, the second one may be too late or inadequate. By making use of several small opportunities, you may achieve more than by waiting for a big one to come along. Get hold of the first opportunity that comes by.

THOUGHTS FOR THE MONTH II

The following sayings were compiled from various sources, many of them from the class-talks of Swami Shivapremanandaji, president and rector of the Sivananda Yoga-Vedanta Centre of Uruguay in Montevideo.

DO THE BEST YOU CAN

Frustration is the mother of evolution, but only when you do something about it.

Nine times out of ten we are disappointed in life because we do not ask enough of ourselves.

Do the best you can with what you have rather than indulging in pious intentions under better circumstances.

You can project only what you have been and what you are doing or cultivating now. By wishful thinking nothing is achieved.

Never ask others what you are not willing to do yourself. Standing on dignity makes a poor footing. Dignity is in how you conduct yourself in the lowliest of work.

A good scavenger looks more dignified in doing his work naturally than trying to be dignified.

You cannot see eye to eye with someone if you are looking down on him or her.

Ultimately it is human qualities that make the difference between success and failure as a human being.

There are three skills: technical, managerial and conceptual. In the last two, human qualities play a great role.

The identification of talent, the kindling of motivation and improvement of relationship in the institutions of society for productive effort constitute a major part in governing.

To understand human nature is to work with human beings, not just files, blueprints and statistics.

Human beings are full of likes and dislikes, and secret resentments. It is very difficult to be objective, but without objectivity you cannot be fair to others.

The most successful people are not those who burn the midnight oil themselves, but those who are able to guide and inspire others to work in team spirit and team effort. One who is able to arouse enthusiasm is the one headed for leadership.

If you do not have integrity, you can never guide or inspire others. A teacher without integrity will not attract respect but contempt.

Honesty once pawned is never redeemed. Once you start cutting corners, you will find that all corners are cuttable.

Once we assuage our conscience by calling something a necessary evil, it begins to look more and more necessary and less and less evil.

Only by being true to yourself can you be true to others.

It is easy to be base, casual, frivolous, cynical and critical. Carping and quibbling are not substitutes for action.

As long as your conduct is straight, you need not bother about being observed and talked about.

Even little courtesies go a long way, like being first to smile, first to greet.

Humanity means not to sacrifice a person for the sake of a purpose.

THOUGHTS FOR THE MONTH III

The following sayings were compiled from various sources, many of them from the class-talks of Swami Shivapremanandaji, founder-president of the Sivananda Yoga-Vedanta Centre of Chile in Santiago.

UNDERSTANDING AND APPRECIATION

Avoid pettiness. Accommodation with and understanding of others are essential in day-to-day relationship. Insisting on having your way all the time shows your insecurity.

One of the deepest urges in human nature is to be appreciated. Give full credit for a work well done, and do so promptly and spontaneously. Be slow to blame.

Nothing kills the incentive of a person as criticism from a superior.

As long as one acts in good faith, he or she should be assured of your support in a team-work.

A character roll is as much a picture of a person writing it as a person written upon.

Only consistency and decisiveness inspire respect and command obedience, not vacillation.

The word of honour is a good thing to cherish, but all important matters should be transacted in writing.

Anger is the wind that blows out the lamp of the mind. Avoid display of emotions. State the facts. Let them speak for themselves.

When you are right, you can afford to keep your temper. When you are wrong, you cannot afford to lose it.

No gem can be polished without friction. So also no virtue can shine without scrubbing the ego.

A person conscious of his or her virtue is not virtuous but self-righteous.

Wounds inflicted by careless words are hard to heal. Do not be rash in what you say under the pressure of circumstances.

Lamenting over something which has gone out of your hand does no good to you or anyone else. Resolve not to make the same mistake again.

Avoid paralysis by analysis. Sometimes there may not even be analysis, just pure paralysis.

What you can do tomorrow, do it today. What you can do today, do it now!

The difficulty is not so much in the choice between good and evil, but in the choice between good and good. So also one has sometimes to choose between evil and evil, but the decision has to be taken. Once having made the choice between the lesser of the two evils, one should endeavour to get out of it.

A Sanskrit saying: It takes a thorn to take out a thorn, but then both the thorns are thrown away.

Trust others, but keep your eyes open.

To manage well you have to delegate responsibility, but do not keep your hands too far away from the controls.

Direction should be with the least show of authority. Firmness should be concealed in politeness.

To be important is a deep human urge. If it is not catered to with supporting qualities to be deserving, you will only make yourself ridiculous!

A good teacher teaches without the least show of teaching.

In a team-work remember that you have to work with the material available, not what you want. Your credit lies in getting the best out of it.

A successful person is the one who can lay a firm character-foundation with the brickbats that others throw at him or her.

THOUGHTS FOR THE MONTH IV

The following sayings were compiled from various sources, many of them from the class-talks of Swami Shivapremanandaji at the Sivananda Yoga-Vedanta Centre of Argentina in Buenos Aires.

RIGHT AND WRONG

One who is sure of oneself lets others be themselves. Trying to impose your will on others is a sign of insecurity.

Listen attentively and respectfully. Encourage those who work with you to speak out, but make sure that they know what they are talking about and that who is in charge.

You should have the capacity to assimilate new information, and apply such knowledge with the best possible judgment of the circumstances.

Be always firm and fair, but also tactful and polite. There is a way to disagree without giving offence or being self-important.

Do not seclude yourself in an ivory tower. Get out and communicate with those you work and live with.

The most difficult relationship is with your superiors, especially when some of them happen to be less intelligent than you. The qualities they are entitled to are loyalty and cooperation. Do not forget that they have risen to where they are because of the qualities such as ambition and will which you do not have in the same measure.

Having one's nose rubbed in the mud helps to dispel illusions and to see things in the correct perspective, as long as one who does so cares for you and is sincere.

One who thinks that he or she already knows what you are saying is generally incapable of focusing attention and filled with a sense of self-importance, which holds the person down to a low level of understanding.

It is your work that will speak for itself, not the certificates apropos that you display.

You can never be happy in a place of work without certain norms of working relationship. It means tact and courtesy, patience and consideration, reliability and understanding.

It is not enough if you do what is needed of you, but it is necessary that your colleague understands what is expected of him or her. Mutual trust, responsibility and accountability are required.

Personal example speaks more convincingly than all exhortation.

You may not be able to do all that you consider to be right, but as long as you are not doing what is wrong you are on the right path.

Rigidity will harm even if you are in the right. Principles are right not because they are principles but the fact of their helping those involved, including you, to be in the right.

Let not right and wrong confuse you. Anyone who is not a hypocrite can know the difference. You have only to ask yourself: Is it only for myself or does it include the good of others? Does it unite or divide? Does it heal or hurt? Is it authentic or deceitful? Will it hold true when the exigencies of the circumstances are gone? Will it speak for itself or have I to do a lot of explaining? Am I sincere or devious? After the heat of the moment will I be ashamed of my deed?

Ultimately, it is the purity of conscience, inspiring steadfast resolve and action, the purity of heart in being free from resentment and desire for vengeance, the humility of spirit to learn and strive that count as blessings of life.

THOUGHTS FOR THE MONTH V

The following sayings were compiled by the Sivananda Yoga-Vedanta Centre of Uruguay in Montevideo.

CHINESE PROVERBS

The higher type of person seeks all that one desires in oneself. The lower type of person seeks all that one desires from others.

Honouring one's debts is the highest principle of honour, not only in monetary dealings, but as to the debt one takes upon in the various stages of life, such as to parents or anyone who has been helpful along the way. Thus, honour is inseparably bound with duty.

If the heart does not break now and then, how would you know that it is there? Hearts break and mend again just as dawn sows the evening and twilight sows the morning.

Great happiness and great unhappiness are one.

You cannot have something without giving. That would be unworthy.

What is life but foolish desires and imperfect choices?

Worldly passions are the thieves of life.

MISCELLANY

The past is never dead. It is not even past. *(Faulkner)*

The separation between past, present and future has only the meaning of an illusion. *(Einstein)*

Man finds an image of himself in the questions he poses, and shows himself more truthfully by the profundity of his questions than by his answers. *(Andre Malraux)*

The history of his soul (in *Confessions* of Rousseau) which he promised us becomes, without his having known it, the legend or the myth of his soul. *(Mercel Raymond)*

There is always a path where no one thought that there was one. *(Euripides)*

Man is but an insignificant dot in the infinite. *(Pascal)*

Man is but a servant of customs, prejudices, self-interest and fanaticism. The bane of man is the illusion that he has the certainty of knowledge. *(Montaigne)*

Truth is a dream, unless my dream is true. *(Santayana)*

What a wee little part of a man's life is in his acts and his words! His real life is led in his head, and is known to none but himself. *(Mark Twain)*

Call no man happy until he is dead. *(Solon)*

Faith in immortality was born of the greed of unsatisfied people who make unwise use of the time that nature has allotted us. For the wise man, one life is sufficient. A stupid man would not know what to do with eternity. *(Epicurus)*

Man is but a foundling in the cosmos, abandoned by the forces that created him. Unparented, unassisted and undirected by the omniscient and benevolent authority, he must fend for himself, and with the aid of his limited intelligence, find his way about in an indifferent universe. *(Carl Becker)*

Only rarely have I paused amid the trivia of living, which make up so much of our existence, and out of which come the setbacks, the triumphs, the sorrows and the rare moments of happiness, to consider how puny and unimportant we all are, how puny in fact is our planet. Even the solar system, of which the earth is a negligible part, is but a dot in the infinite space of the universe. Who can say, then, that the purpose of the universe, if it has a purpose, has been to create man? Who can even say that there are not millions of other planets on which there is some kind of human life, perhaps much further advanced than ours? *(William Shirer)*

THOUGHTS FOR THE MONTH VI

The following sayings were compiled from various sources by the Sivananda Yoga-Vedanta Centre of Chile in Santiago, including some from the class-talks of Swami Shivapremanandaji.

RELIGION AND SIN

From the Judeo-Christian point of view, sin is not of a moral but of a religious nature, defined biblically in terms, not of a behaviour, but of an existential quality, in the sense of a relationship to God.

From the yogic point of view, sin is an error, a deviation from the spiritual path, not from a contractual commandment of a deity. It is we that punish ourselves through our errors, as well as are able to save ourselves from them with the help of the spiritual content of our being.

The Bible is a sacred text, but its prohibitions against riches or public prayers, for example, do not apply directly as exhortations. However, to brand human beings, to snatch away their legal standing, to oppress them with inquisitorial laws, does not reflect a Christian calling.

In the West, morals are understood to be social norms to serve as ligaments of the body politic and the borders of life. They are shaped by the interaction of human necessities and, thus, have a behavioural connotation.

From the yogic point of view, morals are a direct projection of spiritual ideals that flow from our soul, in recognition of each other's soul, and mean much more than social norms, even if they have a behavioural imperative.

The Bible is not a bulwark against changing values, but a reservoir of inspired human experience from religiously heroic ages, the resource amid change for an ultimate and saving reference, the genesis in fact, of our changeability.

FEELINGS

Feelings are not just emotions that come from inside. They are reactions that one chooses to have, even though they may appear to be spontaneous.

One feels that things or people make one unhappy, but this is not accurate. One makes oneself unhappy because of the thoughts one has about people and things.

Since feelings come from thoughts, if one understands and controls one's thoughts, then one is capable of understanding and controlling one's feelings. Feelings are controlled by working on the thoughts that precede them.

The following epitaph is from the tomb of Emperor Hadrian:

My little soul,
charming wanderer,
guest and companion
of my body,
you are leaving now,
and your games with me
and my friends are over.

THOUGHTS FOR THE MONTH VII

Many of the following sayings were adapted by the Sivananda Yoga-Vedanta Centre of Argentina in Buenos Aires, from Leo Reston's 'A Treasury of Jewish Quotations' and some from the class-talks of Swami Shivapremanandaji.

JEWISH QUOTATIONS

God saw that heaven and earth were jealous of each other. So he created man out of the earth, and his soul out of heaven.

Do not be too sure of yourself until the day you die.

Reason serves only in a society which recognises the rights of all.

Passion is a friend of prejudice, not reason.

Passion for truth guarantees dogmatism.

Passion for God guarantees bigotry.

To accept a tradition without examining it with intelligence and judgment is like the blind following others blindly.

No one is as ugly as the person conceited.

When a friend says that the mother and daughter look like sisters, the mother beams, but you should look at the face of the daughter.

It is true that when an old man marries a young woman, he gets young, but it is also likely that the young woman quickly gets old.

At the age of five the child is the master of the parents, at the age of 10 their follower, at 15 their rival, and at 20 their friend or foe, depending on how he or she has been raised or treated.

People deserve the kind of leaders they have. Parents deserve the kind of children they have.

You can tell the nature of a person by how one treats children or subordinates.

It is easy to fool yourself, somewhat difficult to fool your superiors, and most difficult to fool your subordinates.

A basic requirement of a close friendship is, when a doubt arises, to clear it as soon as possible through a sincere and humble dialogue. If such a dialogue is not feasible due to pride or fear on either side, the friendship is not deep enough but circumstantial.

If you keep insisting too long that you are right, you are wrong.

The greatest teaching is to teach how to think.

The greatest help is to teach how to help oneself.

The first step to knowledge is to know that you know very little.

The first virtue is to know that you are not good enough.

The second step to knowledge is, after acquiring it, to apply it.

The second step to virtue is, while practising it, not to show it.

The following sayings are adapted from 'The Book of Abraham' by Mark Halter:

Where there is light, there is shadow. Light can be compared to the soul and shadow to the body.

From the righteous we learn to do good. From the unrighteous we learn to turn away from evil.

He who wishes to be wise, must listen to everyone.

He who wants to be wise must learn something from everyone, for one becomes wise with the help of the examples and instructions received from others.

The Cabala makes the divine human, whereas for the Hassid it is the human that is divine.

The Hassid is saddened by the purity of joy, and he rejoices in the purity of sorrow.

THOUGHTS FOR THE MONTH VIII

The following sayings were compiled from various sources, as indicated, by the Sivananda Yoga-Vedanta Centre of Uruguay in Montevideo.

UNIVERSAL IDEALS

The fault does not lie in our astrological signs but within ourselves, and the remedy is in our hands. *(Indian saying)*

Men are moulded in the furnace of responsibility, and on the anvil of self-reliance. *(Percival Spear)*

In thought faith, in word wisdom, in deed courage, in life service. *(Inscription on the Jaipur pillar in New Delhi)*

Social justice cannot be attained by violence. Violence kills what it intends to create. Society should assure man of his seven basic rights: 1) right to life, 2) to security, 3) to work, 4) to a home, 5) to health, 6) to education, and 7) to religious freedom. *(John Paul II)*

Work expands so as to fill the time available for its completion. Expenditure rises to meet income. Action expands to fill the void created by human failure. *(C.N. Parkinson)*

Far better it is to dare mighty things, to win glorious triumphs, even though checkered by failure, than to take rank with those poor spirits who neither enjoy much, nor suffer much, because they live in the great twilight that neither knows victory, nor defeat. (*Theodor Roosevelt*)

It is not the ministry of culture that you should worry about, but the culture of the minister. *(Anonymous)*

An unjust world raises the question of morality and, in turn, religion. Belief in the goodness of human nature, and projection of mankind's noblest qualities form the basis of religion. God is a unique personal creative entity. Conscience does make Christians. The source of that spark of conscience is God. *(Hans Kueng)*

Although primitive instincts and emotions are the basis of religion, faith actually stems from the sophisticated reasoning process related to a supreme moral and causal agency. *(R. Green)*

It is useless for the sheep to pass resolutions in favour of vegetarianism when the wolf has a different opinion. *(Dean Inge)*

An appeaser is someone who believes that if you throw enough steak to a tiger, the tiger will become a vegetarian. *(Heywood Brown)*

People will ignore an old man sitting on a park bench, but stare intently at a painter's portrait of an old man sitting on a park bench. *(Anonymous)*

ADAM AND EVE AND SIN

The followinq interpretation was adapted from a class-talk by Swami Shivapremanandaji in Montevideo, Uruguay.

The original sin was committed by Adam when his individual soul breathed in by God, became bored with a state of blissful union with the creator. Adam's ego-consciousness felt the need of a companion other than God. So, he asked God for Eve. God obliged him by creating Eve out of his rib.

Eve became a symbol of Adam's mind. His consciousness separated from God-consciousness. He was not content being one with God. He needed duality within himself, to enjoy life apart from God.

The serpent is a symbol of temptation, a necessary stimulant to knowledge, because the mind needs a stimulus to think. Thus, the serpent tempted Adam to eat the apple. God was not too happy with what was happening to Adam.

As long as Adam's will was one with God's, he was not affected by the fruits of his actions, because he had no mind of his own, and there was no Eve either. With a mind of his own, and with Eve around, the apple became the symbol of carnal knowledge.

Adam ate the apple, and became responsible for his action by bearing the consequence, the progeny to come. God became fed up, and expelled Adam and Eve from heaven, with spare fig leaves. Adam turned to Eve and said, "Look, what has happened to us!" Eve replied, "But, darling, we have each other." Adam kept quiet, and kept his thoughts to himself.

The Christian church made the carnal act the original sin, and became obsessed with it. The original sin ought to be the rise of Adam's ego, separating him from God-consciousness. Therefore, the word for religion is *re-ligare*, to re-tie.

THOUGHTS FOR THE MONTH IX

The following sayings were compiled by the Sivananda Yoga-Vedanta, Centre of Chile, in Santiago, from the sources as indicated, and related in the class-talks by Swami Shivapremanandaji.

COMPANIONSHIP OF SOUL

From the Autobiography of the late President of Egypt, Anwar Sadat:

One must seek the companionship of that inner entity, one's spiritual self, the source of hope, strength, creativity, security, of life itself, for only through its help the dark shadows of the mind, its suffering, its uncertainty can be cleared.

Nothing is more important than self-knowledge. Your first duty is to face yourself, recognise the source of what troubles you. Then you have to deal with it by faith in your higher self, in your spiritual values.

Only when you know what you want, you can get rid of what you do not.

There are always solutions to everything, if only you would try hard and long enough.

Love of life can only be derived from the love of something positive. Love of the superficial not only conduces to shallowness but indicates a lack of love in one's own life.

SELF-REVELATION

From The Eighth Sin by Stefan Kanfer:

Not only two people in love are one, but one person in love is two.

Not only the mouth but the eyes can stammer. It is something a portrait painter can reproduce with a canny series of lines between the forehead and the neck; related or isolated, the eyes sometimes lying to the nose, the chin at war with the mouth.

Women reveal themselves with their eyes, and men with their mouths, particularly in the jaw-set through the years of denial or indulgence.

The face is a calendar and a medical chart. Look at the nose to see how the health has been. The eye's white tells about the nights, the margin around the eyes the days. Examine the hair to see the current state of health, skin-tone to find out the future, the mouth to see how things go from day to day.

The girls with deep-brown suntans will have skin like the rhinoceros' hide one day.

There are silences inside silences, just the way there are rooms inside houses, and wardrobes inside roans, and trunks inside wardrobes, and boxes inside trunks, and when you come next to the last silence, watch out, because inside that silence, there is the biggest silence of all, because it is God. *(The above paragraph is a Cabbala saying, and used by Swamiji for meditation.)*

HUMAN RIGHTS

From a speech by Patricia Derian, former US Assistant Secretary of State:

There are three basic categories of rights.

1) The right of the integrity of the person, the right to be free from cruel and inhuman punishment, including physical and mental abuse to squeeze out confession under extreme pain (as a political prisoner of Stalin said later that if they beat you hard enough, you will be ready to admit that you are the King of England). It also includes the right to be free from the invasion of the home without a legal warrant, and from the denial of a fair trial.

2) The right to economic and social justice, the right to work for food and shelter, and the right to education and health care.

3) The right to enjoy civil and political liberties, such as the freedom of expression, including through the media, of assembly, of the practice of religion, and the freedom to participate in government by a free electoral process. All rights should have individual and collective responsibility.

THOUGHTS FOR THE MONTH X

CONSCIENCE AND HUMAN NATURE

Ultimately a highly complex sentiment, having its first origin in the social instincts, largely guided by the approbation of our fellowmen, ruled by reason, self-interest and by deep religious feelings, confirmed by instruction and habit, all combined, constitute our moral sense or conscience. *(Charles Darwin in The Descent of Man, 1871)*

Behavioural geneticists say that the heritability of the cluster of traits they call conscientiousness is between 30 and 40%, that is, about one-third of the differences among people can be traced to their genes. But that still leaves two-thirds traceable to environment. *(Robert Wright in The Moral Animal, 1994)*

Darwin himself saw his moral tuning as beginning early, under the guidance of his kin (and observed), "I doubt indeed whether humanity is a natural or innate quality." (*Ibid*)

Childhood lies are not just a phase of delinquency we pass through smoothly, but the first in a series of test runs for self-serving dishonesty. (*Ibid*)

Integrity in word and deed is the backbone of character, and loyal adherence to veracity its most prominent characteristic. Character is power in a much higher sense than knowledge is power. Men whose acts are at direct variance with their words command no respect, and what they say has but little weight. *(Samuel Smiles in Self-Help, 1859)*

The character of parents is constantly repeated in their children: the acts of affection, discipline, industry and self-control, which they daily exemplify and live and act. (*Ibid*)

In centuries to come Communism is likely to be viewed by compilers of dictionaries much as we view alchemy today. In defence of alchemy, much of the beginnings of modern science may have originated with the alchemists and with those determined to prove that they were charlatans or witch doctors. The century-long struggle to deal with the idea of Communism has given idealists, romantics and pragmatists an opportunity to address the issues of liberty and equality in modern society, but at a great human cost. *(William Luers in Newsweek, 26 June 1989)*

All the vapourings about equality are at best an exercise in naivety and at worst at power grab by astute politicians. The ratio of leadership, a combination of intelligence, will, ambition and the ability to get the best out of others, being only one in ten or even less, society can only try to provide the equality of opportunity to filter out the incapable but require adequate compensation for their labour to have a fair standard of living. *(Swami Shivapremananda in Reflections IV, 1999)*

A society's retardation is guaranteed if equal status and material reward to all its members, if that is possible at all, are sustained for a long time. (*Ibid*)

Perhaps only a malignant end can follow the systematic belief that all communities are one community, that all truth is one truth, that all experience is compatible with all other, that total knowledge is possible, that all that is potential can exist as actual. Note: Gurus, think of it! *(Robert Oppenheimer in Dark Sun by Richard Rhodes, 1990)**

* The above quotations were sent by the students of the Sivananda Yoga-Vedanta Centre of Argentina in Buenos Aires.

THOUGHTS FOR THE MONTH XI

HONESTY, TIIE BASIS OF ALL QUEST

The liberal Buddhist attitude is: It is proper to doubt, to be uncertain. Do not act upon what has been acquired by repeated hearing, nor upon tradition, nor upon rumours. When you know for yourself that certain things are unwholesome and wrong, abandon them. When you know for yourself that certain things are wholesome and good, accept them.

Buddhism places the greatest value on man or woman who alone of all beings can achieve the supreme state of Buddhahood. Each man has in him the potential to realise the truth through his own will and endeavour and to help others to realise it. *(Aung San Suu Kyi in Freedom from Fear, 1991)*

Scientific knowledge is always tentative, always being refined. The history of science shows a progression of theories embraced for a time, only to be overturned or adjusted when contradicted by observation. *(George Smoot in Wrinkles of Time, 1994)*

Something in the evolution of the universe caused matter to condense, to form stars and planets, and ultimately life, not just life on earth but with a possibility approaching 100%, on millions of other planets too, including some in our own Milky Way. (*Ibid*)

Scholars who have devoted their life either to the editing of the original texts or to the careful interpretation of some of the sacred books are more inclined, after they have disinterred from a heap of rubbish some solitary fragments of pure gold, to exhibit these treasures only, than to display all the refuse from which they had to extract them.

But true love does not ignore all faults and failings; on the contrary, it scans them keenly, in order to be able to understand, to explain and, thus, to excuse them. To watch in the sacred books of the East the dawn of the religious consciousness of man, must always remain one of the most inspiring and hallowing sights in the whole history of the world.

What we want here, as everywhere else, is the truth, and the whole truth; and if the whole truth must be told, it is that, however radiant the dawn of religious thought, it is not without its dark clouds, its chilling colds, its noxious vapours. *(F. Max Mueller in The Sacred Books of the East, Vol. I, 1900)*

Our view of man obviously depends on our view of God. Age of Reason exalted humankind but still admitted God as a sort of supreme philosopher-king who ultimately presided over the glories achieved by reason and science. The humanist nineteenth century voted him out. It increasingly saw reason and science irreconcilably opposed to religion, which would fade away. Secular humanism stubbornly insisted that morality need not be based on the supernatural. The ultimate irony, or perhaps tragedy, is that secularism has not led to humanism. Goethe points out the moral: "Only he deserves his life and his freedom who conquers them anew everyday."

(Henry Grunwald in Time, 30 March 1992)

The large majority of the so-called happy marriages are simply habit marriages. *(Anonymous)*

The church recognises the limitations of men and helps them to surmount their mental obstacles by faith. The besetting horror of mental limitation becomes the beatific calm of spiritual consolation. *(Anonymous)*

If the church, any church, went too deeply into the realities of what it professes, it will surely undermine itself. *(Swami Shivapremananda)**

---

* The above quotations were sent by the students of the Sivananda Yoga-Vedanta Centre of Uruguay in Montevideo.

THOUGHTS FOR THE MONTH XII

HEALTH AND HATRED

There is always a direct relationship between mental and physical health. Unless a person has a reason to live for other than himself, he will surely die, first mentally, then emotionally, then physically.

To recover physically involves regaining the ability to get up in the morning. To recover spiritually requires restoring the will and desire to do so.

Defeat is never fatal unless you give up.

When you go through defeat, you are able to put your weaknesses in perspective and to develop an immune system to deal with them in the future.

You tap your strength you did not know you had when you have to cope with adversity.

No one can recover spiritually from a major loss without the help of others.

Spiritual recovery is hastened by overcoming the sense of isolation, by recognising the fact that your family, friends and supporters still stand with you, and by putting the defeat in perspective.

You must live your life for something more important than your life alone. One who has never lost himself in a cause bigger than himself has missed one of life's mountaintop experiences. Only by losing yourself in this way can you find yourself.

The moment that you think the struggle is over, when you have nothing to live for, you are finished. *(Richard Nixon in In the Arena)*

Hate is difficult to discuss. The mind resists it. The subject is amorphous, disorderly, malignant. Why hatred is not one of the seven deadly sins and why the Old Testament is so full of hate?

The reason the subject is hard to discuss is that hate is simultaneously a mystery and a moron. It seems either too profound to understand or too shallow and stupid to bear much analysis—a cretin with a club, violent, repulsive, irrational, a black intoxication, an accomplice of death.

The subjectivists (poets and moralists) look for the seeds of hatred within the human heart. The objectivists (economists, historians, lawyers) dismiss such vapourings and locate the causes of hatred in the conditions of people's lives. "Hard, visible circumstances define reality," said John Kenneth Galbraith.

The typical hater, said Vaclav Havel, has a serious face, a quickness to take offence, strong language, shouting, the inability to stop outside of himself and see his own foolishness.

(Lance Morrow in Time, 17 September 1990)

The stoics believed that the universe was rational, despite appearances, that man could regulate his life by emulating the calm and order of the universe, learning to accept events with a stern and tranquil mind and to achieve a lofty moral worth. They believed that man, as a world citizen, was obliged to play an active part in public affairs. Thus moral worth, duty and justice were singularly stoic emphases, together with a certain sternness of mind. *(Encyclopaedia Britannica)*

Religions often are the codification and sanctification of a people's native character. *(Luigi Barzini)**

---

* The above quotations were sent by the students of the Sivananda Yoga-Vednta Centre of Chile in Santiago.

THOUGHTS FOR THE MONTH XIII

SOCIETY AND HOME

Society is a system of relations between individuals. Human beings cannot be themselves without interacting with their fellows, and society is a field of action common to a number of human beings. The source of action is in the individuals.

All growth originates with creative individuals, and their task is twofold: first the achievement of their inspiration or discovery, and secondly the conversion of society to which they belong, to this new way of life.

This conversion comes about in two ways: either by the mass undergoing the actual experience which has transformed the creative individuals, or by their imitation of its externals. In practice, the latter is the only alternative open by which the rank and file *en masse* can follow the leaders. *(Arnold Toynbee in The Study of History)*

The way to build a better nation is to build better individuals. A successful nation is usually composed of citizens, the majority of whom are efficient and possess a reasonably high sense of duty.

An individual who aspires to be trusted should have character. The foundation of business, as we know, is credit. Credit depends upon confidence and confidence upon character.

Efficiency implies the possession, in a high degree, of the qualities of diligence, ambition, punctuality, discipline, precision and the desire to do one's work as well as possible. *(Sir M. Visvesvaraya)*

It is not the physical part of homelessness that is hard: home and homelessness are also ideas, emotions and metaphysical states. Home is all the civilisation that a child knows. Home is one of nature's primal forms, and if it does not take shape around the child properly, then his mind will be at least a little homeless all his life.

Creation is an onion with many skins, all layering outward from the child's self. If he gets lost in the galaxy, he can find the way back, can fly through the concentric circles to his own house, from outermost remoteness to innermost home. Nostalgia means *nostos algos*, agony to return home.

The womb is the first home. Thereafter, home is the soil you come from and recognise what you knew before: the infinitely subtle distinctiveness of temperature and smell and weather and noises and people, the intonations of the familiar. Each home is an unrepeatable configuration. It has personality, its own emanations, and its spirit of place. Home, like the mind, is a time capsule. Love is home. The myth of Eden is the first trauma of homelessness.

Home, after that expulsion, is what we make, what we build. We build our home again, endlessly, in memory of Eden. The present is never contented, perfection is hypothetical, and home is always incomplete.

(Lance Morrow in Time, 24 December 1990)

A hen is just an egg's way of making another egg. *(Samuel Butler)*

All reforms are brought about by the energy of the reformers and by the apathy of the opponents who are always in a majority. *(Anonymous)*

Intellect without imagination is like soup without salt. *(Anonymous)*

Some use words to express thoughts and some use words to express words. (*Anonymous*)

Nothing can be so alluring or so offensive as a voice. *(Anonymous)**

---

* The above quotations were sent by the students of the Sivananda Yoga-Vedanta Centre of Argentina in Buenos Aires.

THOUGHTS FOR THE MONTH XIV

POINTS TO PONDER

Consciousness precedes being, and not the other way around. The worthiness of being consists in the commitment to the realisation of worthy ideals. For this reason, the salvation of this world lies nowhere else than in the human heart, in the power to reflect, in human meekness and in human responsibility.

The only genuine backbone of all our actions if they are to be moral is responsibility, responsibility to something higher than my family, my country, my company, my success, responsibility to the order of being where all our actions are indelibly recorded and where and only where they will be properly judged.

Hope is not a feeling of certainty that everything ends well. Hope is just a feeling that life and work have a meaning.

(Vaclav Havel, addressing the US Congress in 1990)

When you assemble a number of men to have the advantage of their joint wisdom, you inevitably assemble with those men with all their prejudices, their passions, their errors of opinion, their local interests and their selfish views. From such an assembly, can a perfect production be expected?

(Benjamin Franklin, addressing American Constitutional Convention)

Politics is intimately related to human mediocrity. *(Mario Vargas Llosa)*

The rule of law, the development of the common law, the fact that democracy is more than majority voting, is about justice, about certain human rights which no government can displace because they did not come from government. That is what unites us, the enlarging of freedom backed up by rule of law, backed up by economic liberty, because political liberty and philosophical liberty will not last long without economic liberty. *(Margaret Thatcher in Newsweek, 8 October 1990)*

History is a part of a society's attempt to structure a self-image and to communicate a common identity. No community can exist as a community without common references. In a modern nation they come from history. *(Eugen Weber)*

There is no such thing as a true historical account of anything. Each sees the world from his own vantage point. *(Gore Vidal)*

The worst distortion of all is to turn love, a relation that is founded on natural sweetness, mutual caring and the contemplation of eternity in shared children, into a power struggle. *(Alan Bloom)*

Joy is not the same as gaiety. Destruction accompanies pleasure. When I eat a cake, I get pleasure by destroying it. If I bake a cake, especially by inventing the recipe, then it is a joy. Joys are gardening, building a clock, fixing up a room, writing a book. Reading should be a creative act and, thus, bring intellectual joy. *(Michael Tournier)*

I have puzzled for years over the church's dark, astigmatic view of sex. But sex is merely the narrow focus. The broader perspective, and failure, involves the church's view of women and their role in the world. Women are not ordained priests because Christ in human form was a man and chose male Apostles. But surely maleness was incidental to the essence of Christ's teachings.

Some similar distortion of religion's natural sweetness and profound reciprocity has been too long accepted as part of the Catholic Church's design (male authority, female submission).

The danger lies in the continuing distortion, the airless stasis of a bad tradition.

*(Lance Morrow in Time, 3 October 1994)**

---

* The above quotations were sent by the students of the Sivananda Yoga-Vedanta Centre of Uruguay in Montevideo.

THOUGHTS FOR THE MONTH XV

HUMANITY'S ASPIRATION

It is from God we have received our being, and it is to him we must leave the right to take it away. The bodies of all men are mortal and have been fashioned out of perishable matter. The soul is immortal forever, a fragment of God dwelling in our bodies. (Note the idea of God within.)

Don't you know that those who depart from this life according to the law of nature, and repay the loan they received from God at such time as the lender chooses to claim it back, win everlasting glory, that their souls remain unspotted and obedient, having won the most holy place in heaven, from which when time's wheel has turned a full circle they are again sent to dwell in unsullied bodies? (Note the idea of reincarnation.) *(Flavius Josephus in The Jewish War)*

Stories are precious, indispensable. Everyone must have his story, her narrative. You do not know what you are until you possess the imaginative version of yourself. You almost do not exist without it.

People invent stories to explore their own behaviour and to imagine their possibilities. People require the stabilising, consoling, instructing influence of other human tales.

People without a surrounding atmosphere of myth and example are prone to the stupidity that arises from being isolated and incurious about the nuances of the experience of others. *(Lance Morrow in Time, 21 September 1992)*

Democracy acknowledges the right to differ as well as the duty to settle differences peacefully. Regimented minds cannot grasp the concept of an open exchange of major differences with a view to settlement through genuine dialogue. Democracy, like liberty, justice and other social and political rights, is not given. It is earned through courage, resolution and sacrifice.

Revolutions generally reflect the irresistible impulse for necessary changes which have been held back by official policies or retarded by social apathy. The institutions and practices of democracy provide ways and means by which such changes could be effected without recourse to violence.

(Aung San Suu Kyi in Freedom from Fear, 1991)

Historically, nationalism as distinct from nationality or patriotism is a fairly recent development. For a thousand years, after the fall of Rome, people's loyalties were to their church, their lords, their rights and duties under the feudal system, to their guilds, and eventually to their king. Only in the French Revolution did nationalism burst forth, complete with flag and anthem. Altars were raised to the French nation with the inscription: The citizen is born, lives and dies for *la patrie*. Given such messianic megalomania, national freedom did not lead to individual freedom.

Yet something is happening to the traditional nation state. It is beginning to explode in two directions. Some of the newer, less stable states are exploding downward, as it were, into ever smaller ethnic or religious units, which really is not nationalism but tribalism. The nation state is also exploding upward, into larger units, notably the European Union. Western Europe has learned the momentous lesson that war and conquest no longer lead to prosperity.

The most successful economies in the world are, more than anything else, the expression of people's spirit, will and intelligence. We will need a new sense of drive, less emphasis on rights and more on responsibility.

*(Henry Grunwald in Time, 30 March 1992)**

* The above quotations were sent by the students of the Sivananda Yoga-Vedanta Centre of Chile in Santiago.

SIMPLE RULES TO REMEMBER

If you cannot do what you love to, do with love what you can.

If anything is useful to you, treat it with love.

If you are ready to give an opinion, do something about it.

If you do not know a subject well, do not give your opinion.

If you cannot help someone, do not give advice.

Only a fool gives unsolicited advice.

If you do not know how to do something better, do not criticise.

If something does not concern you, do not interfere.

If something is free, do not fail to appreciate it.

If you do not know how something works, do not take it apart.

If you wish to use something that is not yours, seek out its owner to ask for permission.

If something is lent to you, return it promptly.

If you promise something, do not fail to keep your word.

If you do not know what to say, keep quiet.

Be a listener. If someone is saying something, do not interrupt.

If you manage to offend someone, do not fail to ask for pardon.

If you break a thing belonging to someone, replace it with a better one.

If you dirty a place, clean up. Having eaten, wash up.

If you open a door, close it behind.

If you switch on a light, switch it off.

[These rules were sent by the students of Swami Shivapremanandaji from Buenos Aires.]

Chapter Twenty-one

ANECDOTES

SOME MEMORIES OF AN ENCOUNTER

The caterpillar weaves a cocoon and lives within it. It becomes a chrysalis, always changing, waiting until the proper time. Then the cocoon is broken and the butterfly escapes, and it is beautiful because it is free, and it flies away to no one knows where.

—Bette Bao Lord, in *Spring Moon*

So could be said of the spirit of man. A person is remembered for some time by the memories he leaves behind and longer by the record of his works, kept alive by organisations to promote what he represented. It is difficult to imagine what shape Christianity might have taken without St. Paul, or if the modern history of India would have noticed Ramakrishna without Vivekananda. It is not so much what a person was, concerning his human nature, but what he meant to others, and the impact of his ideas serving as a catalyst to the thinking of people and resulting in the shaping of society, that determines his place in history.

It was on a wintry day, in 1945, that I had the rare tryst with destiny when I saw Swami Sivananda at his still-primitive ashram, north of Rishikesh, when he was a youthful and vigorous 58, bubbling with enthusiasm in what he did. I saw the last of him sixteen years later, by then fairly recognised as a representative of what could be termed modern spiritual culture of India, before I left for Europe and the Americas, in 1961.

The foremost impact of his qualities on me were his immense tolerance and understanding of the shortcomings of human nature, patience and tactfulness, absence of animus and pettiness, the practicality and universality of outlook, his freedom from religious and caste prejudice still distressingly present in many other ashrams of that time but, above all, his unique way of letting others find their own spiritual paths and shape their ideals. It was this last quality that held me at his ashram so long, for never did he try to indoctrinate, never was he doctrinaire, nor require of anyone a blind allegiance, philosophically or personally. Mahatma Gandhi used to say, "If you wish to know the nature of a person, give him power." Swami Sivananda, as founder of his ashram, held absolute authority there, and he came out well in the exercise of it.

Many years later, returning to India on different occasions, I was told by two of his senior disciples that they had been to several other ashrams, before and after, more as well as less well known, but had never met anyone like him, as to the qualities I have just mentioned. Thus, I was happy to know that, without having shopped around, I happened to stumble upon the best teacher accessible then, suited to my temperament. Since then I have never regretted that tryst with destiny.

TRUTH AS IDENTITY

The truth of a person is in what he is, for truth is *sat*, that which *is*, as opposed to what is not. What is and what is not is, of course, in the eyes of the beholder, but truth being universal cannot be an isolated perception, unsupported by fact, for the face of truth is self-revealing, even if what it means to the beholder may vary, in some ways, from person to person. Reality is wrapped up inside layers of illusion, and it is the business of religion to make myths convincing. The point of it is in its usefulness to inspire the search for the unknown and widen the dimensions of the known within oneself, and strengthen the human spirit.

"Truth is a dream, unless my dream is true," said George Santayana, and so true it is about the truth of a person. It will, indeed, be too tall a claim to say that one knows a lot about oneself or of another. Some of the truth, surely, is expressed by words and deeds, but it is in the nature of things that some of it remains veiled. Mark Twain mused that a person's "real life is led in his head, and is known to none but himself." Andre Malraux remarked caustically that the "truth about a man is first of all what he hides."

Swami Sivananda was too uncomplicated a person, nor was he Hamlet-like heavy-laden with self-doubt, to have successfully done that. He spread himself all over the mainstream of his writings, like it or not, although about half-a-dozen of his disciples wrote independent articles in his name, at different times, but these could easily be sorted out as not being his from their style and shape of ideas. Great philosophical problems did not gnaw at the fibre of his conscience, nor was he weighed down by the excess baggage of the glory of other philosophers he drew from. He will surely be known as a prolific anthologist of the religious literature of India, which he presented in a simple form. He knew what he wanted to say, and do, and be known as, and went ahead and did his best to get what he wanted.

No writer can hide his soul in what he writes about, even if he tries to. The personality and qualities of character, with concomitant deficiencies, come through and through: truthful or false, profound or shallow, restrained or blatant, sincere or hypocritical, modest or vainglorious, painstaking or flippant, thoughtful or fastuous, conscientious or unprincipled, knowledgeable or inane, literate or merely literary, self-effacing or blissfully egolatrous. Unbeknownst to himself mostly, the writer is self-revealing.

The strengths and weaknesses of a culture are spun into the fabric of the society it spawns. How important then that one should not indulge in the visions of a glorious past when they are narcotised by fantasies to escape their painfully-evident contradictions in the present! Hypocrisy is an inevitable companion of an exaggerated sense of one's traditional background, and a common fault of a backward society is to be pompous, if not ridiculous, about it, while not really trying to live up to what is relevant, useful, helpful and productive. Singing paeans of praise may be moving at times, if no one laughed.

The role of Swami Sivananda in the future of India will be etched by what impact his teachings have on the minds of the people who have access to them, and by the continued mission of service the Divine Life Society is able to effectuate mainly in this field, and of which it already has a good record. The usefulness of a teaching is in its revitalising effect on the mind: releasing, soaring and guiding, inspiring, ennobling and delighting, not confining, twisting and benumbing, retrogressing, obfuscating and self-absorbing, but helping to form substantial values to live by and save oneself from a life of "foolish desires and imperfect choices."

Swami Sivananda has left for posterity a well-established umbrella institution, The Divine Life Society, of which he would have been proud were he alive today. Ambitious he was to have liked to make it a household word, known as widely as possible, but dispassionate enough in not being frustrated with the less-than-optimum talents available to him. He did not have a Madan Mohan Malaviya* to establish a great Yoga-Vedanta University (later called Academy) he so much wanted, but no one could say that he spared himself in the effort. He laid the groundwork of what he called his mission and lived long enough to see it bear fruit, which it continues to do with even greater fertility and efflorescence than during his lifetime. There cannot be a better epitaph than that it is so.

---

* The late founder and organiser of the Varanasi Hindu University.

ANECDOTES II

The following anecdotes were related by Swami Shivapremanandaji in some of his class-talks at the Sivananda Yoga-Vedanta Centre of Argentina in Buenos Aires.

BE A LIGHT UNTO OTHERS

Long before the glory-hopping gurus of these days, who have their statues installed in their ashrams to be worshipped even when they are alive, apart from their own person on special occasions, marionetting the whole show, there lived selfless gurus who did not even care to make themselves known to the world. The following is an anecdote of one of them.

The guru was on his deathbed, and saying goodbye to his chief disciple who was to succeed him after his demise, he said:

If you are complimented for your integrity, take no credit for it, for you are a son of *sat,* transcendental truth.

If you are complimented for your wisdom, take no credit for it, for you are a son of *chit,* transcendental knowledge.

If you are complimented for your equanimity, take no credit for it, for you are a son of *ananda,* the equilibrium of spiritual fullness.

You should worry when you find yourself lacking in them, that you have not strived hard enough to inherit your birthright, this spiritual inheritance that you have wasted so many years by making a habit of being a guru.

Do not fail to educate your disciples to stand on their feet, for the highest gift is the gift of self-reliance through self-knowledge, to think anew, yourself being a light unto them, so that people may learn to make less mistakes, suffer less and cause less pain to others.

EARN THE RIGHT FIRST

§ A mother once brought her little son to her guru and said, "My boy would not listen to me when I ask him not to eat too many sweets. Please tell him not to do so." The guru told the lady to bring her boy the next week. She did so, and the guru said to the boy not to eat too many sweets, as it was bad for his health.

The mother was surprised, and asked the guru, "But, sir, why did you not tell him so the week before?" The guru replied that he himself was eating too many sweets, and that without practising what he was going to tell the boy, he had no right to do so.

§ Once I knew a guru who was very fond of saying how he liked to cut the egos of others. Having been a medical doctor, he coined the word egodectomy, and thought that it was a great fun. I thought to myself, one has to have a great ego to practise egodectomy on others. The guru, however, rarely did so, and was very patient and tolerant. It was just a manner of saying to feel important.

§ A disciple of this guru once had to get rid of a colleague from the ashram he had later founded, because it was uncomfortable for him to accommodate a rival. Dismissing him he said, "God himself wants me to ask you to leave." I thought, what a crude way to justify a personally-motivated action. Then he told me that, after firing his rival, he had cried. I thought, what a self-deceiving hypocrisy, for I knew he really hated his rival.

§ Once Pope John XXIII was dreaming about the problems of his church, and said to himself, "Tomorrow I will ask the pope for their solution." Waking up he found that he himself was the pope, and it was he who had to solve them.

§ After John XXIII had become the pope, a boyhood friend and a fellow-seminarian came to see him and seek his blessings. The friend had not risen up the ranks, and was only a senior parish priest, whereas the pope, after a lifelong diplomatic service in the Vatican's nunciatures in the Balkans and France, and having been the patriarch of Venice, had become the vicar of the Christ.

The priest said to the pope, he was sorry that he could only do such a little service to the church. John XXIII replied, "After you leave this earth and meet your creator, he would ask you not what great works you did for the church, but how many souls you saved."

HOW WOULD YOU KNOW?

§ Shasta the Zen monk was standing over a bridge in the company of a fellow-monk, and watching the fish swim below. Shasta said to the other monk, "Look, how the fish are enjoying themselves." The monk asked Shasta, "How would you know? You are not a fish." Shasta replied, "How do you know that I would not know? You are not Shasta."

§ Two monks were walking along a path towards their monastery. On the way there was a stream they had to ford. As they were doing so, a young woman, also crossing the stream, was about to falter because the current was strong. One of the monks picked her up, and carrying across, set her down on the road. The woman went her way, and the monks continued to their monastery. Half an hour passed, both the monks walking silently.

The monk who had helped the lady thought, it was odd that the other monk was so quiet, and asked if anything was wrong. The fellow-monk replied, "You are a monk, and you embraced a young woman, carrying her across the stream." The first monk remarked, "Curious! I held the lady in my arms for only three minutes, and you are still embracing her in your mind since more than half an hour."

§ There was a pundit who lived by the side of a great river, very proud of his learning. There was also a boatman who eked out his livelihood rowing his boat back and forth across the river. Rain-clouds were gathering, threatening a storm. The pundit had to go to the other side urgently. He asked the boatman to take him across. The boatman replied that it would be unwise because a storm may soon arise. The pundit said that he would give him whatever fee he asked, for he had important business to do.

So, they both got into the boat and started out, the boatman rowing rhythmically. The pundit became pensive, and started talking about the philosophical mysteries of life. He asked the boatman if he had at least read some of the scriptures. No, the boatman replied, he was too busy rowing the boat to feed his family. The pundit remarked, "Then you have wasted your life." The boatman didn't know what to say.

Sure enough, a storm rose and the boat started buffeting on the waves. It was now the boatman's turn to ask the pundit if he knew how to swim. No, he did not. The boatman remarked, "What good is philosophy if you do not know how to swim to save your life?" Practical knowledge is better than speculative philosophy.

§ Once a Greek Orthodox priest was dreaming that he was being pursued by the devil. However much he told him to get lost, the devil wouldn't just go away. So, the priest abruptly turned around and grabbed the devil's beard. He woke up with a start, and found that he was fiercely pulling at his own beard!

SOME REMINISCENCES

In the mid-1960s, the late Archbishop Fulton Sheen of Rochester, N.Y., told about an amusing experience in his early life as a priest. One Sunday he was asked to give a sermon in a village church. Having arrived there and being new to the place, he asked a boy for direction. The boy offered to come along and show the way. From the priest's collar he recognised him to be a cleric and was curious to know if he was going to the church to give a sermon. Father Sheen replied that he was indeed. The boy wanted to know the subject and Sheen said that it was about the 'Way to Heaven'. The boy was so surprised that he exclaimed "What! How come you are going to show the way to heaven when you do not know the way to the church?" I found Father Sheen's candour disarming. Then based in New York as director of the Sivananda Yoga-Vedanta Centre, I met him a few times. His breadth of vision was remarkable and motivation for helping the poor inspiring.

About that time, I used to see an immigrant rabbi from Hungary, Joseph Gelberman, who used to come to the Yoga Centre and I, too, occasionally went to his Little Synagogue on 20th Street and Broadway (the rabbi has since moved out to a bigger location). He once told a story about a Polish rabbi. As a rabbinical student, at the age of 20, the Pole was so full of idealism about the teachings of the Old Testament that he wanted to save the world through its gospel. At the age of 30, after becoming a rabbi, he found the world was too big but still he could save a small country like Poland through the Biblical teachings. By the time he was 40, he found that all he was capable of attempting was to save his Jewish congregation. When he reached 50, he found that even that was too much for him, but he thought that at least he could save his family. By the time he was 60, the generation gap between him and his children and grandchildren he recognised to be too wide, and realised that the only person he was capable of saving was but himself. Gelberman was very broad-minded, even if some spoke of him as an offbeat rabbi due to his unorthodox, ecumenical spirit.

In 1949, when I was a young novice at the ashram of Swami Sivananda in Rishikesh, I went to see Anandamayi Ma at her ashram in the nearby town of Dehra Dun, also at the foothills of the Himalayas. One evening, after the *satsanga* (prayer meeting), a middle-aged woman approached Anandamayi Ma to ask for a much-needed advice. After a quarter century of a buffeted married life she could no longer live with her husband, and asked if she should seek a divorce. The Mother replied that the fact that she was asking such a question showed that nature had not yet taken its course. When it really became impossible to live together, nature would automatically separate them, and she would not be coming to her for counsel. As long as there was a question about it, she could still continue to live with him. Full of motherly love, Anandamayi Ma was respected for her wisdom and revered as a saintly soul. She passed away early in the 1980s.

APPENDIX

GAYATRI MANTRA

Gayatri means: *Gayantam trayate iti gayatri. Gayantam* is chanting, *trayate* is being protected from sorrow.

The two great mantras of the Vedas are Gayatri mantra and Mrityunjaya mantra. Gayatri mantra is famous and powerful because of two reasons: 1) the vibration it creates, and 2) it asks for the ultimate enlightenment or God-realisation.

If you listen to the Gayatri mantra you will find that there are three *swaras* or tones: *anudhatta*, *udhatta* and *swarita*. Chanting in that dimension creates a vibration. That vibration helps us not to be afflicted by sorrow. Most of our sorrows are born of ignorance. If ignorance is removed, our sorrows are also eliminated.

Krishna in the *Bhagavad Gita* says: "Because of ignorance our intellect is concealed, and because of this we are unhappy and deluded. Gayatri mantra, through creating powerful vibrations, helps us to overcome sorrow. Our sorrow may be real, but it is unreasonable, say the *rishis* (sages).

Listen to this story: Krishnaswami was very drunk, and being drunk, he was walking to his home. On the way his friend Ramaswami wanted to have a little fun with him. He said, "Eh Krishnaswami I went to your home and found that your wife has become a widow." The moment Krishnaswami heard this, he started crying. Then another friend of Ramaswami said, "Hey Krishnaswami, how can your wife become a widow when you are very much alive?" To which Krishnaswami replied, "No, my closest friend said that my wife has become a widow, and he never lies." So he kept crying stupidly.

Hence the sorrow of Krishnaswami is real, even though it is unwarranted. Most of our sorrows are real, even though unreasonable. This sorrow, born out of ignorance, has to be removed. Gayatri mantra, by creating a powerful vibration, is said to help us to do so.

Please listen: We live in a universe. The universe lives within us. Both these dimensions should be understood. That we live in a universe everyone knows. That there is a universe within us, we do not know. Gayatri mantra helps us to draw energy from the external universe, and also from the inner universe. That is referred to by the word *savituhu*, meaning the sun. So Gayatri mantra is a prayer to the external sun, which represents the outer universe. It is also a prayer to the internal sun, the spiritual consciousness within us.

Let us all be enlightened: *dhiyo yo nah prachodayat*. It is interesting to note: Even though an individual is praying, it says: *let us all*. It becomes clear that the sages wanted our prayer to be inclusive, not exclusive. Hence the word *us*. This important principle, called the principle of ladder, indicates that everyone of us on the ladder of spiritual evolution is on one rung of the ladder or the other.

Therefore, if we have to go up the spiritual ladder, we should help others to climb as well. Just imagine, each one fighting to go up the ladder. Then there will be chaos. Hence Krishna in the *Bhagavad Gita* says: *parasparam bhavayantaha*, help each other to become enlightened. *Parasparam* means helping each other, *bhavayantaha* nourishing the ultimate good.

Listen to this story: The *devas* (demigods or angels) and *asuras* (demons) were invited by God in heaven, and offered nectar, drinking which they were to become immortal. The demons were very confused: Why did God invite us? The angels (devas) were also confused: Why did God invite the demons? Then God addressed both of them: "Here is *amrita*, the divine nectar. Please drink it. You will become immortal. But only on one condition. You have to drink by the hand without bending the elbow. Now, the demons tried their best to drink the nectar without bending their elbow. Then they could not, they cursed God, and went back. The angels knew better. They fed each other the nectar, one by one, the drinker not having to bend his elbow. Hence, by *parasparam bhavayantaha* or by mutually nourishing each other, they became immortal.

We have to start with prayer, and God will answer it, like a lover initiates, and the beloved completes the loving. Prayer is a surrender to the spiritual beauty within, and the material beauty without. In such a beauty of surrender there is the beauty of prayer. When our whole being is offered as a prayer, a tremendous wakefulness opens up within. It leads to *prachodayat* or enlightenment.

Somebody asked a master, "What should I do in order to be enlightened?" The master answered, "As much as you can do to make the sun rise and set." Then the student asked, "Then what is the use of all the spiritual practices?" The master answered, "Only to make sure that you are awake when the sun rises, and remain awake until the sun sets." Enlightenment is a wake-up call, to make our consciousness awake. Hence *prachodayat*.

To another enquiry about enlightenment, the master replied, "You have just to see." "Is there a special type of seeing?" "No, an ordinary type of seeing." "Seeing what?" "See the flower, see the stars, see the moon." The student said, "I have been seeing them." The master said, "In order to see, you must be awake. Enlightenment is awakening the inner consciousness. When this inner consciousness is awake, you will be free from sorrow."

Now, what is enlightenment? Listen carefully. Enlightenment is understanding the fact: There is an inner man, and an outer man. When the outer man is in conflict with the inner man, there is bitterness. With bitterness, you can never experience the poetry and the beauty of life. If you look deep within, there is always a conflict between the inner and the external man.

Listen to another story: There was a monk who lived in the Himalayas, chanting mantras and meditating, having renounced the world. But within him another mantra went on: "Oh, I am wasting my time. I am not enjoying the pleasures that a normal man enjoys in the world." Thus, it was his inner mantra, even when outwardly he was chanting spiritual mantras. Thus he was constantly in conflict between the inner and the outer.

Once the monk heard a lady singing a song: "Oh Lord, what can I offer you but the honesty of my song? Whether my song is good or bad, it is honest, authentic. It is this authenticity I am offering to you, oh Lord." When the monk heard the lady's song, he realised that he had not been honest, but inwardly false and outwardly different. He renounced his falseness. Then a magical bridge was created between the inner and the outer. In that bridge there was the experience of inner oneness with the outer. This experience of authenticity enables inner awakening. Authenticity, not by the arrogance of the intellect but by the innocence of the heart.

Listen to yet another story: There is an innocent man who prays to God: "Oh Lord, I do not know how to pray, but one thing I know, that I love you with all my heart." So he repeats from A to Z all the alphabets, and tells God to join them and make the right kind of prayer. Then God says that this was one of the best prayers a devotee had offered to him. It is in this innocence there is an inner oneness that leads to enlightenment. Hence, *dhiyo* means our intellect, and *nah prachodayat*, let our intellect be enlightened. With this inner awakening, one looks at existence from a different angle altogether.

Dattatreya, the son of Anusuya, even when a young man, was very wise. A student asked him, "Who is your guru?" He replied, "The sun is my guru, the moon is my guru, the fire is my guru. My whole existence has become my guru." The student asked, "How is the sun your guru?" Dattatreya answered, "Look at the sun. It gives light, but is not contaminated by what it lights up, such as the gutters of the world. This is what I have learned from the sun. I can live in this world, and not be contaminated by it. Thus the sun is my guru."

Savituhu is the inner sun, the spiritual consciousness within that lights the mind, and its thoughts and emotions, but is not influenced by them, just as the sun is not affected by what it lights up.

Another important aspect of enlightenment is understanding who I am. If you ask who I am, you find that you are more than your body, because the body is seen by a seer within. You are not the thoughts, because the thoughts are seen by a seer within. You are not the intellect, because the intellectual knowledge is derived by a seer within. Therefore, if you closely see, the body is sun, as also your thoughts and emotions are the sun. There is the *drik*, the seer, the inner sun, that is not affected by what it enlightens in the waking state and the dream state, and keeps the life-giving energy alive in the deep-sleep state.

The words *bhuh*, *bhuvah* and *swaha* refer to these three states of consciousness. The monosyllabic sound Om stands for *turiya* or the fourth, transcendental state, while giving life to the three states of consciousness. If you anchor yourself in *turiya*, you will see that you are just a witness to your thoughts and emotions which come and go. But you do not come and go, you remain steady in a state of awareness.

In the Gayatri mantra we meditate on Om, the sun, to enlighten increasingly more our earthly consciousness. This is indeed *prachodayat*, to look at life from a wider spiritual perspective. We try to overcome insecurity, which makes us suffer. The constant changing phases of life make us insecure. If we do not accept this fact, change becomes a surprise. We are not prepared to face it. The Gayatri mantra gives us the wisdom to find security in an insecure world. It helps us to overcome inner conflicts. We learn to live our life spontaneously, as is the case with our breathing.

Now, how should one chant the Gayatri mantra? Rhythmically. It has to be learned from a teacher with a Sanskrit background. It should be chanted when the sun rises, standing in front of the sun with closed eyes, if it is a prayer to *savituhu* or the external sun. If it is a prayer to the inner sun, it can be repeated at any time. In the early morning, facing the rising sun, with closed eyes, chant at least seven times, just loud enough for you to hear.

The mantra can be chanted once each, concentrating on the chakras, beginning from the *muladhara*, then *swadhisthana*, *manipura*, *anahata*, *vishuddha*, *agnya* and *sahasrara*, or correspondingly at the base or end of the spine; below the navel; on level with the navel within the abdomen; in the heart; inside the throat; between the eyebrows; and inside the middle of the head.

The Gayatri mantra also should be chanted facing the setting sun, at least seven times. The rays of the rising and setting sun are supposed to be good for the body. It is equally valuable to chant the mantra any time of the day or night, semi-loudly being the best way, but can be said mentally as well.

If you are chanting the mantra inside a room, make sure that you put a mat or a comfortable seat, on which to sit only for prayers, so that the mantra has an appropriate place to generate its vibrations. No one else should sit on it, so as not to affect the energy field. If the weather is not too hot, the body should be covered by a shawl to retain its warmth. The most important factors are devotion, sincerity and commitment.

AN INTERVIEW WITH SWAMI SHIVAPREMANANDA

By Jane Sill, Editor, 'Yoga and Health'

Jane Sill: I have your brief biographical resume, but a fuller account of your stay at the Sivananda Ashram in Rishikesh, your duties there, your memories of Swami Sivananda as to how he taught, etc., would be interesting. Also, perhaps, some information about the main purpose of the Ashram (The Divine Life Society), its aims and aspirations, and how they are being carried on today.

Swami Shivapremananda: I joined the Sivananda Ashram when I was 20 years old, straight from college, a raw youth, rather naive. It was the mystique of the Himalayas and the stories about the knights errant of the spirit who went there to find themselves—how far they succeeded is another question—and to search for a meaning of what life was about, that drew me. Swami Sivananda was not a mystic, but a down-to-earth, practical teacher with a striking personality. It was a counterbalance to my dead-serious yet romantic approach that I needed. What I liked most about him were his broad-minded, universal vision, immense tolerance and understanding of the difference of opinions of others and the foibles of human nature, his total freedom from any religious or sectarian bias. He gave us the liberty of conscience to think and express ourselves, without imposing or requiring to conform to his ideas.

My first duties at the Ashram were in the circulation department of The Divine Life magazine—of which I became editor four years later—and soon as a junior private secretary to Swami Sivananda, partly answering his correspondence and doing some subeditorial work. His teaching method was mainly by personal example, although in the early years of my stay, after the morning meditation class, he spoke for about three quarters of an hour on the practical aspects of spiritual life, sometimes pointing out the shortcomings he had earlier noticed in some of us, without mentioning any name, but we knew of course who he was referring to. He never reproached us but instructed indirectly how we could go about correcting ourselves. The methods of *sadhana* (spiritual exercise) we learned from his books. We also learned a great deal from his manner of handling the problems of our egos, as they cropped up occasionally, and from his conversation with the visitors.

Swami Sivananda passed away in 1963 at the age of 76, when I was in Milwaukee in the United States, in charge of the Sivananda Yoga-Vedanta Centre which I had organised two years earlier as per his wish. The main purpose of the umbrella organisation, The Divine Life Society, which Swamiji (as we called him) had founded in 1936, is the dissemination of the integral teachings of yoga and their practical application in daily life for a better understanding and improvement of human nature and relationship, for self-knowledge and self-realisation. Having been a medical doctor for 10 years (from 1913 to 1923 in Malaya, now Malaysia) before he became a swami, he was also concerned about the alleviation of physical suffering and, thus, started a charitable dispensary (now an adequately-equipped hospital) and a pharmaceutical works in his Ashram which he initially called Ananda Kutir or joy-permeated cottage.

Being in the West since more than 30 years, every time I go back to the Ashram I find the activities started by Swamiji are continually expanding. His concern was for the betterment of the body, mind and spirit, for which daily classes on Hatha Yoga, meditation and yoga philosophy and psychology are available at the Ashram's Yoga-Vedanta Academy. There are temples for worship and opportunities for Karma Yoga (selfless service) at the Ashram's hospital, printing press, publishing and despatching offices, also at the main kitchen which feeds some

500 persons daily. The Ashram helps to run three leprosariums, situated a few miles away, and gives scholarships to numerous students in India. The floating number of visitors who come there for short or longer periods of stay exceed one hundred. About 200 novices and monks reside there permanently and there are some 100 paid employees. The Divine Life Society also conducts spiritual retreats periodically at the Ashram and Yoga Camps and medical relief camps all over India.

JS: Can you give a bit more information about your life and experiences after leaving India, your work in South America and your impressions on yoga there, mentioning the enormous diversity of the southern continent?

SS: In 1961, after leaving India, on my way to the United States, where Swami Sivananda had deputed me to spread the teachings of yoga I spent a month on a lecture tour in Switzerland, Hamburg and London. Until the end of 1963 I conducted the activities of the Sivananda Yoga-Vedanta Centre in the midwestern city of Milwaukee, very insular and conservative. Meanwhile, I went on an extensive lecture tour of the west coast from Vancouver to San Diego, which was more open-minded. In 1962, invited by a group of people interested in yoga and deputed by Swami Sivananda from Rishikesh, I went to South America for the first time, to found the Sivananda Yoga-Vedanta Centre in Buenos Aires, and also guided for a few months the incipient activities of the same organisation in Montevideo, Uruguay, which Swami Chidananda, now president of the Divine Life Society in Rishikesh, had informally started in 1961. Then I returned to Milwaukee. Subsequently, from 1964 to 1970, I was director of the Sivananda Yoga-Vedanta Centre in New York, which was earlier formed by Swami Vishnudevananda.

While being based in New York, I went back to Buenos Aires and Montevideo, from time to time, to guide the activities of the Centres there. During my second visit to South America, in 1965, I founded the Sivananda Yoga-Vedanta Centre in Santiago, Chile, and reorganised the Centre in Montevideo. After 1970, I stayed for increasingly longer periods of time in these three South American Centres but went on lecture tours almost every year, and since the 1980s once in two years, to the United States and Europe. Now I am based in Buenos Aires and guide the activities of the Centre there and those of Montevideo and Santiago for up to three months at a time in each place as their president and rector.

In the United States the culture is basically oriented to Anglo-Saxon, Protestant values, as in Britain, whereas in South America the cultural pattern is generally Catholic and Latin European in Argentina, Uruguay and Chile, specifically. In the rest of South America it is Latin American, i.e., Latin Europeans mixed with American Indians have formed a distinct cultural milieu. I am not very well acquainted with the latter, since I have been only on a few lecture tours in Brazil, Venezuela, Colombia and Peru. I have visited Bolivia and Paraguay as a tourist and have not been to Ecuador and Central America.

As you say, in South America there is a great deal of diversity, in ethnical mix, culture, climate and geography. The high Andean mountains are fascinating. The Iguazu falls are much larger than the Niagras. Brazil is Portuguese speaking (the rest of Latin America being Spanish speaking) and has a polyglot culture and racial mix, descendents of Portuguese colonisers mixed with the descendents of Negro slaves and, to a lesser extent, with the American Indians. There are also large segments of thriving Italian and German communities in southern Brazil where the climate is milder rather than mostly tropical and subtropical as in the rest of the country. Venezuelans are also a polyglot of Spanish descendents mixed with Negroes and American Indians in a lush, tropical country with shades of Caribbean culture superimposed on that of the

Spanish colonisers. In Colombia the racial and cultural mix is Spanish, overwhelming the American Indian.

The full-blooded American Indians one sees in large majority in Bolivia, Paraguay and Peru, as well as in the Amazonas of Brazil. However, in all these countries the ruling class is of European descent. In the southern cone, where I reside, the climate is temperate, as in the south of France. In Buenos Aires the culture is mainly European. It is the most cosmopolitan city in South America and the second largest after Sao Paulo. Forty percent of the Argentines are of Italian descent, the second largest ethnical block is of Spanish origin and the rest consists of German, East European and, to a lesser extent, of British descent. In Uruguay the ethnical pattern is about the same. Eighty percent of the people in these two countries consider themselves middle class. The Chileans are mainly of Spanish origin and the second largest group is of German descent, there being also a sprinkling of East Europeans. Many Chileans are of mixed origin, as also about 20% of the Argentines, *i.e.,* Spaniards mixed with American Indians.

Except in the metropolitan areas of Rio de Janeiro and Sao Paulo, yoga is more popular and widespread in Argentina, Uruguay and Chile than in other South American countries, percentagewise. In the Buenos Aires area alone there are over 40 yoga groups, the Sivananda Yoga-Vedanta Centre being the largest with about 900 active members (in the 1980s). The second largest is the same organisation in Montevideo and by far the largest in Uruguay, with an active membership of over 600 (i.e., those attending classes at least once a week). Our Santiago Centre is smaller but still the largest in Chile. Hatha Yoga is the main draw, as in Europe and the United States, but there is a greater interest in the spiritual and philosophical aspects of yoga in these three South American countries than what I have seen in the USA and Europe.

Although 27 weekly Hatha Yoga classes are given in the two buildings of the Buenos Aires Centre, over a hundred students attend each of my weekly philosophy and meditation (*satsanga*) classes. At the Montevideo Centre 20 Hatha Yoga classes are given weekly and over 80 students attend each of the philosophy and meditation classes. The attendance at the Santiago Centre is smaller. Each of these Centres are registered as non-profit church organisations and run by a board of directors (council members) and office-bearers. There are also between 20 and 30 staff members in each Centre, consisting of Hatha Yoga instructors and secretaries whose voluntary work, including that of the others, has enabled us to have our own buildings with ample space to conduct the activities.

JS: What is the origin of yoga?

SS: No one can be sure when yoga originated in India. Some teachers claim that it has a pre-Aryan beginning, i.e., in the Indus Valley civilization which flourished between four and five thousand years ago, but there is no hard evidence. Yoga is a Sanskrit word, the language of the Aryan tribes who came to India from the northwest nearly 4,000 years ago. The word, derived from the root *yuj* (to unite) means "union"—of the physical, mental and spiritual aspects of one's being. The English word yoke may also have come from *yuj*. The earliest teachings of yoga are found in the Vedas, mainly as Gyana Yoga, although Hatha Yoga may have an earlier origin, not as a system of physical culture but to develop psychic powers as a part of Kundalini Yoga. However, there is no hard evidence. By the time the *Bhagavad Gita* was composed nearly 3,000 years ago (the present version having been written in the first century B.C.), the spiritual and contemplative aspects of yoga were already well defined.

JS: How would you describe yoga?

SS: As a philosophy of life, with which to develop a sense of being, our spiritual identity, self-knowledge through a psychological understanding, to shape motivation, sublimate emotions and passions, cultivate a balanced state of mind, deepen our relationships with each other and acquire good health by the practice of *asana* and *pranayama*. A tall order, indeed.

JS: What is the relationship, if any, between yoga and Hinduism?

SS: Hinduism is a religion which, like any other religion, consists of three basic aspects: mythology, rituals, and moral and spiritual teachings. Yoga has no mythology. It has no specific rituals but universal prayers for the welfare of all and as expressions of one's spiritual aspiration, although in some yoga groups oriented to Hinduism rituals pertinent to it are performed. The only common aspect of yoga with religion is its moral and spiritual philosophy but without any dogmatism. The goal of any wholesome religion, which does not claim to have exclusive telephone lines to God, is the same as that of yoga. Religion means *re-ligare* or to re-tie, reunite, and *yuj* means to unite—the individual with the universal, the material with the spiritual, meaning an integration of the various facets of life, of humanity with each other and with a common, transcendental source of being.

JS: Is there one ultimate truth accessible through the practice of yoga and is it equally accessible via other systems such as different religious beliefs?

SS: The only thing I can say about one ultimate truth is that it is ultimate nonsense, if there can be an ultimate nonsense. Truth is infinite and therefore endless. Truth is universal and therefore accessible to all. It is neither one nor many in the sense of separateness, but universal with a common convergence (and as such the term "one" is used) in an ever-widening state of consciousness. In a dogmatic mind its understanding is limited. In a broadening vision its perception is far-reaching and profound. In the relativity of its application its aspiration is transcendental. When one arrives at the door of a clear vision of truth, a new door in the distance opens up and beckons for a greater spiritual understanding. However, truth must begin with the requisite of what it exactly means, *veritas*, verify. Then try to deepen your realisation of its meaning.

JS: Do you believe in saints?

SS: Saints are created on earth but they dwell in the heaven, i.e., in the idealised vision of some people—to inspire, pray to in times of need for help. Haven't you heard the Russian joke? Two women happened to meet in a park and started talking. One said, "My husband is an angel." The other replied, "You are lucky! Mine is still alive." Of course there are saintly people with surpassing spiritual qualities, but to expect someone to be perfect and free from any residual human deficiency is to ask for the moon.

JS: Do you see the West's contribution to the understanding and practice of yoga having a beneficial effect upon the practitioners in the East? Do you believe that yoga can help promote an East-West synthesis, providing humanity with a means to improve and evolve itself to a higher state of development and create a greater harmony in the world at every level?

SS: It is a tall order. The West has certainly contributed a lot to the practice of Hatha Yoga through a better knowledge of how the body functions and how the different *asanas* and *pranayamas*, etc., have their effect on it. The claim by some Indians as well as copycat western authors of books on Hatha Yoga that this and that posture and breathing exercise will cure this and that disease is not only stupid but unethical, due to the lack of an adequate clinical data. The medical science and Hatha Yoga can surely benefit mutually by therapeutical use of the postures and breathing exercises under strict supervision.

The western culture, as a product of the age of reason and built on the foundation of Protestant ethics, can surely consolidate the application of the spiritual teachings of yoga and make them more effective. Eastern mysticism can deepen western values such as responsibility and work ethic, and the otherworldliness of yoga can compensate for the rampant materialism in the West, at least to some extent, hopefully.

JS: Is knowledge derived from yoga in one's consciousness finite, i.e., all that is knowable is known through self-realisation, or as in other sciences is knowledge constantly growing and becoming more defined?

SS: Knowledge is infinite and therefore has to grow constantly whether derived through the teachings of yoga or by the experimental means of other sciences. Knowledge, in order to be applicable, has to be defined. Definition is a discipline imperative to understanding. Its dimensions have, however, to be constantly widened through spiritual aspiration. The human mind that has produced all the scriptures, including the Vedas, is very limited indeed. It has caught only some glimpses of the endless light of truth or spiritual realities of existence, just as "scientists have picked up some pebbles of knowledge from the ocean shores strewn with an infinite number of such pebbles," as Sir Isaac Newton is said to have remarked.

JS: Do the laws of yoga as described in the scriptures apply to the whole universe or just a part of it?

SS: I only know a little bit about the planet earth we inhabit in a solar system of a medium-size star in one of the outer arms of the spiral galaxy called the Milky Way, in which there are a hundred billion stars, the Milky Way itself being just one of the fifty to a hundred billion galaxies (according to the English physicist Stephen Hawking). The natural laws of what is in existence have only limited universality and time-dimensional validity or truth, such as the moon whirling around the earth a couple of billion years ago had a different velocity and at a different distance. So also the laws of yoga or the laws of the Old Testament have a limited universality, i.e., at best relative to the life we know on earth within a time frame. The British author J.R. Ackerley once wrote to a friend, "I am half way through *Genesis*, and quite appalled by the disgraceful behaviour of all the characters involved, including God." (Quoted by Lance Morrow in Time, June 10, 1991.)

JS: What is a swami? Does the term vary according to different traditions and how does this relate to what is happening today, especially in the West?

SS: A swami is a title generally given to a Hindu monk and relatively recently extended to others not owing allegiance to any particular religion. He is like a Catholic monk and usually belongs to one of the ten orders (now a few of them not extant) which were organised by the eighth-century Gyana Yogi Shankaracharya. A swami is traditionally ordained by the Guru or the abbot of an Ashram after having stayed there as a novice for several years (the Ramakrishna Order requires 10 years, approximately), learning some of the basic scriptures, including the major Upanishads and the *Bhagavad Gita*, and engaging in selfless service and devotional practices such as prayers and meditation. Centuries ago these orders were supervised by four regional Shankaracharyas based in Jyotirmath (in the Himalayas) for the northern area, Sringeri in the South, Puri in the East and Dwaraka in the West. It was done through many Ashrams affiliated to these four regional headquarters.

The Shankaracharyas are still elected and continue to preside over their seats of theoretically spiritual but not institutional authority. Not many ashrams owe their allegiance to them. Ashrams in India are generally autonomous and are headed individually by a guru or abbot. Swami Vivekananda, at the end of the last century, founded the Ramakrishna Order in the name of his late guru, although Sri Ramakrishna was initiated by a monk of the Puri order. Swami Sivananda belonged to the Saraswati Order, owing its spiritual allegiance to the Sringeri headquarters, but institutionally none at all. As disciples ordained by Swami Sivananda we belong to the Saraswati Order, but only in a spiritual sense. Our bonafides—as that of any others calling themselves Swamis—depend on how we conduct ourselves and on the reputation of the ashram we were trained at.

SETTING UP YOUR OWN YOGA SESSION

By Ronald Hutchinson, the late Editor of 'Yoga Today' monthly magazine, published formerly in the U.K.

Swami Shivapremananda politely balanced a teacup English style until he found that he needed both hands to talks about *asanas*. He then disposed of the cup and quietly slipped into part of a Lotus position which left him cosily balanced in a posture which he obviously prefers to sitting western style.

Apart from the Lotus seat, the Swamiji looks rather like a youngish university don who knows a great deal but has not had the time to grow fusty and bookish. He talks fluently in a very perfect mid Atlantic English which occasionally slips from New York to London and back, which is not surprising, considering that he spent much of his school days at an English school but has been teaching in New York for the last ten years. He doesn't really look old enough to have done all this but he is in fact also a director of yoga studies in South America. He has about him that timeless air that seems to hover over genuine yoga teachers.

With his background of western schooling and a Christian education, Swami Shivapremananda probably understands better than any other Indian swami the problems which beset the westerner who comes to yoga. Not for him the traditional shaven head and the saffron robe. He pads around in neatly creased terylene trousers and a tweed jacket and his concession to the saffron coloured robe extends only so far as wearing an orange coloured cotton gown when he lectures.

The Swamiji had just finished taking a course of beginners, when he sat down to balance his teacup and talk about how to set up a yoga session. He is absolutely clear about the first simple and even obvious rule which gets broken quicker and more often in the west than all the other recommendation put together.

"The body gives the rule" said the Swamiji, "What you do and how much you try to do is governed by what your individual body is capable of doing. There is no point in assaulting yourself.

"There are some practices given by various teachers which are in my opinion too extreme. It is not necessary to be a contortionist to practise yoga. Of course, many of the movements are strange at first and many people are stiff; but do not think that this stiffness is confined to the western world; there are just as many stiff bodies in India as there are in the west. It takes time for people to become attuned but one thing must always be clear, it is the body which sets the rule.

"When you are ready to do a pose, your body will adapt to it. Remember it should be possible to hold *asanas* without strain."

There it is, the besetting sin of most beginners in the west is that we try too hard. It really is important to understand that there is nothing wrong with not being able to do some of the postures right off. It is no sin. You have not failed in any way. It is enough that you have made the attempt, so long as you put your heart into it.

So you have to strike a balance between trying with all your will and concentration but without bullying yourself. Yoga is a path of self-development, and the operative word is 'self'. It is your personally who must ultimately decide how far and fast to go. Because one teacher may say do a thing five times and another fifty times, there is no reason to take either of them as gospel. Five repeats may be too much for one person and fifty too few for another, only the individual himself can know. It is really a form of lessons in responsibility.

The Swamiji went on to say that he tried to set his postures into groups of patterns, each group of patterns providing a sort of miniature balanced session, but before any session began there should be a short preparation.

PREPARING YOURSELF

Preparation is simplicity itself. The first step is to relax and to dismiss from the mind all things other than the session you are about to enjoy. If you can adopt a cross-legged pose, then you can relax in that.

The next thing is to loosen the shoulders. The Swamiji said: "The great majority of people come to classes with tension in the back of the neck—the medulla oblongata and around the shoulders. You should try and get rid of this before your start or the breathing will not be free."

To begin this loosening, the Swamiji advises simple arm movements. Raise the arm sideways above the head and then lower them down. Raise them in front of you, bend the elbows and pull them in a few times. Or put the arms out together straight in front of you at shoulder height then open them outwards as though you were doing a swallow dive.

When the stretching has been done you can sit in a cross-legged posture and begin by chanting Om three times.

At this some people are going to say "Chant Om?" The answer is "Yes, chant Om", if you can do so without causing yourself difficulties. Only you can judge if it matters that someone in a next door bedsitter may think you are a sinister 'nut'. Fortunately Om can be sounded very quietly and there is a sound reason for this chanting even if you are not concerned with the bigger spiritual aspect of yoga.

Chanting the sound Om (pronounced as in 'home') will help you. Om is considered to be the sound of infinity. By making this sound, you tune yourself into the music of the universe.

You can disregard this explanation if you like, but the chanting of Om is valid as a mark in time. It acts as a dividing line between the preliminaries and the session proper. From the moment you have chanted Om, you should think of nothing but the *asanas* you are doing.

THE SESSION ITSELF

"You must balance your flexing," said the Swamiji. "I do not believe in those sequences where for example the Cobra, the Locust and the Bow all follow one another. I believe you should balance the flexing so that if one *asana* bends the spine forward, the next one should bend it back, and the same thing of course applies to the other movements. If you bend to the left, then you must also bend to the right, twist left, twist right, and so on."

"The Shoulder Stand should normally be followed by the Fish pose, and another thing," said the Swamiji warming to his subject. "I don't believe that people should necessarily stay absolutely still when they are in some of the postures, particularly the upside down ones. Once you can balance in a Shoulder Stand, there is no point in having the blood drain upwards and then life around in pools. You can move your legs about, shake your knees, bring your legs down one at a time either straight or diagonally above your head. That is, if you are in the Shoulder Stand, you can try to bring your left leg down to your right shoulder or your right leg to your left shoulder. The other important thing is that you should try to synchronise the breathing."

So here then are some of the basic rules of setting up a session. Relaxation, concentration, alternate the flexing positions, synchronise your breathing the above all allow your own body to tell you when you have had enough.

Here then is a suggested very short session which could last for about fifteen minutes and which is laid out using these principles:

1. Relax for five minutes lying flat on your back *(Savasana)*.

2. Stand and stretch the area of the medulla oblongata and the shoulders by area movements.

3. Sit cross-legged and stabilise your breathing.

4. Chant Om three times.

5. Have two or three minutes of slow abdominal breathing.

6. Change to *Kapalabhati*, 'bellows' breathing, pushing the air in and out at the rate of one breath (in and out) per second. About 30 breaths. Relax.

7. Do the Simple Twist, both sides, synchronise the breath.

8. Then hold the breath and raise yourself smoothly and slowly into the Shoulder Stand to a count of seven. Resume normal breathing, remain stationary for a short time and then,

9. Lower and raise the legs individually. First straight up and down, e.g., right leg to right shoulder, and then diagonally, e.g., right leg to the left shoulder. Shake the legs.

10. Lower both legs straight together into the Plough posture, if you can manage it.

11. Unwind yourself slowly and relax flat on your back in Savasana for a short time.

12. Raise on the elbows to your chest lower yourself into the fish pose. Hold this for a minute or as long as you can manage. Relax.

13. Lie flat on your back, raise your arms back over your head and then bring them forward and gradually roll yourself up into a sitting position and from there bend over to touch your toes. Lie back.

14. Roll over and do the Cobra.

15. Relax face down, roll over and relax face up. Stretch. Sit up. Stabilise your breathing. You have finished.

This is a very basic format. In the beginning, any session much shorter than this would hardly be worth doing, but once you are fit and adept at the postures, even a ten minute session like this will be enough to maintain health through long periods.

WHO IS A SWAMI?

The Sanskrit word *swami* is derived from the root *swa*, meaning one's own. Thus, the word originally meant: one who owns something such as an estate, or being the lord of a realm or even the master of a household. A Hindu god is sometimes referred to as swami, as in the designation of a house of worship, Swami Narayan temple, for example. To South Indian forenames, the word is added as a suffix, as in Krishnaswami or Ramaswami, even if it does not imply a spiritual vocation.

In ancient India, life was supposed to be divided into four stages:

Brahmacharya, the first 20 years devoted to study or learning a vocation and leading a disciplined life of celibacy (child marriage was a consequence of the Moslem rule since the twelfth century and even earlier in Sindh, now in Pakistan).

Grihastha, the following 30 years being the married life of a householder, raising a family, earning a livelihood, the word literally meaning: one who holds a house.

Vanaprastha, the following 10 years or so, the husband and wife retiring to a cottage in the forest (*vana*), and devoting themselves to spiritual study and discipline.

Sannyasa, when generally the male, after the age of 60, renounced his possessions and became a monk, presumably the wife returning to one of her children's homes.

All, however, did not follow the fourth step, probably not even a fraction of one percent, nor did all take to the third but stayed on as householders. It is in this fourth, *sannyasa* stage that the word *swami* became a title of a monk, a renunciate. One did not have to go through the second and third stages, necessarily, but could become a monk after the first, depending on the spiritual and vocational urge.

The *gurukula,* school or abode of a guru, had come into vogue at least 3,000 years ago, as that of Vyasa, Vasishtha, Yagnyavalkya, who were generally married men and called *rishis* or sages, not to be confused with *sannyasis,* although some of them eventually became so.

The title *swami* denotes a monk who is a celibate (not married or, if married earlier, no longer living with his wife), a renunciate, even if being the head of an ashram, to which the property belongs, and whose vocation is spiritual ministry. These are the fundamental requirements of a swami.

Early in the eighth century A.C., the first Shankaracharya organised the *sannyasis* into ten orders, some of which are now extinct, according to their aptitude generally but not indispensably. The Saraswati order preferred the erudite who interpreted the scriptures (Swami Sivananda was one of them). The Puri order based their ministry in urban areas (Ramakrishna's *sannyasa* guru was a Puri). The Tirthas served in the pilgrimage centres.

The Giris preferred the fastness of the mountains, as did the Aranyakas and Vanams the seclusion of the forest, devoted to a life of contemplation like the Trappists. The Bharatis generally came from the upper level of the social order, although *sannyasis* are supposed to be classless.

Ashrams existed in India since nearly 2,000 years before the first Shankaracharya, but it was he who established four regional headquarters to supervise them and the orders, and generally the Hindu religious ethos. Each was headed by a senior swami with the title of Shankaracharya: for the northern region at Badrinath/Joshimath in the central Himalayas, for the South at Sringeri in Karnataka, for the East at Puri in Orissa, and for the West at Dwaraka in Gujarat. Many *sannyasis* continued to be itinerant and typically autonomous. There never was a supreme pontiff.

However, the authority of the regional Shankaracharyas gradually waned as most of northern India came under the sway of Moslem rule, spearheaded by the Turko-Afghan invaders with Arab clergy, since the late twelfth and early thirteenth century. The ashrams became gradually autonomous, under the authority of their founding gurus and designated and/or elected successors. The married gurus, in addition, continued to have their ashrams. The word guru is generally translated as the remover *(gu)* of darkness *(ru)*, by implication, of ignorance.

No record is found as to when the suffix *ananda* designated an ordained monk. Since the late seventeenth century, however, one comes across names such as Samartha Ramdas, the guru of the famous Maratha king Shivaji. Some like Swami Rama Tirtha and Swami Tapovanam did not use the suffix *ananda,* although most of the ordained monks use it these days.

Apart from the vocational aptitude and the vows of celibacy and renunciation, spiritual aspiration is the fundamental requisite of a swami. He is equivalent to a Catholic monk. The vow of obedience to the abbot or guru is implicit as long as he lives in the ashram and the guru is alive, or to the current head of the order, as in the case of the well-organised Ramakrishna Mission based in Belur, near Calcutta. The Catholic monk's vow of permanent residence in a monastery does not apply to all swamis, some of whom could be itinerant monks.

Except this order, there is hardly any supervisory organisation in India on par with the Catholic orders, so that it is difficult to rely on the trained background of a swami or his or her vocational authenticity. The Ramakrishna Mission requires four years of probation and the next four years as a confirmed novice *(brahmachari)* before being considered for ordination as a swami and adding the suffix *ananda* to the name. It is mainly to make sure of the vocational aptitude through years of service, spiritual discipline and acquiring a basic knowledge of the scriptures.

The title *swami* also means one who is vocationally a spiritual teacher like the rabbi, although being a celibate and a renunciate.

In a spiritual sense, the word means one who tries to attain mastery over oneself.

The various shades of the saffron robe indicate the colour of fire, as a symbol of the aspiration to attain enlightenment and remove the dross of earthly desires.

In the West, the title *swami* and the suffix *ananda* are often used with astonishingly unabashed superficiality and, in many instances, with unscrupulous complicity of swamis from India. It is for the public to evaluate the integrity of the swamis, which is fundamental to any religious vocation, by the kind of life they lead and the ethical and moral principles of the institutions they guide.

The Biblical verity that human beings are made of clay is very appropriate, into which God breathed his spirit (in the *Genesis* it is said that we are all made in his image). As a life-principle or *prana,* yes, but as a dormant soul, his image, the *atman,* it remains to be awakened. Made of clay as we all are, it is all the more paramount for the swamis to try to measure up to that ideal, as best as possible, through integrity, unselfish love, humility of spirit, altruism and sublimation of earthly desires and carnal passions.

Avoiding bombastic titles, which is for the posterity to give, and not going around like a canary in public places where people are not used to the robe, speak of a delicate mien.

WHAT IS PRANA?

Generally-speaking *prana* is the energy principle within all that exists, sentient or insentient.

Prana, as understood in the word *pranayama*, may simply be translated as a vital force which is of the nature of electrical impulse that emanates from the brain and sustains all the activities of the body and mind. It can also be called perceptible and imperceptible life-force, perceptible such as in breathing and heartbeat, and imperceptible as energy automatically flowing through the nerves to enable the functioning of the different organs of the body, and also the thinking and remembering process.

Nearly a thousand years ago, or perhaps even earlier, yogis like Swatmarama speculated about this pranic activity and specified its five functions. One should not, however, take them literally but consider the rudimentary level of neurological knowledge in the early-medieval India and not repeat parrot-like what was said in the books such as *Hatha Yoga Pradipika, Gheranda Samhita* and *Shiva Samhita*. Their contents should be interpreted in terms of today's physiology.

Considering how limited the understanding of physiology was in Europe as recently as only two hundred years ago, the speculative insight in these works is remarkable.

Although the word *pranayama* is translated sometimes as restraint *(yama)* of breath (*prana*), its actual meaning is lengthening or prolonging (*ayama*) the breath, according to Swatmarama. It generally means, however, harmonising and regulating the two aspects of pranic energy flowing through the nervous system: passive (*ida*) and dynamic (*pingala*), *yin* and *yang*, anabolic and catabolic, *ha* (sun) and *tha* (moon).

There is no physical nerve called *ida* or *pingala* but the terms may be considered to refer to the flow of these two types of energy impulse.

This harmonising process is also mentioned in the *Bhagavad Gita* (IV, 29) as 'the outer breath flowing into the inward breath and *vice versa*, the aim of *pranayama* being the harmony of breath, flowing in and out peacefully.'

Five *Pranas*

The five functions of the pranic activity are divided as: *prana*, *samana*, *vyana*, *apana* and *udana*. Swatmarama grades them differently, but this order as well as a rather non-traditional interpretation are meant to give a better understanding of how *prana* functions in stages.

1. *Prana*. The *prana* in the air (oxygen-nitrogen) is breathed in to exchange and nourish the forms of energy called *samana* and *vyana,* flowing through the bloodstream to sustain all the organs and cells of the body. This constant replenishing process continues until death, discharging from the lungs used-up energy *(apana)* and filling them up with fresh supply *(prana)*. The yogis of medieval India observed that this *prana* is located in the chest (although all the five *pranas* are actually located in the brain).

2. *Samana*. It serves the assimilative process of converting another form of outer energy such as in food through the glandular system, mainly by digestive activity, and also to nourish metabolically all the organs and cells of the body. Its location was observed in the upper abdomen.

3. *Vyana*. The converted nutritive energy has to circulate freely to enable such a nourishment. Thus, the circulatory function made possible by the pumping of the heart muscles is called *vyana,* an infiltering process. It was thought to be located all over the body.

4. *Apana.* Having converted the energy from the outer *prana* through food-intake *(samana),* circulating it through the blood-stream *(vyana)* and purifying it through oxygenation *(prana),* the residual waste matter has to be eliminated. This eliminatory type of energy impulse is called *apana,* such as in the peristaltic movement in the small and large intestines, cleansing of the blood in the kidneys resulting in urine, the perspiration of the sweat glands, and discharging of carbon-dioxide. Its location, the yogis presumed, was in the lower abdomen.

5. *Udana.* The function of this *prana* was thought to be located in the head and neck (*ud* means upward), indicating the brain and brain-stem. It not only performs the more subtle forms of vital activity, such as in the endocrinal system, but sustains the thinking and remembering process, and regulates the unconscious as well.

PRANA IS ALL-PERVASIVE

Prana is found not only in all forms of manifest life, such as in living beings and plants, but also in stones, waters and air. Some stones 'breathe' better and, therefore, look more alive than the others. Some waters 'breathe' more when not clogged-up by vegetation and, thus, look more limpid. Some airs are charged with refreshing positive *prana* and some emanate negative energy as in a certain type of wind blowing from mountains.

The five vital *pranas* owe their existence to the *atmic prana* or the dormant individual consciousness of the spirit within, also called soul.

The universal form of *prana* is cosmic energy *(prakriti)*. It exists in the space. In the sunlight there is *prana*, as also in the electro-magnetic force, gravity, and in the strong and weak forces of the atomic nucleus of matter. Behind this universal *prana* is the transcendental, immeasurable spiritual force called *purusha*.

From the universal *prana* is born *akasha* or ether, from *akasha vayu* (air or gases), from *vayu agni* (fire) and *apas* (liquid matter) through combustion and condensation, and from *apas prithvi* or solid matter.

From *purusha* is born the individual spirit or soul *(jivatma)*, from *jivatma manas* or the mind, from *manas prana* or the vital force, and finally from *prana* or the body *sharira*.

Thus, within the physical body is the vital force, within the vital force the unconscious, subconscious and conscious mind *(antar-chitta, vahir-chitta* and *manas)*, within the mind is the microcosm (*vigyana*) of the universal consciousness (macrocosm), and within *vigyana* is *ananda* or spiritual plenum.

The body is the chariot, the five senses are the horses, the five reins are the vital *pranas*, the mind is the driver, and the rider is the individual soul. Roads are the value system or the paths of life one chooses. The negative paths give a bumpy ride, and the positive ways a smoother journey. Horses do not move without the urging of the reins, the reins do not move without the prompting of the driver, and the driver directs according to the order of the rider.

PRACTICE OF MEDITATION

(TRANSCRIPTION OF A TAPE)

Preparation: Posture and becoming aware of the breath

We will begin the practice of meditation in a few simple steps. But, first of all, sit in a comfortable position. If you are sitting in a chair, the feet should be together, knees together, back straight, without being rigid, neck and head are also straight, hands can be in your lap, one palm facing up above the other palm. Close your eyes. Feel peaceful, restful, detached. You are not trying to do anything, not even trying to meditate. There is no predisposition to do anything, just feeling detached and relaxed. Your breath is spontaneous as the lungs need to breathe. Now try to be aware of the breath, the inflow you experience by the feeling of its coolness inside the upper nostrils and, gradually, deep inside the head you feel a cool sensation also. As you exhale, try to feel the warmth of the outflow of the breath inside the lower nostrils. Slowly the mind becomes deeply absorbed in the experience, that is the external form of the breath. The purpose of experiencing the *external prana* or the breath is to be aware of the *internal prana* which is the spirit or the life-force within. To breathe in Latin is *spirare* and it is possible on account of the presence of the spirit within. In yoga too, to be aware of the breath is to be aware of the spirit within. The psychological counterpart of the experience of the breath, that is the experience of the spiritual content of our being, is primarily through a sense of inner peace usually associated with the inflow of the breath and the experience of a sense of freedom associated with the outflow of the breath. So for the first minute, we shall try to train the mind to feel the breath with complete attention. The coolness inside the head and the warmth inside the nostrils. Breathing spontaneously. You are not trying to breathe deliberately slowly, but spontaneously. As a result of concentration, the breathing becomes automatically slower than normal. The concentration is gentle. You are not forcing the mind to do anything, just being aware of the breath.

1a. *First Step: Cultivating a Disposition, 'Peace and Freedom'.*

Now, together with the awareness of the external breath, the coolness and the warmth, we try to meditate on inner peace and an inner state of spiritual freedom. These are the two characteristics of the expression of the spiritual content of our being, that is a profound inner calm, in a state of freedom which is to say, the mind being totally free from any state of bondage, anxiety, any conflict. Feeling like a free soul, like a liberated soul, liberated from all that which is negative, deeply immersed in the peace of the soul, feeling like a free soul. That is the first part of meditation. You are continuously aware of the inflow and the outflow of the breath. Now we have to guide the spiritual feeling with the help of two words, *peace* as you inhale and *freedom* as you exhale. In Sanskrit, for those who want to, *shanti* inhaling, *mukti* exhaling, but it is better to repeat in your own language these two words to guide the spiritual feeling of this part of meditation.

Naturally thoughts will come and go but the best way is not to try to prevent thinking by resisting thought. When a thought comes, when you become aware of thinking of something else, you say to yourself, *'I am now feeling profoundly peaceful. I am a free soul'*. And, once again, go back to the mental repetition of these two words, 'peace' inhaling, 'freedom' exhaling. In the course of time, you will not be needing to repeat these two words. You will just be aware of the state of inner calm and freedom automatically without verbalisation. Until then, from time to time repeat these two words, not continuously, only when thoughts come, 'peace' inhaling and 'freedom' exhaling. And only when you need to, amplify these two words by the phrases, *I am full of peace, I am a free soul.* Now continue.

1b. *Addition to the first step: Paripurnam, spiritual fullness; coolness of the inflow of breath.* We have now practised the first step of meditation for about five minutes. In continuation of the first step, which is basic, you can also add an extended aspect of the first step, depending on the time that you have. The mind is again absorbed in the feeling of the breath, both the inflow and the outflow. Now try to be aware of only the inflow, that is the coolness experienced inside the head, exhaling spontaneously, without trying to concentrate on the warmth of the breath, at the same time, trying to imagine the cool sensation inside the head. With each inflow, you renew this sense of coolness, deeper and deeper, raising the sensation inside the top of the head with each inflow of the breath. Exhaling spontaneously, while trying to feel the coolness while trying not to be conscious of the warmth of the breath. The related mantra is, *spiritual fullness*. In Sanskrit, it is called *paripurnam* or *transcendental fullness,* or total fullness. You can paraphrase it. When thoughts come to your mind, *'My heart is full of peace'*, and the short phrase is spiritual fullness repeated from time to time, associating with the experience of coolness, continuously deep inside the head, and with each inflow, trying to renew this sense of coolness. Continue. This optional extension of the first step is meant to deepen the sense of inner peace.

1c. *Second Optional: Feeling in harmony with the whole of creation, and expansive with the outflow.* There is also another optional extension of the practice of *peace and freedom,* to develop an inner sense of spiritual freedom and that is to feel a sense of unity with the entire creation with the help of the repetition of a few phrases. Begin by being aware of the breath, both the inflow and the outflow. Now, before repeating the affirmations, you may choose one of the two points of concentration. Either continue to be aware of the inflow and outflow or, in order to develop concentration, as we tried before to be aware only of the inflow, that is the coolness, let us only try to be aware of the outflow, that is at first, the warmth, of the outflow inside the nostrils, while not trying to concentrate on the coolness of the inflow. Then try to be aware of the outflow, the warmth inside the throat and, gradually inside the lungs, inside the chest. And try to be aware of this outflow continuously, even when you are breathing in, you try to be aware of this warmth of *prana,* inside your chest. If you find it difficult, then just be aware of the inflow and the outflow. This you at first do for a minute at least, before repeating the following affirmations. Repeat to yourself, while feeling the breath, *'My breath is one with the breath of all'* or *'I am breathing with all living beings'*. From time to time, you repeat this affirmation at least half-a-dozen times.... 'My breath is one with the breath of nature. I am breathing with trees, with the waters of lakes, rivers and the ocean. I am breathing with the earth. My breath is one with the breath of nature'.... *'My breath is one with the breath of God. I am breathing with the entire atmosphere. I am breathing with the entire creation beyond this earth. My breath is one with the breath of God which sustains this whole universe. I am breathing with the atmosphere and the entire creation beyond this earth, with the entire universe. My breath is one with the breath of God'*....

Rest period between steps of meditation:

Now a pause. Detach the mind. There is no focus. You are not aware of the breath, nor are you making any affirmation. Keep the eyes closed. If necessary, move your shoulders and the neck. Relax your torso. Move your feet if you have to. Feel detached. Pause for a couple of minutes. We have meditated for a little over half an hour. I shall go over, after a pause, to the second step which is basic. When you are practising meditation alone, without the help of this tape, having learned the first step, if you have less time, practise only the meditation on *peace and freedom* with the synchronisation with the inflow and the outflow of the breath for about ten minutes. If you are doing the extended practice of the first step, in two parts, it will take more time.

2a. *Second Step: Repetition of Mantra*

After a pause of a couple of minutes, wc shall begin the second basic step which is with the help of a mantra. You can choose a mantra by yourself, with the help of the suggestion of someone who has an adequate knowledge of the mantras. Otherwise, you can choose from the three I am suggesting, but only one of the three. It is meant to renew a sense of spiritual belonging to an inner transcendental source, a spiritual source. It is to develop the sense of our identity with the Divine, because it is only through a feeling of the Divine or of the spiritual that our mind is at peace, that we have an inner spiritual peace, an inner sense of fullness.

2b. *Choice of Mantra*

First, be aware of the breath, both the inflow and the outflow, the coolness and the warmth. After at least a minute or a couple of minutes, choose one of the three mantras.

i) A basic *Yogic or Vedic mantra* which is from the *Isha Upanishad* is *Soham. So* inhaling, *ham* exhaling while being aware of the inflow and the outflow of the breath, loving the sense of infinite unity. *So* means the infinite spirit, transcendental, spiritual vision of God, not anthropomorphic but the infinite spiritual presence which is transcendental as well as immanent. *Hum* means *I am one with, I am in, I am of.* This mantra you continuously repeat. Instead of *Soham,* you can also repeat *I am one with You,* the English translation. And, in this case, *You* can be a personal deity, like Jesus Christ.

ii) Those who are Christians and who are deeply tuned to the presence of Jesus, can repeat the second mantra, that is inhaling *Jesus,* exhaling *I love you,* or *Jesus I am one with you.*

iii) A third option is for those with a Jewish background. Two of the most known names of God in the Old Testament are *Adonai,* inhaling, which means *My Lord, Elohim,* exhaling, *the Lord of all beings*.

Continue.

2c. *Substantiation of the mantra by repetition of three phrases.*

After practising for about five minutes, this second basic step to renew our sense of spiritual identity or a sense of spiritual belonging to a higher, transcendental source of life which is in our heart, which is God within, which is God all around, and God beyond all that we know, transcendental. Now we shall substantiate this mantra of spiritual identity by the repetition of three phrases.

i) Be aware of the breath as before. Mentally repeat four or five times, *My body is your temple,* feeling a spiritual presence. either mystical or personal such as in the case of Christians, trying to feel the presence of Jesus within them as in the case of transubstantiation of the Holy Communion. Or, in the Jewish faith, the presence of God. One tries to feel as being one with God. 'My body is your temple' and then feel a flow of harmony, a sense of well-being, health coursing through the entire body. You feel the body is wholesome. 'My body is your temple'.

ii) *My mind is your altar* and this is like a clear blue sky which is your mind, a pure mind, the altar of God, limitless, not a narrow mind but an open mind, wholesome, pure, peaceful. 'My mind is your altar' and feel an inner purity, a spiritual consciousness, a pure conscience, that is the presence of God in your mind, purifying your mind, making it more and more universal. 'My mind is your altar'.

iii) Be aware of the breath, as before. Mentally repeat four or five times. *My soul is your abode*.

Now feel a glow of light filling the inside of your head, and that light flows into your heart, inside the chest, filling it with pure love. And, once again, a feeling of pure love from your heart flows into your mind, flowing inside your head and filling it with pure light, the light of God and the love of God, that is what you try to experience by the affirmation of the phrase, 'My soul is your abode'.

Rest period between stages of meditation.

Now disconnect the mind. Another pause after having practised the second step which would take a minimum of ten minutes, the first part consisting of a continuous repetition of the mantra and the second part substantiating the meaning of the mantra. As before, when you were resting in between two steps of meditation. Keep your eyes closed. If necessary, move the shoulders and the legs.

3a. *Third Step* (Optional): *Repetition of Five Affirmations*

After having rested for a minute or two, begin the third part which is optional but which is also very good for planting the seeds of positive qualities which you want to develop in the subconscious with the help of the repetition of five affirmations. This will take at least ten minutes.

At first, be aware of the breath and, after a minute, begin the repetition.

Repeat each phrase about four or five times, trying to feel its meaning.

i) Inhaling and feeling the breath, repeat *Peace is my real nature,* exhaling and feeling the breath, *not conflict*.

ii) *Love is my real nature, not resentment*.

iii) *Truth is my real nature, not untruth*.

iv) *Strength is my real nature, not weakness*.

v) *Freedom is my real nature, not bondage*.

3b. *Abbreviation of phrases*

Then abbreviating these five phrases, repeat mentally, inhaling,

i) *Peace, exhaling, only peace.*

ii) *Love, spiritual love.*

iii) *Truth, only truth.*

iv) *Strength, mental strength.*

v) *Freedom, spiritual freedom.*

Having done so, this third step will take about ten minutes. Give a pause. Then you will have finished the practice of meditation. Feel peaceful, restful, detached for at least a couple of minutes before getting up.

STRESS MANAGEMENT

Transcription of a talk given on 27 November 1995 at Golden Square Book, in London.

The subject is 'Stress Management'. From the time we are born, we have to cope with life. We can't help it because, fundamentally, we love life. From the very simple fact that we don't want to die, we refuse to give up and those who are on the point of giving up are actually calling for help unconsciously because giving up is not a natural process.

Life begins with some kind of involvement in the sense that without an interdependence we cannot survive. In the process of interdependence as we grow up, we react in a way not conducive to surviving happily or agreeably and that is how stress builds up. So you have to ask the question, 'What is the cause of stress or feeling unhappy, tense?' I found in India at the medical hospital at the Sivananda Ashram, and also at two other hospitals I visited, the tendency I observed was that they were more concerned about treating the symptoms rather than the cause. That was the general trend. I do not know how it is in England. Of course, the immediate need is there to treat the symptom because you want to alleviate the suffering. But, simultaneously, we must treat the cause. If you are not mindful of the cause, treating the symptoms will not be very helpful in the sense of a long-lasting result because the symptoms will recur on and off and be treated from time to time. So the alleviation will only be temporary. We must think of the cause. I shall come back to this later.

There are some basic facts in life which we have to face up to. One is, people are all born differently and this is due to a great extent to genetic make-up. Health is a product of several factors. The primary factor is genetic which most people tend to ignore. I know a case of a swami, a colleague of mine, who died in 1993. His name is Swami Vishnudevananda. He has written a good book, *A Complete Illustrated Book of Yoga*. He had a series of strokes. He became a diabetic. He was very good at the postures and he was quite committed, devoted to practising yoga from the age of seventeen. He joined the Sivananda Ashram at the age of eighteen and started practising in a dedicated way all the aspects of Hatha Yoga, and also partly meditation until he developed diabetes. He ate wrongly and became rather stout. But, as late as in the mid-sixties, he was still healthy. But the genetic factor was there. You can remain quite healthy, even if you are quite stout.

PSYCHO-PHYSICAL FACTORS

In the case of Winston Churchill. He abused all the rules of health. He hardly had any exercise. So is the case of Somerset Maugham. There is a saying attributed to him that all the exercise he did was getting in and out of the car, and yet he lived to a very old age and generally kept healthy. Both died on their 90s. There is a genetical factor which we have to accept. We cannot help this. So some are born with a stressful make-up and others with a less stressful personality.

Then, there is the second factor: the immediate childhood. That is more relatable, more tangible. We can understand and work on yourself. Genes are also adaptive but that takes a long time, takes a lot of work.

There are five basic factors which make up our personality. The first, as we have already mentioned, is the genetic factor which relates not only to physical health but also to psychological make-up. Psychologically, a person may be more fearful and would need a lot of changing to get over the fear complexes. Previously, psychoanalysts tended to attribute the immediate impact of the personalities of the parents, the father and mother, especially the mother during the first two years of a child's life because of the close contact. This is, of course, very true and some child psychologists such as Jean Piaget, the

French child psychoanalyst, would say that by the time the child is five, the future has already been decided because of the impact of the parental influence and the unguarded, unfiltered absorption in the child's psyche of that influence.

I do not know much about child psychology or the irreversibility of the qualities or the touch treatment received by the child in very early childhood. But I am imply reluctant to submit to the theory that it is an inalterable state of being. Approximately, the first five years of a child's life is when the character traits are projected into the child, sometimes with tact, sometimes without tact at all. All the frustrations and hang-ups, unhappiness of the parents can make them react to the child's behaviour and treat the child in a way that may affect his or her future. I am not keen on the theory that this is irreversible but I believe that it is an important factor to be taken into consideration. One has to work a lot to counteract it.

KARMIC THEORY

I am coming back to the old karmic theory. I can't prove about the past life or the theory of *samskaras* or ingrained character traits with which we are born and which are said to have been formed in the life immediately before, sometimes, they say, stretching on to further lives in the past—I can't prove these theories and so I'll fall back on the genetical factor, the parents, because karma is said to bring you to a home according to the nature of one's karma. I do not want to go into this because it is a question of belief.

The point is that any belief that helps you to cope with the day-to-day problems of life and which helps to give you a certain amount of self-confidence and understanding of the problems of life and gives you enough motivation and incentive to move forward is good enough. Whether there is a basic truth, doesn't matter. The truth is in evidence and if a spiritual belief such as a belief in God helps you to be a better person, that is proof enough. I don't speak about the existence of God, depending on how you define the existence of God. If someone says that there is someone up there who is deciding your fate. I don't know about this. I cannot deny it because I don't know, nor can I say, Yes, yes. That would be lying, because I simply don't know about it. But, if that belief helps me to accept things in a more tranquil way with better equanimity and gives me motivation to work on myself and look forward to something good and positive, thinking that God knows best and so I must do my best, accept things that I cannot change after having tried to change what could be changed and, if I fail to change what can't be changed, then to accept it.

This is very much like the prayer of Reinhold Niebuhr: "To have the courage, sometimes translated as strength, to change what can be changed and the serenity to accept what cannot be changed and to have the wisdom to know what can be and what cannot be changed." Sometimes it is disputed as to authorship, but it doesn't matter. The saying contains a truth. So that is very much, I would say, the spirit of yoga because there are five factors. One, as I mentioned before, without going into the karma theory, the genetical factor. In the karma theory, this is called 'the inexplicable state of being', the inexplicable qualities with which we are born. As I told you, genes are adapted, so too the karmas are flexible and can be shaped and reshaped without completely annulling the consequences of what has already been done (to cause them).

GENETICAL FACTOR

So that is the first factor of our life. We have to learn to cope with our genetical background even if we don't like it. Previously it was thought that the genetical factor pertained mainly to the physical make-up, disease patterns and so on, but now it is known that this goes further. Even if you separate a child at the time of birth and put the child in a different environment, the child will grow up in the course of time and he or she will carry the psychological factors of the genes of the child's parents, whether you like it or not. I mentioned that genes are adaptive. The second factor is what they call *griha* karma or the karma of the household and, in this case, (it relates to) the early childhood impressions formed by the influence of the parents, the immediate contact.

In order to grow up (healthy), you need two basic elements, apart from surviving physically. One is the nourishment of love, the protection of love. Love of course is there in the sense of attachment. The mother feeds her child as an extension of her body and takes care of the child. It is natural. But again we must understand, a basic factor. The maternal instinct is not entirely universal nor is it continuous. Whatever the exaggeration of the maternal instinct, it is not universally present in all women. So those children who are born of mothers not having sufficient maternal instinct, to give that protective warmth of love, of being wanted, those who are not lucky enough, they have to struggle a great deal.

So this is what we have to take into account. And then there is the factor of one child being more wanted than the other child, of a disappointment. For example, a mother had, let's say two sons, and then a daughter comes, and the mother wanted another son, like in the olden times when people had large families, especially in the East or countries with somewhat backward social structures in which females were considered to be a burden on the household because they were not productive in terms of manual labour because they are not strong enough.

Although this is a mistaken belief because I have seen in all poor countries women working even harder than men. This is sheer social injustice... and the dowry system, especially in countries such as India. Marriage becomes the primary goal of a female. It becomes a kind of protective continuity apart from its being a 'meal ticket'. But the female also contributes to the economy of a household, especially in agricultural communities where women often work as hard or even harder than men although they may not carry as heavy loads. These factors should be taken into consideration. Also, women have the responsibility of taking care of the house and organising all the household tasks.

So, (let us consider the case when) a daughter is born and the mother wanted a son for the first child. The disappointment that the mother feels will be expressed in the relationship with the child. Of course, she will adjust to having a daughter, but the immediate reaction is very, very unfortunate if it is negative. That factor also needs to be taken into account. There is nothing worse in a child's life than feeling unwanted by the parents. So, the nourishment of love, the nourishment of feeling wanted helps the emotional growth of the child.

ROLE MODEL

Another factor is the role model, or security of character. As I told you, cowardice is imprinted in the genes, cowardice or courage. This is why in the military caste, they always asked (so also in the British army) whether any member of the family belonged to the armed forces. So that factor is there—courage, cowardice…. very much so although it is not in all children born of the parents. The lying habit, dishonesty again are genetical factors. Years and years, generations may be needed to outgrow these (factors) even if the child is placed in different circumstances, environment. So all these factors contribute to stress: not being wanted, being regarded as a person who is careless, who has no responsibility, who is dishonest, devious, prone to cheat whenever he or she gets the opportunity and is, thus, being rejected personally and collectively, and having a 'bad' name in a group. So, that sense of isolation contributes to stress.

So the second factor is the immediate environment, how lucky we are or unlucky to have parents who can give us these two basic needs: one, the emotional nourishment for being wanted, being accepted, the tender warmth of love; and the other is the role model, what we call the protection, the security of love, security of character, that is the immediate influence of what is right and what is wrong, blindly copying. There is a very well known saying of Bernard Shaw, that children start loving their parents because of the very simple fact of dependence, of survival. It is a natural process of identifying and thus feeling some kind of warmth and since there are no other immediate examples around.

Life begins with imitation,—and so, blindly copying the role models one is immediately exposed to, *e.g.*, one's father and mother. And then they start questioning and the third process is that they either start hating the parents or they make a sort of understanding as adults that they are human beings and so their failures have to be accepted and not judged with resentment. But there are some who cannot get over the childhood traumas of bad treatment, of not having the protection of love, of not having character guidance.

RELATIONSHIP

So these two basic factors determine the relationship of the child to the parents: one is the protection of love and the other is character guidance. You can do without the protection of love but, without character guidance, you will suffer and that suffering is greater than the lack of love, for example. Lacking the protection of love, one grows up afraid of relating to people, of success, so that is not having a good marriage because of having seen a failure, for example, a failure in a parental relationship, being born in a home which has seen divorce, a lot of quarrel, a lack of understanding and a lack of acceptance, mutual acceptance, and so such products as adults will find it difficult to relate and will make mistakes.

There is a saying that between a boy and a girl, or between a young man and a young woman, the relationship starts with infatuation leading to marriage, and the second stage is picking faults with each other and the third stage is indifference. So, after getting tired with finding faults, they become indifferent to each other, just being used to each other, like a comfortable chair or an uncomfortable chair, whichever that is. That is a very sad thing to say but we need to have a greater motivation to manage our lives.

The third factor: We are the product of our society; the influence of the surroundings, which is called *samaja* karma, *i.e.*, the factor of actions produced by the influence of the peers or those around us in school and at our place of work; generally speaking the social and economic factors. Marx and Engels exaggerated these factors, suggesting that all social ills were due to economic factors.

One cannot say that all social ills are the product of the bad management of the economy but it is a fact that we are greatly influenced by pressure groups around, social pressures and circumstances and, if one likes to say so, the sheer bad luck of being born in the wrong place where there are no stimuli, there is no incentive around to find work, to stimulate your mind or to have bad influence with very negative results, *e.g.*, the experiments with drugs. In the latter case, it is basically an escape, obviously something is not fulfilling in the lives of drug addicts, they are wanting to 'have kicks', again coming back to home, the parental relationship.

Of the other two factors, over which we have some measure of control, largely in spite of the genetic factor and the previous three factors, one is called selfish deeds impelled by our basic instincts without filtering them through a sense of fairness, of right and wrong, responsibility to each other and to our own selves. So this is the fifth of factor. Do we really want to submit to all our weaknesses, or do we want to have a measure of control over our lives? This is called karma inspired by spiritual ideals.

CAUSES OF STRESS

Now let us consider why does stress build up? There are two basic causes of stress. One is the ego. The ego can be divided into two parts, with many subdivisions. When one talks of a person with a big ego, it indicates self-importance, which is due to selfishness.

Stress is caused by clashing with people. It leads to unhappiness and to a bad relationship. One clashes with people in a place of work and at home. You can clash with a complete stranger due to intolerance. It is a product of the ego. If you do not agree with a person, why not explain your position, and respect the other person's position.

If you are secure in your knowledge, there is no need for an argument. Religious quarrels spring from an unconscious lack of conviction. Intolerance is a result of insecurity. You are not sure of the understanding of your or another's religion. Your concern should be to inform yourself.

In an advanced country like Britain there are laws against blasphemy. You can be taken to a court for it, although it is not generally done. Blasphemy is due to irresponsibility. It is caused by the ego. A selfish person is naturally irresponsible, although could be trained not to be so.

In Raja Yoga the method of counterposing your attitude is taught to overcome a defect. If you are intolerant, try to cultivate patience and understanding of someone or some subject you are intolerant about. In a relationship gone sour, if someone hurts you, instead of being resentful, try to remember a positive experience in the past and be grateful. That is an immediate step to overcame resentment. Then think of someone you love.

If something goes wrong in a relationship, accept your responsibility. It may be that nearly 50% you are to be blamed for it. That is the way to prevent resentment. Due to a bad relationship with one of the parents in childhood, you may have deep roots of resentment. As an adult you could tell yourself that it is no longer valid, and thus it is irrational to be resentful.

SUBSTITUTION AND TRAINING

Self-pity is due to not accepting one's responsibility. It is easy to pass the blame on to others. It is also a cause for stress. It is like slowly poisoning your health. Anger is an immediate reaction which poisons your blood. One should never hurt another when he or she is eating, nor should get angry while eating. It causes an imbalance of the gastric juices and delays digestion. In an extreme case it leads to indigestion.

The desire to be loved is a natural emotion. If you love someone, it is normal to expect a response. You should not expect it from a selfish person. Lower the level of expectation to avoid disappointment. Love is a two-way stream. If it is just one-way, it cannot last long. If you are not loved, ask yourself the why of it. There may be a solution to it.

The mind is a field of energy. Energy is movement, pulsation. The energy pattern can be treated in three ways: by indulging, *e.g.*, if you get angry, get more angry, which will make it worse; by suppressing it, which will cause stress; and by sublimating it. The last is the only way. It is done by cultivating its counterpart, patience, tolerance and understanding. They are interrelated and mutually help each other.

Sublimation needs motivation. It is to love the ideal of what you want to cultivate. In the Bible one reads about the dos and don'ts. It is more important to emphasise what one should do, by which the positive energy of the mind will be strengthened, whereas by stressing on the don'ts the negative energy will become stronger. You should, of course, take into account what you should not do, but then turn your attention to what you should.

The key to success is practice, *abhyasa*. Patanjali in his *Yoga Sutras* insists on it. Practice is a result of motivation, i.e., loving the ideal behind. Then there has to be talent, at least some of it. Whether you have talent or not, you can find out only by trying. It is better not to set your goal too high, but what is accessible. Then the third requirement is effort. Make the best effort you can. Effort is to be combined with learning. Life should he an endless process of learning, until the last day of oneself. It is to work hard.

The next requirement is to learn from mistakes. There is a saying that one should learn from other people's mistakes. One generally does not learn this way. One should learn from one's own mistakes. The foolish fail to learn from their mistakes. Only by trial and error one learns.

SELF-MANAGEMENT

We come again to the subject of the ego. The next cause of stress is the image problem, vanity, being preoccupied with how you are seen. One goes through play-acting in order to be seen well. But the truth will sooner or later come out. A lady told me that her father was considered by others as a charming person, but that was only outside home. His real nature showed at home, where there was no concern for image, so that he behaved as who he really was.

Another cause of stress is being consumed by desires. There is a difference between desire and need. Desire is fed by desire. The more you fulfil one, the more you want it, and then fall for some other desire. We should learn the limitation of our capacity and accept it, instead of getting frustrated. If we do not succeed in what we wish most, you ought to try something else to see if we succeed or not.

We desire something in order to be fulfilled. Objects do not give fulfilment but the sensation of the ego by its possession. The ownership of a house does not give fulfilment but in the harmonious relationship among the persons who live there: a sense of belonging, acceptation, communication, understanding, respect, gratitude. Too much work does not give stress if you love the ideal behind. What gives stress is something that you do not like but are obliged to do.

That money is nothing is a hacknied saying. It is patently false. Economic autonomy is basic to not compromising your values. Money gives option for a better education, health care and wide-ranging travel for learning other people's culture, as well as to learn some audio-visual art, if you have the talent for it.

Unhappiness is another cause for stress. It is mainly due to a bad relationship with someone at home or at the place of work. You should be the first to smile rather than the person you meet to smile, first to be considerate than to expect consideration, to sympathise than to be sympathised, to understand than to be understood. This is the spirit of St. Francis of Assisi.

Do not forget that there are people less fortunate, less talented, having less opportunity, than you. If you are near them, they need your attention than criticism or, worse, contempt. If you do not get along well with someone, cultivate understanding and tolerance, and as a last recourse indifference.

The above points are basic to self-management to cope with stress.

KNOW THYSELF

By John-Paul II

From the Papal Encyclical 'Fides et Ratio'

Faith and reason are like two wings on which the human spirit rises to the contemplation of truth, and God has placed in the human heart a desire to know the truth, in a word, to know himself, so that, by knowing and loving God, men and women may also come to the fullness of truth about themselves.

In both East and West, we may trace a journey which has led humanity down the centuries to meet and engage truth more and more deeply. It is a journey which has unfolded, as it must, within the horizon of personal self-consciousness: the more human beings know reality and the world, the more they know themselves in their uniqueness, with the question of the meaning of things and of their very existence becoming ever more pressing.

This is why all that is the object of our knowledge becomes a part of our life. The admonition Know Yourself was carved on the temple portal of Delphi, as testimony to a basic truth to be adopted as a minimal norm by those who seek to set themselves apart from the rest of creation as human beings, that is, as those who know themselves.

Moreover, a cursory glance at ancient history shows clearly how in different parts of the world, with their different cultures, there arise at the same time the fundamental questions which pervade human life: Who am I? Where have I come from and where am I going? Why is there evil? What is there after this life?

These are the questions which we find in the sacred writings of Israel, as also in the Veda and the Zenda Avesta. We find them in the writings of Confucius and Lao Dze, and in the preachings of the Tirthankaras and the Buddha. They appear in the poetry of Homer and in the tragedies of Euripides and

Sophocles, as they do in the philosophical writings of Plato and Aristotle. They are questions which have their common source in the quest for meaning which has always compelled the human heart. In fact, the answer given to these questions decides the direction which people seek to give to their lives.

Men and women have at their disposal an array of resources for generating greater knowledge of truth, so that their lives be ever more human. Among these is philosophy, which is directly concerned with asking the question of life's meaning and sketching an answer to it.

ROLE OF PHILOSOPHY

Philosophy emerges, then, as one of the noblest human tasks. According to its Greek etymology, the term philosophy means love of wisdom. Born and nurtured when the human being first asked questions about the reason for things and their purpose, philosophy shows in different modes and forms that the desire for truth is part of human nature itself. It is an innate property of human reason to ask why things are as they are, even though the answers which gradually emerge are set within a horizon which reveals how the different human cultures are complementary.

Philosophy's powerful influence on the formation and development of the cultures of the West should not obscure the influence it has also had upon the ways of understanding existence found in the East. Every people have its own native and seminal wisdom which, as a true cultural treasure, tends to find voice and develop in forms which are genuinely philosophical. One example of this is the basic form of philosophical knowledge which is evident to this day in the postulates which inspire national and international legal systems in regulating the life of society.

Nevertheless, it is true that a single term conceals a variety of meanings. Hence the need for a preliminary clarification.

Driven by the desire to discover the ultimate truth of existence, human beings ask to acquire those universal elements of knowledge which enable them to understand themselves better and to advance in their own self-realisation.

These fundamental elements of knowledge spring from the wonder awakened in them by the contemplation of creation: Human beings are astonished to discover themselves as part of the world, in a relationship with others like them, all sharing a common destiny. Here begins, then, the journey which will lead them to discover ever new frontiers of knowledge. Without wonder, men and women would lapse into deadening routine, and little by little would become incapable of a life which is genuinely personal.

Through philosophy's work, the ability to speculate which is proper to the human intellect, produces a rigorous mode of thought, and then in turn, through the logical coherence of the affirmations made and the organic unity of their content, it produces a systematic body of knowledge. In different cultural contexts and at different times, this process has yielded results which have produced genuine systems of thought.

Yet, often enough in history, this has brought with it the temptation to identify one single stream with the whole philosophy. In such cases, we are clearly dealing with a philosophical pride which seeks to present its own partial and imperfect view as the complete reading of all reality. In effect, every philosophical system, while it should always be respected in its wholeness, without any instrumentalisation, must still recognise the primacy of philosophical enquiry, from which it stems and which it ought loyally to serve.

Although times change and knowledge increases, it is possible to discern a core of philosophical insight within the history of thought as a whole. Consider, for example, the principles of non-contradiction, finality and causality, as well as the concept of the person as a free and intelligent subject, with the capacity to know God, truth and goodness. Consider as well certain fundamental moral norms which are shared by all.

These are among the indications that, beyond different schools of thought, there exists a body of knowledge which may be judged a kind of spiritual heritage of humanity. It is as if we had come upon an implicit philosophy, as a result of which all feel that they possess these principles, albeit in a general and unreflective way.

Precisely because it is shared in some measure by all, this knowledge should serve as a kind of reference-point for the different philosophical schools. Once reason successfully intuits and formulates the first universal principles of being and correctly draws from them conclusions which are coherent both logically and ethically, then it may be called right reason or, as the ancients called it, *orthos logos*, *recta ratio*.

On her part, the Church cannot but set great value upon reason's drive to attain goals which render people's lives ever more worthy. She sees in philosophy the way to come to know fundamental truths about human life. At the same time, the Church considers philosophy an indispensable help for a deeper understanding of faith.

FAITH AND REASON

Therefore, following upon similar initiatives by my predecessors, I wish to reflect upon this special activity of human reason. I judge it necessary to do so because, at the present time in particular, the search for ultimate truth seems often to be neglected. Modern philosophy clearly has the great merit of focussing attention upon man. From this starting point, human reason with its many questions has developed further its yearning to know more and to know it ever more deeply.

Yet, the positive results achieved must not obscure the fact that reason, in its one-sided concern to investigate human subjectivity, seems to have forgotten that men and women are always called to direct their steps towards a truth which transcends them.

This is to say that with the light of reason human beings can know which path to take, but they can follow that path to its end, quickly and unhindered, only if with a rightly tuned spirit they search for it within the horizon of faith. Therefore, reason and faith cannot be separated without diminishing the capacity of men and women to know themselves, the world and God in an appropriate way.

There is, thus, no reason for competition of any kind between reason and faith. Each contains the other, and each has its own scope for action. The desire for knowledge is so great, and it works in such a way, that the human heart, despite its experience of insurmountable limitation, yearns for the infinite riches which lie beyond, knowing that there is to be found the satisfying answer to every question as yet unanswered.

In acting ethically, according to a free and rightly tuned will, the human person sets foot upon the path to happiness and moves towards perfection. Here, too, it is a question of truth. It is this conviction which I stressed in my encyclical *Veritatis Splendor*: "There is no morality without freedom. Although each individual has a right to be respected in his own journey in search of the truth, there exists a prior moral obligation, and a grave one at that, to seek the truth and to adhere to it once it is known."

It is an illusion to think that faith, tied to weak reasoning, might be more penetrating. On the contrary, faith then runs the grave risk of withering into myth or superstition. By the same token, reason which is unrelated to an adult faith, is not prompted to turn its gaze to the newness and radicality of being.

Faith will, thus, be able to show fully the path to reason in a sincere search for truth. Although faith, a gift of God, is not based on reason, it can certainly not dispense with it. At the same time, it becomes apparent that reason needs to be reinforced by faith, in order to discover horizons it cannot reach on its own.

My thoughts turn immediately to the lands of the East, so rich in religious and philosophical traditions of great antiquity. Among these lands, India has a special place. A great spiritual impulse leads Indian thought to seek an experience which would liberate the spirit from the shackles of time and space, and would, therefore, acquire absolute value. The dynamic of this quest for a liberation provides the context for a great metaphysical system.

CONCLUSION

A survey of the history of thought, especially in the West, shows clearly that the encounter between philosophy and theology and the exchange of their respective insights have contributed richly to the progress of humanity.

Precisely in the light of this consideration, and just as I have reaffirmed theology's duty to recover its true relationship with philosophy, I feel equally bound to stress how right it is that, for the benefit and development of human thought, philosophy too should recover its relationship with theology. In theology, philosophy will find not the thinking of a single person which, however rich and profound, still entails the limited perspective of an individual, but the wealth of a communal reflection.

I appeal to philosophers, and to all teachers of philosophy, asking them to have the courage to recover, in the flow of an enduringly valid philosophical tradition, the range of authentic wisdom and truth, metaphysical truth included, which is proper to philosophical enquiry. Let them always strive for truth, alert to the good which truth contains. Then they will be able to formulate the genuine ethics which humanity needs so urgently at this particular time.

Finally, I cannot fail to address a word to scientists, whose research offers an ever greater knowledge of the universe as a whole and of the incredibly rich array of its component parts, animate and inanimate, with their complex molecular structure. I would urge them to continue their efforts without ever abandoning the horizon within which scientific and technological achievements are wedded to the philosophical and ethical values which are the distinctive and indelible mark of the human person.

May Mary, seat of wisdom, be a sure haven for all who devote their lives to the search for wisdom.*

---

* To celebrate the forthcoming Easter, the students of Swami Shivapremanandaji at his Sivananda Yoga-Vedanta Centre in Buenos Aires, Argentina, selected the above excerpts from the encyclical *Fides et Ratio* of Pope John-Paul II, published by the Vatican in September 1998.

A WINDOW OF YOGA IN ARGENTINA

By Ana Hosmann de Sarasin

In territory, Argentina is the eighth largest country in the world after India. Its 1,068,301 sq. miles of area compares to that of 94,249 sq. miles of the United Kingdom, the inhabitants being some 32 and 57 millions, and the density about 30 and 600 persons per sq. mile, respectively. Stretching from the tropical borders of Brazil and the uplands of Bolivia, above the latitude of Capricorn, all the way towards the Antarctic, the country has the whole range of climate. The southernmost town in the world is Ushuaia on 55S latitude. On the West the lofty Andes demarcate the 2,800 miles of frontier with Chile. The northern border is along Bolivia, Paraguay and Brazil. On the East are Uruguay and the Atlantic ocean, and on the South the Tierra del Fuego peninsula juts into the Antarctic ocean.

The capital Buenos Aires is on the southern bank of nearly 30-mile-wide River Plate, striding on the same latitude of Adelaide, Australia. The climate is like that of Rome, hot and humid in the summer and cold and moist in the winter. One-third of the country's population, some 10 millions, live in Greater Buenos Aires, as in Montevideo and Santiago de Chile. The people are mostly of European origin, the majority of whom are descendants of Italian and Spanish immigrants. The national language is Spanish like the rest of South America with the exception of Brazil where Portuguese is spoken. At least 20 percent are mestizos, that is, mainly Spaniards mixed with Red Indians. Pure-blooded Indians are few and located in the North and Patagonia in the South. As in North America, there being no large and powerfully structured Red Indian communities, the coming of the Spanish conquistadors resulted in their decimation and absorption.

In the beginning of this century there was a thriving British community of at least a hundred thousand, mostly in the Buenos

Aires area, but now reduced to some thirty thousand, who have left their legacy in a few fine schools, cricket, football, rugby and polo clubs and some cultural institutions. In Patagonia there is a large group of Welsh descendants who are generally sheep farmers. In the southern lake region, there are German, Swiss and Austrian communitics, as also in and around Buenos Aires. The Jewish population is the largest in South America and next only to that of France and Britain, some four hundred thousand, most of them Ashkenazim, with strong religious and cultural institutions. There are immigrants, from all parts of Europe, as also some from the Middle-east, specially from Lebanon, Japan, China and South Korea, but only a few thousands from the Indian subcontinent. Italian descendants comprise about 40 percent of the inhabitants, the next largest being Spanish, as in Uruguay.

The country wrested its independence from Spain in 1813, the mother country having been invaded by Napoleon and, thus, unable to put down the rebellion. Agricultural produce dominates the Argentine economy, although there is a large industrial sector led by automobile manufacturing. In grain and meat export, our country competes with the U.S.A., Canada and Australia, but only 39 percent of the cultivable land is used, 61 percent remaining unutilised on account of the glut in the world market. Argentina can, indeed, be a future breadbasket for those countries with agricultural shortfall. Our land is also rich in mineral resources and just about self-sufficient in petroleum.

Since independence we have had a tumultuous political history, alternating between weak democratic and moderately dictatorial governments. Since 1983, there is political stability, and the free market policy of the present government has arrested inflation and encouraged growth. We have a welfare state. As usual, the middle classes, claiming to be 80 percent of the population, that grumble most. There are many large pockets of poverty, but not as extreme as in many other South

American countries. The Catholic church has widespread influence over society, but there is complete freedom of worship for other faiths. The political changes did not affect the activities of the Sivananda Yoga-Vedanta Centre, although the Hare Krishnas and Jehova's Witnesses were banned by the military government.

Buenos Aires is a cosmopolitan city. In the newspapers one sees that more than two dozens of cultural activities, including free public lectures on various topics ranging from nuclear science to yoga philosophy, are available every evening. The Colon Theatre is the most prestigious in South America, where world-famous artistic ensembles like the New York Philharmonic and the Bolshoi and Kirov (now Marinsky) Ballets regularly perform. It is also interesting to note that, percentagewise relative to inhabitants, Buenos Aires has the largest number of psychiatrists and psychoanalysts in the world, and a district is unofficially known as Villa Freud. Since the Second World War the British influence in commerce has declined, even though the Harrod's continue to be the largest department store in the city.

ABOUT MYSELF

After acquainting the readers with my native land, now I shall give my background and that of yoga in Argentina. My father was a fourth-generation German and a country-squire. Mother was born in St. Petersburg, of Swiss-German parents who moved the family to Switzerland after the Bolshevik revolution. As a young woman she migrated to Argentina and married my father. I was born in Buenos Aires on Easter Sunday 70 years ago, the first of their four children. Although parents were Protestants and respected other faiths, religion did not have a significant role in our family. They sent me to a Catholic school belonging to the order of St. Vincent de Paul, whose headmistress was a German. It is there that my incipient spiritual longings were stirred by the candlelit ceremonies redolent with incense, and melodiously moving chants.

My childhood was pleasant in father's estate, not too far from the Atlantic ocean resort of Mar del Plata. I studied music and languages, and married Max Sarasin, a Swiss-German, who had migrated to Argentina. We had a loving relationship until death parted us 26 years later. Like my parents he was a Protestant and equally ecumenical in spirit, but we were not churchgoers. My aunt, who had a cottage in Capri, off Naples, introduced me to the works of Carl Gustav Jung. She made me interested in arts and literature. Psychology prepared me for yoga.

In 1961 and early in 1962, Ulrich Hartschuh, a Uruguayan German from Montevideo, organised a few meetings in Buenos Aires to invite Swami Shivapremanandaji who was at that time staying in Milwaukee, U.S.A. Along with my husband and Renate Gradenwitz, I was among those who participated in them, which resulted in Swamiji's arrival in June, 1962. At that time my husband and I were just curious about yoga. We did not know what a swami meant. After putting Swamiji up in a hotel for sometime, we had the honour of having him as our houseguest for two months. His presence, classes and public lectures made a deep impression on both of us, although we took our time to come close to him.

In 1932, a group of Argentines, mainly from the literary scene, invited a spiritual teacher from India, the first ever to come to our country. He was Swami Vijoyananda of the Ramakrishna order, who pioneered the knowledge of yoga in South America, even though at that time only a few were interested. His work was limited to the Buenos Aires area, but he also visited periodically Rio de Janeiro and Sao Paulo. He founded the Ramakrishna Ashram in the suburban town of Bellavista, where he passed away 32 years later, ripe in age, in 1974. Like all swamis of the Ramakrishna order, he did not teach Hatha Yoga, but was the first to introduce Raja Yoga and Vedanta philosophy in Argentina, even if in limited circles. He translated some of the works of Ramakrishna and Vivekananda and wrote a few texts himself in Spanish. Since the late 1950s, numerous books on the various branches of yoga are available, but Hatha Yoga is what interests people most.

When Swami Shivapremanandaji came in 1962, there were only two or three small yoga groups in town teaching Hatha Yoga and holding lecture and meditation meetings, but they were not known for erudition or spiritual depth. In fact my tentative contacts with them made me withdraw due to their neurotic behaviour, backbiting and infighting. On a sunny, winter afternoon, on 24 June 1962, a large group headed by a reception committee received Swami Shivapremanandaji at the Ezeiza airport. From the same evening he started giving public lectures and philosophy and meditation classes almost daily for three months in Buenos Aires. On 17 July he founded the Sivananda Yoga-Vedanta Centre of Argentina. It was a very special day, dedicated to spiritual teachers. At that time we did not know what Gurupurnima meant. Yoga was so very new to us.

THIRTY YEARS OF YOGA

As we celebrate the thirtieth anniversary of our Centre, we look back upon all these years with nostalgia. Years of effort of so many wonderful souls, several dozens of them, headed by Swamiji, his constant coming and going to keep their enthusiasm alive and the light of aspiration burning, their love for him and his for them, have made the Centre a spiritual home for so many of us. Some of them are no longer present, my husband included, who passed away at the age of 61 in 1975. The loving memories of many of them warm our hearts, and the ethos of their spirit soundlessly resonates, in the ambience of the Centre. We had, of course, our share of disappointments. Otherwise it will be too unreal.

We functioned at first on a small scale in rented places until, in 1968, we bought our flat in the town centre where the activities rapidly grew. The Centre's main building was completed in 1983, where most of the work is concentrated. The active membership hovers around 900, the majority of them coming twice a week to attend any of the 27 Hatha Yoga classes available weekly, and the *satsanga* on Saturdays draws quite a few, as also Swamiji's lectures on Wednesdays.

The Indian embassy in Buenos Aires has always given us their wholehearted support and encouragement, sponsoring many of our activities and jointly holding some of them. As a founding member my husband served the Centre in various capacities, as treasurer, vice-president and president. He was also a Hatha Yoga instructor and a council member, the Centre having got its charity status in 1964. At present I am the vice-president and take care of public relations and organise Swamiji's programmes. I enjoy giving Hatha Yoga classes and continue to be a council member. Since the 1970s, Yoga Centres have mushroomed in our country, nearly 50 of them in Buenos Aires. Most are run on a commercial basis. As with Swamiji's other Centres, everyone of our staff members does voluntary service.

Over the past 30 years, thousands of students have passed through our Centre. To hundreds of them it has been a transforming experience to come in contact with Swami Shivapremanandaji. Like anywhere else, all sorts of people come and go and, as generally irk the West, the majority are interested mainly in Hatha Yoga. Many come to listen to Swamiji out of curiosity and to talk to him due to a transitory psychological need. However, I can honestly say that to many others knowing him and coming to the Centre have been something beautiful, consoling and healing, fulfilling and enlightening, as it was in my case, meeting him soon after my father passed away. Father, along with my husband, were closest to me. I know that Swamiji has filled a void in the lives of many.

Serving at the Centre has been a remarkable experience to most of us, not only educationally but in knowing ourselves. We have our share of excitement and tiffs, warm rapport and raillery, as in any family and community work. The Centre is a home like any solidly-structured hearth, with its share of personality differences, posturing of egos, ups and downs of moods, admirable spirit of service, deep friendship and warmed-up camaraderie. Yet, we all hang on together for the sake of our ideals, some working like industrious ants, some inclined to bovine repose, some painstakingly meticulous and dutiful, and some excelling eels to come to grips with responsibility. Yoga has been a marvellously enriching experience in my life, and to which I owe my physical, psychological and spiritual health. Now I will ask my good friend and colleague, Oscar Cabos, to relate his.

* * *

By Oscar Cabos

My interest in yoga originated due to a health problem. Since childhood I suffered from respiratory insufficiency. A friend of mine recommended a book, *Science of Pranayama,* by Ramacharaka. This book not only changed my breathing habit but awakened in me a longing for a higher meaning in life. I also became interested in naturopathy and organically-grown food, an interest I still maintain. I was then in my mid-twenties. Practice of Hatha Yoga improved my health but did not fill an inner spiritual void I became increasingly aware of.

My parents were of Spanish ancestry. They were both loving and caring. I grew up in a Catholic culture, without being influenced by religious dogmas. We were not a church-going family. From my parents I learned responsibility, to take care of the invalid, spirit of service and a sense of duty. However, there was something missing in my life. This made me join, successively, two Yoga Centres in Buenos Aires for short periods of time, but I did not find there what I was looking for, a spiritual fulfilment. In 1961, I also attended three lectures by Swami Chidanandaji when he came to town from Montevideo.

In 1962, Swami Shivapremanandaji came to Argentina for the first time. Destiny has its strange ways. I attended all his lectures and became a founding member of the Sivananda Yoga-Vedanta Centre he inaugurated on 17 July 1962. Since then I have never separated from him spiritually. I am not a religious man and am aware of Swamiji's innate distaste for hyperbole. He says, "No one is good enough to be another's spiritual master" and likes to spell the words master with a small 'm' and guru with a small 'g'. He would like to do so even with the word God but does not in order not to offend the religious-minded. However, I wish to be forgiven when expressing my sincere feeling in saying that, since knowing Swamiji, his life has become my life and that it is through him I have found a sense of purpose which I did not have before.

In the early years, Swamiji was disinclined to suffer fools, much less gladly. Now-a-days he does so, patiently. To me he is a model of humility, even if at times expressing himself energetically. He has made me understand how few material things are needed to live happily and enjoy each moment without unnecessary anxiety and self-pity, and with a lot of inner strength cultivated through a living faith in spiritual ideals and practice of selfless service. Swamiji is a true image of his teachings, although often self-deprecating. With a few simple words he used to put an end to my worries that had earlier kept me awake all night. He has a great capacity to simplify complex issues and find a solution to problems which seemed to have had no answers. He has taught me to live as best as I can without complaints, to think and act positively, and consider life to be a blessing rather than grumble about.

In have been the treasurer and assistant treasurer of the Centre and a council member, having been a joint secretary earlier. I am also an instructor of Hatha Yoga and serve in the building construction committee. Earlier I had a small business., but now occasionally I go to the Buenos Aires stock exchange. I have no financial worries, having learned when enough is enough. I am fortunate to have the three boons that I have read in some yoga books: to be born a human being, to have spiritual aspiration, and to find a real teacher.

From Swamiji I have learned the relativity of things in determining what is more important and what is less, never to think to be a possessor of truth, to know that its understanding can always be better, and never to lose the capacity of wondering, as a child does, and to learn anew. By his side, I have discovered hidden traits of my character, to strengthen as well as to correct. With each of his stay among us he brings peace and solace, and renews our spiritual aspiration, as well as the desire that he should never leave us, for that would be as if peace, simplicity and transparency of our nature were leaving us.

Swamiji is one of those who practises what he teaches, although he reveals a cynical streak when he says, "A spiritual teacher is, indeed, great if he practises some 50 percent of what he preaches, for most of them does only 10 percent." He speaks from his heart and is not impressed by the title, social standing or material riches of others. What he cherishes most in us are integrity, compassion, selflessness, constancy, positive thinking and broadmindedness. These lines of mine he may consider rather exuberantly Latin, but they truly represent what I have learned from yoga over more than 30 years, and to speak of which is to speak of my teacher, who has certainly brought a meaning to my life, which is like kindling the sacred fire in me.

* * *

By Salomon Birman

My parents were of Jewish origin. As children they migrated to Argentina with their parents from what is now Moldova and was at that time known as Bessarabia. They grew up here under the influence of the local Catholic culture, but respected the religious tradition of their parents, even though they did not practise their religion or go to a synagogue. I was brought up as such, being rather ignorant of the Old Testament. However, I held in deep respect the high holy days of Judaism.

My introduction to India was through a book of Victoria Ocampo who had translated into Spanish some of the writings of Rabindranath Tagore. Mircea Eliade's book, *Yoga, Immortality and Freedom*, and some articles of Aurobindo and Yogananda stimulated my interest in yoga. In 1968, I visited India as a tourist, more out of curiosity to know the culture of the land. Through reference by some friends, I joined the Sivananda Yoga-Vedanta Centre in Buenos Aires more than 23 years ago and began to attend the Hatha Yoga classes. When Swami Shivapremanandaji came to town, I attended his philosophy classes and *satsangas*, which appealed to me so much by their quality and clarity that, in the course of time, I became a staff member.

I am a married businessman, and we have two grown children who have their own families. My wife and I are very fond of our grandchildren. I have asked myself several times why I am in yoga and serving the Centre. The answer has invariably been that because it does me a lot of good, pure and simple. The teachings of Swamiji have brought me peace and taught me to be more tolerant of and love others. They have inspired in me the spirit of Karma Yoga. What has been particularly important to me was that they have made me study my own religion in order to find my spiritual roots.

Having served as treasurer of the Centre, I am at present its joint secretary, while continuing to be a council member. I am also an instructor of Hatha Yoga and a desk secretary. Swamiji has taught us that no work is too low, relative to one's position in life or in an organisation. My professional background being in air-conditioning large buildings, I had the honour of supervising the construction of the Centre's main building, a role I am still fulfilling in the continuation of its Annexe. Although professionally retired, I also help one of my sons in his computer business. My association with Swamiji and the Centre has made my life more complete. I understand the world much better than before and I am able to handle the problems that come by with inner strength and balance. As Patanjali says, yoga is after all a state of inner balance and fulfilment.

* * *

By Mercedes von Pieschel

When I was 14 years old, in 1928, I chanced upon a book written by Swami Sivananda, *Practice of Yoga*, his very first. I was then a student in one of the best British schools in Argentina. Having been brought up in a Catholic family, the book probably was an introduction to a wider horizon of thinking. My father was a well-known architect of Spanish descent and a personal friend of Le Corbousier. Mother's parents were French, who drew their inspiration from St. Vincent de Paul and were as such dedicated to the service of the poor.

As father moved around his family constantly due to his work, I grew up with no childhood friends. That inner solitude in early life may have contributed to my coming to yoga much later. Meanwhile, however, Mahatma Gandhi entered my life. Before the Second World War, the British empire was the most powerful in the world. I thought that his non-violent means of obtaining India's independence was fabulous and never heard of before, and of which Jesus Christ would have heartily approved. Since then I have admired him and the mysterious land, India, which produced him. Rabindranath Tagore's visit to Buenos Aires sometime in the 1930s, invited by the grand dame of letters, the late Victoria Ocampo, made quite a sensation in the Argentine literary circles. She later translated some of his works.

In the course of time, I married a German, and we had four children who have their families. In 1965, I was passing through a difficult time when father was in his deathbed. Being very close to him, it was painful for me to see him suffer. Swami Shivapremanandaji was then visiting Buenos Aires, and I started to go to his lectures and philosophy classes. It is said that when the *chela* (disciple) is ready the guru appears, although Swamiji does not initiate anybody, nor calls himself a guru of anyone, but wryly says, "Even supposing the *chela* is ready, it is not sure that the guru will appear. Instead of waiting forever, the *chela* should seek out a suitable teacher to learn from."

Since meeting Swamiji, yoga has helped me enormously through life. The construction of the main building of the Centre was finished in 1983. Soon after, I became the first resident there. My stay has been very rewarding and happy. I have peace and the time to read and practise Swamiji's teachings. At the age of 78 now, in spite of two successive hip operations, I continue to be an instructor of Hatha Yoga. The surgeons at the local British hospital and my family and friends were astonished at how rapidly I recovered and started moving around in just a few days and resumed giving classes, thanks to my regular practice of yoga. I am also a member of the Centre's finance committee.

There are, of course, many different ways of teaching yoga, both physical and spiritual aspects of it. However, I have always felt that Swamiji's way is what has helped and taught me most to find my path, although I know that I have a lot to learn philosophically and is doing my Karma Yoga more efficiently. Living in the Centre, I became more aware of myself. Having to cope with the human side of my fellow-staff members has been an education in itself. Before I used to judge people by their formal educational background rather than by the values that shape their character. As Swamiji says, "Knowledge is not the determining factor of a person's culture but behaviour."

To me, along with the rest of the staff, the Centre is a great field of self-development. Everyone being a voluntary worker, with no risk of losing an income, our egos are put to a greater test, a new skin is laid upon thinner skins without being insensitive, and we learn to understand better each other's points of view, instead of imposing our own. The way Swamiji has organised the Centre and the line of his teachings I find extraordinary, and consider myself very fortunate to be a part of it. We have the maximum autonomy of living our lives, experimenting with and finding our truths, and be creative in our teaching activity while being within the broad outlines laid down by him.

Swamiji says: "Each one of us should grow according to the law of our own spiritual growth and through our individual effort in the line of our best understanding. The human being is not like a clod of earth to be kneaded into a shape by the superimposition of an ideology, religious or political, neither by a guru nor a messiah. One can only inspire the heart and mind by the purity of aspiration and clarity of reason, so that the individual may learn to choose, be personally responsible and walk his or her own path, and society may do so by consensus." To communicate with the students while teaching a class and the feeling of mutual affection and understanding have been a moving experience in my life. What greater reward can one expect at my age than to be active and useful and be loved?

HOW I CAME TO YOGA

By Renate Rikke Maria Gradenwitz

I was born in Hamburg of a German father and Norwegian mother. Father was a martinet, and mother oozed with warmth. I had rather a strict Lutheran upbringing. When I was a child, Hitler came to power. My parents were quickly disillusioned by the dangerous extremism of his fascist and racist ideology. We were an international family. Mother was courageous and outspoken, which were perilous traits under Nazi rule. As a child I was deeply scarred by the unsettled times in which I grew up. That may have unconsciously planted in me the seeds of spiritual search by which I do not mean religious beliefs; that unfolded later in life.

In Hamburg I went to a private school. Religion was a part of its curriculum, which bored me. Nazi fanaticism, like an octopus, grabbed all aspects of German society, including our school, which bewildered me. Father had been doing business in Argentina. He happened to be there when the war broke out. Mother followed him sometime later. I was at that time in a finishing school in the French part of Switzerland. Theatre interested me. While going to a commercial school in Basel during the war to prepare for a career, I took acting lessons. Father died in an accident in Buenos Aires and, as mother felt lonely in a foreign land, I migrated to Argentina in 1947 to be with her for sometime.

Feeling somewhat uprooted and pulled between mother's Norwegian and father's German roots, having to adjust in Switzerland and Argentina, it was kind of logical that one day the questions will arise : where do I really come from, who am I, where I am going to, and what is the meaning of it all ? Yet all these questions were not deep enough to search for higher values. I lived a normal, worldly life with its ups and downs, hopes and frustrations, pleasures and disappointments. In 1958, when I was staying in Switzerland, I met a yoga student, meanwhile having already read a few books on yoga. I began to get interested, at first in Hatha Yoga and then mainly in the Vedanta philosophy.

That year, I started to go to Selvarajan Yesudian's Yoga School in Zuerich and to his Yoga Camp in Caslano near Lugano. He had a calm disposition. I liked his simplicity and the stories about India. He had pioneered the teachings of yoga in Switzerland since 1948. These were my first steps in a long path which became more and more a part of myself. It was an inner need, a search, without being able to say what was it that moved me. It was something that somehow had to happen, which pushed me forward, without being able to explain why. I came back to Buenos Aires in 1959 to nurse my mother who was very ill, and continued my interest in yoga. I kept reading a lot of books on the subject. On those days I thought that I could answer all sorts of questions, having quite firm ideas about the teachings with preconceived notions and in spite of doubts and prejudices.

A SPIRITUAL JOURNEY

Here in Buenos Aires, in 1961, I joined a Yoga Centre but was disappointed. The same year I also listened to a couple of lectures by Swami Chidanandaji. The next year Swami Shivapremanandaji came and inaugurated the Sivananda Yoga-Vedanta Centre, and I became one of its founding members. A managing committee had already been formed, inspired by Ulrich Hartschuh of Montevideo. His enthusiasm was infectious. I was also charmed by its secretary, Marina Gonzalez del Campo. I became her friend. In 1962, Swami Shivapremanandaji did not speak Spanish. I interpreted nearly all his lectures and classes. Although at first I did not realise it, the longer I listened to him the more I became aware how little I knew, that a revealed truth is only a part of the truth and the rest of it one has to find by oneself, stretching out into the infinite, and that such a spiritual journey is so very personal, so very private and so full of trials and errors.

It is now more than 30 years that I have known Swamiji. From the very first encounter I have never been separated from him spiritually or the Centre he founded. In due course, I passed through various roles such as a desk secretary, instructor of Hatha Yoga, editor of the Centre's bulletin, its accountant, Swamiji's housekeeper. Now having retired from a multinational German company, I continue to be the administrator of the Centre as its general secretary and council member. I am also Swamiji's secretary and cook for him when he is among us. There could not have been a better education for me than in all these years of association with him. When I see what goes on in the name of yoga and read such a plethora of unproven myths in books and magazines, I feel like running away from it all. Yet, as Swamiji would say, everyone has a right to think and believe and express as one chooses, but "truth is first of all *veritas*, that which has to be verified by its evidence, its consequence, and then the dimensions of truth have to be widened by spiritual search, deepened by self-realisation, which is an infinite process, that a self-realised soul is an institutional creation like a saint."

Swamiji has awakened in us the hunger for learning, saying that no one can reveal us the truth but only speak about it in the light of one's realisation, that walking the path is totally personal and private, and should be spoken of as little as possible. When I read fantastic stories about yogic experiences, I wonder how much self-promotion is involved with how little seriousness, knowing well that a deeply spiritual experience at once becomes sacred and inexpressible. I have read that yoga is not going somewhere, for you are already there, that being is not becoming, for you already are. That is all well and good for a saint to say, but what about us, ordinary souls, knowing so little about the various layers of our persona, or what about the individual wrapped up in a spiritual ego and concerned with promoting a self-important role, well equipped with cameras and taperecorders? Swamiji jokes: "Blessed Immortal Self, you are fired; you need not bother to come back to the ashram, thy own Self."

REALITY AND ILLUSION

Do we really learn by the *neti-neti* (not this, not this) doctrine? It is like emptying the ocean with a blade of grass until one finds the truth. It is too depressing a goal, for when would I finish emptying the ocean? Discarding and discarding the layers of superimposition, and what guarantee is there that what reveals itself at last is the truth? Deep down I know, of course, that I am a soul, the spiritual content of which is, as Swamiji would say, "transcendental love and truth, beauty and goodness, peace and harmony, purity of heart and clarity of wisdom." But I also know that I am a body composed of and sustained by its primordial instincts in my unconscious, that I am a mind with layers upon layers of my personality formed in the subconscious since my mother brought me to this world. To negate them would be hypocritical. Swamiji says:

"We are a contradiction unto ourselves. We are both spirit and matter, light and shadow. The pure light of our soul is veiled by many layers of our personality, revealing it in various hues according to their transparencies, sometimes obscuring it, sometimes shining a facet of it through. We are in this world to cleanse these layers, not deny them by fiat, to harmonise and sublimate them with the help of the inner light, not repress and make them atrophied. Until the day we die, we will be both spirit and body, the mind serving as a bridge between the two. We are happy when the consciousness is closer to the spirit, in and through and beyond our relationship with others. We are unhappy when it suffocates inside the ego in the relativity of its feedback from others or the lack of it."

There was no conflict in my coming to yoga on account of my cultural background. Both my parents were a product of the age of reason, with a highly developed moral sense. To the contrary, it was due to many unanswered questions that I came to yoga. At first, yoga was a means to a better health, to be more self-confident and to do well in material and professional life. It did not represent a spiritual goal until I met Swamiji, and then that goal meant how could I be a better human being and how could I learn to love, for infinite love and God then became synonymous to me. Earlier, I could not cope with the injustice of birth, some having better advantage than the others, some of the wicked having better luck than some of the decent ones struggling to be fair and virtuous.

The theory of reincarnation I found to be a better alternative to the theory of being given the chance of a single lifetime to deserve eternal heaven or hell. I could not cope with the idea that there was only one valid religion, only one gospel truth, that by believing in it alone could one be saved. What about the thousands of millions of human beings who did not share that truth? Is it not egomaniacal to think that they are lost? The spirit of reconciliation in yoga and its philosophical and religious broadmindedness drew me to it.

On the other hand, harping on the need to be free from the cycle of birth and death, that life on earth is unreal, that the world is an illusion and all such mealy-mouthed assertions leave me cold. It all sounds so hypocritical and patently illogical. As Swamiji says: "We cannot understand the world if we reject and curse it. We cannot learn from the mistakes of a past life because their memory is not carried over to the present one, but can only learn from what we do now and what we remember." Whereas, rationalisation about the inequality and inequity in life through the theory of reincarnation brought me peace, I learned that I could improve myself here only by regarding the world as a reality. There are, of course, higher and lesser realities, but one can only cope with and be responsible to what is tangible. Swamiji says, "To regard this world as an illusion is like brushing the dirt under the carpet, not cleaning it."

SHAPING OUR BELIEFS

So, I was indeed searching for a teacher who would not fill my head with fantastic ideas for daydreaming, nor tempt me with the promise of freeze-dried illumination like through *samadhi* in six months, but would make me face myself as I am with the light of my higher self. In Swamiji I found such a teacher who taught us that we were not created in the image of God but with potential rudiments of it in the form of vague spiritual longings, and that our happiness lay in realising them through our relationship with others and identity with inner self yet to be awakened.

In my Christian background I was told to believe in what the scriptures said, meaning accepting without questioning. From Swamiji I learned: "Believing is not conforming. You can really accept, assimilate, what you know. To know is to search. Without searching you cannot know what you are asked to believe to be true or not." My religion taught me to accept suffering as a means of purification, that the poor are heaven worthy and the rich not. I have always rebelled against such ideas. Then I found my peace in Swamiji's sayings:

"Suffering by itself does not purify. Otherwise, the majority of us would become saints. Only when we are willing to correct the cause of suffering can we learn from it, and by sharing the suffering of those while helping to alleviate it, we purify ourselves. When suffering is prolonged, we become anaesthetised to it and, therefore, cannot learn from it.

Overcoming suffering is the goal and, only when suffering cannot be avoided, we should accept it stoically.

"Poverty is degrading and dependence demeaning. Economic freedom is the first freedom because it gives one the freedom of choice, autonomy. Money is not the root cause of all evil but attachment to it can lead to a great deal of evil. Poverty and wealth can both be bondages from which we should try to free ourselves. It is not true that the poor will sail to heaven through the eye of the needle of misfortune and the rich will stay behind with the camels."

I have learned to accept life as a blessing because, in spite of my lower self, Swamiji has awakened in me the hunger for higher values. In spite of the dark hours, the moments of doubts, I have the urge to go on, for life has many more beautiful hues than the uglier ones, and maybe that is what faith means, faith in ourselves, faith in God. Swamiji has deeply influenced my vision of God, even if it is only a faint glimpse of what God might be in the light of spiritual aspiration.

From time to time, I have the urge to run away from it all, from God, yoga and the Centre, and let my hair down, be my worldly self. Is there anything wrong in it? I do not think so, as long as I am not harming anyone or acting unethically. In fact, I enjoy being with my non-yoga friends who live a normal, worldly life, without a thought about God crossing their head. I enjoy going to the theatre and dinner with them, going to the beach, the fjords and the mountains, visiting my classmates in Germany, relatives and friends in Norway and Switzerland. Swamiji approves of it as a part of life, just as healthy as any, but as long as we do not forget our basic spiritual values. I have no problem in keeping the both together.

Overt spirituality I cannot stand, just as I dislike crash courses on yoga or using terms as "having a good workout" in Hatha Yoga. Levitation, reading the minds of others, claims that half-an-hour of meditation daily would change one's entire life, promise of salvation, repel me. Swamiji says that, there being so much unhappiness in life, spiritual teachers should never be "merchants in human misery" (his words), that they should be all the more responsible due to the gullibility of people. I have seen how false overt humility is, and supposed holiness of some swamis or spiritual teachers.

I have now turned 70 (in 1992) and accept life as it comes, neither feeling burdened by it, nor being too light-hearted about it. Swamiji has taught us to keep our feet firmly planted on earth and heads looking upward into the sky, losing neither, the ground nor the sky, reality nor idealism. I can again say that life is a blessing. How yoga has helped me in daily life? It is like the air I need to breathe, like the water to drink. It has become a part of me, sustaining my faith, my hopes, my ideals, giving me self-confidence and peace by substantiating them, encouraging me onward and keeping my lower self on the leash. I know that it is there, even when I feel like running away from it all, because I know that I cannot simply run away from myself.

A WINDOW OF YOGA IN URUGUAY

By Mario Caffera

Uruguay is relatively a small country, with its northern frontier along the southernmost state of Brazil, Rio Grande do Sul, and the western border along the eastern province of Argentina, Entre Rios. On the south and east lies the Atlantic Ocean, the River Plate flowing into it. In size it is nearly three-quarters the territory of the United Kingdom, but has a small population, a shade less than three millions. The land is very fertile; agricultural and rolling grassland stretching endlessly, almost empty, and streaked with a few low slung mountain ranges.

The industry is mainly agronomic: grain producing and cattle raising, as well as sheep farming, its woolen and leather products being among the finest. The second largest industry is tourism, due to the hundreds of kilometres of beaches along the South Atlantic coast, with fine-grained white sands, and free from rocky shoals. The tourists are mostly from Argentina, fewer from Brazil and also some of the rich from North America and Europe.

The climate is temperate, rather like the Cape Province in South Africa or California, but with abundant rainfall and plenty of sunshine. The capital Montevideo, where one-third of the Uruguayans live, is exactly on the same latitude as Adelaide or one degree south of Sydney or Cape Town. The population is wholesale of European descent, the Spanish conquistadors having virtually and swiftly exterminated the sparse Red Indian settlements, there being no mestizos as in most other South American countries.

Only one percent of the Uruguayans are of African origin, Montevideo having been a slave-market town during the Spanish rule. There is no racial discrimination in our country. Some 80 percent of the people are of Italian and Spanish ancestry, the rest being of other European countries, including a tiny portion from Britain, all souped up by intermarriage, while yet each ethnical group keeping its cultural roots alive, like the Germans through the Goethe Institute, the French by the Alliance Francaise and the British through some excellent schools run by the British Council. There are no Asian immigrants. It might be interesting for British readers to know that for nearly 70 years the United Kingdom was the largest trading partner of Uruguay, from the 1880s until displaced by the United States around 1950.

DEMOCRATIC TRADITION

In Uruguay one does not see extremes of wealth or poverty as in Brazil and most other South American countries. About 80 percent of the people are middle class. The lifestyle is easy-going, rather Mediterranean, with a resigned idea that tomorrow will take care of itself. The shops and offices warm up only after 10 o'clock but they do not close in the afternoon. The siesta habit is fast disappearing. The language is Spanish, spoken with a River Plate accent. The upper class imitates the French intellectually, and the general population looks to Italy and Spain for cultural identity. However, Uruguayans are not gay like the Italians, or proud like the Spaniards, but rather sombre and modest. They are a friendly and hospitable people, with a laissez-faire attitude.

After statehood in the beginning of the nineteenth century, followed by a few years of civil war, the country has enjoyed democratic forms of government all along, except for a decade of military rule brought about by leftist terrorism in the 1970s. Uruguay is probably the first country in South America to separate the Catholic church from the state, in the beginning of this century. Two centre parties, both with its centre-left and centre-right wings, take turns in governing the country, with vociferous parliamentary debates, the two houses of the congress and the presidential form of government being modelled after the United States. Like the United Kingdom, we have a welfare state.

Among the Uruguayans interest in India was, and still is, limited to a tiny group of persons looking for an otherworldly attitude to life through the writings of Tagore and Mahatma Gandhi and a few others. A stretch of the embankment in Montevideo is named Rambla Mahatma Gandhi. Since the 1930s, some of the works of Ramakrishna and Vivekananda became available, subsequent to those of the Theosophical Society. Uruguay had the first direct contact with an Indian philosopher when J. Krishnamurti visited Montevideo in the mid-1930s.

Since the late 1950s, some books on Hatha Yoga, including one by Swami Sivananda, began to circulate. One of those interested in this branch of yoga was Mateo Magarinos, then a junior minister in the Foreign Office. In 1961, one day he wrote extraofficially to his friend Orlando Nadal, then our ambassador in New Delhi, as to the feasibility of an Indian teacher visiting Uruguay for a time. That is how Swami Chidananda came to Montevideo in that year and stayed for four months, giving almost daily classes on the different branches of yoga. A small group formed around him and, in July 1961, he laid the metaphorical foundation stone of the Sivananda Yoga-Vedanta Centre in Uruguay.

Our country was quite lucky to have Swami Chidananda who made a very good impression and inspired a few souls by his personal example of holiness, among whom was a German-born officer of the I.B.M. (Uruguay), Ulrich Hartschuh. If our Sivananda Yoga-Vedanta Centre exists today, it is due to Ulrich's boundless enthusiasm, childlike devotion to yogic ideals, untiring selfless service and organisational skill. After Swami Chidananda left in October 1961, Swami Shivapremananda came here one year later and also stayed for four months. Although then resident in the United States, he assumed the leadership of the Centre and began to come at first for short stays and then for longer residence. It is his constant attention to keep the spiritual ideals alive, continuous selfless service and inspiring teachings that made the Centre what it is today, a well-established, highly prestigious and the largest institution of its kind n the country.

ULRICH HARTSCHUH

Swamiji was specially fond of Ulrich Hartschuh, who unfortunately died of a heart attack at the age of 57, in 1983. All those who came into contact with him, including myself, were inspired by his example of what a Karma Yogi is like. Robert Dix, also German-born and then an officer of the Hoechst (Uruguay), succeeded Ulrich as the Centre's administrator. In the output of hours of dedicated service few could match him. He also served as Swamiji's secretary. His calm disposition was admirable and goodness of heart unforgettable. Swamiji held him in deep affection and used to say that it was "Robert's sweat that built the Centre." His wife, Lotti, was also a prominent worker. Swamiji's book *La Inmanencia de to Eterno* is her production, consisting of a series of class-talks in English which she transcribed, edited and translated into Spanish.

Several others helped to form the Centre through their years of exemplary service, most prominent among whom was Margarita Mendoza who passed away at the age of 82, in 1988. Another colleague whom I would like to mention was Richard Brown, grandson of a British admiral, who died accidentally rather young, in 1971, and whom I succeeded as the Center's treasurer. It would be fair to say that the Sivananda Yoga-Vedanta Centre pioneered the teachings of yoga in Uruguay. Since the 1970s, more than two dozens of yoga groups, including one known as Asociacion Sivananda de Yoga, operate for private gain, mostly in Montevideo. Many of their teachers have been former alumni of our Centre. As of February, 1992, our active membership is 631, *i.e.,* those who come twice a week on the average to participate in any of the 20 weekly Hatha Yoga classes or the philosophy and meditation *satsanga* (prayer meeting).

I came to yoga in 1965 by reading Swami Shivapremananda's book *Platicas sobre Yoga* (Talks on Yoga), the first of his works published in Spanish in that year. At first I knew nothing about yoga and, although my longtime interest was in athletics, it was the spiritual teachings in this book that stimulated my interest in yoga. In our country, however, yoga means mainly a system of physical exercises. I recognised their benefit immediately, for calming the mind and relaxing the nerves, which I needed because of my profession as a chartered accountant, requiring constant concentration.

It is now more than a quarter of a century that I am associated with the Centre, as a student at first, then as a staff member, mainly taking care of the accounts which I still do, as an instructor of Hatha Yoga which I still am, and finally as administrator with the title of vice-president. I also guide the philosophy and meditation meetings during Swamiji's absence. After I retired as a director in the Uruguayan Ministry of Economy and Finance, I am happy to serve as a full-time worker at the Centre.

My parents were descended from Italian immigrants, as that of my wife, and my upbringing was secular and liberal, exphasising self-effort, respect for law and one's teachers, decency and affection in the family without being demonstrative, and duty and responsibility overall. Practice of Catholic religion in my family consisted of baptism, confirmation, church marriage and little else, but I was taught to respect spiritual values and not to be dogmatic. As such, coming to yoga did not cause any conflict in me.

Being trained as an accountant, I found Swami Shivapremananda's teachings precise and pragmatic. His idealism fitted into my formation and his interpretation of yoga was something I considered fortunate to have encountered. It became a positive influence in my life, as much as the happiness I derive from my work at the Centre. In yoga I found a great realism in the understanding of human nature, a means of finding peace within, cope with the problems of life with a greater equanimity, improve my conduct, and deepen love and friendship. What more can one ask for from a transitory life of light and shadow?

YOGA IN URUGUAY II

By Humberto Cairoli

I came to yoga through medical advice about 20 years ago, when I was above 40 and suffered from chronic migraine. The condition of my spine was that of an old man, according to my doctor. The medications gave me only temporary relief but caused gastritis. My prognosis was not very encouraging. One day, my doctor said, "Why not try yoga?" I had then a very superficial notion of yoga, associated with a man standing on his head or sitting cross-legged with closed eyes.

The same doctor recommended me to go to the Sivananda Yoga-Vedanta Centre in Montevideo. Thus more out of curiosity than conviction, I started practising Hatha Yoga. My body was very stiff to start with. Soon, however, the chronic headache disappeared, the muscles and joints loosened up, and the condition of my back improved remarkably. This naturally made me an enthusiastic practitioner of yoga. Noting such a rapid improvement of my health, I encouraged my wife, Blanca, to join the Centre, as she suffered from asthma since a long time, and as also both of us liked to share our interests outside home. Soon enough, she felt a great relief through the practice of Hatha Yoga, specially the *kapalabhati pranayama*. She learned to breathe better and, believe it or not, gave up the cortisone drugs she was dependent on for 25 years, much to the surprise of many, including her doctor.

After two years of regular practice, we were trained to become instructors, which we still continue to be, not having lost a bit of our initial enthusiasm after so many years. We both had our favourite Hatha Yoga teachers who inspired us by their dedication and friendship. About the exercises I learned a lot from the late Matias Guasch, an immigrant from Spain, and about yoga philosophy, other than Swamiji, from Robert Dix, then in charge of conducting *satsanga*. When Swamiji came to

Montevideo, my wife and I never missed any of his classes, meanwhile having read all his books, which shaped our ideas about yoga.

Both of us became voluntary workers and came under the inspiring influence of Margarita Mendoza, then general secretary, a position I succeeded to in 1988 after she passed away, having been a founding member and one of the chief architects of the Centre. I have rarely met a person like her with such unblemished integrity, self-effacing service, immense sense of duty and responsibility, unfailing reliability and devotion to Swamiji. She was very close to him and served as his secretary, a position to which I also succeeded after she left us physically.

Like most Uruguayans, I am part Italian and part Spanish, my father's family having migrated from the Lake Como region of northern Italy and my mother's from northern Spain. I had a very happy childhood, with loving parents, and was raised in traditional Christian values, but without an adequate knowledge of our religion. In addition to being an instructor, my wife is one of the two auditors of the Centre. Both of us feel quite at home with the teachings of Swami Shivapremananda. "Spirituality," according to him, "consists in the practice of integrity, compassion, purity of heart, selflessness, sublimation of passions and humility of spirit." Swamiji's role is explaining what they actually mean and their relativity to practical life, under different circumstances. He says:

"All of us on this earth are different from each other just as each leaf is different from the other while belonging to the same tree. Thus, individually apart, we all belong to the common tree of our species, drawing the psychological sap from the same mixed source of creation, from the reservoir of good and evil, positive and negative, God and devil in us. Our fears and anxieties, hopes and disappointments, desires and frustrations, all have a common streak in each of us, welling up from the same primordial psyche that is being shaped and reshaped, refined and tarnished, anchored and let flow freely for a while by the forces of history, with religions and ideologies serving as handmaidens, popping up ideas as to who we are, what we want to be, where we have supposedly come from and where we want to go."

SWAMIJI'S IMPRESSION

Swamiji's teachings have made a vivid impression on our thinking, specially his knowledge of the human nature as much as the scriptures, including the Bible. As his secretary, I have observed him closely and learned to appreciate his straightforwardness, even if at times expressed rather bluntly. Most of his students like and enjoy demythification, including about yoga. He has reminded us often:

"Emotionalism in Bhakti Yoga experienced by singing *kirtans* and *bhajans* (devotional chants and songs) by itself does not purify the heart, although they can be momentarily uplifting, nor long hours of *japa* or saying the rosary mechanically, nor getting up before dawn to practise concentration and meditation as per Raja Yoga, nor contemplation on the *mahavakyas* (great affirmations) and the *vidyas* of the Upanishads (metaphysical themes) as per Gyana Yoga. Real *sadhana* (spiritual discipline) consists in leading a life of ethical idealism and selfless service, watchfulness over one's motives and freedom from hypocrisy and egolatry, passions and prejudices. *Sadhana* is more a process as to how we think and express ourselves through attitude and conduct, rather than merely an act in itself. Without such a basis, spiritual exercises are like pouring water in a leaking pot."

As a production manager in a large factory, I have a lot to cope with the problems of human nature among the work force. Swamiji's teachings have helped me much to promote accord through a common sense of purpose, discipline by motivation, harmony through mutual appreciation, performance by attention to individual welfare. A wide window of yoga has opened up before me by the way Swamiji teaches about God and spiritual values, as much as by his personal example. Without being bound by dogmas, nor indulging in self-serving fantasies about God, I have found peace in my heart by feeling his presence, within and around, as an "infinite spirit expressed through love and truth."

Having found so much benefit at the Centre, both physical and spiritual, it gives me great joy, as also to my wife, to be able to serve others through it. I come to the Centre everyday after work. Swamiji has gathered around him such a fine group of persons to make it for all of us a real spiritual home. I remember with fondness those of my friends who are no longer physically present but whose inspiring memory of love and kindness brings so much peace and happiness to me. As Swamiji says, a Centre does not consist of well-furnished, splendid buildings but the human element, of those who serve idealistically to make it a spiritual home for all those who need such a refuge. My wife and I are proud to be a part of it.

YOGA IN URUGUAY III

By Sofia Aguiar

Since my adolescence I developed an interest in India and admiration for the spiritual ideals of that remote land, mainly from the stories I heard from my grandmother who was a German. I thought that some day I would learn more about India and yoga. In 1968, from a friend, I learned that in Montevideo there was a Sivananda Yoga-Vedanta Centre, of which she was a student. She also told me that the Centre's guide, Swami Shivapremananda, was known for his integrity and had pioneered the teaching of yoga in our country on a sustained basis.

However, due to circumstantial reasons and my interest being still incipient, it was only in 1974 I joined the Centre, when I came to know that Swamiji had just arrived and was about to give courses on Vedanta and Raja Yoga. I attended all his classes, which made a deep impression on me due to their wisdom, expressed in a practical manner. Then I read all his available books. Regular practice of Hatha Yoga improved my health as well. The teachings of yoga have helped me a great deal to overcome my mental rigidity on account of my childhood formation. My mother being a German and father of Basque and Galician origin, I was brought up very strictly. No longer I see things in black and white terms. Yoga has broadened my attitude to life and improved my understanding of others.

In course of time, I became an instructor of Hatha Yoga, which brought me in contact with many students, and this helped me not to be distant and self-absorbed. The past 18 years of association with the Centre has been a rich experience in my life. I became a council member and secretary for public relations. I am not a practising Christian in the sense that I am not a churchgoer, but I find so much similarity of Christian values with the teachings of yoga as taught by Swamiji. I have learned that the practice of any religion consists in living up to its ideals in daily life, that prayers are not so many words said in the act of worship, but mean spiritual aspiration, as Jesus said "God hears what is in your heart." Yet I like the *satsanga* at the Centre and also participate in spiritual retreats conducted by Swamiji.

Being an architect and a follower of yoga, I know that it is far easier to design a building and structure it according to one's drafts, but how difficult is the inner reconstruction, to know the intricacies of what has already been made within and to restructure it according to one's ideals. Swamiji says: "Destiny is what you make of what you have, within and without, tapping inner resources, potentialities,. and making the best use of the circumstances, opportunities, not sitting around and saying that it is my karma as to what I am and how I suffer, but through self-effort trying to overcome suffering and better yourself and your situation. It is only after doing so, accept with fortitude what cannot be helped. You do not know what your destiny is without trying to find out what it can be by self-effort."

Thus I am learning more and more about my destiny, listening to Swamiji's teachings: "Get hold of the first opportunity for anything good that comes by. Do not wait for a better one to appear the next time, for there may not be a next time. If you have found a friend or a teacher of integrity, do not let that person move away through your indifference or selfishness, but sustain such a friendship by sharing of the best in you."

YOGA IN URUGUAY IV

By Olga Gutierrez

When I was about 40 years old and my daughter old enough to take care of herself, and my husband being content with a settled and predictable household life, I felt like many other housewives of my age that as if I was in a spiritual vacuum. Thus, in the beginning of 1973, I came to the Sivananda Yoga-Vedanta Centre on recommendation of some of my friends. The Hatha Yoga classes were of high quality and the *satsangas* inspiring. What impressed me most was, however, that all those who served there were motivated by a selfless, spiritual idealism. At first I had thought that they were paid personnel, but soon I knew that they served there only for the love of their ideals.

Since childhood I have felt the protection of strong family ties and the security of ethical and moral values that I learned from my parents. My ancestry is part German (on father's side) and part English (on mother's), and I am married to an Uruguayan of Spanish descent. I was raised as a Christian like most of my countrymen, but without dogmatism. I married early, and my husband and I have an understanding family life, each respecting the other's sphere of interest outside home. My daughter pursues a lawyer's career, as does her husband, and I have two handsome grandchildren who bring much joy to my life. Like many others, I have passed through ups and downs since my early years. The traditional religious teachings did not help me much and troubled my spirit with contradictions and doubts. By and by, listening to Swami Shivapremananda's classes and reading his books, I found my path and made peace with myself.

Soon after joining the Centre, I came under the influence of Margarita Mendoza. Her selfless devotion and dedication were exemplary. She was then the deputy headmistress of a grammer school and had spent a lifetime in the teaching career. In a few years I became an instructor of Hatha Yoga and a staff member. After Margarita passed away four years ago, I succeeded her as Swamiji's housekeeper when he is in town. I became a council member and am at present in-charge of training instructors. I am also a deputy to the General Secretary.

The teachings of yoga never had any conflict with my liberal Christian background. On the other hand, they helped to clear many of my doubts and enabled me to understand myself better. However, I must say that it has been possible mostly through Swamiji's line of interpretation. For example, I found in the *Bhagavad Gita* Krishna's threat of punishment in hell as distasteful as that of the Bible. Swamiji's sayings found a common cord in many of our hearts, such as:

HEAVEN AND HELL

"Heaven and hell are within each of us and in our surroundings. When truth and love, goodness and kindness, justice and commonweal, understanding and tolerance, clarity of reason and purity of devotion reign in our hearts and in our relationship with each other, at home and in the community, we experience heaven and the presence of God. In their contradictions we are in hell, both within and without, suffering the absence of God. In work ethic, in a work well done, in a duty carried out as best as one could, in an obligation well fulfilled, in nourishing and tending carefully a loving relationship, in the inspiration of realising a spiritual ideal, we experience heaven. Whereas, when our hearts are ruled by passion and prejudice, and contort with resentment and malice, when our heads simmer with anger and nerves tense up with bitterness, when words and looks are used as daggers, and actions are plotted and executed to destroy the welfare and happiness of others, we experience and *are* in hell.

"Eternal heaven and hell are wishful thinking. The roots of *satchidananda* in our souls give an inner awareness *(chit)* of an eternally existing *(sat)* heaven *(ananda),* but due to our attachment to physical existence, we like to make it an abode of happy denizens enjoying forever rivers of milk and honey (in Islamic heaven even *houris* are provided). How cloying that can be! Naturally, not wanting our enemies to be around, we want to invent a befitting place like hell for them.

"It is doubtful if inducement for heaven has made anyone behave better, or punishment in hell has been threatening enough to prevent people from evil deeds, for otherwise society would not need so many arms of law enforcement. It is also equally unfair of God to send anyone to an eternal hell when an imperfect judge in a civilised society does not punish the worst criminal for more than 15 to 30 years of life-imprisonment, with a provision of one-third remission for good behaviour. Nor does it make sense when God, who is supposed to be merciful, threatens to punish not only the idolators but up to the fourth generation of their descendants (second commandment in the Bible), when an ordinary judge would not deem it just to punish children for the crime of their fathers."

The above quotations from Swamiji's class-talks are indicative of his line of teachings, providing a wholesale reassessment of the scriptures. According to him the classical texts of yoga as well represent the "vision of their authors in the light of their spiritual search, their minds reflecting the shape of values and thinking in their times, as also their own wishful thinking like the yogis attaining omnipotence and omniscience (so much for modesty), or their bodies becoming as light as a feather (*anima*) or as heavy as a mountain (*laghima*), as per Raja Yoga.

The *siddhis* (occult powers) never attracted me, nor did psychic experiences. I only wanted to be a better mother, a better wife, a better friend and a better human being, to have a measure of control over my destiny, to come to terms with adverse conditions that are beyond my power to change, without complaining, to find peace in my heart and be in peace with others. The Centre has provided me a unique field to fulfil this need. It is surprising that how many people come to it, not only to attend Hatha Yoga classes and the *satsangas*, but to find someone to talk to, unburden themselves, seek a sympathetic understanding, even a shoulder to cry on. That I can be useful not only as a Hatha Yoga instructor and a staff secretary but as a spiritual friend of those who need me, has been and is an ample reward in my life and given me much happiness.

A WINDOW OF YOGA IN CHILE

By Anita Palma

Yoga came to Chile relatively later than to Europe and the USA, or even to Brazil and Argentina. Chilean people, however, have deep spiritual roots. Most of them are Catholics but not close-minded. Being so near the high Andes over a length of some 2,500 miles with a width of only less than 150 miles between the mountains and the Pacific Ocean, there is a mystical tendency in the Chilean unconscious. The Red Indians had very sparsely settled the region since over 10,000 years ago until the coming of the Spanish conquistadors early in the sixteenth century.

The native tribes were rather primitive unlike the Incas in Peru, Mayas in Central America and Aztecs in Mexico. Not being numerous, they were absorbed in the Spanish culture in the course of the centuries. Although Chileans are mainly of Spanish descent, German immigrants started coming in since the middle of the nineteenth century. From the beginning of the twentieth, other immigrants from Europe like Italians and Yugoslavs also arrived. Thus, Chile looks more like a modern Mediterranean nation with a dash of Red Indian blood. There are 13 million inhabitants.

My grandparents were descendants of Spanish colonisers and were devout Catholics, but for reasons unknown to me my parents converted to the Baptist faith. In my adolescence, I was obliged to read the Bible daily, but even then many doubts arose in my mind as to God's wrath in destroying Sodom and Gomorrah, including innocent children, why the human being was imperfect in spite of being created in the image of God, why there were so much suffering and calamities in the world? All these questions worried me and, when once I spoke about them to my parents, they took me to our pastor who thought that I was possessed by the Devil and made me kneel down and he put his hands on my head to drive him out of me.

It was not a pleasant experience, and soon I became anti-religion and started doubting in the existence of God. I studied biochemistry to have a profession, which I still practise part-time at the age of 83 (in May 1991). In due course, I got married and later lived, for some years in La Paz, Bolivia, and Montevideo, Uruguay, on account of my husband's business career. In the 1950s, after years of indifference to religion, when I was already over 40, I came across a book of Yogananda, Autobiography of a Yogi, which was my first introduction to yoga. It fascinated me. I began to read all the books on yoga I could lay my hands on in the libraries of Santiago and Montevideo, and bought those available in the bookstores.

MEETING TWO SWAMIS

Chileans have been interested in the spiritual culture of India through the writings of Rabindranath Tagore, Vivekananda, Aurobindo, Annie Basant, J. Krishnamurti, Mahatma Gandhi, Yogananda and others. In the late 1950s, a small group in Santiago formed a branch of the Self-realisation Fellowship of California and in the early 1960s another small group organised itself as Suddha Dharma Mandala. However, to my knowledge, Swami Shivapremanandaji was the first to pioneer a comprehensive teaching of yoga in Chile since 1965. I met Swamiji for the first time in 1962 in Montevideo where I was staying at that time. He was then the Director of the Sivananda Yoga-Vedanta Centre in Milwaukee, USA, which he had founded in 1961, having been deputed by Swami Sivanandaji of Rishikesh to spread the teachings of yoga in the West.

The universal spiritual message of yoga and its broad vision of God had since many years opened up within me deep longings to search for a higher meaning of life. Religious dogmas never appealed to me. I disliked the fundamentalists and ideologues. Exclusive claims to truth did not make sense because they made groups of humanity antagonistic to each other. It was before Pope John XXIII had initiated the Second Vatican Council in 1962 that I found my spiritual home in yoga.

One day, in 1961, I read in a Montevideo newspaper that a Swami was coming to town. His name was Swami Chidananda, now President of the Divine Life Society. He was at that time travelling in the USA. A small group of people interested in yoga had written to the Uruguayan ambassador in New Delhi if a Swami would be willing to come to Montevideo for a few months to teach yoga. Through some reference, the ambassador went to Swami Sivanandaji in Rishikesh. As Chidanandaji was already in the USA, Swami Sivanandaji asked him to go to Uruguay. It was as per the suggestion of Shivapremanandaji, although Chidanandaji had suggested that Swami Vishnu-devananda should go instead.

Chidanandaji stayed in Montevideo for four months and pioneered the teaching of yoga in Uruguay. I attended all his classes. A group was informally constituted as the Sivananda Yoga-Vedanta Centre. A year later, this group in conjunction with a group in Buenos Aires, Argentina, wrote to Swami Sivanandaji to send another Swami who could come to South America periodically to consolidate the Centre in Montevideo and establish a Sivananda Yoga-Vedanta Centre in Buenos Aires. Chidanandaji having already returned to India and Shivapremanandaji having been sent to the West, which was to be on a permanent basis, the latter was the obvious choice of the great master Sivanandaji.

Thus, in 1962, I met my future Guru. Shivapremanandaji at first came to Buenos Aires, where I went to receive him with the Montevideo group. He taught there for three months, founded the Sivananda Centre and registered it as a charity. He came then to Montevideo to consolidate and expand the already-existing Centre and also register it as a charity. Swamiji stayed in Montevideo for four months and I attended all his classes, almost everyday, on the Upanishads, Raja Yoga, *Bhagavad Gita,* meditation and Hatha Yoga. It was through him that the students in Montevideo, including me, got a deeper insight into the comprehensive knowledge of yoga. The same can be said about the yoga students in Buenos Aires where he went back afterwards.

Soon, however, Sivanandaji asked Shivapremanandaji to return to Milwaukee, as he was needed there. In 1963, I came back to my country, resolving that the next time Swamiji came to South America, I will invite him to Chile to found a Sivananda Yoga-Vedanta Centre in Santiago. Swami Sivanandaji passed away in 1963. The second visit of Shivapremanandaji to South America was in 1965, when he was Director of the Sivananda Yoga-Vedanta Centre in New York, which Swami Vishnudevananda had earlier founded while being based in Canada.

YOGA COMES TO CHILE

Shivapremanandaji at first came to Buenos Aires and then to Montevideo to help the consolidation and growth of the two Centres. I lost no time to invite him to Chile, having already formed a group with my friends with similar interest. Thus, the Sivananda Yoga-Vedanta Centre came to being in Santiago. Swamiji gave a series of lectures at the University of Chile, the National Library and some cultural institutes, and registered the Centre as a charity in August 1965, for which we had no difficulty with the Charity Commission (Personaria Juridica), as in Argentina and Uruguay, although it is not easy to get a charity status. However, our bonafides would have been vouched by the Indian ambassadors and probably our embassies in New Delhi had also vetted the Divine Life Society in Rishikesh.

Gradually our Centre in Santiago came to be regarded as the most prestigeous institution of its kind. Swamiji again came to South America in 1967 and 1969 but stayed for short periods of time, because he had more responsibility in New York. From the early 1970s he came for longer periods of time almost every year and eventually took charge as President of the three Sivananda Yoga-Vedanta Centres on a permanent basis (earlier he had appointed others as Presidents who were elected by the membership). Since the 1970s yoga teachers have mushroomed in Chile, as in Argentina and Uruguay. However, ours is the only Centre, as in Buenos Aires and Montevideo, which is entirely run by voluntary workers without remuneration, including Swamiji, all trained by him as Hatha Yoga instructors and as spiritual seekers to run the other activities such as conducting *satsanga* and meditation and philosophy classes, and looking after general management. The only paid personnel are the accountant and the caretaker who also cleans the premises.

We keep our membership fee low, so as to make it accessible to all. The philosophy and meditation classes are free, which are on Wednesdays and Saturdays. We have daily Hatha Yoga classes, morning and evening. Swami Shivapremanandaji stays with us at least three months every year or two months at a time twice a year, the rest of his time being given to his other two Centres in Buenos Aires, which is his headquarters, and in Montevideo. He also visits Europe once in two years, stopping over in New York, to and from. Swamiji has frequently lectured in the Catholic University, the University of Chile and the cultural institutes of the municipality of Santiago.

The Catholic Church has a benevolent attitude towards us and to yoga in general, probably because yoga is not considered a religion and it is not strong enough a movement to make the hierarchy sit up and consider it a threat. The public regards yoga mainly as a physical culture, although we have our share of the Hare Krishnas and Transcendental Meditation, Theosophy and Baha'i groups and the likes of them. Except us, Hatha Yoga teachers operate on a commercial basis. When in town, Shivapremanandaji also conducts for his students spiritual retreats in the nearby Catholic monasteries, the doors of which are open to us because they do not regard us as cultists.

NO RELIGIOUS CONFLICT

As such, the church-going students of our Centre do not find a religious conflict, since yoga regards Jesus Christ an incarnation of God and Moses a leading prophet of humanity. There are many like me who are not the Church-going type. The committed Christians, *i.e.,* the dogmatists of course stay away from us. However, more than half of our members are interested only in Hatha Yoga. Socially, we are a mixed bag. There are professionals, businessmen and women, office secretaries, housewives. As can be expected, women predominate and it is not because they have more time. Many of them have regular jobs in addition to housework. It is simply because women are more interested in keeping fit and men are generally lazy. After getting back from work, men would rather watch television than come to a yoga class. It may be also because women have more emotional and spiritual needs.

To me and to many others like me, Swami Shiva-premananda has made a profound impression through his philosophy of life and his interpretation of not only the spiritual teachings of yoga but in making us look at our own Christian background in a brighter light on account of his Biblical scholarship. Although a renunciate monk and born in a Brahmin family, whose great-grandfather was a cousin of Ram Mohan Roy and a cofounder of the Brahmo Samaj reform movement in India in the last century, Swamiji cannot be pinned down to any particular religion. To him "anyone who loves integrity, compassion and selflessness, duty, honour and responsibility, sublimation of passion, moral courage and humility, is a religious person, whether he or she goes to a church or not, believes in a heavenly deity or not, gets up in the early morning to meditate or not."

To Swamiji, "God is not an anthropomorphic deity localised in a heavenly abode, but the eternal, infinite, universal and transcendental spirit immanent in all and present everywhere, whereas a personal God like the Father in Heaven or Krishna or Jesus Christ is an idealised spiritual form of the individual's devotion and aspiration that the same infinite spirit assumes in order to be relatable to the seeker." Swamiji says, "Integrity and purity of heart are the highest practices of religion, and compassion, devotion and ethics are its soul, irrespective of whether you are a Christian, Jew, Hindu, Moslem or Buddhist." Such a Window of Yoga he has opened in Chile, through which the "fresh breeze of the infinite spirit can flow in, to clear the cobwebs of religious exclusiveness and bigotry, pride and prejudice, malice and dogmatism, selfishness and egolatry."

SWAMIJI'S WAY

Shivapremanandaji does not like any showmanship, religious or political, himself being totally free from it. He is uncomfortable in the company of those whom he sometimes calls "performing holy men and holy women" but takes them in stride as a part of life, himself avoiding flowing robes and trying his best to appear like a simple human being. He does not give any Sanskrit name to his students, even though acknowledging a need in some to put on a persona if it helps him or her to be true to or measure up to its meaning. Otherwise, the farce of it does not escape him.

Swamiji has not given *sannyasa* initiation to any of his long-devoted students, because he says that *sannyasa* or renunciation is in one's heart, and as long as it is kept pure it does not matter whether a robe is put on or not. If anyone asks him for *sannyasa*, he tells him or her to go to the Sivananda Ashram in Rishikesh if not content with what he has just said about his philosophy of life. When a student asks Swamiji for mantra initiation, he gives him or her a few pertinent mantras to choose from, explaining the meaning of each to fit a specific personal inclination, and reminding at the same time that it does not make him a *guru*, because he simply does not like the idea of being a *guru* of any, although in effect he is so to numerous people without such a title. Swamiji says that the real *guru* is God in your heart, even if one could have many little gurus as Sage Dattatreya had, like a fly who taught him tenacity and a dog devotion and loyalty. This is also a contribution of Swamiji to the Window of Yoga in Chile.

A favourite joke of Shivapremanandaji is that "no one is good enough to be a spiritual master of anyone, human nature being so deficient." He says, "Knowledge can be taught but spirituality is a personal responsibility and cultivated by oneself alone, because no one can impart it or trigger it by a magic touch." There are half-a-dozen books of Swamiji in Spanish containing his teachings, mainly transcribed and edited from his class-talks, which have made him widely known in Chile as well as in Argentina and Uruguay. He has taught us, "Freedom of thought is a basic right for all, and no one should impose on others a particular ideology or belief through undemocratic means, including the dictat of a *guru*. Rights and obligations are interrelated, as are liberty and responsibility, personal freedom and self-discipline." Swamiji has made his students very aware of these values. He cannot stand self-important people. I have actually seen him squirm in their presence out of displeasure. He is a stickler for punctuality, and the Centre is run by a liberal-minded and highly responsible crew.

ON BEING TRUSTED

I would like to relate two cases to illustrate how Swamiji is trusted by those Chileans who know him, although he does not care about politics while being highly democratic in outlook. During the Marxist regime (1970-73) of the late President Salvador Allende, his deputy foreign minister once sought Swamiji out for an interview to clarify some of his thoughts. I remember, soon after the military coup, when Swamiji was visiting Chile in 1974 and when our Centre was located at a large, rented flat near the Government House, a major of the Chilean Intelligence Services in civilian dress used to come to our *satsanga.* He had earlier met Swamiji in New York while working there for the Chilean government, and became a devotee. He trusted Swamiji so much that he used to keep his shoulder-holstered service revolver in Swamiji's bedroom because he did not like to bring a gun hidden under his suit jacket to the *satsanga* hall during our prayer meetings. He is now retired and comes to the Centre when Swamiji is in town.

In 1978, we bought our present building in the middle-class suburb of Providencia in Santiago. As Swamiji does not like to ask for donations, we did not make a fund-raising drive but paid for the property gradually through membership fees, one of the council members having loaned the down payment and given the collateral. After the military coup, we had to display on the wall of the reception hall a permit signed by the general in charge of the Santiago district to hold any public activity which was then prohibited without permission. The Centre's prestige was such that we were allowed to conduct all our activities without interruption, although even karate schools were closed down.

I also remember that one of the daughters of General Pinochet joined the Centre for some time and used to come to the morning Hatha Yoga class when, unknown to others, two of her bodyguards in civilian dress patrolled the footpaths around the building but did not enter it. She was correct and decent and never made her presence felt. Our Centre must have been vetted and found safe enough for the dictator's daughter to come to. Since 1990, Chile has an elected civilian government headed by Patricio Alwyne whose ancestors came from Wales, UK. He is a leader of the Christian Democratic Party which is now (1991) in power, as in Germany and Italy. Our Centre continues to function as usual, unaffected by any political change.

Now I will let two of my colleagues relate briefly how they came to yoga and give their backgrounds.

YOGA IN CHILE II

By Hector Calderon

By training I am an electrical (now electronic) engineer. My ancestors came from Spain a long time ago. Somehow I chanced upon a book on Hatha Yoga by Yogi Vitthaldas 27 years ago and started to practise the exercises on my own. A year later, I saw an announcement in a newspaper about a public lecture to be given by Swami Shivapremananda. I went to listen to him. It was his first visit to Chile. In spite of my childhood Catholic formation and having gone to a Jesuit school, I liked what he said. It made sense. The message was clear and rational. It fitted into my engineering mind, and I was among the first to join the Sivananda Yoga-Vedanta Centre when Swamiji formed it.

At first I had thought that yoga meant only physical exercises and that was enough for me because I had my Catholic religion after all, but listening to Swamiji and later on reading his books and that of others, I knew that there was more to it. I learned that yoga has a universal philosophy and it was not opposed to traditional western values. Swamiji told us, "Yoga was a state of mind, a way of life, that material and spiritual aspects of it could not be separated, that improvement of our human nature and conduct was its goal, without dogmatism or imposition of any doctrine claiming a divine origin, that life should be ruled by moral and spiritual values."

This broadened my idea of religion and fitted into my pragmatic outlook, having observed how close-minded some of my committed Catholic friends were and the contradiction of their beliefs and actions. Swamiji's teachings have helped me to have a better understanding of myself and the people I relate to. Except for five years in Rio de Janeiro, where my professional career took me to, I have been continuously associated with the Sivananda Yoga-Vedanta Centre in Santiago in different capacities, even as an instructor of Hatha Yoga. The teachings of yoga, as interpreted by Swamiji, have made me happier, more self-confident, more of a realist and helped me to find inner peace.

We have learned a lot of things from him apart from the classical teachings and Hatha Yoga. He simply cannot stand self-pity and says, "If anything goes wrong, you are at least 50% to blame, and so accept your share, learn from your mistakes and do not pass on the blame to others to feel sorry for yourself." He has taught us personal responsibility and the value of commitment. A favourite joke of his is, "Do not tell me that you have not been able to keep your word because you were run over by a lorry."

YOGA IN CHILE III

By Lucila Broughton

My father was of British ancestry and a Free Mason, and my mother of Spanish origin and a Catholic. Religion did not mean much in my early life. As a child, I was fascinated by the pictures and statues of the Buddha seated in the lotus posture in deep meditation and holding mudras. This inward, contemplative aspect was the first thing that drew me to yoga, to the Orient, to India. In the 1940s, as a child I could not find in Chile anyone who would satisfy my spiritual hunger. As a student of music, however, I learned that Yehudi Menuhin had benefited greatly through the practice of yoga. So, I started buying books available on the subject and began to practise Hatha Yoga by myself. Then I joined for two years an organisation called Great Universal Fraternity which taught yoga, in the mid-1970s.

In 1978, one day I saw an announcement in a Santiago newspaper that Swami Shivapremariandaji was coming to town and went to listen to his public lecture. Since then I have been a devoted follower of him. I joined the Sivananda Centre and eventually became an instructor and worked in other roles. The ancient wisdom of the Vedas found an echo in my soul. Swamiji's teachings have been vitally important in my personal development, have given me strength which I had thought I did not have and depths to the understanding of life I knew not. I am a housewife and a piano teacher. Yoga has taught me to be creative in music which I love, more honest, and to appreciate more the happy moments and take in stride the unhappy ones without bitterness. It has prepared me to look forward to the next life with peace and strength and, when the time comes, to leave this one without reproach or sadness. Yoga has helped me to be in peace with myself and with others.

CONCLUSION BY ANITA PALMA

After my three friends have spoken about how yoga has influenced their lives, I would like to conclude with my impressions. Now pushing 84, my only regret is that I could have started much earlier. Over 30 years of practice of yoga has kept me fit, physically and mentally. As I said before, I still work part time to keep my mind active. I go to concerts and come to the Centre three times a week to supervise the management and attend a meditation class and *Satsanga*, even subbing as a desk secretary. When Swamiji is in town I attend all his classes. I have made my peace with the Biblical God because I have learned from Swamiji that the "same infinite spirit is reflected in different forms in the mind of man according to the nature of his spiritual aspiration, insecurity and anxiety, and the pure light expresses itself as per the clearer or darker transparencies of his individual consciousness."

Swamiji has taught me that the essence of my soul is a spark of the same infinite spirit in a state of embodiment, and the "same spark twinkles as myriads of God's light in the souls of humanity, awaiting individual discovery and realisation." Thus, I have lost the fear of death. In the spirit of the *Bhagavad Gita*, although I know that in a few years my body will return to earth "from dust to dust and ashes to ashes," my soul will continue to burn in the light of God and merge in it eventually, "for winds cannot blow it out and torrents cannot drown it."

I have learned that it is through my errors that I punish myself, not God, that "heaven and hell are within our minds and the circumstances of life". This philosophy has inwardly strengthened me and given peace of mind, because I know that I am not alone, that God is in me and I am in Him. I have a deep respect for the Christian values of peace and love and forgiveness which, according to Swamiji, represent the soul of my religion. I have come back to Christianity through yoga. Ours is the smallest of Swamiji's three Centres in South

America, the one in Buenos Aires being the largest and the one in Montevideo much bigger than ours, but our hearts are as big as any of those who are closest to him over there. Can there be anything greater than pure love for one another among all humanity?

ABOUT THE AUTHOR

SWAMI SHIVAPREMANANDA

Swami Shivapremananda was born in India on 26 July, 1925. He studied at St. Paul's Collegiate School in Darjeeling, and subsequently at the St. Xavier's College in Calcutta (now Kolkota) University. In 1945 he chose the vocation of spiritual ministry and entered the Ashram (Divine Life Society) of Swami Sivananda in Rishikesh at the foothills of the Himalayas.

He studied there various branches of yoga and comparative religions and philosophies. From 1949 to 1961, he taught at the Yoga-Vedanta Academy, and was the editor of *The Divine Life* and *Wisdom Light* monthly magazines and other philosophical publications. During this period he was also a private secretary to Swami Sivananda and a trustee of the Divine Life Society.

Swami Shivapremananda took part in social work for the poor under the auspices of the Sivananda Eye Relief Camps, in 1957-58, in Sourashtra. His interest in Eastern mysticism drew him to some monasteries in the Himalayas and Tibet in the 1950s and later to Thailand, Cambodia and Japan. Swamiji stayed with Gurudev Swami Sivananda for 16 years and eight months.

In 1961, invited by educational and cultural groups and urged by Swami Sivananda, he went to Europe and the USA to share his knowledge and experience gathered in the course of many years. He has since lived in the USA, Europe and South America, and founded and guided yoga centres in many countries.

From 1961 to 1963 he was the founder-director of the Sivananda Yoga-Vedanta Centre in Milwaukee, Wisconsin, and from 1964 to 1970 president and director of the Sivananda

Yoga-Vedanta Centre in New York. Since his arrival in the West he has been guiding yoga centres in Europe and the Americas.

At present Swamiji is the president and rector of the Sivananda Yoga-Vedanta Centres in Buenos Aires (Argentina), Montevideo (Uruguay) and Santiago (Chile), which are the largest and most prestigious organisations of their kind in these countries, built up over the years since their inception under his guidance.

Swamiji is the author of eleven books on yoga philosophy and psychology in Spanish which he wrote for his thousands of South American students. They are: *Talks on Yoga* (1965, 1990), *The Universal Philosophy of Yoga* (1969, 1991), *Introduction to Yoga Philosophy* (1971, 1975), *Philosophical and Psychological Aspects of Yoga* (1972, 1984), *The Immanence of the Eternal* (1973), *Window of the Soul* (1983, 1987, 1988, 1988, 1989, 1993), *Integral Yoga* (1992), *Yoga, an Attitude Towards Life* (2000), *Tryst with Destiny* (2002), *To Live Is to be Happy* (2003) and *Meditation* (2004). More than a dozen booklets of his teachings are also published. From time to time he has lectured in the national universities of Argentina, Uruguay and Chile and the Catholic universities in Buenos Aires and Santiago de Chile.

Swami Shivapremananda goes to Europe periodically to give seminars at various places, mainly in Great Britain and also in Belgium and Ireland, having done so in Holland, France, Germany, Switzerland and Italy. He is also well known as a teacher of Hatha Yoga, and conducted spiritual retreats in many countries, his inclination, however, being basically to Gyana Yoga and Raja Yoga.

To promote a greater understanding of the spiritual teachings of the East through Western interpretation, Swamiji has given lectures in many universities in the USA, such as Columbia in New York, Wisconsin in Milwaukee, Stanford near San Francisco, the East-West Cultural Centre in Los Angeles,

St. Mary's Seminary in Baltimore, and the American Academy of Asian Studies in San Francisco.

He has also lectured in the universities of Oxford, Stuttgart and Antwerp and other educational institutions in Europe. Invited by the late Thomas Merton, he twice visited the Trappist monastery in Gethsemane in Kentucky in the early 1960s.

His book *Yoga for Stress Relief,* published in 1999 and 2000 by Gaia Books, England, and Random House, USA, has been translated from the original English and published in six other European languages.